Traffic-ruts on Postern Hill, above Marlborough
(see pages 58 and 70)

ARCHAEOLOGY
IN THE FIELD

by

O. G. S. CRAWFORD

C.B.E., D.LITT., F.B.A.

Editor & Founder of
'Antiquity'

J. M. DENT & SONS LTD

LONDON

Made in Great Britain
Printed by Lowe & Brydone (Printers) Ltd
Victoria Road · London NW 10
for
J. M. DENT & SONS LTD
Aldine House · Bedford Street · London
First published 1953
Second impression, revised, 1953
Third impression, revised, 1954
Fourth impression 1960
Fifth impression 1970

ISBN: 0 460 07662 0

CONTENTS

Field archaeology nearly co-terminous with archaeology: reasons for great modern expansion of knowledge about the past: pre-nineteenth century archaeology, the hand-maid of history: the Bible and Julius Caesar: the early English field archaeologists (Aubrey, Stukeley, Colt Hoare, etc.): their bookish background and illogical reasoning, illustrated by an example: the first finds that books could not explain (Picard and Boucher de Perthes): historic visit of Sir John Evans and Sir Joseph Prestwich to Abbeville in 1859: their report established authenticity of finds proving the great antiquity of Man: the year 1859 a decisive one and a turning-point in human thought: the problem stated at the beginning of the chapter now solved: the modern expansion of knowledge results from the application if a new method—that of observation and deduction.

When did modern archaeology begin? With Schliemann, though still under the spell of books: followed by complete emancipation by Flinders Petrie in Egypt and Evans in Crete: English archaeology somewhat stagnant in second part of nineteenth century, the heyday of collectors and of typology: all this changed by General Pitt-Rivers, the inventor of modern methods of excavation, who demonstrated the importance of the object-in-juxtaposition and of common things as contrasted with rarities: his anthropological outlook and its impact on archaeology: the new view-point which he represented gave new life to archaeology: illustrated by examples from Africa and Bulgaria: the world looked at as culture-patterns instead of as periods of history arbitrarily divided: the past in the present (Poti and Southampton).

Origin of the term 'field archaeology' and its connotation: resumption of narrative, beginning with General Roy and his circle: Guest one of the pioneers of field archaeology: later work in Scotland, culminating in the subsidized productions of Cole, Christison and Romilly Allen, the forerunners of state-organized archaeology: the German Limes-Kommission and the British Royal Commissions: the Ordnance Survey and archaeology: their early association (Roy and Colt Hoare): the original 1-inch map: the large-scale survey, its merits and defects: failure to utilize existing data: the objects of the topographical record enumerated: philosophical, practical, geographical: the distributional method marks the achievement of complete independence in space as did the stratigraphic in time: now a recognized normal technique, based ultimately on field-work.

the population-pattern: evolution of the modern Bath road taken as an example and its courses from Roman to modern times described in detail: continuity of use discussed and some exceptions cited: factors which made for continuity and disuse: bush clearance and bridges, involving constant attention: roads other than made Roman ones and the difficulty of identifying such: parallel examples of bush clearance for roads in Sudan and the habits of their users: existing tracks improved: methods of upkeep, and results that would follow from a short period of neglect: task of discovering main prehistoric thoroughfares: the great open plain of Salisbury and the three corridors of approach, and the Jurassic (Cotswold-Lincoln-Humber) thoroughfare: description of the southern corridor along the South Downs to Winchester and beyond: and of the narrow corridor (Pilgrim's Way and Harroway) past Stonehenge to the west, possibly to Ictis: the third corridor is the Icknield Way from the Wash to the same southern chalklands: its course described with the bars, loops, fords and ancient sites along it: the two ridgeways (Chiltern and Berks) merely alternative, perhaps older, routes: the 'oldest cross-roads in England' near Stonehenge, whose exact siting acquires significance: the fourth corridor is the Jurassic belt from the Humber to Bath: its track on Lincoln Edge and from Northampton to Stow-on-the-Wold with an earlier (?) loop: the continuation by Iron Age sites to Bath: evidence of age and purpose: cross-communications between the people of the Cotswolds and those of Wessex and the probable routes followed: a passing note on a road, probably medieval, along the Corallian ridge from Malmesbury to Oxford and Abingdon: summary of preceding paragraphs: some other routes not discussed.

Filling the gaps: barrow-hunting: Britain as a training-ground for field archaeology elsewhere: 'passed R.B.': lynchets (long known) explained: negative and positive lynchets: double-lynchet-ways: plough-marks: dene-holes (Pliny): Celtic fields and linear earthworks: dating by contact (examples): distribution of prehistoric fields briefly described: the Curwens' field-work in Sussex.

Reasons why querns are regarded as important by modern archaeologists, who put greater value on functional and necessary objects than on others: why querns are both: some remarks on them in general: the material they are made of and its source: the Pen Pits and their relation to the road system: history of their discovery: General Pitt-Rivers involved: his excavations prove them to be pre-Norman quern-quarries, thus discomfiting Thomas Kerslake and his theories: Cole's Pits in Berks probably quarries for mill-stones and no evidence of pre-medieval working: geology and roads show close resemblances to those at the Pen Pits: the rôle of Faringdon as a market and road centre: a new hill-fort described: its possible connection with the 'bridge-road' connecting Wessex with the Cotswolds via the Corallian ridge: Worm's Heath: why this chapter was required.

PLATES

TEXT FIGURES

Acknowledgments

The plans, except where otherwise stated, have been drawn by Mr Frank Addison, F.S.A., from my pencil models. I wish to thank Mr Addison for the care and efficiency with which he has done the work. The basis is in many cases the first edition of the six-inch Ordnance Survey maps, whose copyright has expired. Thanks are due to the Director-General of the Ordnance Survey for permission to reproduce part of an unpublished O.S. map (Fig. 15) and for other help. Plate 5b is from a photograph kindly lent by Mr F. G. Roe, pioneer of the study of animal tracks. I wish also to thank Sir Cyril Fox for supplying most of the material about linear earthworks in Wales (pp. 248–51). Specific acknowledgments have been made in the text and thanks are due to all those who have allowed use of their material; it is hoped that, if any have been overlooked, they will be indulgent.

The photographs were taken by me except where otherwise stated.

The first part of the book was written originally for a series of lectures which were not delivered; the lecture-form of address has been retained. The book contains, I fear, much irritating repetition, caused by the fact that the writing of it was carried out at intervals over a period of years. This may, however, serve to emphasize certain aspects regarded as important, and save a certain number of cross-references. Some personal reminiscences have been given when it seemed desirable to put them on record as forming part of the history of the subject.

Nursling, September, 1952   O.G.S.C.

A few misprints and errors have been corrected, and four items under Hampshire, accidentally omitted, have been inserted in Appendix 3. Otherwise there are no alterations.

March, 1953.   O.G.S.C.

Minor corrections only have been made, and page references added to the Plates. A new illustration has been used for Plate 5a.

February, 1954.   O.G.S.C.

Preface,

or, What Is Archaeology?

IN CASE SOME of those who read this book may be hazy about what archaeology is, a few words may perhaps be said of it as a branch of knowledge. That is all the more necessary because the conception of archaeology which I and most of my colleagues in this country hold is quite a new thing, and it has hardly had time as yet to influence the thought of educated people and to become a normal part of their outlook on the world. That may seem to be a large claim and expectation. I do not, of course, mean to suggest that every educated person will eventually become qualified to conduct excavations; that would be absurd. What I mean can best be explained by discussing what archaeology is and what its aims are. Archaeology is that branch of science which is concerned with past phases of human culture; in practice it is concerned more, but not exclusively, with early and prehistoric phases than with those illustrated by written documents. Archaeology is concerned with the culture of the Stone Ages and the other prehistoric periods; but its techniques can also be used to discover things about such historic periods as the Dark Ages, and Saxon and medieval times. There is no period whose remains are not susceptible to archaeological investigation. A little book has just been published describing the excavation of a Jesuit mission-station in Canada, and the results were of a kind that will prove extremely useful to future workers in that country.

Archaeology, then, is concerned with culture. What is culture? Tylor, the founder of anthropology, defined it as 'that complex whole which includes knowledge, belief, art, morals, law, custom, and any other capabilities and habits acquired by man as a member of society'. Culture traits, he continued, were to be regarded and studied as a distinct class of phenomena; and he classified them into such categories as weapons, myths, rites, social customs, etc. It was the business of the student to 'make out their distribution in geography and history and the relations which exist between them'. Tylor was, of course, thinking primarily of still living primitive peoples, the subject of anthropology, and naturally he emphasized those traits which, being immaterial, are as a rule not available to the archaeologist. But archaeology is merely the past tense of anthropology, and it is concerned with material culture-traits chiefly because the others, by the accident of their nature, have vanished and left no trace.

Archaeology studies these culture-traits as a separate and distinct class of phenomena, which can be explained in terms of culture. They are explained geographically by distribution maps, historically by their evolution. Axes, for instance, are culture-traits; their distribution tells us much about the culture of Britain in, say, the Early Bronze Age, especially when compared with the distribution of certain types of pottery called beakers, also culture-traits. The evolution of the bronze axe can be studied without any regard to the men who made it; but when we have finished we shall know more about the movements of culture and population during the period covered. Similarly we may study the evolution and distribution of hill-forts, burial mounds or field systems. There is no culture-trait that cannot profitably be studied in this way; and outside archaeology the method can be used by the folklorist and historian. For instance, the distribution of certain folk-tales associated with megalithic monuments is very enlightening, and so is that of gavel-kind and the three field system. The study of place-names in time and space is a valuable auxiliary technique for the historian, whose method conforms precisely with the principles laid down by Tylor.

A few words about explaining culture in its own terms. The method is best illustrated by examples from art criticism. In the old days it was usual to explain art motifs as originating from some innate disposition. Anglo-Saxon art contained many animal and plant motifs because, it was said, the Anglo-Saxons were particularly fond of animals and plants. How did the critics know? Simply because their art contained such motifs—a beautiful example of argument in a circle. Such a pseudo-psychological explanation explained nothing. Actually, one of the commonest motifs of Anglo-Saxon (Northumbrian) art is the vine-scroll, in which birds are represented within the coils of a vine. The makers may have been fond of birds and vines, though few Northumbrian artists in the seventh and eighth centuries can ever have seen a vine-plant; but we know that, so far from being an Anglo-Saxon invention, it originated in Syria and was introduced into England by artists imported from the Mediterranean by Benedict Biscop. The culture-trait is thus explained culturally, not psychologically. It originated simply in the spread of a fashion.

The gradual growth of archaeological knowledge—that is to say, of knowledge derived from a study of the material culture—has brought about a complete change in our method of thinking about the people of past periods. When I began to study archaeology it was usual to refer to the earlier inhabitants of Britain by racial names, such as Iberian, Celts, Picts and Scots, Goidels and Brythons. People derived much consolation from those blessed words, and were quite content to be told that a long barrow was an Iberian grave, that hill-forts were Celtic, brochs Pictish, and most of what remained to be attributed to the Goidels or Brythons. Did that convey much meaning to them? Do we not know more that really matters about the builders of our hill-forts from knowing, thanks to archaeological excavation, that they were agriculturalists who tilled a certain type of field (which we can see and plan), used certain kinds of pottery, lived in certain kinds of house, used certain types of implements and weapons? Is not that better than a mere name? I was recently asked by an earnest enquirer to tell him who the Celts were, and was tempted to reply 'the people who spoke Celtic'; so too one might describe the Iberians as the ancient inhabitants of Spain, the Picts as those of Northern Scotland, the Scots as displaced Irish, and the Goidels and Brythons as Celts. These terms have no place in archaeology which does not now need to borrow its labels from philology and should never have done so.[1]

Nor do we bother much to-day about the head-shapes of prehistoric peoples. That is, of course, an important branch of knowledge, but it is the concern of physical anthropologists and anatomists, to whom we leave it, just as we leave the Goidels and Brythons to the philologists. The earlier interest was based largely upon a false premise—that culture and physical anatomy were causally related. That was the racial doctrine of Gobineau and the Nazis, which is now exploded. Cultures are explained in terms of culture and not of philology or anatomy. The result is a great enlargement of knowledge. We see, for instance, the succession of cultures that have occupied Britain, each developing into the other and influenced or even partially replaced by others. We give them special names such as the Beaker-folk, the Wessex culture, Iron Age A and so on; these names are not jargon; they are technical terms necessary for clarity of thought and expression, and they are fully and authoritatively explained in the popular books which anyone can now buy. The connotation of these names is cultural, and it is far wider than the connotation of such earlier terms as Iberian, etc. could ever be. Why? Because it covers all the culture-traits that have been brought to light by archaeological research. To explain a long barrow as an Iberian grave was not really to explain it at all; it was simply a camouflaged anthropological description based on the head-shape of the skeletons and on a theory of their origin. It was, in fact, an explanation of culture in terms of race. But to say that long barrows belong to Neolithic A brings them into relation with a culture of which we know something, or, if we don't, it is our own fault and can easily be remedied by reading.

Now it is natural that the culture-traits which the archaeologist finds most often are just those common objects which are in daily use and serve the basic needs of existence—food, clothing, shelter, protection against enemies. Thus he acquires an essentially sound point of view. He classifies past cultures on these principles—as those of hunters, food-gatherers, farmers; or by the types of houses they lived in and their methods of defending them. Such things are still basic; we need no reminder to-day of the importance of food, housing and defence; and if we are apt sometimes to overlook the importance of clothes the advertisements will soon put us right. Thus from his training and experience the archaeologist learns to look at both past and present from the same point of view. He will perhaps feel more at home when on holiday he visits some primitive people who may still be in an Iron Age stage of culture, for his training will direct his attention to just those things which are important in their lives—their agricultural system, method of grinding and stor-

---

[1] I am fully conscious of having sinned myself in this respect and have been justly reproved; but that was a generation ago, at the tail end of an earlier epoch, before we had, as archaeologists, achieved our independence. See *Antiquity* vi. 1932, 156–60.

B

ing corn, weaving, houses, choice of site for villages. Incidentally, he will find that his interest in these matters evokes an immediate response; the villagers will be surprised and pleased to find that he attaches the same importance to these things as they do themselves; and they will often disconcert him by asking questions about corresponding things in his own country.

Thus we find that the modern archaeologist looks at both past and present from the same view-point. It will now be clearer what I had in mind when I said (in the first paragraph) that the modern conception of archaeology had not yet had time to influence the thought of educated people, and to become a normal part of their outlook on the world. I meant that people still regard archaeology as concerned with isolated bits and pieces of past cultures—the churches, ruined buildings, coins, potsherds—or with the 'higher' traits such as art, temples and palaces, richly-furnished tombs. All these things are, of course, culture-traits and the concern of the archaeologist; but he is interested in a ruined building (to select one example) not because it looks picturesque but because it is a building. The thrill of excavating a rich interment is quite real and genuine and very enjoyable; but it is not an unalloyed archaeological thrill such as one experiences, for instance, in finding and tracing a new piece of Roman road or linear earthwork. Having experienced both I can say that I have derived a deeper and more lasting satisfaction from the latter. Why? Because it satisfied my ego? That explains nothing; why did it do so? The only reason I can suggest is that my ego has had a sound training in modern archaeology and craves for appropriate nourishment.

But to return to archaeology and culture. The basis of culture is technology. A hunting people depends for its existence on certain technological instruments such as the bow and spear, an agricultural one upon the hoe or plough. The one is usually nomadic and the other sedentary, and each has its appropriate social system closely adapted to its mode of living. The technology of military defence is also an important determinant of social and political organization. The Turkish Empire of the sixteenth century was founded upon gunpowder, and modern weapons have made old-fashioned revolutions impossible. This is not the place to develop this theme with which the works of Professor Gordon Childe have made us familiar. My point now is that this view of the past (which extends down to present times) is based upon the data provided by history and archaeology, and that it is not only legitimate for an archaeologist to be interested in social and political forms of organization but inevitable that he should be. The sequence is as follows: archaeology deals with the remains of material culture which include technological instruments; technology is a determinant of social and political organization not only in past ages but also to-day. One therefore who has studied the technologies of the past and their influence on society will be better qualified to detect their influence on modern society than one who has not so studied. It was archaeologists who discovered the Agricultural Revolution that begat civilization. May they not have something to say also about the social effects of the Industrial (or Fuel) Revolution? Yet when they say it they are told to stick to archaeology!

Where does archaeology end? We are allowed to use archaeological technique in dealing with a well-documented 'historical' period like the Dark Ages, or one that is less well documented such as ancient Egypt or Mesopotamia. Future archaeologists will perhaps excavate the ruined factories of the nineteenth and twentieth centuries, when the radiation effects of atom bombs have died away. These technological matters will then be legitimate. Why are they not so when they are so much better known?

I am not, of course, suggesting that anyone should start excavating a bombed factory site to-day. I am merely pointing out that it is impossible, if technology is admitted to be an archaeological concern at all, to restrain the archaeologist in drawing deductions from it in all periods, including the present. If they are valid for the past, they are equally valid now. Such fascinating problems as the relative influence of great men and great inventions on history—though this is an old-fashioned mode of expression—are perfectly legitimate subjects to be dealt with in an archaeological publication. Human culture is one and undivided in fact and only split up into past and present, pre-history and history, for convenience of study.

This book is concerned with some of the ways in which archaeologists can pursue their task. These have to be learnt by long practice and there is a risk that, in course of learning and of becoming eventually a specialist, the student may get lost amongst the trees. As their headings indicate, I have tried, in writing these chapters, to avoid this danger by relating particular facts to general principles.

CHAPTER 1

Archaeology before 1859

THIS BOOK IS entitled *Archaeology in the Field*, and it will in fact be concerned chiefly with open-air work. The best way of explaining my title is to show how archaeology began as the handmaid of history—that is, of books—and how, by developing its own techniques, it has become a subject in its own right. Since those techniques all begin in the open air, it becomes evident that field archaeology is in fact nearly co-terminous with archaeology itself.

It is very pertinent to this enquiry to ask—Why is it that our knowledge of the past has so greatly expanded in modern times? Remember that the evolution of man from the ancestral primate, and the origins of civilization, are discoveries that have been made during the span of two lives, one of which is still running. Why did not other earlier generations make these discoveries? There have been people in every period of the past who were, in their way, archaeologists. An ancient ruler of Mesopotamia excavated a temple and recorded the result. Pausanius the Greek (*fl.* A.D. 174) was a typical local antiquary. There were museums in ancient Rome. William of Malmesbury has left the only description of some antiquities at Glastonbury that must have been about five centuries old. The nucleus of the Ashmolean Museum at Oxford was formed just three hundred years ago. But in spite of this age-long interest in the past, the accepted view in the early nineteenth century was that the earth itself was not more than about six thousand years old! Why this sudden spurt forward? Why has the advancement of knowledge during the last hundred years been so infinitely greater than during all the preceding millennia? Is it merely a coincidence that this advancement took place *pari passu* with that in material culture? I put the last question without attempting to answer it here, and would merely say that *technique* is responsible for both advances.

All archaeology before the nineteenth century was pre-scientific and inductive. It accepted certain postulates found in books and attempted to square the facts of observation with those postulates. Herodotus, the father of history, got his account of Egyptian history from the priests, who got it presumably from a hotch-potch of written records, not from the ancient monuments. By employing the technique of archaeology we have caught up and surpassed him in this subject, though we had a handicap of $2\frac{1}{2}$ millennia. For the classical Greeks history began with Homer, as it did for the Romans—so far as they thought about it at all. Virgil gave the ruling family a respectable Homeric ancestry; and the fashion spread to England in the Middle Ages. But then the temporal power of the Christian church enforced the acceptance of certain dogmatic views about the history of man and nature; and those who differed did so at their own peril. A few travellers like William of Worcester (1415–82 ?) recorded their observations of antiquities seen during their journeys. An occasional historian such as Hector Boece or Boethius (1465 ?–1536) and George Buchanan (1506–82) mentioned the remains of material culture in the course of their narrative. But they were primarily historians for whom the written document came first, nor were they in any sense field archaeologists. Even William Camden himself (1551–1623), the founder of British archaeology, came to archaeology by way of the classical writers, with whom, as a schoolmaster, he must have been familiar. Though his concern was primarily with antiquities rather than with written documents, he consistently explained the former in the light of the latter. He had of course read the Commentaries of Julius Caesar, and was therefore familiar with the Belgae who are often mentioned in his *Britannia* (first edition 1586) and marked on his maps. From Caesar too he got those 'ancient Britons' who were to dominate the archaeological scene for three subsequent centuries. They were the aborigines responsible for everything that was not obviously medieval or Roman, and for much that was in fact attributable to one or the other. They built Stonehenge and all the barrows, and the hill-forts or 'camps' as he called them. Influenced no doubt by Caesar's narrative (which is naturally concerned with warfare) they were regarded as perpetually fighting battles with each other. The hill-forts were military camps, and the barrows the graves of soldiers killed in battle. A line of barrows marked the retreat of a defeated army—which must have been leisurely and unharassed.[1] That there is some truth in this view is proved by Caesar's own remark[2] that Cassivelaunus had been at perpetual warfare with the other states. But the nature of the warfare was wrongly conceived, and all the centuries of prehistoric times were telescoped into a single 'ancient British' period. The 'military' view lasted into the nineteenth century.[3] Camden's *Britannia* was a 'best seller' and 'though written in Latin, it quickly ran through six editions.' Appearing first, in 1586, at a moment when the new vitality released by the bourgeois revolution was at its zenith, its publication was well timed and its popularity great. But its author 'was no mere child of the moment. He created an organic whole out of a vague, incoherent, ill-understood material. The scholar who does this creates an epoch in historical writing as surely as a Vergil or a Tennyson creates an epoch in literary style'.[4]

Camden was a schoolmaster and later became a Herald. From about 1571 he travelled about England collecting materials for his *Britannia*. Some of his notes were subsequently acquired by Sir Robert Cotton and are now in the British Museum.[5] From this and from the *Britannia* it is evident that his interests were all-embracing and included not only

[1] This portion of my book is based upon the first part of my paper on 'The distribution of Early Bronze Age settlements in Britain' read before the Oxford University Anthropological Society in 1910, and again before the Royal Geographical Society in 1912, and published (without this first historical part) in the *Geographical Journal*, Vol. XL (Sept. 1912) 184–203; 304–17. A much fuller and better account is now available in Kendrick's *British Antiquity* and Stuart Piggott's *William Stukeley*.   [2] *De Bello Gallico*, v, 11.

[3] Lysons, for instance, says of Berkshire that 'having been frequently the scene of military operations in remote times [it] exhibits the remains of many ancient camps' (*Berkshire*, 1806, 213). But that does not necessarily follow. Defences are constructed against a threatened attack that may never take place. The forts built by Henry VIII, those built during the Napoleonic wars and in 1940 were never the scene of any fighting. They were brought into existence by war-scares. But in prehistoric times it must be admitted that such war-scares would not occur until invaders had actually landed somewhere on the island. Even so, many hill-forts may never have been the scene of fighting.

[4] Haverfield in *The Roman Occupation of Britain*, p.69. Haverfield himself performed precisely the same task for Roman Britain.

[5] Cotton, *Julius F. vi.* See Haverfield on this, *Trans. Cumb. and Westmorland Arch. Soc. NS.* XI, 1911, 343–78, from which I have taken the facts here summarized.

inscriptions but also camps, barrows and medieval sites. But it was inscriptions that bulked biggest in his mind, both those of Roman origin and also others of later date, such as the Bodvoc stone in Glamorganshire and the Bewcastle cross in Cumberland (with runes). That was to be expected of a schoolmaster whose chief concern was naturally with the classical writers. It was only natural, therefore, that the Roman Wall should occupy much of his attention, for along it were scattered very many inscribed stones, some of which have since disappeared. Camden and his correspondents were, I think, the first to copy and record these; there is no trace of any such record before the Reformation. His idea of writing a book about British antiquities stimulated others to record and describe them in letters to him. It was an original idea, made possible by the invention of printing and (even more perhaps) by the Bourgeois Revolution, which created a class with money to buy the books and leisure to read them. This class included schoolmasters and university teachers as well as the new landed gentry.[6]

There had been people interested in antiquities ever since Bede, but they were isolated phenomena and their work ended at their death. Camden's did not; copies of his books, being multiplied by printing, fell into the hands of others and bore fruit. The archaeological correspondence he began was thenceforth a regular and recurring phenomenon that has continued down to the present day. The Honorary Correspondents of the Archaeology Branch of the Ordnance Survey are merely the modern phase of an activity begun nearly 400 years ago by Camden.

One of Camden's most helpful correspondents was Reginald Bainbrigg who was born about 1545 at Hilton, four miles east of Appleby in Westmorland. Bainbrigg was probably related to that Christopher Bainbrigg, also born at Hilton, who became Provost of the Queen's College at Oxford in 1495 and subsequently a Cardinal (he was poisoned at Rome in 1514). Reginald became headmaster of Appleby grammar school in 1580, and his books were still preserved there in 1911 when Haverfield wrote his account of the Cotton Julius collection. He had read the 1590 and 1594 editions of the *Britannia* which appear to have begun, or more probably encouraged, his interest in antiquities. In 1599 and 1601 he made archaeological tours, recording his observations in letters to Camden. The first began on 15th August, and proceeded along the line of Hadrian's Wall from Bowness to Birdoswald, and included visits to Netherby and Bewcastle; from Birdoswald he went on to Risingham and Rochester in Redesdale.[7] The second tour was from Bowness to Carvoran and from Sewingshields to the North Tyne.[8] Though chiefly interested in inscriptions he did not neglect other antiquities and he has left an account of the stone circle called Long Meg and her daughters.[9] He not only recorded inscriptions but also collected them, and even made them! He kept these harmless 'forgeries' in his garden and showed them to visitors; some still survive. Though not an expert epigraphist, he was, says Haverfield, who had himself been a schoolmaster before he came to occupy the chair founded by Camden at Oxford, a 'scholar with some knowledge of Roman history and literature, and he wrote a respectable if not very racy Latin'. He is an interesting figure out of a bygone age, when classical teachers in England did not ignore their national antiquities. In his humble way, he is a fitting counterpart to his great contemporary,

[6] It would be very interesting to know who actually bought the early editions of the *Britannia*.
[7] Cotton, *Julius F. vi*, ff., 317–31 (*olim* 300–13).
[8] ib. id., ff., 339–40 (*olim* 320–7).
[9] ib. id., f., 335.

who issued the first four editions of his *Britannia* while successively usher and headmaster of Westminster. It seems that he and Camden never met, having failed to do so when Camden was touring in the north. Bainbrigg died in 1606.

Amongst Bainbrigg's friends were two Germans, Crispin Gericke and Servaz Reichel, who visited North Britain about 1602–4, perhaps together. They too copied Roman inscriptions.

The strong start made by British archaeology in the north was continued and extended there and eventually became a sort of department of its own, developing there on parallel but distinct lines. The next famous name there is that of John Horsley (1685–1732), a scholar of the first rank whose *Britannia Romanæ* appeared in the year of his death. He was followed by others who have throughout maintained a high standard of scholarship and later of excavation. That standard has never been higher than it is to-day, thanks to the work of Haverfield, Collingwood and Macdonald and others still living. But 'the Wall' is a subject in itself, and the very excellence and quantity of the work done on it has had the effect of scaring off southerners, who in any case are preoccupied with those prehistoric remains that are more abundant in their region. The present writer's field-work has chiefly been done either far to the south of the Wall or north of it, and he must plead ignorance of its archaeological history.

How far north the influence of Camden extended is unknown. The earliest evidence of field archaeology is a tract of a certain Commissary Robert Maule, doubtless a relation of the first Earl of Panmure.[10] But the first serious major work was that of Sir Robert Sibbald (1641–1722) who was followed by others, working (it seems) independently and without much or any intercourse with their southern fellow antiquaries. The two lines of development converged in General Roy (1726–90); and although there continued to be a distinct school in Scotland (and a very good one, too) there was not, during the nineteenth century, so much isolation.

But the next field archaeologist after Camden and his correspondents was John Aubrey (1626–97), who was the effective founder of British field archaeology, and a good deal more than that as well. Not only did he discover the stone circle of Avebury—and what a discovery that must have been!—but his *Brief Lives* mark the first essays at modern biography. He left copious records of his observations in his *Monumenta Britannica* (still unpublished, in the Bodleian Library). He was an acute observer and a careful recorder, and blessed with an attractive style and a knack of vivid portraiture. After him, in the eighteenth century, came William Stukeley (1687–1765) whose best work was done about 1720. Stukeley was a good observer and the plans and drawings he made are faithful records and invaluable to-day. But he had a vivid imagination and in later life allowed himself to wander into realms of speculation that have done his reputation much harm. Finally came Sir Richard Colt Hoare (1754–1838) and his collaborator William Cunnington (1754–1810), links between the old age and the new. These field archaeologists of the eighteenth and early nineteenth centuries belonged to what may be called the 'country gentleman' school, whose outstanding merit was that they rode about the country and saw things for themselves. Stukeley gathered round himself a coterie of kindred spirits with whom he used to exchange correspondence; they even did some desultory excavation,

---

[10] For this see my *Topography of Roman Scotland*, 97–8, note 3. The tract is still amongst the muniments of Brechin Castle. It appears to have been written about 1606–12.

but left the scantiest records. William Cunnington was a wine-merchant of Devizes, where his great-grandson, happily still alive, carried on the business in recent years. It was Cunnington whose opening of the barrows on Salisbury Plain aroused Colt Hoare's curiosity, and most fortunately so; for Colt Hoare published a sumptuous and remarkably good account of both Cunnington's and his own excavations. To Colt Hoare is due the honour of publishing, in his *Ancient Wiltshire*,[11] the first archaeological section of an earthwork (Wansdyke), and of drawing certain conclusions from the stratification that it revealed. Colt Hoare also was the centre of a group of field archaeologists, two at least of whom have left ample records of their observations. Thomas Leman (1751–1826) rode about the country along Roman roads, staying with the local gentry, and has left manuscript notes now preserved in the Library of the Bath Literary and Philosophic Institution and in that of the Wiltshire Archaeological Society at Devizes. John Skinner (1772–1839) bequeathed ninety-eight volumes of notes, all recording his own first-hand observations, to the British Museum. None of these valuable manuscripts have ever been published, except in the form of brief extracts, nor has Aubrey's *Monumenta Britannica* in the Bodleian Library. Aubrey and Skinner have been the victims of literary men, but Leman remains completely unknown. At the time when they rode abroad there was far more to be seen than there was when I began to do the same on foot; and now that the Army, the Royal Air Force, the Forestry Commission, the builder, the gravel-digger, the water-works engineer and the modern farmer have joined forces to obliterate what little was left, their records have gained additional value.

The background of these early field archaeologists was, as I said, an exclusively literary one. They explained what came to their notice by reference to some literary source. Caesar spoke of the Druids; and Stukeley explains the bronze axes which we called 'socketed celts' as a special kind of implement used by the Druids to cut off the boughs of oak and mistletoe required for their rites. He explained the loop, which was actually used to tie the axe to its handle, as put there so that, when not in use, the Druids could 'hang them to their girdles'! Others regarded them as the chisels of statuaries, used in making graven images, or as war-flails, spearheads or some kind of Roman weapon. The socketed axe was explained by the books; it was not itself used as a clue, as evidence. It is as if the detective, on finding an old revolver on the ground, should consult the files of the local paper, discover that a murder had been committed recently and announce triumphantly that this was the weapon used by the murderer. Centuries earlier the monks of St. Albans followed precisely the same line of reasoning. A skeleton had been found in an adjacent barrow, and they at once proclaimed that it must be the body of St. Alban the Martyr—as if no one else had ever died or been buried in that neighbourhood.

Roman villas, are, of course, amongst the commonest of British antiquities. Their discovery has gone on continuously from Saxon times to the present day, and no doubt the last has not yet been found. The Saxons called them 'spotted floors' (faga flora), and at one place so named (Fawlor in Oxfordshire) the mosaic pavement which gave its name to the place has come to light again in modern times. The attribution of Roman villas to the Romans was an easy one that could hardly be missed, for the Romans were named

[11] North Wilts, 1819, 123. The section is through Wansdyke near Tan Hill. Hoare's engraving (on p. 225 here) shows that the bank was raised to a greater height at some date long enough afterwards for a turf-line to have formed on the original bank. Thus, said Hoare, were the conjections of his ingenious brother antiquary, Mr. Leman, confirmed; for he had always considered Wansdyke as the work of two distinct nations.

in the source-books. But even here the military obsession originating with Julius Caesar led some astray. Thomas Hearne (1678–1735) deserves an honourable place in the list of the early field-archaeologists, if only because, when the Roman villa at Stonesfield was found, he walked over from Oxford to inspect it, starting before breakfast, a distance of some seven miles each way. He was, however, essentially a bookman, an indoor student, and far more at home amongst the books of the Bodleian, of which he was Librarian, than in the country fields. The mosaic pavement at Stonesfield puzzled him and he racked his brain to produce explanations. In accordance with current practice he turned to his books and found that in the Roman army there was a person who held an office called *tesserarius*.[12] Mosaic pavements were made of *tesserae*; *ergo* the *tesserarius* was obviously the official concerned. And he then evolved the delightful theory that the duty of the *tesserarius* was to pave the general's tent each night, as they marched conquering through the country, with a mosaic pavement! Could there be a more amusing instance of the futility of the bookish mind? It is only fair to add that Hearne, to whom I say we owe a great debt of gratitude for what he has left on record, eventually abandoned this theory, not on commonsense grounds, however, but for some incompatability of a learned kind which I forget.

But this accumulation of evidence could not go on for ever being explained from the books. Sooner or later something was bound to turn up that the books could not explain away, and it did. The truth emerged, not from a well but from a cave, and from a gravel pit. A gentleman called MacEnery dug in Kent's Cavern near Torquay and found what were certainly stone implements of human manufacture associated with the remains of mammoth and other extinct animals. This was all wrong, and to MacEnery, who was a Catholic, it appeared not only wrong but positively dangerous; and he therefore held his peace, thus forfeiting his claim to one of the epoch-making discoveries of history. That honour goes therefore to a Frenchman, Boucher de Perthes (1788–1868) who claimed to have found similar associations in the gravel pits of the Somme valley near his home. Interest was at once aroused in England, and in 1859 a small, unofficial (but most authoritative) commission of enquiry was instituted. The evidence on which the claim rested was both archaeological and geological; it had to be proved that the stone implements found were really of human manufacture, and that they were found in an undisturbed deposit of gravel whose age could be geologically determined. The Commission consisted of Sir John Evans and Sir Joseph Prestwich,[13] representing archaeology and geology, and they returned home fully satisfied that the claims made by Boucher de Perthes were well founded. This was a revolutionary event, for it proved that the antiquity of man was far greater than was allowed for by any of the books, and that it must be dated in hundreds of millenia. The date was most opportune, for in the same year Darwin published the *Origin of Species*. Dr Joan Evans has well stated its repercussions:

'The establishment of the existence of palaeolithic man . . . did more than add chapters to human history. It added vast stretches of time to those ages which even the most

---

[12] The *tesserarius* was the army officer to whom the commanding officer gave the watchword or orders of the day, to be passed on to the men.

[13] The commission, as I have named it, was originally instituted as a private party of geological friends by Sir Joseph Prestwich; but of those invited only Sir John Evans actually turned up. See Joan Evans's life of the Evans's, *Time and Chance* 1943, 100–106, and the article in *Antiquity* XXII, 1949, 115–125.

anthropocentric philosopher must consider; it destroyed the conventional chronology of Church and University; it brought a new proportion into man's view of the cosmos, that was only comparable with the change of proportion brought about by the Renaissance discovery of a new world. No discovery of a new civilization of historic or nearly historic date could have had the same scientific and philosophical repercussions: for the establishment of the existence of man in Quarternary times involved a fundamental re-orientation. It was the proof by Evans and Prestwich of the validity of Boucher de Perthes' discoveries in 1858,[14] that by its extension of the time of man's habitation of the earth made the theories of Darwin's *Origin of Species* . . . directly applicable to *Homo Sapiens*.'

The year 1859 marked a decisive turning-point in human thought. It marked the triumph of the scientific method of observation and deduction over the authoritarian method which argues from the general to the particular, from statements in books to the facts of nature. The road had been prepared by geologists who were, and still are, closely associated with the earliest discoveries of man and his works. William Smith (1769–1839) had already by his observations established the main sequence of stratigraphical succession at the end of the eighteenth century; and early in the nineteenth he went further and proved that those strata could be dated wherever they occurred by the fossils found in them. Darwin's own work had a geological foundation, being closely concerned with time—and geology is the measure of time in the history of life upon the earth. (Two of the chapters in the *Origin of Species* are purely geological.)[15] Stratification is, of course, the record of lapses of time; and it is because stratification was later to enter so closely into archaeological technique that I have given space to these geological remarks here.

At the beginning of this chapter I asked why our knowledge of the past had so greatly expanded in modern times, although an interest in the past is as old as history itself. The question has already been answered; the expansion is the direct result of the application of a new method, that of observation and deduction. But that answer merely suggests another question. Why was that method not applied before? To say that the time was not ripe until the eighteenth and nineteenth centuries is merely to evade the problem. It is easier to explain why the advance did not occur during the Middle Ages than to give a satisfactory reason why it was not made in earlier periods. The existence in England and France of a long series of stratified rocks accounts for much; there was no such easily observed sequence in the Mediterranean basin or further east. But the rocks existed here and were available for observation and deduction throughout the Middle Ages. The prime cause is, I think, social. I have developed this idea elsewhere,[16] and here will say only that I am sure the great advance in knowledge was closely connected with the industrial revolution, which created a leisured class whose members could say what they thought without fear of economic sanctions or social ostracism. The decisive battle was won by the great protagonist Huxley at the Oxford meeting of the British Association in 1860. Since then things have changed. The storm of abuse with which the new discoveries were greeted has subsided. Now that the war is irretrievably lost we are told that the issues so hotly contested were in fact irrelevant, that Genesis doesn't really matter and you can

[14] (*sic*) for 1859. The discoveries themselves had been made over the preceding decade.
[15] For evidence of the decisive importance of geology on Darwin's work see 'Darwin and the forgotten Mr. Lonsdale'. by Paul Tasch, *Geological Magazine*, LXXXVII (July–August 1950), 292–6.
[16] *Sociological Review* XXIV, 165.

take it or leave it as you like. It is ironical that some of the greatest advances in recent knowledge have been made by a Catholic priest in those very gravels of the Somme valley where the trouble began. The sceptic notes that while Boucher de Perthes is conveniently forgotten, Henry VIII is not, and he wonders whether the loss of temporal power may not be something that really does matter.

CHAPTER 2

Archaeology Achieves Independence

TOWARDS THE END of his long life I asked Professor Sayce when, in his opinion, modern archaeology began, and he replied 'With Schliemann.' What gave exceptional value to his opinion was the fact that he had lived right through the whole development himself and known most of the protagonists, from the Abbeville days down to Ur. Schliemann was a German business man who achieved the plan he had cherished for many years, and dug Troy. He was the first person who dug purely for knowledge on any considerable scale, and dug with method. That method has been criticized, but it has emerged with credit. Schliemann published his results in book form, and those who expect to find there the plans and sections that adorn the best modern excavation reports will be disappointed. But his unpublished notes show that he was a keen observer of all those things which the excavator should look for, first and foremost of course stratification. He also admitted his mistakes. Judged by modern standards his technique was primitive, but judged by the only legitimate standard—that of his predecessors and contemporaries—it represented a great advance. One has only to read Mr Seton Lloyd's history of excavation in Mesopotamia[1] to realize this, and to understand why Professor Sayce did not date the beginning of modern archaeology with Layard or Rawlinson.

But when all due honour has been paid to Schliemann it must be admitted that he was still under the spell of books. He selected for his attention the famous sites of the Iliad, and he began at any rate with the idea of finding relics of the world of Homer, and achieved his ambition in full measure. That was a perfectly proper sort of ambition, and it still is; but as I am trying to trace the development of archaeology from a servile to an independent status, it is right to emphasize certain aspects. Interesting though it will always be to dig a site made famous by history and thereby greatly to amplify and illustrate that history, it is no longer necessary to confine ourselves to such sites. By the progressive refinement of technique we can now select a completely undocumented site and reconstruct its history. Archaeologists welcome historical and epigraphic evidence, but they can exercise their function independently of such and in their own right. Their business is not merely to illustrate history but to remake it.

The first to do this on a big scale was Flinders Petrie.[2] When he went to Egypt he found

---

[1] *Foundations in the Dust*, Oxford University Press (Cumberlege) 1947.

[2] Petrie, though he was one of the first to free archaeology from the spell of books, was himself learned in all the wisdom of the classics. There is not of course, any *antagonism* between archaeology and books, or between archaeologists and scholars; but merely the assertion by archaeologists of their ability to make history by employing their own technique both on sites that come also within the sphere of history and on those that do not.

there a complete absence of excavation-method, and he got to work to build up some system. This is not the place to describe it, but it may be said that by inventing methods of recording finds, by typological study and by making and promptly publishing annual reports illustrated by plans and drawings he revolutionized excavation methods in the east. He discovered an early 'prehistoric', or rather predynastic, age, and by an ingenious method of sequence-dating of the pottery was able to assign relative dates to what was found. Following in his steps his pupils later added yet earlier periods to the original ones. Petrie introduced method and refined the technique of digging. In his books he laid stress on the uniqueness of every ancient site, and the corresponding responsibility thus thrust upon its excavator who by the mere act of excavation must also to some extent, and sometimes entirely, destroy it. 'Henceforth,' he said, 'that site exists only on paper. Your business as an archaeologist is to record everything so that future generations, who will have only your record, may be able in imagination to reconstruct that site, and visualize its life. For the whole business of the archaeologist is the reconstruction of past life.'[3]

That was the crowning achievement of one of Petrie's contemporaries, Sir Arthur Evans (1851–1941), son of Sir John who verified Boucher de Perthes' discoveries. Sir Arthur's life covered the whole span of modern archaeology, for he once told me that as a boy he well remembered the excitement at home caused by Abbeville discoveries; and that although he did not accompany his father on that first historic journey, he did accompany him on later visits to the Somme gravel pits. The great achievement of Sir Arthur Evans, fully comparable with Schliemann's and in most respects far surpassing it, was to discover in Crete the remains of a completely forgotten civilization, to excavate it mainly at his own cost, and to carry to a triumphant conclusion the masterly volumes describing his work. I have compared Evans' work with Schliemann's, and Schliemann as a pioneer will always be secure in his niche of fame; but Evans accomplished more. Schliemann found the great Homeric sites of Troy, Mycenae and Tiryns and revealed their glories; but Evans found a new civilization, a new art and a new and still unread language, of which there survived only the dimmest of memories in the great days of classical Greece, when that civilization had already been dead for more than half a millennium. Its rediscovery was the greatest achievement up to date of archaeology, excepting only those of Abbeville in which his father played so leading a rôle.

I am not setting out to write a history of archaeology; if I were I should have to mention many people and undertakings that I have passed over unnoticed. There would be an account of the work of Scandinavian archaeologists, of the Swiss lake-dwellings and much else. But my theme is field archaeology and the development of its technique, and for that many otherwise important matters are irrelevant. For my present purpose it is hardly necessary to mention such important work as that carried out in Palestine by the Palestine Exploration Fund, or in the Aegean and Greece by those who followed the lead given by Evans: that of course implies no disparagement.

You may be wondering what was going on in England all this time. It was a period of very slow progress. Local societies were pottering about, not quite understanding perhaps what they were really trying to do. Squires and parsons were 'opening' barrows, and stripping Roman villas, doing irreparable harm to everything they touched. Collectors were

---

[3] I have put in my own words the sense of various passages in Petrie's book *Methods and Aims in Archaeology*, which is still an admirable exposition of them.

snapping up the prehistoric and other antiquities that flowed in a steady stream from the gravel pits, dredgers and fields, often neglecting to label them. Canon Greenwell, who was both excavator and collector—a dangerous combination—and J. R. Mortimer were removing the contents of hundreds of burial-mounds from the earth to their cabinets. The Canon published an account of his work which was regarded as a classic forty years ago, though it did not contain a single plan or section. Mortimer's book was better, but still rather a painful production. Sir John Evans, a far bigger man, had published two great books on the stone and bronze implements of Great Britain and Ireland, largely based on his own collections; and had reduced to order the coins of the 'Ancient Britons'. The accumulation, from barrows and workmen's diggings, of a large quantity of objects created the need to group and classify them by types. Long before, in Denmark, a similar accumulation had provided a similar result, and was in fact responsible for the recognition of the existence of the Bronze Age. Classification was based upon types, and typology became a subject in itself. The French excelled at this game, and a vast number of subdivisions of the cave-period were invented, based partly upon stratification but chiefly upon typology. The objects themselves, so long the victims of the bookmen, were having their revenge; the socketed axe, once a Druid's tool for cutting mistletoe, became a subtype in an artificial scheme hatched in the study. It was forgotten that (for the archaeologist) these axes and things were not ends in themselves but means to an end—the fuller understanding of life (in Britain) during a period of the past. The older archaeologists seldom got behind the objects to look for the people who made them, in whom they were not interested. It was a sort of game played with antiquities as symbols, and like the machines in Erewhon the symbols threatened to take charge of their masters. This might still be going on (though I doubt it) had not General Pitt-Rivers changed it all. Of that great man (whom many readers of this book may never have heard of) I shall have a good deal to say later. For the present it is his work in South Wilts and Dorset that matters. He demonstrated there (amongst much else) that it was not the object in isolation which revealed the past but the object in relation to its original surroundings. A Roman coin picked up in a field is evidence of nothing except a hole in a Roman tunic; but one found under the undisturbed rampart of Bokerley Dyke (as he found it) was proof that the rampart had been built after the coin was lost, and must therefore be Roman or later (Fig. 1). That sounds simple and obvious enough, but so do many things after a genius has invented them. It did not appear so to many of his contemporaries, and it was not until the generation to which I belong grew up and acquired an influence that the outstanding importance of Pitt-Rivers was generally appreciated. There were some, of course, who recognized it; Haverfield was one, and I well remember an occasion when he exhibited a single potsherd of Arretine ware at a meeting of the Society of Antiquaries of London.[4] The Society was then dominated by dilettanti and collectors, and I am sure Haverfield did it to provoke them into some reaction. His point was, of course, that a single potsherd found in the right place has a value as *evidence* far outstripping its intrinsic value, which is almost nil; and he made this quite clear in the note which he read out to the Society.

Pitt-Rivers is usually described, and correctly, as the inventor of the modern method of excavation. Looked at from a different angle his achievement was to show the supreme importance of what is generally called stratification, but what might in Dorset be better

[4] *Proc. Soc. Ant. Lond.* 2 S. XXII, 1907, 461–2. The sherd was found at Bicester.

called juxtaposition.[5] In other words, it is not the object found which is important, but where and under exactly what conditions—not what he says but the way he says it! Remember that the whole point of Boucher de Perthes' finds was not the shape of the axe but the place of its discovery, in undisturbed gravel. Pitt-Rivers brought archaeology back to its starting-point after forty years' wanderings in the deserts of antiquarianism. To-

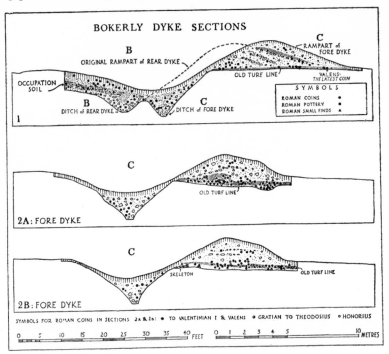

FIG. 1. Pitt-Rivers' sections of Bokerly Dyke (after Hawkes).

wards the end of his life he excavated sites in Cranborne Chase, especially two hill-top villages at Rotherley and Woodcutts. By his method of record of apparently trivial matters he was able to reconstruct models of these villages and to recreate in imagination the life of those who lived in them; and he has left a masterly description of that life as he visualized it. The things found were not ends in themselves, curios for the collector's cabinet or whatnot, but means to an end, the life of the past. He was the first to use the post-hole technique to restore the plan of wooden huts. All this told us much more than mere barrow-opening such as Greenwell's; though the General did excavate many barrows himself and did it in a way that has never been surpassed and rarely equalled. He emphasized the importance in archaeology of common things; they are, he said, of more importance than particular things because they are more prevalent.[6] He had, moreover, the humility to learn from his mistakes; most excavators before him had been afraid to admit error, and loath to do so in print. Pitt-Rivers didn't give a damn for what other people

[5] The point is trivial, but on the chalk downs there is little chance of stratification as a rule, though it does occur on densely occupied sites such as Maiden Castle.
[6] *Excavations in Cranborne Chase*, IV, 1898, 27.

thought about him; he had the superb independence of the aristocrat and went his own way regardless of gibes.

Pitt-Rivers reached archaeology by way of anthropology and an unexpected inheritance. His interest was first aroused when he was charged, as one of his official duties, with an enquiry concerning the improvement of the army musket of the day. He found that improvements in the past had been by means of the successive accretions of minute variations. He then turned his attention to the implements of modern primitive peoples and found that the same thing happened there. Upon this basis he built what was then a new branch of study, the technology of primitive peoples, forming a large collection himself, which is now divided between Oxford and his own museum at Farnham in Dorset. When he inherited the large family property of Cranborne Chase, replete with prehistoric remains, he decided to excavate there. He trained a staff of excavators of whom one (Mr St George Gray, the excavator of the Glastonbury and Meare lake-villages) is still happily with us. This is not the place to describe his method in detail; the essence of it is exact record, in plan, section, letterpress and tables, of all the facts observed, so that future generations may be able to read the record and get from it the facts that they, with their other and till then unforeseen requirements, wish to utilize. His records have in actual fact so been used to great advantage, both by myself and others.[7] That such is possible is the greatest tribute that can be paid to the soundness of his methods.

It is as the initiator of the modern method of excavation that Pitt-Rivers is most famous. But he also stands for the impact of anthropology upon archaeology. This means that he had learnt to see, imaginatively, the villagers of prehistoric Cranborne Chase as just the same sort of people living just the same sort of life as those in some existing modern village in, say, the Balkans or North Africa. Most of the earlier antiquaries never succeeded in doing this. To them the 'ancient Britons' were a race apart, perpetually fighting each other or engaged in bloodthirsty rites. I remember talking to such an antiquary myself and being shown what he called an altar, set up in his garden in Gloucestershire. It was an ordinary Roman tombstone, but he showed me a groove, cut, he assured me, to allow the blood of human sacrifices to run away. Now of course there was a lot of fighting and a lot of savage ritual in Europe then; and there still is. But people had to live in between the battles and the orgies. It was the General who showed us these people at home, living at peace, growing and grinding their corn and tending their flocks and herds. He showed us, by finding the marks on the side of a chalk trench, that the so-called bronze battle-axes were also used for other purposes. He even went further, found the broken bronze axe used to make that very trench, and that the marks corresponded exactly, flaws and all, with the edge of the axe (Fig. 2).

The impact of anthropology upon archaeology, which the life of Pitt-Rivers symbolizes, was an altogether healthy one. It made one see the past, not in terms of historical and archaeological periods, but of stages of culture, stages which are still represented by living communities. The picture it presented of human society was that of a continuum in time and space, consisting of peoples at varying stages of culture, from the Stone Age onwards. It gave a point of view, and that was perhaps the most valuable gift, for it is the key to everything else. Anthropology began with Tylor, whose *Primitive Culture* is generally

[7] Particularly in writing my article on the invasion of the late Bronze Age, *Antiquaries Journal*, II, 1922, 27-35. For fuller and more recent use see Professor Hawkes, *Arch. Journ.*, CIV, 1948, 27-81, from which Fig. 1 comes.

c

recognized as marking the birth of a new branch of science. I know that the acquisition of this way of looking at the world is one of the most valuable things that I got from Oxford, where as a student I well remember seeing Tylor taking parties of students round the cases of the Pitt-Rivers Museum. Let me give a few examples to illustrate how a visit to a primitive community enlivens one's view of the past.

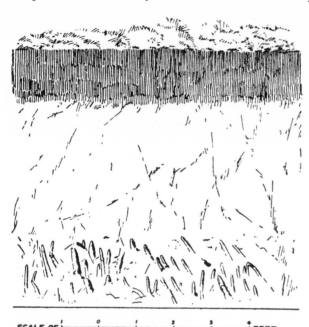

FIG. 2. Pitt-Rivers' drawing of a section of the Angle Ditch showing, at the bottom, the marks of the bronze axe used to make it. From his *Excavations in Cranborne Chase*, Vol. iv.

There are several places in Wessex—Badbury Rings is one—where a village of the Romano-British period is found immediately outside the ramparts of a hill-fort, on the lower slopes of the hill. The usual (and doubtless correct) explanation is that, when the *pax Romana* put an end to tribal warfare and the need of seeking safety behind the ramparts, the people came and settled outside it. One day on a holiday I was sitting on the side of a hill in Algeria, talking to one of the inhabitants of the village below, where I was staying. On the top of the hill were a number of houses, mostly deserted and half ruined. I asked him why this was. 'Oh,' he said, 'the people don't need to live there now the French are here; they have gone to live in the village down there.' The village on the hill corresponded exactly to our hill-fort, and the French, just like the Romans, had stopped the inter-tribal raiding. It was a perfect example of the anthropological method of the present throwing light on the past, or if you prefer it, of the past living on in the present —of the continuum of culture in time. Exactly the same thing seems to have happened at Mardin in Kurdistan, to judge from an old woodcut, which shows the modern town on the (probably exaggerated) slopes of the hill and the remains of the old one on the top. Another excellent example is in the Naga hills of Assam where the people can still be seen erecting megalithic monuments. Nor is it necessary to go so far afield. There are still a few villages left in the north of Lewis, largest island of the Outer Hebrides, consisting mainly or entirely of black houses (as they are called) built in a tradition of prehistoric antiquity: they have survived for the same sort of reason that the Dodo survived, because they are admirably adapted to their windswept environment. The villagers of Lewis are, as Dr Curwen has said,[8] a modern survival of the culture of the prehistoric Iron Age.

You can get illuminating sidelights on prehistory from almost any country. The timber-and-stone walls that were used in some Iron Age forts in Scotland and France are still built in Bulgaria and Abyssinia. Rotary querns of Iron Age type are still sold in the market at Houm Tsouk in Jerba, off the coast of Tunisia, and saddle-querns—a more primitive type—in Omdurman. Life in the Sudan, as I remember it some forty years ago, was extraordinarily like life in Roman Britain in many of its administrative and social features. And one could go on multiplying instances indefinitely. I have given enough to illustrate my point, which is that one can travel in time as in space. You can have an Iron Age holiday in Algeria or Lewis, a megalithic (Bronze Age) holiday in Assam, a medieval one in Spain, or in the still almost medieval towns of Alcudia and Pollenza in Majorca.

The world thus looked at is like a geometric design whose various colours represent the culture-patterns of communities of uneven cultural level. Each stands for an attempt to come to terms, the best possible terms, with the environment. Some have remained in the Iron, Bronze or (in New Guinea) in the Stone Age while others, living perhaps only a short distance away, have progressed further in material culture. A map of the world thus classified would show small patches of the earlier ages interspersed amongst large patches of later ones. Such a map would be like a map of the stars, for although we can see them all at once, what we are really looking at is not all contemporary, but of many different periods. We find the same thing in nature where many whole species have remained unchanged from remote geological periods. Nor will it, I fancy, ever be otherwise. Even in countries regarded by themselves as most modern there are still great variations of culture. When I went to Poti (the ancient Colchis) in the U.S.S.R. in 1932, they were still using horse-trams there. At Erivan, the capital of Soviet Armenia, they were in a fever of excitement about the new electric trams they were installing in the same year. But in the south of England electric trams are regarded as prehistoric monsters that should be extinct. If I ever return (which is most unlikely) shall I find electric trams at Poti, or trolley buses at Erivan? Even in the United States there are rumours of backward hill-folk. Such inequalities of culture will surely persist. It is unlikely that the productive methods of, say, Tibesti or Tibet will be as advanced as those of, say, North America at any time in the near future.

[8] *Antiquity* XII, 1938, 261–89: The Hebrides, a Cultural Backwater.

CHAPTER 3

Archaeology and Maps

IN THE LAST chapter I traced in very brief outline the stages by which archaeology progressed from a servile status as the handmaid of books to complete freedom. I showed that this freedom was in fact achieved by the discoveries of Boucher de Perthes in the middle of the nineteenth century; but that it was not fully exploited until half a century later, by Pitt-Rivers, Petrie and Evans. The latter part of the chapter was concerned with the development of the technique of excavation, by means of which the things found were made to tell their own story. It is now necessary to consider more closely what the term field archaeology connotes. It was invented by Dr Williams-Freeman, who told me that he coined it from the term field naturalist, which was used to distinguish those who studied plants and other living things alive and in the open air as contrasted with those who studied them in museums. He embodied the term in the title of his own book,[1] which is a survey of the earthworks of Hampshire. In this sense the field archaeologist is one who walks over the country observing and recording the remains of the past that are visible on the surface or are indicated by superficial remains such as potsherds, flints, soil-discolouration or the growth of crops. Field archaeology thus did not cover excavation; the invention of the word came about in response to the need for a word that would describe the activities of those who were archaeologists but not necessarily also excavators. It indicated that there was a wide field of research available for those who did not or could not conduct excavations. Many field archaeologists of course did excavate, but some, including Dr Williams-Freeman himself, did not. Aubrey did not, and it would have been much better if Stukeley, whose field-work was excellent, had also refrained from excavation. Colt-Hoare was both field archaeologist and excavator.

I shall now take up the thread again where I left it in the last chapter, because this is primarily a book about field archaeology, and is only concerned with excavation because that too is a branch of archaeology; and the history of the part cannot be divorced entirely from the history of the whole. I shall now, therefore, go back to the eighteenth century, and show how field archaeology also gradually became emancipated from the bookman's spell, and developed a technique of its own.

Modern field archaeology began with General Roy (1726–90) who was the effective, if not the actual, founder of the Ordnance Survey. Roy was both a soldier and a map-maker; and it was therefore natural that when he made his great map of Scotland in the middle of the eighteenth century he should have become interested in Agricola's campaigns

[1] *Field Archaeology as illustrated by Hampshire, 1915.*

in that country. At the same time another army officer, Captain Robert Melville (1723–1809), also became interested, and in August 1754 he discovered no less than four Roman marching-camps in the vale of Strathmore.[2] Roy subsequently made plans of these and many others, which were published posthumously in 1793, in his great book *The Military Antiquities of the Romans in Britain*, a classic and a landmark in the history of field archaeology. Roy himself was a field archaeologist only; he did not excavate. The fact that so monumental a work as the *Military Antiquities* could not only be written, but retain its value for a century and a half is proof, if proof were needed, of the value of mere field archaeology and of its place in the discipline of archaeology. What gives it this value? Chiefly the fact that, since his day, several of the camps he planned have been obliterated by cultivation. That has a moral which is topical to-day. Cultivation is obliterating ancient sites far more quickly now than ever before; field archaeology can at any rate preserve a record of them in the form of plans and sections.

There were of course people who did good field-work in the north before Roy; Horsley was one, and there were others.[3] Roy may, however, be said to have 'put it on the map' in a double sense, and it is convenient to start from him. (I am not writing a complete history but merely trying to trace the main development in outline.) Roy not only did good work himself but he was also the prime cause of it in others, whose output altogether was both large and of a high quality. Their interpretations of earthworks were often at fault, and they were prone to see the Romans everywhere; but that was merely because, like the rest of their contemporaries, they were still under the spell of books. Their observations were made and recorded as a rule with scrupulous regard for accuracy. A great stimulus was given by Sir John Sinclair, whose ambitious and successful venture, the *Statistical Account of Scotland* (1791–9) embodied the replies to a questionnaire circulated to every village in the land and filled in usually by the ministers. The volumes of the Proceedings of the Society of Antiquaries of Scotland contain a long series of articles of a topographical kind—far more than those of the London Society. But when everything has been said, and our debt of gratitude paid for even wrongly interpreted observations, it must be admitted that the technique of field archaeology did not advance much either in Scotland or England during the nineteenth century. In England Dr Edwin Guest (1800–80) was one of the first moderns to go out into the country and look at earthworks for himself, and write articles about them; and he was the first to concern himself with those linear earthworks which, still under the spell of books, he called Belgic ditches. (The name was not so far out as was once thought, for some of them *are* Belgic.) His articles were collected together and published posthumously in 1883, under the title *Origines Celticae*, edited by Stubbs & Deedes. Guest was ahead of his times, and although his writings contain much speculation, some of it rather fantastic, they have an honourable place in the history of field archaeology. They contain the first mention in print of many now familiar earthworks.

Towards the end of the nineteenth century there was a strong revival of interest in out-door archaeology, marked in Scotland by a series of excavations conducted by the Society of Antiquaries of Scotland, and by such surveys as those of Cole and Christison, which were subsidized by grants. Cole made an elaborate field survey of stone circles,

---

[2] For further details see my *Topography of Roman Scotland*, 1949, 93 ff.
[3] E.g. Sir Robart Sibbald (1707), Alexander Gordon (1726).

which was published serially in the society's Proceedings. Christison did the same for earthworks, mostly native forts, and also published his results in book form, *Early Fortifications in Scotland* (1898). Unfortunately he was no draughtsman, and his plans are extremely amateurish. He was also a poor observer, with no eye for the things he was observing. He often failed to distinguish modern or recent field-banks from earlier work, and he was curiously blind to the characteristic features which marked Roman work. But in spite of these deficiencies his articles and book contain much valuable information, some of it supplementary to that on the large scale Ordnance Survey maps and not elsewhere recorded.

But undoubtedly the most valuable and important summary of field-work that appeared about this time was Romilly Allen's splendid corpus, *Early Christian Monuments of Scotland* (1903). It is an astonishing achievement for one man, and is all the more valuable because it is fully illustrated by photographs. Romilly Allen himself seems to have inspected every monument he describes, or at any rate the majority of them, which alone is an outstanding performance adding greatly to the value of his book. The stones he deals with are not only those carved crosses of the Christian period which are analogous to those of England and Ireland, but also the symbol-stones of an earlier pagan period that may be put at roughly A.D. 600–800. Some of these are not only archaeologically interesting but also aesthetically pleasing; the animals carved in low relief (wolves and bulls) are works of art of a high order. I wish to call special attention to Romilly Allen's work because it is of a kind that may well appeal to some who find earthworks and Roman roads dull, or who hanker after art. Although he covered the whole of his chosen field, there is still plenty of work to be done in it. Some of his photographs are very unsatisfactory and should be replaced. Moreover he did not make, or at any rate publish, a complete survey of each stone. Each of the crosses has four sides; and it is always desirable to have a photograph of the carving on the narrow sides as well as of that on the faces, which is usually more striking and interesting. For instance, on the side of the so-called Sweino's Stone at Forres is a design that represents the famous vine-scroll in a very degenerate form; but there is no illustration of it in Romilly Allen's book, and the only one available when I wanted one was a poor drawing in Stuart's (pre-photographic) *Sculptured Stones of Scotland* (Vol. I, 1856). After my immediate need had passed I managed to go there and take a complete set of photographs of Sweino's Stone, one of the finest crosses in Scotland. It is interesting work because one has to take each side in a different light, which involves many visits. But unless the photograph is taken in the right light, which must be sunlight falling at an angle of 45 degrees or less, the low relief of the carving does not stand out. I shall return later to this subject.

Cole, Christison and Romilly Allen were forerunners of a new order of things; they were all virtually professional, that is to say whole-time, archaeologists, and were paid for some of their work. They foreshadowed the Royal Commissions that were to come a decade or two later. Archaeology was gaining recognition as a subject of national importance, and not only, or even chiefly, in this country. In Germany a special Limes-Kommission was set up by the State in 1904 to survey the line of the Roman frontier between the Rhine and the Danube.

The creation of the post of Archaeology Officer of the Ordnance Survey in 1920 was entirely due to the then Director General, Colonel Sir Charles Close (now Arden-Close). It was the culmination of a long and fruitful association between the national map-makers and field archaeologists. Thanks in the last resort to the personal qualities of General Roy, thanks also to the wide culture of some of the early Directors of the Survey, antiquities were marked on the original one-inch-to-mile Ordnance Map, the first sheet of which (Kent) was published in 1801. Some of the credit for this must certainly be given to the squires and parsons whose initial interest rescued the antiquities from oblivion and was the cause of their being marked on the county maps that appeared in the eighteenth century. For these maps were certainly used by the surveyors who made the first Ordnance Map; that at any rate seems to be a safe inference from the fact that a fairly complete set of these county maps, mounted and folded in cases, was once among the archives of the Ordnance Survey. I imagine that the surveyors used them as guides to find their way about with. They may well have derived from them a knowledge of the existence of certain antiquities which were subsequently inserted on their maps from their own field-measurements. There is evidence also that the Ordnance Survey was in close touch with the leading field archaeologist of the time, Sir Richard Colt Hoare, for when I went to the Ordnance Survey I found a proof of the Wiltshire sheet of the one-inch map (dated about 1811) with corrections of the antiquities in Sir Richard's own handwriting. (This happily has survived the war.) There is also a close resemblance between the maps in Hoare's *Ancient Wiltshire*, drawn by his own surveyor, Crocker, and the Ordnance Map.

The original manuscript plans, on a scale of two inches to the mile, from which the published edition was engraved, are also happily still in existence. They mark the course of Roman roads which were sometimes, for some unknown reason, omitted from the engraved maps. They are a mine of valuable information about the topography of the country, and should be consulted by all who are studying any particular district.

When the large-scale Ordnance Survey was undertaken, an official memorandum was drawn up by certain archaeological bodies and sent to the appropriate ministry, praying that due regard might be given to antiquities, and this was agreed to, on the understanding that local archaeologists would help with their advice. Accordingly the surveyors consulted these people when they were at work. The result of the scheme was the incorporation of a large number of ancient sites on the 25-inch and 6-inch maps, and this has been of the greatest service to archaeology. But it had many drawbacks. So far as topographical detail was concerned—the mapping of the actual features of hill-forts and other earthworks—there is little to complain of. Though, as Haverfield long ago pointed out,[4] this is often imperfect, it is better than nothing and far better than anything the field archaeologists of the day could have done. But the descriptions reflect the current ideas of the time, and are often absurd. Megalithic remains are called 'Druids' altars', cromlechs and dolmens. Many things called 'Roman' are not Roman at all; and, worst of all, the forged itinerary of Richard of Cirencester, which duped Stukeley, was accepted and the names embodied on the map. It was primarily to eliminate these errors, and restore to the Ordnance Maps the accuracy for which they were in other respects so rightly famous, that I was appointed Archaeology Officer there. The appointment, though generally welcomed, was just half a century too late. If it had been made when the large-scale survey of England was first undertaken, these errors would probably either never have been made, or been less numerous. One of the R.E. officers might well have been given this task; and if either

[4] 'The Ordnance Survey maps from the point of view of the antiquities on them.' *Geogr. Journ.*, XXVII; 1906, 165–76 (read 20th December, 1905). For a similar critique from the next generation, see my article on the same subject in the same Journal, Vol. LIX, 1922, 245–58 (read 16th January, 1922).

Major Bayley or Captain Courtney[5] had been appointed Archaeology Officer, the work would certainly have been well done. For the omission to press for such an appointment the blame rests primarily on the archaeologists of the day, and more especially upon the Society of Antiquaries of London. But it may be doubted whether, even if they had done their duty, the Treasury would have agreed.

For another shortcoming the blame must rest directly upon the shoulders of the Ordnance Survey. We have seen that antiquities were marked upon the original one-inch map, and that the Ordnance Survey agreed to continue this good practice on the new large-scale maps; and one would have thought that the obvious course would be to consult the older maps during the new survey, and use them as a guide to the location of antiquities on the ground. Some of them might have been destroyed in the interval of half a century by ploughing or other agencies; but even so the sites would still be easy to locate, for many of them are still visible, and would have been much plainer eighty years ago. And most of the antiquities were still there and are so still. But this was not done. There was no attempt at collation, either by the surveyors or their archaeological advisers, with the result that many earthworks that were marked on the maps at the beginning of the nineteenth century and are still intact were omitted. The survey of antiquities, as of topography, was begun again *de novo*, as if nothing had ever been done before. I suspect that one of the reasons for this strange neglect was that the responsibility was now divided, and the Ordnance Survey shirked its share. Whatever the cause the result was a great loss to knowledge: and one of my first and chief tasks there was to study the original one-inch maps and, after field-work, to restore those antiquities whose sites could still be identified. There is of course much more to be done, and it can be done by anyone who can read a map. It is exciting work, for there is the opportunity of making discoveries. The field-location of a site that appears on the original one-inch map but not in the later ones may reasonably be regarded as a new discovery.

At this point in the story it will be profitable to stand back and look at the picture as a whole, as does a painter. It is a story that is full of details, but we must not get lost amongst them. What, for instance, is the justification for all the labour involved in recording on the Ordnance Maps all these ancient sites? One such is of a philosophic kind, and without going too deeply into philosophic matters one may say that the data of archaeology cannot be fully used until they are located as accurately as possible both in time and space. The time-aspect demands a chronological system, and the space-aspect a series of distribution maps. Archaeologists were quicker to realize the need of the former than the latter; but both are important. The archaeologist and historian who has not disciplined his thought so that he thinks in terms of these two fundamental dimensions will never really understand his subject. I could quote amusing instances of lapses that, though trivial, reveal undisciplined thinking. An account was published in *Archaeologia* of the excavation of a Roman villa, but the writer forgot to say where it was. A professor of Egyptology reported the results of a season's excavations in Nubia and made the same omission. An American professor published an account of his excavations at Kourion, but forgot to say where it was, and one can only infer that it was in Cyprus from his use of the adjective 'Cypriote'. These are small matters, but revealing. An ancient site has no meaning isolated from its environment, nor indeed has a modern one. Stirling, for instance, has been called

[5] For them see my *Topography of Roman Scotland*, index.

the gateway of Scotland, and Southampton the gateway of England, the one because it is on an important river crossing and the other because it is a port of a certain kind. You cannot understand either of these terms without a map; in other words you cannot isolate things from their environment. It is, on a much larger scale, exactly the same as juxta-position. The object excavated derives its meaning from its juxtaposition, its relation to its environment, in exactly the same way as does its site. Juxtaposition is of course con-cerned with time rather than space, but the analogy is nevertheless exact. As an instance of the importance of exact location I would quote the position of groups of barrows, long and round. Several of these groups are found to be near the sources of rivers; that is a fact that can only be revealed by a map or a visit to the spot. We are not now concerned with the inferences from the fact, except to note that they are important.

Another justification for the exact location of ancient sites on maps is purely practical; it helps you to find them on the ground. Archaeologists have not always made full use of the data provided by the Ordnance Maps. One such of the older school, in an article which catalogued a certain type of monument, gave the most careful description of the way leading to one of them, which he said was very difficult to find. He did not know, apparently, that it was marked on the one-inch Ordnance Map, even on the first edition. Another published a fine detailed survey of all the ancient remains round Avebury in Wiltshire, accompanied by a map which was enlarged, very crudely, from the one-inch map. He had never, apparently, heard of the six-inch map, whose use would have saved all the labour and expense of enlargement, and been far more accurate and useful to his readers.

The third justification is perhaps the most important. The marking on the Ordnance Maps of a large number of ancient sites is the essential preliminary to the publication of special period-maps such as those of Roman Britain and of the Dark Ages. It also greatly facilitates the compilation of distribution-maps of certain types of sites and objects. At this point we come back to the main line of the history of archaeology. You will remember that we found that archaeology achieved independent status and unfettered freedom of action towards the end of the nineteenth century in the hands of Petrie and Pitt-Rivers, when by gradual refinement of technique the objects were made to tell their own story. That was a great achievement, but it was chiefly concerned with the time-aspect. The story was a sequence of events, or a process of development, that occurred in time. If our philosophical principle holds good, there should be also a corresponding achievement in the space-aspect. Objects should be capable of being so marshalled spatially, that is to say geographically, as to yield new knowledge comparable with that which ensued when they were marshalled temporally. As one whose interest in geography has always been as great as his interest in archaeology and history, this possibility intrigued me at an early date. Forty years ago I was much mixed up with the early developments of human geography and the Oxford school of Professor Herbertson, who was teaching the import-ance of environment in the study of modern communities. The subject was in the air and was reacting upon history. Professor Myres had just written[6] his masterly account of the Mediterranean, which was a study of the influence of geographical environment upon the ancient civilization of that basin. Abercromby had published a distribution-map of beakers in Great Britain.[7] My own interests were then chiefly in British archaeology; and it seemed

[6] I remember him telling me at the time that he had done it in three weeks.
[7] *Proc. Soc. Ant. Scot.*, XXXVIII, 1904, 366.

to me that similar methods applied to Britain should yield good results. I therefore took a certain period, the Early Bronze Age, and mapped the distribution of certain selected types of object—flat bronze axes (the earliest type of metal object) and beakers—and found that they not only roughly coincided but that there was a very obvious geographical explanation of the grouping of the sites. It was not quite the first time this had been done; Schliz[8] had done it for the band-keramik of Central Europe, pointing out how its distribution coincided with that of loess-formation. Lissauer[9] had also published distribution-maps of selected bronze objects of the Bronze Age; but he had not gone on to suggest any causative geographical explanation. Nor had Abercromby, whose lists and maps of beakers inspired my own and gave the necessary data for them. But the method was fundamentally sound and had in fact been used in other branches of science with good results.[10] In Germany the geographical study of archaeology gave rise to the valuable concept of Kulturkreis which are based upon the groups that distribution-maps reveal; but the maps themselves often left much to be desired, and the method was not always used to full advantage, generally because the archaeologists who used it had not the necessary geographical training and outlook.

The distributional method is now a recognized part of all archaeological work in this country, and distribution-maps illustrate all articles that are concerned with the study of particular types of objects. It stands for the achievement of complete independence from all outside sources such as written documents, and corresponds in space to the method of stratification (or juxtaposition) in time. Armed with these two implements of research the archaeologist can go to a land that had no history and make it. He can do this, for instance, in Nigeria or the southern Sudan. He will select a stratified site, get his sequence of stratigraphically determined types, and then—though this must of course wait for the long accumulation of data—map their distribution and discover his Kulturkreis. This is being done in America, where written history did not begin before the sixteenth century, and it is being very greatly helped by the American techniques of dendrochronology and radio-carbon dating (C 14). The distribution-method has recently been applied for the first time in Asia, by Piggott and Wheeler, who learnt it in England.

The employment of the distribution-method is based ultimately upon field-work—somebody's field-work. The user may not have collected all or any of the facts he uses himself, but each one of them must ultimately represent field-work by someone—the person who found and recorded the site or object. It may have been the surveyor who put it on his map, or the field archaeologist who found it and inserted it there, or wrote a verbal description of where it was found. The record may have been made centuries ago, but it could not have been made if someone had not once left his house or study. These are platitudes, glimpses of the obvious, and I only state them in order to justify my mention of them in a book about field archaeology.

---

[8] Der Schnurkeramische Kulturkreis und seine Stellung zu der anderen neolithischen Kulturformen in Sudwest-Deutschland: *Zeitschrift für Ethnologie*, 1906, 312–45 (map, with no scale, marking loess and pots).

[9] Lissauer's articles were cast in the form of reports to a committee; there are four of them, published in the *Zeitschrift für Ethnologie* in 1904 (537–607), 1905 (793–847), 1906 (817–62), 1907 (785–831); and there is also in the 1905 volume (519–25) an article on the distribution of copper double axes, illustrated by a sketch map.

[10] e.g. It had explained the origin of sleeping-sickness (though I was not aware of the fact till later): see *Man and His Past*, 1921, 88.

CHAPTER 4

The Modern Phase of Field Archaeology

It may perhaps be thought that I am dealing at excessive length with the history of archaeology and of field archaeology, and the reader may be wondering when I am going to tell him what the field archaeologist actually does when he is out for the day. That will come in due course; meanwhile may I remind him that our subject itself has a time-aspect, a history. The archaeologist sees man as a time-product and his culture as an intermittent time-phenomenon; he is convinced that this time-aspect which pervades and colours all his thinking is something fundamental, and that thanks to it he can understand a little more than those who regard things statically. This applies also, of course, to archaeology itself, which is itself a part of human culture; I do not think you can make the fullest and best use of the technique of archaeology or of anything else unless you know something of how that technique has been developed; or, if that is a little too sweeping, I would say that without some such knowledge, which is historical, you will not be likely to improve a technique.

Time-thinking is an art that can be acquired, and of course it moves in both directions and not only in reverse gear. I do not mean that time-thinkers have the gift of accurately forecasting the future, but that, other things being equal, and given the relevant facts, they are more likely to do so correctly than static thinkers or, as they are more usually described, people with one-track minds. Weather-forecasting is an excellent example of the historical method working in forward gear.

At the lowest estimate a knowledge of the history of a subject is useful in forming judgements. For instance, the history of science shows that progress in any branch of it usually comes from some outside influence and not from its professional workers. Geikie, who wrote a history of geology,[1] found that the majority of the pioneers were men normally engaged in other pursuits; several were doctors, and amongst the rest were clergymen, a retired soldier, the superintendent of a porcelain manufactury, a civil servant, an engineer and surveyor, teachers and persons of independent means. Only a small proportion were professional geologists. The same is true of archaeology, whose advances have derived from outside; military science is represented by Roy and Pitt-Rivers, and it contributed largely to the development of archaeological air-photography; geology has contributed varve study, and much in the earliest human history would be unintelligible without it; pollen analysis and dendrochronology are based upon botany; some knowledge

---

[1] *The Founders of Geology*, by Sir Archibald Geikie, 1905, 468 ff.

of survey and of cartography are necessary to produce the best sort of period map. In judging, therefore, of the merits of any particular claims that may be made by those whom the professional would call outsiders, we should remember that outsiders have in the past contributed more than insiders, and should therefore beware of hasty or too sweeping judgements. That does not, of course, mean that every wild theory must be treated seriously. There is no need to waste time, for instance, refuting the speculations about Atlantis which every geologist knows to be preposterous, or claims of the Pyramidiots whose facts have many times been shown not to be facts at all. But every honest factually-based claim deserves serious consideration, at least once.

So much for the reasons for studying the history of a subject and for giving so much time to it here and now, for which I make no apology. One more chunk of history only is needed to bring us down to the present day.

In the previous chapters of this book I have not attempted to draw any hard and fast line between the different branches of archaeology in the field, of which the chief is excavation. From now onwards excavation will be excluded, and I shall be concerned only with field archaeology proper, which as I said above consists of the observation and record of the things seen on the surface of the ground. That is the sense in which it was used by Dr Williams-Freeman, the inventor of the term; and as he was himself one of the pioneers of the modern phase, his background is of historical importance. He was a doctor with a country practice, and he lived at Weyhill on the edge of Salisbury Plain. His interest in earthworks was first aroused, I believe, by the late Mr Percy Farrer, whose official duties were connected with War Office property on the Plain and who was himself a competent surveyor. Mr Farrer made plans of those puzzling linear earthworks which wander over the downs; and he had also helped the Cunningtons by making plans of Casterly Camp and the other sites they dug. There was then a very lively group of archaeologists whose interest was aroused by the earthworks of the downs. Field archaeology was, so to speak, in the air. It was in Wiltshire that I first got interested in it myself over forty years ago. One of the books that had a great vogue at the time was a curious compilation called *Neolithic Dewponds and Cattleways*, by Hubbard. It was full of the wildest ideas, but it did have a freshness that was in marked contrast to the dreary stuff that then often passed as archaeology. It was a sort of earlier precursor of *Downland Man*, no more trustworthy but less bookish. At the least it showed that there were a lot of interesting things lying about all over the downs, waiting to be explained.

It was a little before this time that the Congress of Archaeological Societies had established an Earthworks Committee which attempted to classify earthworks, not with much success, and to co-ordinate the work of interested amateurs. It collected information and published an annual report, recording new discoveries, damage and the clearance of woodland and undergrowth that made earthworks visible and capable of being planned. It was a move in the right direction, and both Dr Williams-Freeman and Mr Heywood Sumner gave it practical support, stating that their books had been written as the direct result of the appeal of that Committee for such surveys. Hadrian Allcroft's *Earthwork of England* (1908) was, I believe, also inspired by the Earthworks Committee. It was the first book to deal with earthworks of all periods over the whole country, and was profusely illustrated by excellent plans; it remains the only book that covers the same ground and is still a very useful textbook for the beginner, though naturally it is now a little out of date. There were other books written and surveys made, and it is impossible to measure the amount of good work that must be attributed directly and indirectly to the existence of the Earthworks Committee.

The part played by provincial archaeological societies in field archaeology varied greatly. Counties that contained large stretches of open downs and moorland naturally produced more field-work than those which were mainly under cultivation; but there were exceptions. A much higher level of output was maintained in Wiltshire, for instance, than in Dorset or Hampshire, and in Cumberland and Northumberland and the Border than in Wales. The Midlands and East Anglia, which are intensively cultivated, produced little because they afforded less scope. Sussex has now an excellent record, thanks to Allcroft, the Curwens, Holleyman, Toms, Margary and others. Berks, Bucks and Oxon could only muster a single journal between them, and their record is undistinguished.

Oxfordshire might have been expected to do better, but the other-wordly interests of Oxfordians attracted them away from the homeland. Lately this long neglect has been amply made up for, and *Oxoniensia* us full of good things. It would be a fascinating task to study the influence of topography upon field archaeology, and the respective rôles of man and of the environment. This is a minor parallel to the old problem of whether history is made by great men or by economic causes, Do earthworks produce field archaeologists or vice versa? Both questions are of course wrongly put; you cannot practise a technique without raw materials; you cannot, to give an extreme instance, do field archaeology on the Antartic Continent. But the existence of abundant raw materials does not necessarily produce field archaeologists. There are, for instance, plenty of earthworks and Roman roads in France, but no field archaeologists.

The modern phase of field archaeology began with the Earthworks Committee and the workers inspired by it. The growth of interest was cumulative and rapid. People with common interests like to meet and discuss them; new ideas are shared and criticized; the knowledge that others are also interested in your work is a stimulus and an encouragement. Ploughing a lone furrow is dull work. The young especially are encouraged to emulate their elders. I am sure that I should never have gone in for field archaeology so enthusiastically if it had not been for the encouragement of Dr Williams-Freeman and others, books like that of Hadrian Allcroft, and the prestige given to it by the Earthworks Committee. One felt it was a subject worth pursuing, in which there was ample scope for making new and valuable discoveries, and one in which many people were interested. There was too the amusing game of trying to prove one's elders wrong.

We now come to the discovery of a technique which revolutionized field archaeology, that of air-photography. I have given elsewhere[2] the main facts of its history and need not do so again. I would merely point out that the advantages of the vertical view of earthworks was fully realized by both Dr Williams-Freeman and myself long before we had either of us ever seen an air-photograph, and before our time by Colonel Sir Charles Arden-Close and by the late Sir Henry Wellcome, who actually had vertical photographs taken from a box-kite of his excavations in the Sudan in 1913.[3] What neither Dr Williams-Freeman nor I realized was the extraordinary clarity and sharp definition that would be

[2] *Wessex from the Air*, Introduction.
[3] See the report of his excavations at Jebel Moya written by Mr F. Addison and published by the Oxford University Press, Vol. I, 1949, 6.

given to earthworks by air-photographs. We were accustomed to look at them at close range; we used occasionally to see in the corn the track of a ploughed-up ditch showing as a broad greener band; but seen from near by from the opposite hill the outline was rather blurred. We longed to see it, not obliquely but in plan, as would be possible in an aeroplane, but we did not then realize that the greater distance given by the height would so greatly improve its appearance. It is exactly the same thing as the reduction by photography of a coarsely-drawn plan; the rough edges disappear, and what looked coarse becomes fine and pleasing.

I made several unsuccessful efforts after the 1914–18 war to get hold of some British air-photographs, and tried to interest the Earthworks Committee, also without success. Through the failure of their then honorary secretary to do anything the Committee lost the chance of its life-time. My expectations were at last satisfied when Dr Williams-Freeman asked me to come over to Weyhill and see some air-photographs with curious markings on them that had been shown to him by Air Commodore Clark Hall, then in command of the R.A.F. station there. What I saw far surpassed my wildest dreams, and I felt much the same excitement as, according to the poet, did stout Cortez on a memorable occasion. Here on these photographs was revealed the accurate plan of field-systems that must be at least 2000 years old, covering hundreds of acres of Hampshire. There followed a period of intensive field-work over the area, supplemented by fresh air-photos taken in Hants and Wilts. The results were announced at a meeting of the Royal Geographical Society on 12th March 1923. The paper which I then delivered was published in the *Geographical Journal* for May of that year, and subsequently reissued with some alterations as an Ordnance Survey monograph (*Air Survey and Archaeology*, 1st edn. 1924, 2nd edn. 1928). In 1929, after we had had time to study air-photos more thoroughly, I wrote another monograph (*Air Photography for Archaeologists*) dealing not so much with the new discoveries themselves as with the ways in which they were revealed by photography. There was not, as some were almost inclined to think, any magic power in the camera; as a matter of fact it sees no more than does the naked eye. What it does is to make a document, the photographic print, which has all the properties of an original historical manuscript except its uniqueness—for it can be replaced if lost. This document can be studied at leisure in the home or office, and compared with others and with maps of the region—things that are impossible when observing from a fast-moving aeroplane. In this second monograph I classified the ancient sites revealed by air-photography into three groups: (1) shadow-sites, (2) soil-sites, (3) crop-sites; and that classification has been found adequate and still holds good, not only in this country but all over the world.

During this same decade I took some air-photographs myself, working in collaboration with Mr Alexander Keiller in a specially chartered aeroplane from a base near Andover. The results were published in a joint book, *Wessex from the Air* (Oxford, 1928). Soon after this, I think about 1930, a private flier, Major George Allen, happened to pick up one of my Ordnance Survey monographs in an hotel at Southampton, and was immediately interested. He wrote to me about it and began work on his own account. Having his own aeroplane he was a free agent and could go where he wished and take his own photographs. For a decade he continued to explore the country round Oxford and sometimes further afield, and gradually accumulated a magnificent collection. The majority of his sites were crop-sites and new discoveries. He did more than anyone else to advance the new technique; and his untimely death by accident in 1940 was a very severe loss. He bequeathed his collection of photographs and records to the Ashmolean Museum at Oxford, where they are now available for the use of students. Comparable with Major Allen's work is that of Father Poidebard in Syria, where with the co-operation of the French Air Force he has surveyed the Roman frontier defences and discovered an enormous number of new Roman forts and roads. He has also succeeded in adding a fresh triumph, the photography of ancient remains beneath the sea (at Tyre) both from the air and below the water. (I tried out the possibilities of this myself in December 1928, when I flew over the harbour of Alexandria looking for the submerged quays there; but the sea was rough and muddy and I could see little or nothing.)

To return to the technique of air-photography, however. Shadow-sites are those whose surface is irregular, consisting of banks, mounds, ditches and terraces whose presence is revealed by the shadows they cast when seen in the low light of the rising or setting sun.[4] There is of course nothing at all mysterious about this process, which can be observed (though far less effectively) on the ground. Exactly the same principle is employed in photographing inscribed stones and carvings in low relief, where a side-light is necessary to bring out the detail. In explaining by examples how the shadow technique works I am necessarily anticipating somewhat, for I have to assume a familiarity with certain types of remains which I have not yet described; but it will be quite enough if for the moment they are regarded simply as banks (or whatever they may be) without worrying about their archaeological significance, which will appear later. The simplest and most familiar examples of banks are the ramparts of prehistoric hill-forts like Maiden Castle or Badbury Rings, or to take examples from Hampshire, St Catherine's Hill at Winchester, Tachbury Mount and Toothill near Romsey. These are all shadow sites of the most obvious kind. An observer visiting these hill-forts sees of course the shadows on the slopes away from the sun, but he gets no clear view of the hill-fort as a whole nor of its plan, for he is too near it. Returning to my analogy of the carved stone he is in the position of a fly on its surface. It is unnecessary to labour this point further; the basic principle is very easy to grasp.

Under the head of shadow-sites must also come, rather paradoxically, those where there are no shadows at all. When the land slopes towards the sun the banks on it reflect the light at a different angle and appear as brighter lines than the rest of the terrain. The light thus reflected is foreshortened and condensed and therefore brighter. The banks of prehistoric fields show up in this way.[5]

Shadow-sites can all be seen by an observer on the ground. Many of them were already known before they were photographed from the air; but even so air-photography has often revealed new features which had not been observed before. The classic example is the Trundle, a hill-fort near Worthing, where an air-photograph[6] revealed within the ramparts a hitherto unnoticed circle which Dr Cecil Curwen subsequently excavated and proved to be the rampart of an earlier neolithic habitation-site, This led to a re-examination of other well-known hill-forts in some of which similar remains were found.

[4] See for instance Plates iii and iv of my *Air-Photography for Archaeologists* (Ordnance Survey, 1929), of Steeple Langford Cowdown in winter without sunlight and in summer with it.
[5] See for instance the air-photo of strip-lynchets at Winspit Bottom, *Antiquity*, I, Plate iii, 272, where those on the left illustrate this, and those on the right are made visible by their shadows.
[6] *Antiquity*, IV, Plate iv, p. 40.

When taken in a good low light an air-photograph will reveal undulations in the surface so slight and broad that they might, and often did, escape the notice of a field archaeologist. When, however, with his attention thus drawn to them, he goes over the ground (as he always should) with the air-photograph in his hand, he can generally see something of them however faintly. One of the chief services of air-photography has been to sharpen our eyes so that we can see these faint undulations. To the inexperienced eye they seem so slight as to be negligible; but no clue, however faint, should be neglected. Others brush them aside as products of the imagination, but air-photography has vindicated them, and their observers. It must be remembered, because it is a fundamental axiom of field archaeology, that in the chalk regions and in some (but not all) others, every irregularity of the surface is of human origin and demands an explanation. Broad low banks may seem trifles, but every gardener and every farmer knows that they are not. The cubic content of a bank that, though now only a few inches high, is several yards broad, represents long hours of human labour; and people do not undertake that for no purpose, or merely to mislead field archaeologists. The same remarks apply conversely to a silted-up ditch whose present depression may be a matter of a few inches only. Its original depth is probably not far short of its present width; the ditch of a levelled hill-fort may appear as a depression of a foot only with a width of fifteen feet representing perhaps a depth of ten feet. That is quite a formidable affair.

Soil-sites are those which are revealed by disturbance and consequent discoloration of the surface. Except in deserts (where the few human sites are mostly shadow-sites) soil-sites usually occur on cultivated land when it is not bearing a crop. The marks are usually caused by the dispersal of the soil of banks and mounds and of the causeways of Roman or other made roads. In the chalk country such banks will have been made by digging a ditch and piling up the white chalk, which causes the resulting bank to remain visible even after many years of ploughing. Ditches and pits are sometimes revealed in bare soil even when they have become completely filled in and invisible as surface irregularities because their filling retains more moisture and thus has a darker appearance. For the same sort of reason a wet towel is darker than a dry one. Soil-sites are more common in winter and early spring, especially in a dry spring, than at other times of year. Many sites that appear as soil-sites then, become visible as crop-sites later on in the year. In the case of hill-forts it is usually the bank, or what remains of it, which shows up a soil-mark, and the ditch as a crop-mark. It is therefore a good thing to photograph such sites more than once at different times of the year and under the different conditions of moisture.

Crop-sites are perhaps the most important and the most numerous of all. Most of those known represent completely new discoveries. A crop-site is one that is revealed by the differential growth of a crop; the causes are excess and defect of moisture; ditches, pits, and post-holes, when they silt up, remain soft spots whose filling is of a different composition from that of the ground in which they are dug, whether that be chalk, sand, gravel, hard rock or even clay. When a crop of corn (and some other plants) is sown in a field containing such silted-up holes, the corn will grow better in the moister, more fertile soil of the silting, and will therefore be of a darker green colour. When seen from above those patches of darker green corn stand out in sharp contrast to the rest; and a vertical photograph of them gives an accurate plan of the bands or spots, which appear on it of course in black. No matter how long the holes have been filled up, the pattern is sharp and precise. The ditches of barrows that were ploughed flat in the Iron Age, some 2000 years ago, have come to light again in this way as perfectly sharp, clear circles.

Even to give a list of the important discoveries of crop-sites made during the last quarter of a century would be impossible here, and I must confine myself to mentioning a few of them. The first and one of the most famous was the continuation of the avenue leading to Stonehenge. I saw it first in 1923, not on a print but on a negative that was taken in 1921 by the R.A.F. at Old Sarum, in the ordinary routine of practice. The existence of the ditches of the avenue was proved by excavation the same year. A little later, in 1926, Squadron Leader Insall, V.C., discovered not far away the timber circles which have been called Woodhenge, whose post-holes showed up as concentric ovals of dark spots enclosed within a dark ring marking the ditch. It was excavated later by the Cunningtons, who published their report in book form. One of the most striking crop-sites was that of Woodbury.[7] I found this myself in 1924, but was unable to photograph it, and it was rediscovered independently and a remarkably good photograph taken of it by a member of the R.A.F. photographic staff at Old Sarum in 1929. The site was selected for excavation by the Prehistoric Society, and two seasons' work were done there in 1938 and 1939, under the direction of Professor Bersu. It proved to be an Early Iron Age habitation-site. It was very well reconstructed by Jacquetta Hawkes in consultation with Professor Bersu, at Denham, and used in the film of prehistoric life.[8] Major Allen discovered innumerable crop-sites in the Oxford district; and during the 1939–45 war Flight-Lieutenant D. N. Riley found more both in the same region and in the Fenland and other parts of East Anglia.[9] Since the war Dr St Joseph has discovered many important crop-sites, including dozens of new Roman forts and marching-camps.

In Iraq, Squadron Leader Insall discovered the site of Seleucia, the Hellenistic capital of Mesopotamia, by observing the rectangular lay-out, revealed partly by vegetation and partly by soil discoloration.[10]

The remains of ancient irrigation-systems provide ideal subjects for both crop- and soil-sites. Those of Iraq can generally be seen as shadow-sites, for the ancient canals silted up their beds till they grew into great embankments. But there is a very good silted-up canal to be seen (as a soil- or crop-site) near Ur, complete with its distributary channels.[11] The Romano-British drainage channels and associated field-systems and tracks are revealed in copious detail by air-photography, but remain for the most part unpublished.[12] Extinct irrigation systems have been reported from Nubia,[13] Turkmanistan and Soviet Azerbaijan, but neither Egyptologists nor apparently Soviet archaeologists have published any air-photographs of them.

One of the most important discoveries of crop-sites was made in Italy at the end of the last war by Mr John Bradford. Here turned up a wholly unsuspected group of Neolithic or Early Bronze Age hill-forts whose encircling ditches can be seen with astonishing sharpness and accuracy of outline on some air-photos taken partly during the war and

---

[7] Actually there are two sites here, close together. The one here described is sometimes called Little Woodbury, to distinguish it from the other, whose ditch is much wider and deeper. See air-photo (1929), *Antiquity*, III, opp. 385.

[8] *Antiquity*, XX, 78–82.

[9] Aerial reconnaissance of the Fen Basin, *Antiquity* XIX, 1945, 145–53; groups of circles in the Silt Fens, ib. id. XX, 1946, 150–3; Archaeology from the air in the Upper Thames Valley, *Oxoniensia*, VIII–IX, 1933–4, 64–101; A Late Bronze Age and Iron Age site on Standlake Downs, Oxon, ib. id. XI–XII, 1946–7, 27–43.

[10] See *Antiquity*, XIII, 1939, 441.   [11] See *Antiquity*, III, 1929, 342, Plate iii.

[12] See, however, *Luftbild und Vorgeschichte*, 1938, 57.   [13] W. B. Emery, *Nubian Treasure*, 1948, 42.

D

partly on special archaeological reconnaissances undertaken by Mr Bradford immediately after it.[14]

Crop-sites as yet unpublished have been recorded by photography in Siam and French Indo-China; and they have been seen also in North America by Dr St Joseph.

There are therefore crop-sites to be found in every continent (except, up to the present, Australia), and it is evident that we are merely at the beginning of discoveries. There is no reason to doubt that in favourable regions whole epochs of lost history may be re-covered by air-photography followed up by scientific excavation. Obviously not all can be excavated; but when some have been and the plan-type thus securely established, air-photography will provide the data for distribution-maps of these types.

If one were to attempt to indicate where the most abundant harvest of crop-sites was likely to be gathered, one would find it difficult to exclude any country in the world out-side the Polar Regions and the tropical forests and deserts. I did in fact intend at this point to make such an attempt, but on getting out my atlas and looking through it I gave it up. There are so few regions that are likely to be completely barren, and so many that will almost certainly be rich and productive. The harvest is indeed ready but the labourers are few, and often frustrated by official apathy or by their own lack of enterprise and initiative. I will confine myself to a bare list of some obviously promising regions: China, Indo-China and Siam, northern India, western Turkey, Thessaly and Thrace, central Europe from the Russian steppes (which must abound in crop-sites) to Hungary (where I have seen them myself), Nigeria, the corn-lands of North and South America. One would not look for crop-sites except where large level areas are under cultivation and where prehistoric man has been busy digging holes and ditches. The former considerations exclude many Mediterranean and most mountainous lands, and the latter such regions as Australia and parts of Central Asia where existence has been chiefly nomadic. But there is quite enough left to keep archaeologists busy for many centuries.

[14] See his articles in *Antiquity*, XX, 1946, 191–200; XXI, 1947, 74–83; 197–204; XXIII, 1949, 58–72; XXIV, 1950, 84–95.

CHAPTER 5

Deciphering the Palimpsest: Roman Roads

THE SURFACE OF England is a palimpsest, a document that has been written on and erased over and over again; and it is the business of the field archaeologist to decipher it. The features concerned are of course the roads and field boundaries, the woods, the farms and other habitations, and all the other products of human labour; these are the letters and words inscribed on the land. But it is not easy to read them because, whereas the vellum document was seldom wiped clean more than once or twice, the land has been subjected to continual change throughout the ages. The existing pattern, which is that we see on the six-inch Ordnance Map, was formed very largely at the end of the eighteenth and beginning of the nineteenth centuries, when the medieval field-system was swept away by the enclosures. That system was one in which the arable fields, on whose products the largely self-sufficient villagers lived, were divided up into long, narrow acre and half-acre strips. It was introduced by the Saxons, and although there must have been many changes during the medieval period, they were the changes due to growth, not (like the enclosures) to drastic replanning of a revolutionary kind. The evidence of Saxon land-boundaries proves this. The Saxons, however, did alter the pattern completely, sweeping away the whole of the pre-existing Romano-British system. To what extent that system itself developed from the earlier Iron Age system is still doubtful. The evidence of centuriation in England is still debatable, and the agricultural system associated with Roman villas is unknown. Centuriation corresponds topographically (but not socially) to the modern enclosures, but it may have been used not in areas already under cultivation but in land that was still in a virgin state. Thanks entirely to air-photography we actually have the plans of large blocks of fields belonging to the pre-Roman Iron Age; and it is even possible to detect evidence of a drastic change that occured in at least one area during that period—the abandonment of cultivation in favour of ranching.[1] Beyond this we cannot see anything clearly.

To sum up:— There are three agricultural periods discernible in the surface-pattern of the land; (1) the Iron Age, covering roughly the period from 500 B.C. to A.D. 500, with perhaps two or three modifications; (2) the Saxon-medieval period, one on the whole of orderly evolution; (3) the modern, dating from the enclosures. To revert to the analogy of the palimpsest—the writing was completely erased twice, by the Saxons and by the

[1] The evidence consists of a ranch-boundary which runs across a field-system near Bulford; it will be available if the Ordnance Survey publishes the Amesbury Sheet of the series of maps called *Celtic Fields of Salisbury Plain*. This sheet and the accompanying letterpress were already in the proof-stage when the 1939 war broke out. Part of it (reduced) is reproduced by permission here (Fig. 15).

authors of the enclosures; and there were several alterations of letters, words and whole sentences within those periods.

How does one set about beginning to study the palimpsest? Perhaps the best way of explaining will be to describe how I have proceeded myself on several occasions. I have usually gone to reside temporarily in a district for some specific purpose. I am sure it is a good thing always to have some definite objective, such as the tracing of a Roman road, the location of an ancient site recorded in some old record or revealed by an air-photograph, walking along and verifying the course of a linear earthwork or of some old territorial boundary recorded in a document. (I shall say more about what these are later on). One begins by studying the six-inch map, a pleasant task that one can enjoy every evening after the day's field-work. One asks one's self questions—why do those field-boundaries run where they do? Why, for instance, are some geometrically straight and others not so? Does that continuous line of field-boundaries mark the course of the Roman road? Is the pond that falls about in the place where a *mere* is mentioned in a Saxon boundary an old pond or a modern one? Is there any visible remains of a barrow (also mentioned there) at a point which may be capable of approximate or even exact location beforehand on the map? One then works out a detailed route to follow next day, and walks over the ground looking for evidence. Sometimes one finds visible remains of the causeway of the Roman road along the line of the straight hedges. The pond perhaps has every mark of antiquity, and there are obvious remains of a mound, perhaps ploughed nearly flat but revealed by stoniness or soil-discoloration, just where we expected to find it. The days when one finds these things are the lucky days: they form ten per cent or less of the total. But days in the field are never wholly barren or unprofitable. In looking for one thing one often finds another, which is sometimes a more valuable discovery than that which we hoped to make. Twice I have by pure chance discovered an entirely new Roman road running at right angles to the one I was looking for and failed to find. At the worst one may make no discoveries at all, but at least one has got to know a bit of one's chosen district intimately in the only way in which that can de done, namely, by walking over it.

The next stage is to become acquainted with any old maps that cover the district. There are certain stock sources—the first Ordnance Maps, the pre-Ordnance county maps, such as Isaac Taylor's 'Hampshire' (1759), Rocque's 'Berkshire', Andrews & Duruy's 'Wiltshire'. Then there are the Tithe-maps which can be seen at the Ministry of Agriculture in London, or the Enclosure Award Maps that can be seen in the office of the County Council in the county town. These are earlier and more useful than the Tithe-maps, which date about 1840; but the Tithe-maps contain more field-names, and these often provide valuable clues. Then there are the old estate-maps which are sometimes stored in the muniment rooms of country houses or in the County Archives, but now more usually in lawyers' offices, where they are less easy to get at. Air-photos should of course always be used when they are available. Last come the secondary sources such as local histories and articles in the proceedings of the provincial archaeological society. These always contain something of value, and often the transcriptions of original documents. Thus equipped one explores the region by book and by foot, gradually acquiring an ability to read some parts at least of the palimpsest.

The whole of this armoury of research, except the field-work pure and simple, is a modern, and primarily a British invention. The old field archaeologists walked and rode about the country, and some of them sometimes may have occasionally had recourse to an old map, but they had not the large-scale Ordnance Maps nor of course had they air-photographs. Without large-scale maps showing field-boundaries the finer points of field archaeology cannot be appreciated, nor can one's discoveries be adequately recorded, for verbal description is not enough by itself; it is necessary to insert one's observations on the map. It is the existence of the large-scale Ordnance Maps which makes modern field archaeology possible in Britain; but large-scale maps alone are not enough. There are such maps in other countries such as Germany, which has a series on a scale of 1:25,000, but their field archaeologists lack many of our older sources, and their output suffers accordingly.

The programme I have just described assumes that one has plenty of time to devote to a region that may comprise no more than two or three parishes. It is perhaps a programme more adapted for a permanent resident than a temporary visitor. My own opinion is that, unless and until one has studied at least one district on these lines, one will not properly understand the topography of any district. But such a programme is of course often impracticable or irrelevant. It is not, for instance, necessary to know the detailed topographical history of a district to be able to trace a Roman road or a linear earthwork that runs through it. The best course of action in most cases is a compromise: find out all you can, so long as it doesn't interfere with your programme. It is not a bad thing to have a rather rigid time-table, for otherwise one tends to get drawn more and more deeply into the fascinating but not wholly relevant byways of local topography. You are not going to write the parish history of every place you stay in. There are, in fact, two ways of doing field archaeology; one is to master the topographical development of a region, the other to trace a Roman road, let us say, from Biggar to Edinburgh via Dolphinton. You probably set out to do the latter, but you may very soon find yourself deep in the local history of Dolphinton. That may help your quest, but it may also hinder it by drawing you from the field into the library (if there is one at Dolphinton, which I doubt). When this stage seems to have been reached, it is advisable to move on.

Opinions are divided upon the problem of whether to seek out the local antiquary (if there is one) or remain incognito. A good deal depends upon how much time you can spare to listen to him. If you do seek him out it is advisable not to do so until you have yourself got to know the district somewhat, by which time it may be unnecessary. In my own encounters with local worthies it has generally been I who contributed the facts and they the theories. The old-time local antiquary, who knew every inch of his home ground and all that had been written about it by his predecessors, is practically extinct. Such knowledge requires a life-time to acquire, and the leisure and freedom from mundane cares that cannot now be had. Walking is therefore preferable to talking. That does not necessarily exclude the use of a car or a bicycle to reach the point where walking begins, but it necessitates a tedious return to pick it up again and much loss of valuable time and energy. For this reason it is often better to use a bus, and to plan one's day's operations in some detail the night before. It is rarely possible to follow the Roman road continuously, getting accommodation at a different place each night; that involves carrying all one's luggage and maps all the time and risking the chance of being refused accommodation at the end of the day. Moreover you will seldom find accommodation right on the line of the road, and this often means time wasted. A further drawback is that you don't know beforehand exactly where the road will go, and if you lose the trail you haven't time to go back and hunt for it again. Even if you had time, you will be tired, and you can't do this sort of work properly except when fresh. If you lose the trail in the afternoon it is generally better to quit and start afresh next day. For all these reasons it follows that it is best to work from a centre rather than to follow a direct continuous itinerary.

Before beginning to look for new Roman roads it will be best to follow the course of a well-known one, in order to get to know what Roman roads look like and how they behave. One of the best is Ackling Dyke, the Roman road from Old Sarum (Sorbiodunum) to Badbury Rings (Vindogladia?). The distance from Salisbury (a mile from Old Sarum) to Badbury is a little over twenty miles. The first few miles may be omitted or (if walked) should be done in the reverse direction from Bokerley Dyke. It would be best to take the Blandford bus and leave it a mile beyond (S.S.W. of) Woodyates Inn, now a private house, but once a bleak hostel where the bare necessities of a night's lodging were reluctantly conceded. Here the Roman and modern roads diverge, and the Roman causeway is well preserved. Where it lies near the modern road it has been used and mutilated as a quarry for it; but when it gets further removed therefrom it is found intact and most impressive, and continues so for some distance. There are of course gaps where it is less well preserved, but it is impossible to lose it, and from Gussage Hill to Badbury its alignment is undeviatingly straight. At Badbury it crosses the Roman road from Bath, in a ploughed field immediately north of the hill-fort, and then runs across the open down where it is bounded by side-ditches some seventy feet apart on each side.

Another good example to begin with is the Roman road over Beaulieu Heath. (This was the first one I walked myself, in company with Dr Williams-Freeman in 1911). It is quite easy to reach by taking the Hythe ferry-boat and walking along the Beaulieu road till it comes out on the heath where you turn left along a track (the New Forest boundary) for about half a mile. The causeway is well preserved and consists of gravel dug from quarry-pits which may still be seen beside it.

For Southamptonians there is an even more accessible Roman road on the outskirts of their own town on Fremantle Common, which is nowhere near Freemantle, but is a piece of open land close to (S. of) the Portsmouth road above Bitterne. The causeway here is very low and not too easy to find, but it links up with other fragments further east and is quite certain and authentic.

There are many other stretches of perfectly preserved Roman causeways in other parts of the country. There is Stane Street as it runs over the South Downs north-east of Chichester; the road along the Mendips leading to the lead mines at Charterhouse; the one on Whitby Moors and that over Blackstone Edge near Manchester; that which runs north from Halton (Hunnum) on Hadrian's Wall, by High Rochester (Bremenium) and the forts at Pennymuir in the Cheviots to Newstead—a lovely walk for those who can manage it, but it is near the limits of a day's march. There is a fine stretch of Roman road between Biggar and Edinburgh whose course is marked on a special Roman edition of the quarter-inch Ordnance Map (Forth, Clyde and Tay sheet) which was printed and a few copies distributed in 1941.[2] This road eventually reaches the western route at Craw-

---

[2] The map was on the point of publication in November, 1940, when most of the stock was destroyed by bombing and fire at the Ordnance Survey Office. A few copies which escaped destruction were sent to some of the chief public libraries, including the Bodleian and British Museum, where copies of it can be seen.

ford on the Upper Clyde, where it forks. One branch runs south-west to near Thornhill, Dumfriesshire, and is very well preserved over the open moorlands. The other runs south to Annandale and long stretches are visible, with accompanying forts, signal-posts and quarry-pits, on the moors north-west of Moffat. The most northerly Roman road of which plainly visible remains survive is the main east coast route, especially near Ardoch and Strageath and on the Gask ridge.[3]

The above is not a complete list but only a selection, intended to provide examples of Roman roads within reach of residents in the different parts of Britain. Not all of these examples are as well known as one might expect, but all are good, well-preserved fragments, sometimes a mile or more long, from which the beginner can learn what a Roman road looks like.

The next stage is to try by field-work to discover lost portions, or wholly new roads. When walking along any of the better preserved roads, you will come to places where the causeway has been more or less completely levelled by ploughing or by use as a quarry for modern road-metal. (I pass over the obvious cases where it is not to be seen because still in use). Sometimes the causeway ends abruptly at a hedge; near Chandler's Ford there is a good such instance. The causeway is high-raised and obvious in a grass meadow that has not been ploughed, but when you come to the next field, which is arable, there is not, at first sight, the slightest indication of a causeway, or any inequality of the surface. If, however, you walk on, continuing along its line, and examine the soil of the ploughed field closely, you will find (in this instance) a greater number of white flints, last relics of the causeway, forming a belt across the field. Had you not actually seen the causeway continuing this line of flints in the next field , you might have suspected that it marked the course of the road, but you might have hesitated to use it as evidence. Now, however, with this and other examples to support you, you can use even such slender evidence when you find it elsewhere, at any rate as giving a reasonable hypothesis for the course followed, even when the mound of the causeway itself has been completely ploughed away.

Other evidence may be found in the presence of a belt of gritty soil running across a field. If you suspect this, it is a good thing to walk to the side of the belt and then walk across it at right angles, comparing the nature of the soil on each side with that in the middle. This grit is the result of horse-traffic which reduces the flints to comminuted fragments. Those who can remember the old flint roads of pre-motor days will recall how, when such roads were in need of repair, all that was done was to unload cartloads of flints upon them, which were left to be battered up by the traffic. This took time, but in the end a very good surface resulted, in which a sandy grit was the chief constituent. That, being indestructible, remains to-day as evidence of similar traffic in Roman times.

In rocky country the same grit occurs, but a more useful and common guide are the larger boulders which once formed the foundations of the causeway or the curb-stones. The bigger ones are gradually removed by the farmer, but the rest remain. Ploughing destroys the metalled surface but not the stones of which it is made; it merely distributes them over a wider area.

When the road has been made across low ground which, being marshy, often has black soil, the remains of the causeway are sometimes very plainly visible because it consisted of lighter-coloured material. There is a good example near Cadnam in the New Forest

---

[3] Full descriptive details and plans will be found in my *Topography of Roman Scotland* (Cambridge, 1949).

where the road remained as a broad causeway of yellow gravel contrasting vividly with the black peaty soil of the rest of the field.

Except in iron-mining districts such as the Weald and the Forest of Dean, Roman roads in Britain were not as a rule paved; and even in those regions paving is exceptional. The surface there was made of the by-products of iron-smelting, such as iron-slag and cinders forming a layer six to twelve inches thick and occasionally thicker. These Roman *chemins-de-fer* are a special study in themselves, and I would refer to Mr Ivan D. Margary's *Roman Ways in the Weald*, which, as I said in the Introduction, 'is a record of the most important investigation of the Roman roads of England that has ever been undertaken'. A peculiar, though not unique, feature is that these iron roads are sometimes entirely covered up and buried a foot beneath the surface. For that reason they are not ideal subjects for the field archaeologist, who must also excavate, like Mr Margary, if he is going to make a thorough job of it. For one thus prepared the Forest of Dean and its iron-works presents a virgin field, if the various enemies of archaeology and of the amenities have left anything to investigate.

The field-worker should, however, try and see for himself some of these iron roads of the Weald, which are amongst the most remarkable things of their kind in Britain. A section, exposed by Mr Margary at Holtye near East Grinstead, has been left open and now belongs to the Sussex Archaeological Trust. A photograph of it forms the frontispiece of Mr Margary's book; you can even see the cart-ruts on it.

The materials of which these iron roads were formed must often have been transported for a considerable distance. But the roads in question are both later in time and different in purpose from the majority of those here discussed. The iron roads were of civilian, the others of military origin. The military roads (which we are chiefly concerned with here) were probably all made during the first century A.D., to facilitate the movement of troops during the subjugation of the island. They were probably constructed by gangs of native prisoners working under the direction of Roman soldiers. The materials were certainly obtained from close by, because the quarry-pits can still be seen. I first noticed them on the very first day I ever saw a Roman road, on Beaulieu Heath; and since then I have seen them often elsewhere. They accompany the Roman road over the Moffat moors and were photographed from the air in 1939 near Bushel Beck.[4] A more accessible example is on the hill above Walstone, north-east of Carlops, thirteen miles south-west of Edinburgh on the Biggar road. Here the causeway has gone, but the quarry-pits are very clear.

In tracing Roman roads the causeway is the thing to look for. One must not be satisfied unless some pretty perfect fragments, however short, of the original causeway can be located at intervals. Unfortunately the Romans were not the only people who made causeway-roads. They were also made in the eighteenth century, and in Scotland it is often extremely difficult to distinguish them from Roman roads. Here again the quarries help. The eighteenth-century roadmakers obtained their materials, not (as did the Romans) from a large number of small pits beside the road, but from a smaller number of larger pits dug into the slope of the hillside.[5] On Mendick Hill near Dolphinton and near Beattock Summit (between Moffat and Crawford) the Roman and eighteenth-century roads run

---

[4] See *Antiquity*, XIII, 1939, 280, Plate iii (*Air Reconnaissance of Roman Scotland*, by O.G.S.C.).
[5] See, for examples and illustration, my *Topography of Roman Scotland*, 5 (and Plates ii and iii) from which the following paragraphs have been abridged.

close by the side of each other, and the later of the two can sometimes only be distinguished by these hillside quarries which occur at intervals of about a quarter of a mile apart. The causeways themselves may sometimes be distinguished by the fact that those of the eighteenth century have rather sharply-defined edges, consisting of small scarped slopes, two feet wide. The edges of a Roman causeway merge almost imperceptibly into the ground on either side. The eighteenth-century causeways are usually flatter and less steeply cambered than the Roman, and sometimes have no camber at all. When cleared of vegetation the metalled surface of a Roman road is seen to be bounded by curbstones at the side and to have a setting of stones in the middle as a central rib.

It will be seen from the above remarks that it is rarely possible for even the most experienced archaeologist to express an opinion about an *isolated* fragment of causeway. If he does so in Scotland, it is at his own peril. Those who expect him to be able to do so are themselves at fault. Causeways must be judged not by what they look like at a given point, but by how they behave over a stretch of country. If, for instance, you are tracing a causeway over the moors and you find it crossing streams by culverts, you may be sure it is not Roman, for no Roman road ever does such a thing. Still less would it cross a ravine and torrent on a modern bridge. (One such near the Beef-tub helped to disentangle a complex of Roman and eighteenth-century roads.) When a Roman road comes to a stream you will find, as a rule, nothing but the occasional remains of an earthen ramp, once the support of a wooden bridge. Even these rules, however, need qualification, for near the Beef-tub the eighteenth-century roadmakers did actually use and modify the Roman causeway for short lengths. The road they made would here, therefore, *appear* to be merely a modern one if one were content to examine only this portion of it. Only when one has walked the whole length does its composite double nature become evident. In the case in point I succeeded in disentangling and mapping the two roads on the ground, and later confirmed my observation from the air.

As instances of the behaviour which distinguishes Roman from later roads may be given their alignment and their avoidance of ravines. Of the alignment it need only be said that it was from hilltop to hilltop. There are occasional exceptions, but it is a fairly safe rule that roads which change direction on low ground are not Roman. This rule does not apply to short changes of direction made in order to circumvent natural obstacles, such as very steep valleys. Such obstacles were avoided either by going round them (as does Chute Causeway on the Hants and Wilts border), or by a sloping descent. By avoidance of ravines I refer not to the crossing of them thus diagonally, but to the curious and quite well established fact that a Roman road will never be found running along the side or at the bottom of a long, steep hillside. There were occasions, of course, when it had to be done; but in all the Roman roads of Scotland I do not know of more than two or three exceptional instances. For a time I imagined that there must have been one such in the Clyde Valley below Crawford, but I subsequently found that the road avoids the valley and climbs up the Raggengill Pass (by a series of remarkable and unique graded hair-pin bends). Was it because steep slopes and ravines are good places for an ambush and for the rolling of rocks upon marching troops?—a favourite device employed also by modern Italians in the early days of the Fascist movement. One such boulder occupied a prominent place in the Fascist Exhibition in Rome in 1932, where I saw it. It was, of course, a red boulder, and was described as 'stained with the blood of martyrs'. Probably the Caledonians and ancient Britons also stained their boulders when they got the chance.

Often quite steep slopes were negotiated directly without a change of direction; but when they were too steep a terrace was formed diagonally down the slope. These terraces, being on steep hillsides that are unsuitable for cultivation, are sometimes the only surviving remains of a Roman road, and should be watched for. They will probably have lost their original sharpness of contour through soil-creep or landslips. The ground at the top end should be very closely examined for traces of a causeway.

The course of a Roman road may be indicated by the presence of deeply cut ditches accompanying the road on a hill. These traffic-ruts, as they are called, are very common and of all periods down to the nineteenth century (see Frontispiece). They are the natural result of traffic following a route across country, and they ceased forming when that traffic was canalized on a metalled road between hedges or fences. Their origin is curiously difficult, it seems, for some people to understand, though they may be seen actually forming to-day in roadless countries like Turkey and the Balkans. The traffic forms a beaten track that kills the protective mantle of turf (or the hard crust of the topsoil) so that rainwater can erode the surface and form gullies and eventually deep trenches (Plate 6b). The traffic-ruts are usually multiple because, as one route becomes churned up, another parallel to it is used. Traffic-ruts probably formed during the Roman period because they are often found beside Roman roads which were abandoned before the Middle Ages. But in practice it is hardly ever possible to say whether any given set of traffic-ruts is of Roman or medieval origin. Some, such as those beside the Roman road near Figsbury, west of Salisbury, may have begun in Roman times and remained in constant use ever since. Another example, in Ashdown Forest, is illustrated by an air-photograph in Mr Margary's book (Plate xii, opp. p. 145). Not one of these traffic-ruts is older than the Roman causeway beside it; if any were, an instance would be found where the causeway crossed it, filling it and being demonstrably later; but there is none. What happened was that the Roman causeway showed the way and was followed as a guide; but most of the actual traffic would go not along it but beside it. A precisely similar phenomenon occurred in the Sudan, where traffic, mostly (when I was first there) camels and donkeys, followed the line of the railway between Sennar and El Obeid, but *beside* the rails. The chief service performed by the railway was that it cut a clearing through the dense, thorny mimosa-scrub; and I suspect that the making of Roman roads may have done the same for the native Britons.

In Scotland the predecessors of the eighteenth-century causeway-roads were mere cart tracks which can often be seen as slightly sunken lanes wandering over the moors. Near the Beef-tub—one of the finest spots for the study of roads—such a track may be seen running alongside the two causeway-roads, Roman and eighteenth-century. Near Elvanfoot, south of Crawford, the Dumfriesshire Roman road is cut into by another such medieval track, which in turn is itself obliterated by an eighteenth-century causeway-road. Here is a very nice example of a kind of stratification, enabling the field archaeologist to date his evidence. It was not, in fact, until I had worked out on the ground and on the map the courses of these three roads and studied the intersection carefully, that I felt justified in regarding one of them as Roman.

To sum up: the palimpsest of the surface can be deciphered by patient, unhurried field-work combined with the study of old maps and other documentary sources. But because of the fascination of this task one tends to become absorbed in it and to dissipate one's efforts on innumerable minor problems of topography. For this reason it is better always to have a definite objective such as the tracing of a particular Roman road. (There are of course many other objectives, which will be dealt with later). To begin with, a well-known road should be walked and its behaviour observed. Then it will be possible to select some road whose course is imperfectly known and attempt to fill the gaps. A technique has been evolved for doing this.

The procedure which I have described may possibly seem dull or difficult, but speaking from experience I can confidently assert that it is not. Field-work does demand certain qualities—patience and perseverance, enthusiasm, constant scepticism and self-criticism. It requires and produces physical fitness and the ability to put up with some discomforts. One must be able to withstand the rigours of the British climate in winter and early spring, and of the British hotels at all seasons of the year. But the counterbalancing pleasures are, in my opinion, more than a sufficient recompense. There is an immense satisfaction in discovering a hitherto unknown Roman causeway and in walking along it for a mile or two, inserting it on the map as one goes along. It is a pursuit that combines both physical and intellectual enjoyment. There is only one pastime that is more exciting than field-work on the ground and that is observation of the same kind from an aeroplane, to which is added, in the mountainous parts of Scotland, just that spice of risk that is needed to bring out the full flavour.

CHAPTER 6

Tracks and Roman Roads

ROMAN ROADS, whether military or civil, differed from nearly all others made before modern times in having been deliberately planned beforehand, and then constructed in accordance with a definite method. They may occasionally have been improved versions of existing tracks, though of this there is never any but presumptive and usually, therefore, quite inconclusive evidence. Such pre-Roman tracks certainly existed; there must have been a close network of them connecting the hill-forts and farms of pre-Roman Britain. And here I would call your attention to a fundamental difference. All roads, ancient and modern, fall into two groups: those in the first group may be called 'Natural Tracks', and those of the second 'Made Roads'.

Natural tracks are not made or designed but *grow* in response to the need of going from one place to another. There were natural tracks long before the human race came into existence. They were formed by animals and led from pasture-grounds to drinking-places, or, like the buffalo tracks[1] which preceded the made roads of America (Plate 5b), were the routes followed by migrating herds. Such sheep and cattle tracks may be met with to-day on the downs, and on the Scottish uplands I have often followed them myself. There is even evidence of conscious selection of a route by animals. On Salisbury Plain[2] in 1922 I found a sheep-track plainly marked along the bank of a prehistoric linear earthwork called Old Ditch. For more than a mile the sheep had followed this earthwork, which had been somewhat levelled by former ploughing but was still quite plainly visible. Presumably it led in the direction in which the sheep wished to go, and they used it as a guide, just as the natives used the causeway of Roman roads. It was not for any other practical reason because the surface of the chalk down beside it was just as good. Hares and rabbits also have their regularly-used tracks, and I have no doubt that smaller animals have them also. Ants certainly follow regular routes, even crossing chasms by using fallen grass-stalks as bridges.

The formation of animal tracks does not cease when man comes upon the scene; they are merely diverted to human needs. The caravan or small party of mules carrying merchandise, food, fuel or building-materials from one settlement to another, or from the wood or quarry to the village, will choose that route which combines directness with the avoidance of natural obstacles. River-crossings and bogs will be avoided; valleys that must be crossed will be crossed at their narrowest points; the heads of valleys will often not be

[1] See *Antiquity*, III, 1929, 299–311.
[2] At the N.E. end of the parishes of Norton Bavant and Bishopstone.

crossed but circumvented, for it is better to go a little further round than have to descend and climb again. The best route between two places was not, we may be sure, discovered at once; it was the result of a long process of trial and error during which difficult passages were gradually eliminated and short cuts discovered. A natural track is therefore a product of evolution, of accumulated acts of artificial selection, chiefly performed by human beings but to which animals have, I am sure, made many contributions. Such natural tracks, once formed, will remain fixed so long as the terminal points remain fixed. They will not change until either the settlement is moved or abandoned or the quarry or wood exhausted.

The shorter tracks leading from a village to its water-supply do not, because of their shortness, exemplify this process so well, but they are natural tracks as much as the other longer ones, and there are many examples of them.

The chief natural tracks are ridgeways which are found not only in Britain but all over the world. The main highway of Abyssinia, along which the Italian advance was conducted, is a perfect example of a ridgeway, and it has been in use from the earliest recorded times. The Italians made it into a metalled road just as it may be imagined the Romans converted parts of the Cotswold ridgeway into the Foss-way. The Icknield way from Norfolk to Wiltshire was another such natural track whose existence in prehistoric times, though incapable of proof, may safely be presumed. All caravan-tracks across deserts are natural tracks whose routes are determined by the presence of wells, water-holes and oases, and by the course of dry valleys or wadis which may provide good going and serve also as guides to direction.

Natural tracks, then, differ from made roads because they grow gradually and are not made or deliberately designed at a given moment of time. They differ also in the fact that they are much wider. When travelling over open country the party will spread itself out over a considerable width of frontage, for there is no metalled road to follow and no hedges or fences to confine them. Air-photographs of camel-tracks over the deserts of Syria and Libya reveal a broad belt of paths, the foot-tracks of innumerable camels formed during centuries of travel. Sudanese motor-tracks do the same, especially over bad ground. Similar tracks can be seen on Salisbury Plain, formed by traffic during the Middle Ages, between the market towns of Salisbury, Devizes, Warminster and Marlborough. On sloping ground these tracks, as I pointed out above, cut up the turf and gullies are formed and traffic-ruts produced. When a natural track has to negotiate low-lying, clayey ground it will still be broad, for it is necessary to avoid pools and quagmires. When, however, a metalled road was made, the great width was no longer required. Often the full width of the pre-existing track was retained and delimited by hedges; and a vacant space remained on either side as a grass verge. This was a favourite place for squatters to erect houses on; the house in which I live myself was one of these, built on the grass verge of an old lane called Redbridge Lane. The house abuts on the metalled road, and at one end is a long narrow strip enclosed from the former track and used as a garden. There are thousands of wayside cottages with a similar origin.

I emphasize this difference between natural tracks and made roads because experience shows that it is not appreciated in these days of sophistication. With a few minor exceptions all medieval roads were natural tracks, unmetalled and wide. Even to-day natural

[3] See for instance *Wessex from the Air*, Plates i (Hod Hill) and xxii (Combe Down, Enford).

tracks are in the majority, even in some countries where there may be a network of made roads. In Algeria, for instance, I have ridden on a mule for a distance of sixty miles across a tract of country not more hilly than Herefordshire, where there was not a single made road. Taking the world as a whole, it is probably correct to say that even to-day natural tracks are the rule and made roads the exception.

This long excursus on roads in general was necessary to bring out the special nature of Roman roads and to show how they, as made roads, differ from others. In respect of Roman roads the account of natural tracks is not irrelevant because it shows, by contrast, what Roman roads were not; and it is just as necessary for the field archaeologist to know that as to know what they are, if he is not to waste his time in the field. I shall now proceed to give a few hints about what to do when actually working over the ground following a Roman road.

It goes without saying that a large-scale Ordnance Map is essential, to find your way about, to record your observations and to understand the topography. For recording new discoveries it is not necessary to use a tape-measure; pacing is quite accurate enough. A pace varies in length from $2\frac{1}{2}$ to 3 feet; it is not necessary to take long strides; if you hanker after unnecessary accuracy, you can find the length of your usual pace by counting how many you take over a measured distance. The limit of accuracy on a six-inch map is the width of a pencil-mark, which will be something of the order of ten feet. Your errors in pacing will not usually be as much. For transferring measurements to the map an ordinary visiting card is convenient; it can easily be scaled off from the scale on the map itself. Failing this in an emergency a grass-stalk may be used, or the edge of another map, or a postcard. It is easiest to mark the point where the road (or linear earthwork) crosses a hedge-line. You can pace this point to the nearest intersection of another hedge, i.e. to the corner of the field. Over open moorland accurate insertion is often more difficult for lack of detail, but even there some streamlet or derelict fence will often be found marked on the map. If long distances running into hundred of paces are unavoidable, it is a good thing to pick up a pebble or stick at every hundred; it is very easy to drop a hundred in a long walk.

Tracing roads through woods (other than beech woods) is a maddening business, possible only in late winter and early spring. It is very easy to lose the causeway in a wood, and for this reason one should stick close to it, walking along (not beside) it even when one has to fight one's way through undergrowth. Location is by pacing along paths cleared through the wood, but as these are apt to change (and the Ordnance Map may be as old as your self) they must be used cautiously, and checked at intersections with other paths. Roman roads have an infuriating habit, which I cannot explain, of fading out altogether in a wood.

The best time of year for field-work in these islands is from January to May (or in Scotland, June), after which the crops are too high for walking on. March is the ideal month, especially when dry. The vegetation is then at its lowest, and every fold in the ground plainly visible, especially in the still, low afternoon sunlight. In bracken country (which includes much of Wales) field-work is quite impossible from June onwards, not only because it hides the surface of the ground but also because of the swarms of flies which rise from it. The worst time for field-work is July and August. For those who can stand it Scotland is at its best between January and May, but it is often very cold. The low, yellow sunlight in midwinter is ample compensation for the slight discomforts endured, and ideal for photography.

Observations should be written on the margin of the map *on the spot*. There is no harm in supplementing them later at home, but even then some brief mark should be made at the time. Actual topographical insertions on the map itself should always be made on the spot, never from memory. If it is raining or blowing hard and there is no shelter, you can protect the map while writing on it by bending down over it and covering it with your body. A map is not seriously harmed by getting wet, provided it is not rubbed. Maps can be carried rolled during field-work, but should be kept flat at home. Hotel bedrooms do not usually run to tables, but one can keep them on the floor.

It will be obvious that what one records on the map is not just the 'course of the road', but the actual evidence observed, e.g. 'causeway plain and well-preserved', or 'visible but spread by cultivation', or 'wide stony belt across field', and so on. When no such observations are made there is nothing to insert; the 'probable course' can be left to look after itself later.

When, as often happens, you lose the trail and cannot pick it up again, there is a golden rule to follow: Go back to the place where you last saw it for certain and start again. Observance of this rule must be blind: don't argue with yourself, obey the rule. It may seem silly or hopeless, but do it. I have often got back on the right trail in this way. What really happens is that you have been working on a false hypothesis, and must abandon it and find a new one.

Visual alignment, though strictly speaking unnecessary if one has a six-inch map, is often useful, especially in open, featureless country. You may mark down some fairly distant point as a true alignment of the road, or you may line up trees, gates and so forth behind you. Both methods are very useful in scrubby country when it is necessary to know whether what looks like the causeway is in fact on the right alignment. It can be assumed, unless there is evidence to the contrary, that the alignment will remain unaltered between high points that are mutually intervisible. In scrubby country and open woods it is often only by some such alignments that one can keep direction.

A walking-stick is a very useful implement of research. Mr Margary has proved that the whole causeway of a Roman road may sometimes be buried a foot or more beneath the surface. Even when less deeply buried there may be no superficial evidence of the causeway. In such cases I have found it useful to walk along a shallow ditch, or field-drain, taking soundings with a walking-stick. You will feel at once when you come to the causeway, because you will not be able to ram the point of the stick into it at all. In one instance, on the Silchester-Speen road east of Shalford Farm, Berkshire, I was able, by taking soundings along the bottom of a ditch, to feel the rounded hump of the causeway right across its whole width. On the crest the stick refused to be driven in at all. Similarly in ploughed fields one may apply the same test along the deep furrow between the lands. When found, a distance should be paced to the nearest hedge and then plotted on the map; the edge of a card will then show whether the point marked is, as of course it should be, on your alignment.

Having got to know your ground thoroughly by field-work, you may then, if you can, go up and look at it from the air, preferably more than once, and if possible about March

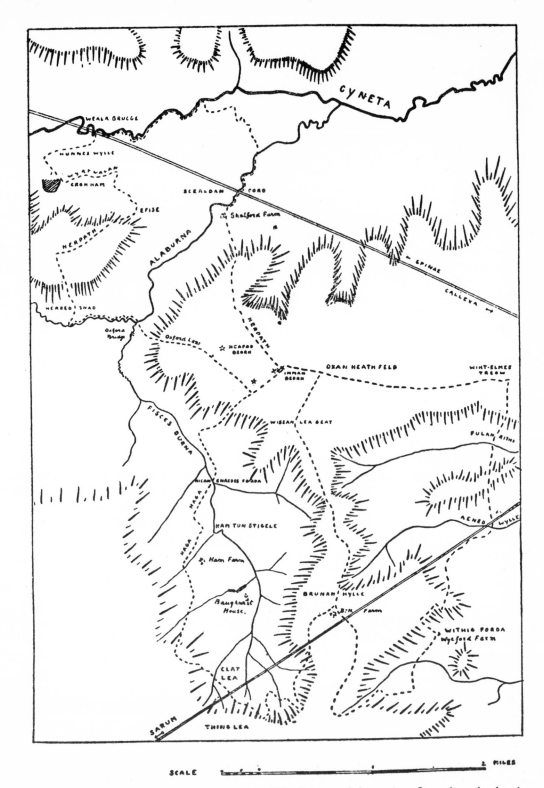

SCALE ⊢ ⊢ ⊢ 1 MILE

FIG. 3. Sketch-map drawn to illustrate an article in *The Antiquary* (July 1915) on Saxon bounds; showing the course of the Roman road from Silchester (Calleva) to Thatcham (Spinae).

and again when the crops are well grown in June or July. Knowing the topography you will not only identify more rapidly and see more, but also distinguish at sight what is new from what is already known. You should mark the new sites at once on a one-inch map, and when you get home check up all you have seen on a six-inch map. My Scottish reconnaissance[4] in June and July 1939 was of this character.

During field-work the evenings and wet days may be employed in studying the map, or better still if you can get them, air-photographs. Such documents often provide valuable clues. It was in this way that I re-discovered the lost Silchester–Thatcham road. After vainly looking for it elsewhere (accepting the then orthodox hypothesis) I came across a footnote in Samuel Barfield's *History of Thatcham*[5] which put me on the right track; but before I could test it in the field, I observed on the map a diagonal hedge-line just north-west of Silchester Walls, which was roughly in alignment with the fence of a pinewood farther on and also with a portion of the modern road where it crosses a valley at Aldermaston Soke. Field-work proved that the line was authentic; the causeway was found to be very well preserved along the edge of the wood and could be traced back to the gate of Silchester and in the other direction without a break to the village of Thatcham (Fig. 3).

The formation of the Roman road system was a factor of the utmost importance in the history of Britain. There was nothing like it in pre-Roman times, nor after it until the eighteenth century. We are not now concerned with their historical aspect, however, but rather with their outward and visible form, and that of other roads. They were not, as was thought until quite recently, the first made roads in Britain, though they were certainly the first comprehensive *network* of such. Thanks to the work of Dr H. Godwin, F.R.S.,[6] we now know that the Bronze Age inhabitants of the islands in the Somerset fens built wooden roads from those islands to the mainland. It seems that during most of the Bronze Age, that is, down to about the middle of the first millenium B.C. or a little before, the peat-moors were raised and the surface hard and dry enough to be readily crossed on foot. But when the dry sub-Boreal climate began to be replaced by the wet sub-Atlantic, that was no longer possible. The flooding which ensued must have made uninhabitable the Bronze Age settlements on the margins of the islands, and it is even suggested that these roads were made of the timber foundations of those settlements themselves; and that they were designed primarily for evacuation rather than for regular use. However this may be, the fact remains that they could not have been long in use for they are in fact covered by peat which formed between then and the Roman period. As they are not visible on the surface, they are not strictly subjects for field archaeology, and this brief notice must suffice.

Though the oldest known made roads in Britain these are not the oldest roads. That which can so be called is a well-defined sunken track leading to the flint-mines near Harrow Hill in Sussex. It is quite short, but that is probably only because we cannot follow its course beyond the slopes of the hill where the flint-mines were worked. It has therefore no more than rarity value. The same does not, however, apply to the quite numerous tracks that may be seen near hill-forts and native villages of the Iron Age. One such track leading to the water-supply can generally be found near every one. There is a good

---

[4] *Antiquity*, XIII, 1939, 280–92.
[5] Vol. I, 1901, 14. See *Man and his Past*, 1921, 182.
[6] *Philosophical Transactions of the Royal Society of London*, Series B (Biological Sciences), No. 599 (Vol. CCXXXIII 1948, 249–73): 'Prehistoric Trackways in the Somerset levels'.

E

example at Hod Hill,[7] leading from the hill-fort to the River Stour. There is another from the Iron Age village on Coombe Hill, Salisbury Plain, to the pond, now dry, in the bottom of the adjacent valley. A very good one can be seen climbing the escarpment of the North Hampshire Downs to the camp and Celtic fields on Ladle Hill, near (E. of) Beacon Hill, five miles south of Newbury. A little search will reveal such hollow tracks near every prehistoric settlement. They answer the question which I have been asked many times when conducting archaeological meetings and giving lectures—Where did they get their water? The answer is, from the nearest available source. One may see the process at work to-day in Algeria. There is an endless procession of donkeys carrying water ascending the sometimes precipitous paths that lead from the village on the hill-top to the pools in the bottom of the ravine. Water was no doubt stored in these hill-forts, but no more than a day or two's supply could be kept. There was no need for more, because sieges were impossible in the primitive society of those days.

In the rocky country of Wales and North Britain, and occasionally in the Cotswolds,[8] these water-tracks are sometimes bounded by settings of large stones, remnants probably of a dry-stone-wall. If you find such a track leading to a gap in the ramparts of a hill-fort, that is good evidence that it was the main entrance. The wall may have been built to prevent cattle and sheep from straying as they were driven down to drink. The same purpose may account for the earthen banks, originally perhaps reinforced by a stockade, which bound some of the Wessex tracks.

I mentioned the water-roads of modern Algeria as an illustration of life in our British hill-forts. That was merely because I happened to have been there and seen them in use. There must be similar scenes to be observed in every hilly country where primitive life survives and villages are set on hills. It will add interest to your travels to watch for such scenes, and it will add value to them if you will photograph them for the benefit of others. They will not last much longer, for like all primitive and laborious tasks they will be abandoned at the first onset of the modern world. The donkeys will lose their employment and become extinct, and the people will have electric windmills and of course be much happier.

[7] *Wessex from the Air*, Plate I.
[8] At Freezing Hill; see below p. 84, note 38.

CHAPTER 7

Some Tracks and Roads Described

AT THE BEGINNING of the last chapter I alluded briefly to those natural tracks which were formed gradually by men and animals who together eventually found the best route and maintained it so long as the track was used. I did so primarily to bring out the contrast between such tracks and the made roads of the Romans; it is a contrast as fundamental as that between the growth of towns during the nineteenth century and the deliberate planning of them in the twentieth. Between the two processes there is a constant struggle; the town-planner designs new shopping-quarters, ignoring perhaps the principle of 'shopping precincts', and when they are built he finds that age-old custom and convenience—or indolence—renders them useless, while the old shopping-quarters still flourish. The same thing happens with roads and paths whose course alters in response to new needs or shifts in the population centres. As those needs and centres change, so do the habits of the people; roads and paths are a most sensitive register of those habits which exercise a constant pressure that in the long run usually proves irresistible. A good example occurred at Southampton during the war, when the railings round the parks—open grass spaces in the middle of the town—were removed. People no longer used the asphalt paths but made new ones across the grass to suit their convenience. At first there were complaints, but the authorities had the sense to perceive that the newly-made paths were an automatic register of needs, and they asphalted them.

When, therefore, we set out to study the road-system of a country at any given period, we must know first of all whether that system came into existence gradually, by a process of growth in response to needs, or whether it was designed as a whole without regard for such needs. The Roman road system was,[1] in my opinion, an example of the latter process; it was probably designed in the first instance for the purely military needs of the conquerors. Once in existence, however, it created a new set of factors; instead of roads following people, people followed roads. New centres of population grew up where roads met or crossed, or where they crossed rivers. The military centres, such as we may be sure London, Cambridge, Winchester, Dorchester (Dorset) and several other towns were originally, developed rapidly into urban centres, and the process was encouraged by the Romans. But the process is extremely complicated, because it is possible that, although the actual alignment and course of the Roman roads was dictated by purely military considerations, the centres from which they radiated may have been selected with regard to existing population centres, such as tribal capitals. That certainly happened at Verulamium

[1] With the exception of certain mining areas in the Weald and the Forest of Dean: see above, page 56.

and probably at Winchester (Venta Belgarum), Chichester (Noviomagus Regnentium) and Cirencester (Corinium Dobunorum). The exact site selected by the Romans was not, however, that of the old settlement, but one whose topography was most suitable for military reasons. These requirements were laid down and can be inferred with some exactness from known fort-sites (e.g. in Northern Britain). Thus the old tribal capital of the Belgae is thought to have been on St Catherine's Hill, of Chichester at the Trundle, and the predecessor of Verulamium was in Prae Wood.

Not only did towns come into existence thus, but also smaller wayside settlements and ribbon-development. Thus were formed the villages of Spinae, where the Roman Bath road crossed the Kennet Valley at Thatcham, and of Cunetio where it crossed it at Mildenhall. At Nursling, where the Roman road connecting the populous chalk uplands of Hampshire (and Winchester) with those of Dorset (and Dorchester) crossed the Test, grew up the village which may have borne the name of Onna.[2] Dozens of others sprang up in the same sort of way.

But a population-pattern brought into existence and maintained by an artificial system of made roads lasts only as long as the roads, and the even more important bridges, are kept in repair; and that in turn is a function of organized administration, such as that which ended with the departure of the Romans. Most of the bridges, in the south of England at any rate, were timber constructions, and although the framework might last for a long time with little or no upkeep, the plank floor of the roadway across it would soon decay and not be renewed. A faint echo of some such a sequence seems to survive in the bound-mark *weala brucge* (now Quaking Bridge) which occurs in the tenth-century bounds of Brimpton, Berkshire, exactly where the Roman road from Silchester to Thatcham (Spinae) crossed the Kennet (Fig. 3).[3] That was the Roman road to Bath, and as the story of how its course gradually changed into that of the modern Bath road is probably typical, I propose to tell it now at some length.[4]

The Roman road left London as what is now Oxford Street and went from Marble Arch through Brentford to Staines (Pontes) where, as the name shows, the Thames was crossed by a series of (wooden) bridges. Then came a long desolate stretch of twenty-six miles, first over barren heaths near the Berks-Surrey border (later part of Windsor Forest) and then through the forested clay lowlands of the Blackwater and Loddon (Fig. 4). From Silchester westwards it ran for four miles over heath, so that there was a distance of thirty miles where habitations were few and (we may safely guess) highway-men many in post-Roman times. The road running northwestwards out of Silchester (which I discovered about 1913) is the road to Gloucester; but it would be followed by Bath traffic to Wickham, five miles north-west of Newbury, where the road to Bath branched off from it. This latter—the road we are now concerned with—crosses the Kennet above Hungerford, but there is a gap of six miles between the Wantage-Hungerford road and Hens Wood. It recrossed the Kennet at Mildenhall (Cunetio) below

---

[2] *Archaeologia*, XCIII, 1949, 43. It may be added, in support of this identification, that one of the headwater streams of the Test is the river Ann, which gave its name to Andover (An-defer—O.C. *Onno-dubron).

[3] See my article in the *Antiquary NS.*, XI, No. 7 (July 1915), 253 and the original document in Birch, Cartularium Saxonicum ii, No. 802.

[4] I had hoped to be able to study it in much greater detail, but that would require access to many documents and is not now possible.

Marlborough, and thence to Silbury Hill, south of Avebury, coinciding occasionally with the present Bath road. From Silbury (which was used as an aiming-point) it ran over the downs to Sandy Lane (Verlucio) and thence in a dead straight line to the heights above Bathford where it entered what is now Somerset and joining the Fossway at Batheaston coincided again with the modern road on the north-west bank of the Avon.

The modern Bath road diverges in places as much as ten miles from the Roman; but they leave London and enter Bath together, and the two are united again for brief sections at Thatcham and Marlborough, the first divergence being at Hounslow. The Roman road continues still in use to Staines, and west of that the modern Basingstoke road only gradually diverges from the Roman near Virginia Water, continuing as a well-authenticated Saxon and medieval road over Hartford Bridge Flats to Basingstoke. The reason for the abandonment of the Roman road west of Staines is to be looked for in the decay of Silchester, whose place was taken by Basingstoke on one side and Reading on the other. Travellers to Bath would thereafter have the choice of breaking their journey at either place, and I think they chose Reading; to reach it they would take the road which branched off at Hounslow making for Slough, Maidenhead, Henley, Benson, Dorchester and Oxford; follow it to Littlewick Green, midway between Maidenhead and Henley, and go thence by Ruscombe and Twyford to Reading.[5] Thence they would follow the gravel terrace on the north side of the Kennet valley to Newbury—or more accurately, to Speenhamland, skirting Newbury itself; and thence similarly to Hungerford.

The medieval route between Hungerford and Marlborough was certainly almost the same as that now followed, whose eastern portion may coincide with the Roman road, and cannot be far off it. The hollow traffic-ruts of the medieval route can be seen to-day running unbroken for two miles in the northern part of Savernake Forest (Fig 5). They begin on the south side of the road west of Puthall Gate and proceed in broad, sweeping curves up the hill, going round the outside of the Hospital grounds and then running due north down the steep hillside to where the road crosses the railway, where they join it. But there was a period between the first use of coaches and the construction of turnpikes for them when the route followed was along the Kennet Valley by Chilton Foliat, Ramsbury and Mildenhall. An amusing story is told[6] of an old driver of the Marlborough stage-coach who in 1752 would cling to 'the old waggon-track called Ramsbury [way]' instead of using the then newly-made road (by Puthall Gate). Passengers would remonstrate with him, but he always refused, saying that he was an old man, his father and grandfather had driven along the Ramsbury way before he was born and he would continue to do the same until he died. It was probably a better road for wheeled traffic than the deeply rutted medieval track, which may have been abandoned for the other when coaches first came into use; for the Ramsbury road has cottages, farms and villages along it, and may have been roughly metalled, whereas the route by Puthall Gate had only one farm in the seven-mile stretch between Froxfield and Marlborough.

The divergence of the Bath road from the Roman in the western part of this stretch

[5] That is the route of the present Bath road; but it is possible that before Maidenhead Bridge (already in existence in 1297: see *Antiquity*, V, 1931, 167) was built, and earlier, when Windsor Park did not bar the way, travellers may have followed another route by Old Windsor, Clewer Green, Fifield, Foxleighs, the Walthams, Ruscombe, and Twyford. This route between White Waltham and Clewer follows a direct but irregular course and has the same marks of ancient ribbon-development as the sector passing Gastard Court, near Bath (mentioned below).

[3] *Cornhill Magazine*, July, 1864, 60.

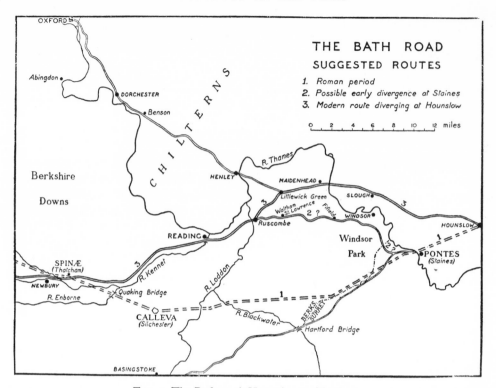

FIG. 4. The Bath road: Hounslow to Newbury.

is easily accounted for. The original settlement was on the hill at Folly Farm, where Roman finds have been made within the ramparts of what looks like a hill-fort (Fig. 5). But the Roman village of Cunetio was below in the valley in Black Field, where the Roman road to Gloucester crossed the Kennet. The Saxon village, as so often, was founded a little distance away on the north side, and its ancient origin is attested by two early Anglo-Saxon saucer-brooches, doubtless from a grave. But Marlborough, whose existence is not recorded until some four centuries later (in 1086), superseded Mildenhall, as it had superseded Cunetio. Marlborough was probably, like Devizes, a new growth round the castle, and would deflect the north-and-south roads from their crossing at Mildenhall to a crossing a mile and a half higher up. The traffic-ruts of those roads are still conspicuous on the hill above the station on the skirts of the forest (see Frontispiece).

West of Marlborough the modern road almost certainly coincides more closely with the Roman road now than did the medieval one, and again, as at Ramsbury, the older route may have been abandoned when coaches came into use; it passed by (south-west of) Manton House (where is a field called 'London Road Ground') and threaded its way amongst the sarsens on Fyfield and Overton Downs. Here are many deeply-cut traffic-ruts.[7] Passing through (or by) Avebury and Beckhampton it followed the same course as the

[7] The 'herepath' mentioned in earlier impressions of this book was due to an erroneous identification of Dr. Grundy's; see H. C. Brentnall in the 87th Report of the Marlborough College Nat. Hist. Soc. (1938) pp. 123–4.

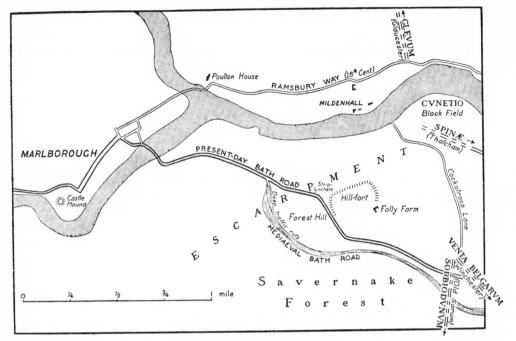

FIG. 5. Roads at Marlborough.

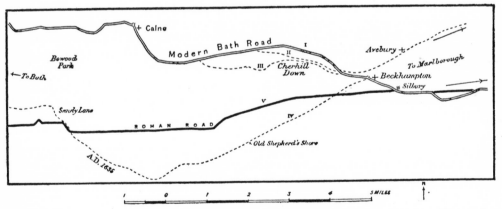

FIG. 6. Roads over the downs west of Marlborough. (Reproduced by permission from *Wessex from the Air*, fig. 57).

modern Devizes road (Fig. 6); but at two miles from Beckhampton it left it, continuing straight on, going through Wansdyke at Old Shepherds' Shore and then curving round to the north on Beacon Hill, south of Heddington, to Sandy Lane (Verlucio).[8] Here it again crossed the Roman road, and passing through the gap—only 100 yards wide— between the park banks of Bowood and Spye went on to Bowden Hill, 583 feet high and a

[8] For the importance of Sandy Lane as a road junction see my letter in the *Wiltshire Gazette* (Devizes), 8th September 1921.

landmark that can be seen even from the Cotswolds. From it, too, there is a magnificent view, extending westwards to the Mendips. But the hill itself was a formidable climb a mile long, dreaded by the early coach-travellers, who were said to have made their wills at the posting station at the foot where extra horses were attached. The Bristol Avon was crossed at Rey Bridge. Passing a quarter of a mile north of Lacock along what is now called Mons Lane it reached the modern road from Lacock to Bath at the 12th milestone from Bath, just south of its junction with the Chippenham road.

At this point a digression may be made to explain how the rest of its course was discovered. Up to this point the existence of a road to Bath following the route described is fully authenticated by documents and confirmed by field-work. Studying the map to discover how it went on, I noticed what looked like traces of ancient ribbon-development along a road which, though for the most part continuous, had small gaps bridged only by footpaths. (The course led through Gastard and Wadswick). This looked very much like an abandoned medieval highway; if such it were there would certainly be traffic-ruts, and the best place to look for them would obviously be one of the gaps, preferably on a steep slope. The biggest gap, of one-third of a mile, was between the 12th milestone aforesaid and a stream rising at Corsham and joining the Avon at Lacock. In order to test the validity of this map-theory I made a special journey to Lacock. The gap is crossed by a footpath and old disused lane running from the milestone south-westwards to the stream where is a house, called Potters Mill in 1808. Sure enough I found a deep hollow way, representing prolonged use, leading down to the stream from the east; this led into Wick Lane, whence a footpath—often the only survival of a right of way—joined the modern road again near Sandpits Farm. The road passed on by Gastard Court, a medieval manor house, then became a footpath again to the south end of Monk's Park, then went as a road to Neston and so to Wadswick. Here at Chapel Plaster it crossed the medieval pilgrim-route from Malmesbury to Glastonbury, and the chapel (which is still used) was no doubt built at the cross-roads to secure the offerings of the faithful on both routes. On the open down immediately south-west of the chapel are many parallel traffic-ruts, the marks of an important and ancient highway. The road now coincides with a modern one curving round the south side of a small park at Hatt House and passing three large round barrows— rather a rarity in these parts. On King's Down the traffic-ruts are evident on the south side of the modern road, as a bow of which the latter is the string. They cross the road at the 5th milestone from Bath, just east of Kingsdown Farm, and the deep hollow way which curves down the hill on the north is marked by hachures on the Ordnance Map (Wilts 25 SW.). It joins an old lane and after passing the Swan Inn comes into the modern road again 250 yards before entering Somerset. The Roman Bath road (represented by Gover's Lane) unites with it in Bathford itself. After passing through Bathford it joins the modern Bath road at the railway-bridge, and goes on to Bath (Fig. 7).

Between Sandy Lane and Bathford, a distance of twelve miles, this road follows a course that is never more than a mile and a quarter to the north of the Roman road, of which it is obviously the successor. Over this stretch the Roman road was destroyed and used by the makers of Wansdyke, so that the need to find another route must have been forced upon travellers early in the Dark Ages. It is even possible that the route here called medieval may have come into existence during Roman times; for it will be noted that it passes through the three known and named Roman settlements of Spinae (Thatcham),

Cunetio (Folly Farm and Black Field) and Verlucio (Sandy Lane). It looks rather as if those places were regarded as necessary points to pass, whatever diversions may have been made otherwise from the Roman road. This probability is strengthened by the name 'here-path' given to it on Overton Down; if it was, as this word implies, an important thorough-fare in the tenth century, it may well have been in existence for several centuries.

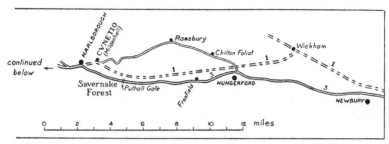

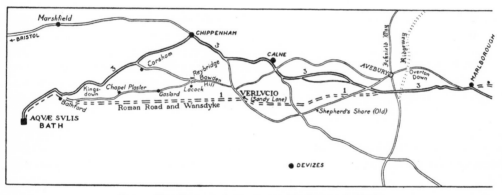

FIG. 7. The Bath road: Newbury, Marlborough, Bath.

Before concluding, I must return for a moment to the point where this medieval route crossed the modern Bath road at Beckhampton. I have dealt with the details elsewhere;[9] it consists of the parallel tracks of two successive roads, precursors of the present road to Bath by Calne, and running parallel to it over Cherhill Down. But though this is now the road to Bath, it became so only after the mid-seventeenth century at the earliest, and probably during the eighteenth century. It is not, in origin, a Bath road at all; to reach Bath by it one has to make a right-angle turn to Chippenham, the other road continuing on to Marshfield and Bristol. It is therefore the old Bristol road which may well once have joined our medieval Bath road at Beckhampton and gone with it by Avebury over Manton Downs.

The foregoing account has necessarily gone rather deeply into topographical details and will only be intelligible if read with an Ordnance Map at hand to consult. That is inevitable; it is not possible, nor profitable, to discuss such matters as the origin of our existing roads merely in general terms. Each road can be explained only in terms of its

[9] *Wessex from the Air*, 235.

own history; roads are cultural traits and, as Professor Leslie White would say, must be explained culturologically. But having just done so in a particular case, it may be permissible to indulge in a few general remarks.

A fixed point in the study of British roads is the Roman road system. Its main outlines are now fairly well known and have been recorded on the Ordnance Survey Map of Roman Britain. To what extent, even during the Roman period, were those roads used? I think it is quite likely that some of them were very little used after the military necessity which created them ceased—and that was before the end of the first century A.D. Professor Collingwood long ago demonstrated this for the Foss-way.[10] I very much doubt whether the so-called Portway, for whose name there is no ancient local evidence, was ever much used between Silchester and Andover. Evidence of use is primarily topographical—the existence of deep traffic-ruts beside the causeway where it descends a hill, and these are not found along the very hilly course of the Portway. Mention of a Roman road (as a 'strete') in a pre-Conquest charter is not necessarily evidence that it was then in use, but merely that its nature and origin were known. If a Roman road is called a 'herepath' it is perhaps a little more likely that it was then still being used, for the term was also applied to other roads that certainly were; but the word means 'army road' and may again merely reveal knowledge of purpose, not current use. Nor does the use of a Roman road as a parish boundary necessarily mean more than that the causeway was found convenient for the purpose. The fact that a Roman road coincides with a modern one does not prove *continuous* use since Roman times, least of all when the original straightness is maintained. Long usage causes wobbling, and it is those modern roads whose course continually wobbles and occasionally diverges slightly from the straight which are most likely never to have gone out of use since Roman times. A good instance is Akeman Street between its junction with the Bicester road on the west and Aylesbury on the east; it was probably a market road between those two places. Another is the Roman road from Canterbury to Rochester and London, which has certainly been in continuous use since its construction.

But the exact coincidence of existing roads with Roman ones may sometimes date only from the beginning of modern road-making in the eighteenth and nineteenth centuries. The reasons why a modern road may have followed a derelict Roman road are quite easy to see: it saved labour, for the road could be made upon it, or else beside it, using its materials; it automatically gave direction; and as it was often already a property boundary, there was a minimum disturbance of existing rights. The use of its material for road-making is on record in many cases; it can be seen on Oakley Down in Cranborne Chase where the crown of the great causeway was used so long as it was near enough to the modern road. We are apt to forget that, down to well within living memory, flints were the main source of road-metal over the whole of southern and eastern England, and Roman roads provided a ready-made supply. (Elsewhere farmers would collect them off the fields and dump them beside the road; and these stone-heaps used to be picked over by 'flinters' looking for stone axes—I have looked over hundreds of them myself).

What were the factors that kept Roman roads in use? Obviously they would continue to be used so long as they satisfied the needs of travellers by providing the safest and most convenient route between inhabited places. Failure to keep the road surface in repair would not greatly inconvenience travellers, for the hollow ways (traffic-ruts) *beside* the causeway

[10] *Journal of Roman Studies*, XIV, 1924, 252–6.

show that they did not use it exclusively; I have always suspected that the chief service performed by Roman roads was the clearance of a passage through forest and bush, and that the causeway itself was followed only when it crossed soft alluvial ground. They thus cleared the way and provided a guide to direction. But failure to keep the bridges in repair was another and more serious matter, for if a bridge became unusable a ford had to be found and that might cause a deflection in the route of a mile or more. Once that happened the approach to the ford would leave the Roman road at a point some distance from the river on either side, and eventually the rest of the route might become changed also.

The Roman road system is central to the study of old roads in this country. Even though many Roman roads may have gone out of use, wholly or in parts, the general framework was the point of departure from which the Saxon, medieval and post-medieval system originated. It must also be remembered that many modern roads conceal Roman ones that cannot, for that reason, be identified as such with certainty; it would often be difficult to do that even by excavation, which is usually impracticable. And it must be noted also that, besides the somewhat artificial system of military roads—which are what we usually mean when we speak of Roman roads—there was also a maze of native tracks, which remained in use during Roman times and afterwards, and which were equally ancestral to the later styems. Unfortunately it is impossible to identify most of them. Many so-called prehistoric or 'British' trackways are merely medieval market-roads. Much rubbish has been written about them by writers who have overlooked the fact that, during the two millennia that have since elapsed, many of these minor prehistoric tracks must have been nearly obliterated by the footsteps of other travellers. Here and there one can recognize, as I have shown in the previous chapter, a few yards of genuine pre-historic road; and in favoured regions where Celtic fields survive or can be seen on air-photographs fragments of a system of field-ways may be detected. In certain regions a combination of good field-work and an eye for the country has done something to restore a few roads.[11] But most attempts to reconstruct in detail the network of minor tracks are foredoomed to failure.[12] Nor can one do much more than guess the main thoroughfares that we assume to have existed before the Romans came. I propose to do so here, but just a few general remarks may be made about a modern parallel which has, as it seems, much in common with Roman Britain. Once more we turn to the present to understand the past.

One can learn much about the habits of road-users by travel over the extremely primi-ative motor-tracks of the Sudan. Although nothing could be much less like Britain than those arid stretches of desert and scrub, yet there are a few points of resemblance, and the habits and preferences of motor-drivers are not wholly different from those of other travellers. One rule the driver seems always to observe is not to lose sight of the track altogether. He does this partly so that he may not lose his way, partly because he knows that where others have gone before he can follow. He is loath to blaze an entirely new track, and when he is obliged to do so he always follows his own track on the return journey, for the same reason, driving often in the actual wheel-marks. He leaves the track only when for some reason it is, or seems, so bad that he may stick in it, and he always does so with extreme reluctance. One imagines that prehistoric man would have done much the same. But

[11] For an example see Aileen Fox in *Arch. Camb.*, XCIV, 1939, 30–41: Dark Age inscribed memorial stones were often set up beside roads and so help to fill out the pattern.

[12] The late Mr Watkins's theories, set out in his book, *The Old Straight Track*, were based upon a misconception of primitive society, and supported by no evidence. His writings on the subject are quite valueless.

one cannot press the comparison very far because the particular factors involved are so different. One which is common to both areas is the existence of bush[13] and dry (or in Britain wet) forest. Tracks (and also, as Sir Cyril Fox has shown, linear earthworks) through country of this kind are never straight but follow a winding course. That is caused by the need to go round big or fallen trees, or to use a natural open space in the vegetation. An excellent example of the diversion of a 'motor-track[14] to avoid a fallen tree was met with on the road from Sennar to Roseires along the east bank of the Blue Nile (Plate 2a); one can see both the old tracks used before the tree fell across them and blocked the way, and the new ones swerving aside to avoid it.[15] Many road-bendings in England must have come into existence from a similar cause, which is often cited, but I do not think that a photograph of the actual thing in operation has been published before.

I have suggested that the most important function (from the native traveller's point of view) performed by the road-making of the Romans in Britain was the clearance of vegetation rather than the making of a causeway. Sudanese experience amply confirms that theory. Except in the towns and across dry river-beds there are no made roads; all that is done is to clear a way through the bush, cutting down the trees and thorn-bushes, and to remove surface obstacles such as large stones and boulders; usage does the rest. Roads thus formed are not mathematically straight, but oscillate slightly on either side of the direct line, avoiding large trees such as tebeldis (in the south) which it would be waste of time to cut down when they can so easily be circumvented. Similar clearings have been made for the railway, and traffic follows in its wake. The roads are either new cuts or pre-existing tracks improved and widened for the use of motors. Just such may have been some of the non-military Roman roads in the Weald, except that there a metalled foundation was needed for the transport of heavy iron ore. The Roman paved ford at Benenden has its close parallel in the causeways of earth (not sand), stones and bushes laid across the sandy beds of wadis in Darfur to enable cars to cross without sticking.

These Darfur tracks are kept in repair by local labour, certain leading persons in each district being made responsible for their upkeep. Besides the wadi-crossings it is necessary to see that the bush does not encroach and to cut it back when it does. The felled bushes are then laid on each side of the road and serve to delimit it. Bushes are also laid beside the road when it crosses open patches, to mark the way, and stones are also so used. Along little-used tracks wheel-marks soon vanish; the passage of a single herd or flock will obliterate them, and it is quite easy to miss the way and get into difficulties. Bushes are sometimes placed upside down on the edge of the track for guidance. If this repair-work is neglected the track will become impassable in a very short time. Now that is exactly what must have happened in Roman Britain in the fifth century. With no central authority to keep the scrub from encroaching many of the Roman roads must have become over-grown, so that the route would be unusable quite apart from the condition of the surface or of the bridges. One imagines that the wilderness would soon return over the heath-lands and forest round Silchester, and indeed that may have been a contributary cause of the town's decay and abandonment.

These Sudanese motor-tracks are topographically equivalent to the Roman roads of

---

[13] But Britain had nothing so formidable as the *Kittir* with hooked thorns that must not be touched, even lightly.

[14] The track followed a clearing deliberately cut for it through the forest, but that does not invalidate the comparison.

[15] The wheel marks of our own car are the plainest; they stop abruptly because, when I stopped it, we reversed and went back so that I might take the photograph from the best view-point.

Britain. (Functionally it is the railways which correspond, for they were first made for military and administrative purposes). They differ chiefly in being far less durable; they are merely cleared ways, not (except over wadi-beds and a few other sandy or muddy tracks) causeways, and would quickly vanish if not regularly used, leaving no trace. They also differ in being designed for civil rather than military needs. (It is significant that the longest stretch of *made* road in the Sudan, from Khartoum to Gordon's Tree, was made during the last war for purely military purposes). They therefore follow pre-existing tracks for the most part, occasionally shortening them by cutting a new track across a bend, as for thirty miles on the west bank of the Blue Nile between a point near Disa and Qalqani. The Romans did exactly the same, and the occasional references to a 'strete'—a word which invariably denotes a made road—in Saxon charters in places where a Roman road of the original military kind seems unlikely, are probably examples of similar improvement of native tracks. As I said above, it would be hopeless to attempt to restore the pre-Roman track-system as a whole; the most that can be done is to see how far certain routes which seem likely on purely geographical grounds to have been used as main thoroughfares do seem to have traces of such usage.

Pre-Roman Britain was still largely covered by forests, but there were certain forest-free areas and belts of limestone (oolitic and cretaceous). The largest such open tract was Salisbury Plain with its adjuncts to the north (the Marlborough and Berkshire Downs), east (north Hampshire) and south (Dorset). To it led two corridors along the North and South Downs respectively, and another along the Chilterns, continuing north-eastwards along the margin of the Fens into Norfolk. North-west of this central chalk area were the Cotswolds, a region of oolitic limestone continuing also north-eastwards (though less open because of the deeper drift soil of glacial origin) by Northamptonshire and Lincolnshire to the Humber. Along each of these belts run ancient trackways all of which (except the last) were known and recognized as such long before their probable geographical origin was suspected. They are predominantly ridgeways, but they leave the higher ground when occasion demands (Fig. 8).

The South Downs ridgeway starts from the English Channel somewhere near Beachy Head, and passing through a thickly populated prehistoric region reaches the Hampshire one at Old Winchester Hill, coming from Corhampton past Millbarrow and Cheesefoot Head. West of Winchester there is no single track that could be called its continuation, but a number of tracks spreading out over the once populous chalk downs. The obvious route to Salisbury Plain crosses the bare chalk region between the clay-capped Buckholt hills in the south and the wooded uplands (later called Chute Forest) round Andover. An old track following such a route is marked on Dr Williams-Freeman's map past Danebury;[16] it is the natural continuation of a track crossing the Test at Stockbridge (where hill-forts dominate the ford on either side, at Woolbury and Meon Hill), and it would reach Salisbury Plain somewhere near Stonehenge.

The tracks which followed the escarpment of the North Downs reached the same point. The eastern portion is called the Pilgrims' Way; and Canterbury is usually taken as the terminus. But there must also have been feeders branching off to the ports on the Thames estuary, where so many hoards of the Late Bronze Age have been found. Mr. Margary

[16] See his *Field Archaeology as illustrated by Hampshire*, 1915, 45–6.

has recently described a little-known but undoubted ridgeway running parallel with the Pilgrims' Way on the lower slopes (*Arch. Cant.* LXIV, 1951, 20–23). The track then goes

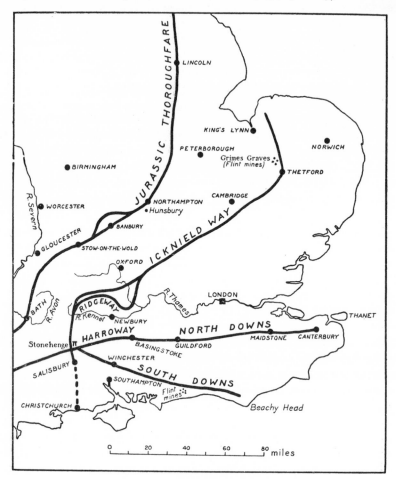

FIG. 8. The four main prehistoric thoroughfares.

along the Hog's Back and entering Hampshire is called the Harroway. There are no early forms of the word on record; a possible derivation is from an Old English **hearg-weg*, the shrine-way, i.e. the way to Stonehenge. This would be closely parallel in form to the name 'Pilgrims' Way', which in fact is a branch of it. The Harroway goes north of Andover—a bronze hoard was found in watercress beds where it crosses the river Anton —and by Weyhill on to Amesbury and Stonehenge. It is, as Dr Williams-Freeman said, the great trunk road of Southern England; and if we like we may think of it re-appearing in Devon and Cornwall, where an ancient road runs down the spine of the peninsula, with ribs going off to ports north and south, ending at Marazion opposite Ictis where those 'shy traffickers, the dark Iberians, came, and on the beach undid their corded bales.'[17]

[17] For the Spanish trade see E. T. Leeds, *Archaeologia* LXXVI, 1927, 227–35.

But the Harroway may well have been trodden long before those shadowy Iberians of the Iron Age. The only long barrow known in the whole eighty miles of chalk corridor, between the Maidstone group in Kent and the outermost example (at Twinley) of the Central Wessex concentration, is on the western slope of the Hog's Back, less than a mile from the mesolithic settlement at Farnham.[18] And amongst the non-local stones found by Dr Grahame Clark in the settlement is one which 'can be matched very closely with a sandy bed in the Gramscatho beds, exposed near Helford, Cornwall,' while two of the others 'could well have come from the Devonian sediments of S. Cornwall or Devon.'[19] It seems not unlikely, therefore, that the Long Barrow people of Surrey may have maintained contact along the Harroway with their congeners in Kent and Wessex, and that their mesolithic predecessors too may have used it for even longer journeys. Nomadic people travel very long distances.

The third great trackway is the famous Icknield Way, already recognized but ill-comprehended by our learned and 'curious' forebears in the eighteenth century, and even dimly seen by the medieval clerk who invented the Four Great Roads of King Belinus.[20] Starting on the Wash it may have been joined near Thetford by others from coastal ports in East Anglia. Through Cambridgeshire its existence is proved not only by medieval references to the existing trackway but also by the great dykes[21] which bar its course. I have given elsewhere[22] an account of it thence through Hertfordshire. Near Luton it passes under the ramparts of Lygeanburg (Limbury), one of the four towns taken by Cuthwulf in 571; battles in those days were always fought on important thoroughfares, the only ones that large bodies of men could use with safety and often for that reason called *herepaths* (war-paths). Between Dunstable and the Thames it has not been studied as a whole by a field archaeologist, and there is an opportunity for someone who will do so, combining the evidence of Saxon· charters, references in local medieval documents and in old cadastral maps. It seems, however, to divide at Ivinghoe, one branch becoming a ridgeway and the other going past (but usually not through) the spring-line villages at the foot of the Chiltern escarpment. I have referred to it in my article on the Chiltern Grim's ditches,[23] and the accompanying map of the roads embodies much field-work not described in the text. The lower road crosses the Thames at Goring-Streatley, and then curving round to the north passes through Blewbury and Wantage (looping between Upton and Wantage), and goes close along the foot of the escarpment through (not past) the spring-line villages to Wroughton, south of Swindon, where it turns south over the downs to West Kennett, where it rejoins the Ridgeway. This, the Chiltern ridgeway, crossed the Thames at Pangbourne and went to Aldworth, near which it was barred by defensive linear earthworks,[24] and thence by the Roman farm on Roden Downs and across Churn Plain back on to the top of the escarpment. Here it becomes the famous

[18] For the mesolithic site see Dr Grahame Clark and Mr W. F. Rankine in *Surrey Arch. Collns.*, Vol. XLIV; *Proc. Preh. Soc.* and *Antiquity*, XI, 1937, 476–8. For the Long Barrow see *A Survey of the Prehistory of the Farnham district* (Surrey Arch. Soc. 1939), 133–49.   [19] *Proc. Preh. Soc. NS.* XV, 1949, 193–4.
[20] A well written but literary and therefore mapless account of its course will be found in Edward Thomas's book (*The Icknield Way*, 1913). Mr Thomas got some of his medieval references from Mr Harold Peake, who got them from me. I was then a student at Oxford and working in the Bodleian. In the summer of 1912 I walked along the Icknield Way from King's Lynn to Dunstable. The course is marked on the Ordnance Survey Map of Britain in the Dark Ages, South Sheet.   [21] See Chapter 17.
[22] *Proc. Preh. Soc. NS.* II, 1936, 97–105: map of district opp. 102.
[23] *Antiquity*, V, 1931, 161–71.   [24] See *Antiquity*, V, 1931, 162–4; XVIII, 1944, 119–20.

Berkshire Ridgeway, well attested by the Saxon Chronicle and charter references. It went by the White Horse, Uffington Castle and Wayland Smith's Cave (a chambered Long Barrow) to the hill-forts of Liddington and Barbury. At the last hill-fort it crossed the track-way (Old Sarum, Marlborough, Cricklade, Cirencester) followed by the invading army of Cynric and Ceawlin, who fought at Barbury (Beran burg) in 556. Passing over Hackpen Hill it joined the lower road on Overton Hill near Avebury (Fig. 7) and crossed the Kennet at a place called *Sealtham* in A.D. 939.[25] Going southwards it then passed the Long Barrow now called Adam's Grave and formerly Woden's Barrow (Wodnes beorg) where battles were fought in 592 and 715. The path across the then difficult ground in the Vale of Pewsey below was carefully chosen, but beyond it climbs the escarpment and is lost on the wide expanses of Salisbury Plain. Intensive research in field and library might well recover the exact course, though the army has robbed field-work of its attraction here. But its general direction is clear; if it did not lose its identity it must have gone southwards between the Till and the Avon past Druid's Lodge along the former Devizes-Salisbury road. This course would take it close by Stonehenge, and bring it to an end at the Iron Age village of Highfield, outside Salisbury. Here in the fork between the Nadder and Avon was a defended village, the first where the fine red-burnished Iron Age A pottery was found, though not recognized as such at the time.[26] That is a fitting terminus for so famous a track-way; but one can hardly believe that the village was its original objective—it must surely be much older than that. How much older one can only guess. The late Mr Harold Peake, who once studied the Ridgeway and drove along it in a dog-cart with Mr Hippisley Cox, liked to assign it to the Early Bronze Age, and he was the first to show, from the evidence of Saxon charters, that the Ridgeway and the Icknield Way were quite distinct.[27] (The two had become confused, and the older Ordnance Maps gave 'Icknield Way' as an alternative name for the Berkshire Ridgeway). He regarded the Icknield Way as of the Early Iron Age, and attempted on that basis to classify roads elsewhere, inventing a class of 'hill-side' roads, all of which were of Iron Age origin. But it is not possible to make so rigid a distinction. The Ridgeway was certainly still used long after the Iron Age, and the Icknield Way may well have been used long before it. Moreover the mere fact that the one obviously branches off from the other proves contemporaneity of use. In the north-east it passes the flint-mines of Grime's Graves, and it may have been used by itinerant pedlars trading stone axes with the people of Wessex. Along it too may have come amber from the east coast and jet from Yorkshire.

The three roads we have been discussing all converge on Salisbury Plain; and if the course suggested for each is even approximately correct they must have crossed within a couple of miles of Stonehenge. The exact point is that known as 'Long Barrow Cross-roads', where there is a celebrated group of barrows. When Mr Peake and I were talking about these things, he told me that he thought he had read in one of Andrew Lang's articles a statement that this was the oldest cross-roads in England—which it would be. At his suggestion (for he had lost the reference) I wrote and asked Andrew Lang, and received from him a postcard with only these words: 'Never heard of the Harrow-

[25] Birch, *Cart. Sax.* No. 734: in No. 1285 (A.D. 972) the place is called *straedford*.
[26] See Frank Stevens in *Wilts. Arch. Mag.*, XLVI, 1934, 579–624 (plan opp. 580).
[27] I write from the memory of many conversations with him rather than from any published account he may have written.

George Allen

1. A Roman road: Tangley to Winchester

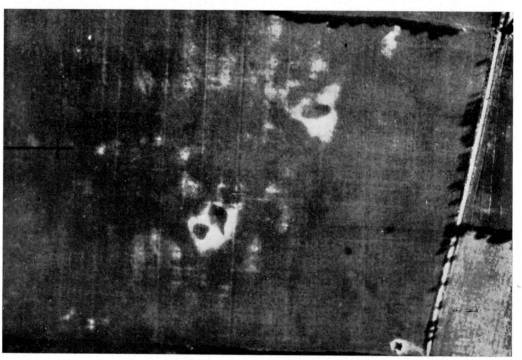

2a. (*above*) How fallen trees divert tracks (Blue Nile); see page 76
2b. (*below*) Dene-holes, near Basingstoke, Hampshire; see page 234

way; never seen Stonehenge.' That seemed conclusive; the author of the statement has never been found, but if he did say that he may well have been right. If he was, then a new reason appears for the siting of our most outstanding prehistoric monument. We know that its builders traded far afield, and that one of those fields, whence amber came, lay to the north-east. They may have traded eastwards and south-eastwards also. It is a mere guess, but might not the flint-mines of Sussex have supplied them? Such a suggestion may seem absurd when flint is so common in Central Wessex. But except for a small undertaking on Easton Down (Wilts)[28] flint-mines are unknown in Wessex, whereas it is certain that its inhabitants got stone axes from as far afield as the factories at Graig Lwyd in North Wales and Pike of Stickle in Westmorland.[29] Some special quality in the raw material, combined probably with a tradition of good craftsmanship developed locally, may have popularized these northern axes, and the same causes may have operated to popularize the products of Sussex flint-mines and those of Grime's Graves already mentioned. Here again a modern parallel is enlightening. Leather is as common all over Central Africa as flint is in the chalk regions of England; but the best shoes are made at Geneina and everywhere command a higher price than the local ones. One can buy them at places 1,000 miles from the source of manufacture, the price naturally increasing in proportion to the distance. (I am at this moment wearing a pair bought at El Fasher, 300 miles from Geneina). Their superiority is due not so much to better skill in shoe-making as to better preparation of the leather beforehand. Flint axes are as transportable as shoes.

The fourth and last of the great trackways follows the Jurassic[30] corridor which runs from the Humber to the Bristol Avon. Fox was the first to recognize this corridor as an artery of prehistoric times.[31] He was led to recognize it partly by geological considerations, partly by the distribution of prehistoric objects and sites of the Iron Age. At the northern end were the Yorkshire Wolds with a rich Iron Age culture. Southwards he suggested the corridor led, by the limestone country round the headwaters of the Thames, to Salisbury Plain and the south-west. But he did not attempt to identify the route followed beyond the Oxford district. My approach was from the other end. I knew of the great Cotswold trackway described below before Fox provided so obvious and convincing a setting for it. I began where Fox left off, and while I agree with his general thesis, I should regard the line leading towards Oxford as rather doubtful, or at the best a branch of the main route.[32]

The trackway starts at South Ferriby on the Humber and follows Lincoln Edge, an

[28] See J.F.S. Stone in *Wilts. Arch. Mag.*, XLVI, 1934, 225–42.

[29] *Arch. Camb.*, 1922, 1–32; 1927, 141–6 (Graig Lwyd): *Proc. Preh. Soc.* NS. XV, 1949, 1–20 (Pike of Stickle).

[30] For the benefit of non-geologists it may be explained that the name is a geological one applied to limestone formed between 110 and 150 million years ago and named after the chief European example, the Jura mountains. It is the great source of building stone (formerly called free-stone) of which the Oxford and Cambridge colleges are built and the famous Cotswold villages. It is also the stone of the pre-Conquest crosses of Wessex and East Anglia. The most celebrated quarries were those of Barnack, Bath, Chilmark, Portland and, in France, Caen.

[31] *Arch. Camb*, LXXXII (7 S., part 1), June, 1927, 96–100.

[32] Since writing this account a full study of the Jurassic Way has been made by Mr W. F. Grimes and published in *Aspects of Archaeology*, 144–71. Neither of us was aware of the other's work until Mr Grimes's was published; and while we agree pretty generally in our views about the course followed, there are slight divergencies in places, especially at the northern end. It seems best to leave what I have written as it stands, since for the most part we both agree, and the very fact of our agreement is evidence for the existence of a trackway. More than one route may have been in use at the same time, and in any case Mr Grimes has studied the subject much more closely than I have, and knows the country better; so that more weight should be given to his views than to mine. He has kindly allowed me to reproduce his two main maps here (Figs. 9 and 10).

F

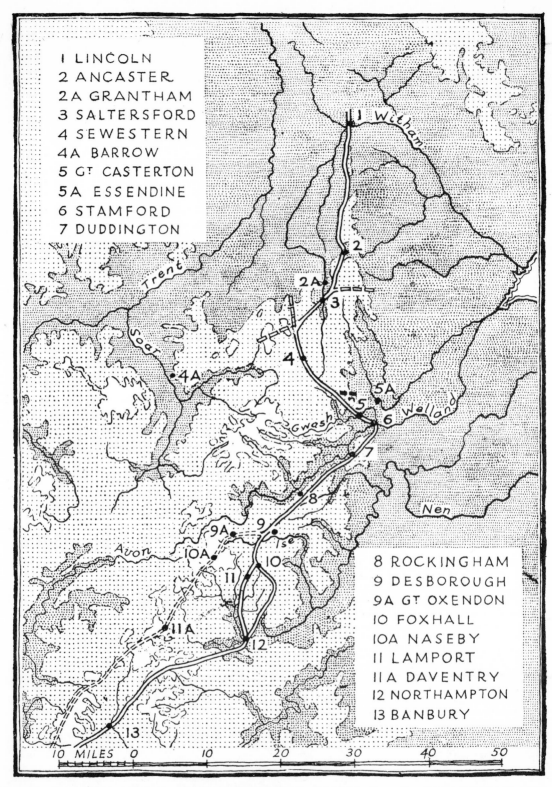

1 LINCOLN
2 ANCASTER
2A GRANTHAM
3 SALTERSFORD
4 S⸱E WESTERN
4A BARROW
5 G⸱T CASTERTON
5A ESSENDINE
6 STAMFORD
7 DUDDINGTON

8 ROCKINGHAM
9 DESBOROUGH
9A G⸱T OXENDON
10 FOXHALL
10A NASEBY
11 LAMPORT
11A DAVENTRY
12 NORTHAMPTON
13 BANBURY

10 MILES 0   10   20   30   40   50

Fig. 9. The Jurassic Way according to W. F. Grimes: northern part. (Reproduced by permission from *Aspects of Archaeology*, fig. 38).

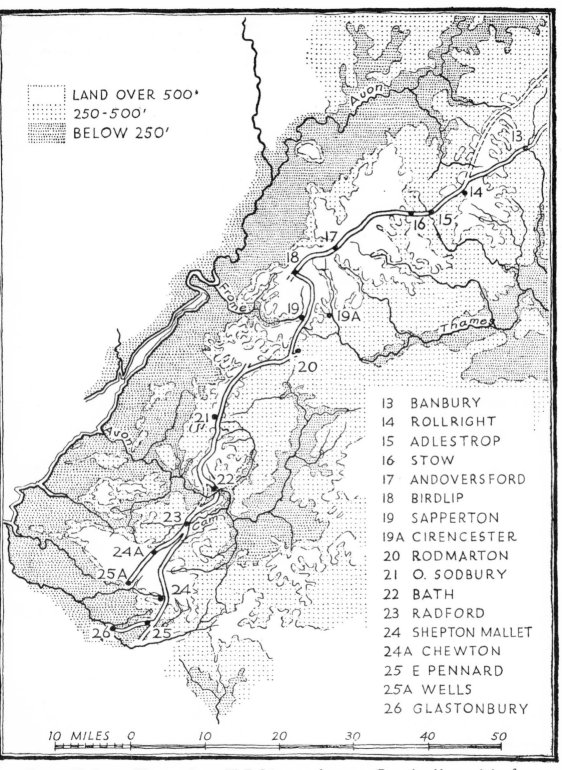

LAND OVER 500'
250-500'
BELOW 250'

13 BANBURY
14 ROLLRIGHT
15 ADLESTROP
16 STOW
17 ANDOVERSFORD
18 BIRDLIP
19 SAPPERTON
19A CIRENCESTER
20 RODMARTON
21 O. SODBURY
22 BATH
23 RADFORD
24 SHEPTON MALLET
24A CHEWTON
25 E PENNARD
25A WELLS
26 GLASTONBURY

10 MILES 0 10 20 30 40 50

FIG. 10. The Jurassic Way according to W. F. Grimes: southern part. (Reproduced by permission from *Aspects of Archaeology*, fig. 39).

obvious predecessor of the Roman Foss-way. South-west of Grantham we may get a hint of its course from King Lud's Bank on Saltby Heath (unless this earthwork was erected rather across that other [Romanized] trackway, Sewestern Lane). Fox suggests that the route went by Stamford, but I should much prefer a more westerly course which would take it over higher and drier ground, with fewer awkward river-crossings, past Pitchley, where there is a long barrow, the only one between Lincolnshire and the Cotswolds,[33] a gap of 100 miles. We reach surer ground, however, at Northampton, just south-west of which place, at a distance of 1½ miles, is the once famous hill-fort of Hunsbury, formerly a type site of the Early Iron Age but now somewhat eclipsed by subsequent discoveries elsewhere. From it runs an old track called throughout its 20-mile run 'Banbury Lane'. It is clearly a medieval market-road, but is probably older, though evidence is presumptive only. From Banbury the same direction is continued by a track to the next market-town, Stow-on-the-Wold, also 20 miles distant. The existence of this stretch of 40 miles as a continuous used way is proved by its description in the bounds of Adlestrop, Worcestershire 4 miles east-north-east of Stow-on-the-Wold, Gloucestershire, as 'regia strata de Norhamtun'.[34] At Oatley Hill, the great projecting tongue of land north of Great Rollright, this track joins another (at a spot-level marked 785 feet); and if we follow this other track northwards we find that it follows the main Jurassic escarpment (here much complicated by outliers) to Edge Hill, past the hill-fort on Meon Hill, and then curves round to Fenny Compton; then it turns eastwards to Byfield and continuing in the same direction joins Banbury Lane at Cold Higham on Watling Street. The 'great road' is an arc of this loop, and looks like the medieval shortening of an older way. The latter not only passes close beside the megalithic circle and other remains at Rollright, but also connects at least three hill-forts—Meon Hill, Chastleton and the one called in Saxon times Maethelgar's burh, within whose ramparts Stow-on-the-Wold was built.[35]

West of Stow the track continues in the same direction to Harford Bridge, passing near the great group of long barrows at Swell. Here its course is attested by Saxon charters. Thence it goes to Andoversford where is a large Roman settlement, regaining the Jurassic escarpment at Birdlip above Gloucester and passing close beside the burial in which the famous Iron Age mirror was found.[36] (At Birdlip there is also a small promontory-fort behind the hotel). Southwards its course is not everywhere obvious, but it probably crossed the Stroud Water near Stroud, where (at Rodborough) parts of a bronze-mounted bucket have been found; after which its course is quite clear. At Old Sodbury it passes a large and almost undescribed hill-fort,[37] and then another equally little-known one on Freezing Hill, four miles north-west of Bath.[38] Crossing a col it ascends Lansdown, a level plateau with ancient remains, and then goes down to Bath.

[33] *Antiquity*, XXIII, 1949, 218–20. For Sewestern Lane see Proc. Preh. Soc., 1950, 185, quoting C. W. Phillips in *Arch. Journ.*, XC, 147.

[34] Kemble, Cod. Dipl., no. 1367 (eleventh century); Grundy, *Saxon Charters of Worcs.*, 1931, 12, 72–3.

[35] See *Antiquity*, VII, 1933, 347–50; also Birch, *Cart. Sax.*, No. 882, A.D. 949.

[36] For the latest account of its discovery, giving fresh evidence and a bibliography, see Charles Green in *Proc. Preh. Soc.*, NS. XV, 1949, 188–90. He concludes that 'the Birdlip group of burials seems to belong to the period 50 B.C.–A.D. 47, when there is evidence of Belgic penetration into the Cotswold region.' That penetration might well have been along the road here described. For the mirrors in general (with distribution map) see Dunning in *Arch. Journ.*, LXXXV, 1930, 69–79.

[37] See *Ant. Journ.*, VIII, 1928, 520.

[38] Called 'Royal Camp' on the 2-inch Ordnance ms. drawing of 1813–14. It is more than ¼ mile across, has a single rampart with stone walling revealed near N.W. corner. From an entrance at the south end well preserved hollow ways lead to a spring 500 feet south of the rampart. The ridgeway passes alongside the eastern rampart; there is a deep hollow way beside the modern road on the west. There is a mound in the north part of the enclosure.

The ancient sites along this trackway have a strong Iron Age flavour, and although that does not preclude greater antiquity, it does strengthen the case for an Iron Age date. Apart from the hill-forts strung along it, (many passed over without mention above), note that iron currency bars have been found at three of the associated habitation-sites (Hunsbury, Meon Hill and Bourton-on-the-Water).[39] Since these prehistoric thoroughfares may be regarded as trade-routes, is it not likely that this one led to iron mines in Northamptonshire, where iron could easily be obtained (as now) by surface quarrying? If we continue the direction another twenty miles we come to Wells and the margin of the Somerset levels where the Iron Age pile-dwelling villages were. (The most obvious route would be up over Odd Down and Duncorn Hill to the hill-fort on Tunley Hill, and thence by Paulton, Chewton Mendip and Green Ore). But such a continuation is purely speculative. From Northamptonshire to Bath there is evidence of an almost continuous trackway, well attested in many places not only by its existence to-day, but also by references in medieval and earlier documents.

The distribution of population in prehistoric times was much denser in the southern portion of the Jurassic belt, and especially in the Cotswolds. There must have been communications between the inhabitants and their southern neighbours on the Wessex chalklands, and it is tempting to speculate on the routes followed. Unfortunately the original prehistoric pattern seems to have been obliterated by Roman and medieval traffic. A road still called Welsh Way near Cirencester branches off from the Roman road to Gloucester 4½ miles north-west of the former and goes by Barnsley, Ready Token, Quenington, Stanford Hall, Lechlade and Buscot to Faringdon, continuing by Challow Station to the foot of the Berkshire Downs. (The same direction is continued by Old Street, a road of proved Saxon age going through Farnborough and Beedon). But the Welsh Way, in its present form, is obviously subsequent to the two Roman roads which it encounters and follows for part of its course. Faringdon also, a great medieval road-junction and market, is for that reason suspect. From it a shorter route to the chalklands is by Fernham (under a hill-fort).[40]

The shortest and best route between Wessex and Cotswold is along the road already mentioned above, certainly (as I think) the one used by the Saxon army after Barbury. It goes down off the chalk escarpment at Salthrop House and then northwards by the Lydiards and Purton to Cricklade, where it joins the Roman road to Cirencester. By this route there was only a short four miles of bad, heavy clayland to be crossed (between Purton and Cricklade).

In passing it may be noted that there may also have been an early highway along this Corallian ridge from Malmesbury to Abingdon and Oxford. An old track (whose existence is proved by references in forest documents relating to Braden and by a map of that forest dated 1632–3 [8 Chas. I], now in the Public Record Office) can be traced from Malmesbury through Garsdon and Dodridge to Purton.[41] Then it turns north[42] for just over a

[39] When writing this I had forgotten that Sir Cyril Fox had already suggested the Forest of Dean mines as a source (*Antiquity*, XIV, 1940, 427-33: see also *ib. id.* XV, 87–8). But, even so, the Jurassic Trackway may still have played a part in distributing them.   [40] See pp. 104–5, below.

[41] Called in 1632–3 'the high waie coarse from Malmsburie to Creklade'. Purton is a large village, deriving its importance from the crossing here of this road with the one from Barbury to Cricklade just mentioned. It has grown as a ribbon-development beside both roads. For details see *Wilts. Arch. Mag.* XLV, 549–67; XLVI, 176–84.

[42] A possible alternative route here is suggested by the names Ridgeway and Broad Way given in Saxon documents to the road between Lydiard Millicent and Upper Stratton. This may be a better route, but I do not know the ground.

mile, goes by Purton Station, and then (eastwards) by Blunsdon Station to the Blunsdons, Highworth and Faringdon. East of Faringdon it fans out into a series of roads leading to Oxford, Radley and Abingdon. It is of considerable antiquity, for at Kingston Bagpuze it is barred by a cross-dyke called *Ælfthrythe dic*, mentioned in a charter of A.D. 942.[43] That the Corallian ridge was inhabited in prehistoric times is proved by the presence of several hill-forts (Ringsbury, Fernham, Badbury). The ritual circles discovered from the air by the late George Allen, though not on the ridge itself, must belong to the people who lived, or roamed, on it. But the track described has obvious medieval uses, connecting three great ecclesiastical centres, and we had better leave it at that.

To sum up:— There are at all times and in all places two kinds of ways—Natural Tracks and Made Roads. Before the Romans came to Britain there were, with a few exceptions, only the former, and the main channels of intercourse can only be inferred. Three corridors converge on Wessex, two coming from the east along the North and South Downs, and one from the north-east along the Chilterns and Berkshire Downs: the three meet on Salisbury Plain near Stonehenge. A fourth corridor was the Jurassic belt, and its track ran from the Humber to the Cotswolds, ending at Bath or a little further south-west. The tracks may all have been in use in the Early Bronze Age, if not before, and the last one has certain features which suggest use in the Iron Age. There were probably ways connecting the Cotswolds and Wessex.

One might continue to write at great length about the old roads of all ages. One might discuss the Cloven Way as a possible invasion route of the West Saxons,[44] or the Lower Salisbury Avon as a corridor to a Bronze Age port at Christchurch, or the routes by which the foreign stones were brought from Pembrokeshire to Stonehenge;[45] but, except for the first (which has been fully dealt with elsewhere), field archaeology cannot help much except in a general sort of way. There are other kinds of roads, such as Salt-ways, where it does help; but these would require a chapter to themselves.[46]

[43] See p. 240.
[44] For a detailed description see my article in *Antiquity*, V, 1931, 441–58; for some drastic criticism of the theory, see my later article in the same, Vol. XXVI, 1952, December.
[45] See for these H. H. Thomas in *Ant. Journ.*, III, 1923, 239–60, and W. F. Grimes, O.S. map of S. Wales (Long Barrows and Megaliths), 1936, 7–10.
[46] The best account is 'Salt-Ways', by F. T. S. Houghton, *Trans. Birmingham Arch. Soc.*, LIV, 1932, 1–17 (maps).

CHAPTER 8

Celtic Fields[1]

In studying the history of archaeology we found that the modern phase begins when the things themselves—the stone axes, earthworks and such like—were made to tell their own story. There is no need to labour this point any further, but I would like to expand it a little. What does it imply? The things we see as we explore a piece of country are both fragmentary and much altered. The site of a prehistoric village or farm shows little more than a confused jumble of banks and hollows. Even where the sites are thick on the ground as in Sussex, Wilts and Dorset, the intervening country is broken up by cultivation and no longer in the state it was at the time when the villages were inhabited. But with the aid of a map and of such fragments as survive, it is possible to reconstruct imaginatively a picture of its former appearance. Field-work alone makes possible such a reconstruction, and the creative imagination gives it life. For the ultimate purpose of archaeology is to recreate past life, and that can only be achieved by a mind that feeds on facts. Minds that starve themselves of facts produce only fairy tales about lost continents and the pyramids.

Wherever, therefore, he may find himself, whether on the Wessex or Sussex Downs or in Central Africa, the field archaeologist will keep his eyes open for unusual features and will question them until they are found to yield an answer. The English countryside is an admirable training-ground for such observations. Amongst the commonest things which one sees there, for instance, are groups of mounds, which are the burial-places or barrows of prehistoric man. In certain districts, particularly on the chalk downs, one will rarely do a day's field-work without seeing several barrows, and one will usually find one or two new ones. (At one time my daily average of such new finds was three, and my maximum, in the Cotswolds, over twenty). The ability to detect barrows comes from constant vigilance and the inspection of all suspicious irregularities of the surface. With practice one acquires the knack of distinguishing artificial mounds from natural ones. No hard and fast rules can be laid down, nor can it be acquired from books, so I will not say any more now; *solvitur ambulando*. I will merely cite an instance where a major discovery was missed for lack of just such preliminary training.

One of the great discoveries of recent years has been that of the Royal Tombs of the barbaric Kings of Nubia at Ballana and Qustal on the Sudanese frontier below Wadi Halfa. These tombs were brick chambers, covered with huge mounds of earth. They form

---

[1] The majority in England belong to the period *c.* 500 B.C.–A.D. 500, so that the term 'prehistoric' is not strictly applicable to the later ones; but we cannot date them at sight, and a single all-covering word being needed I adopted the term 'Celtic' for them in 1923. It is not a good one, but no one has suggested a better, so I retain it.

two big groups which look not unlike some of the barrow-groups on Salisbury Plain. They were first discovered by Burckhardt (whose keen eye missed very little) and he actually used the word 'barrow' to describe them. Yet they were missed by some of the later explorers of the region, one of whom actually stated positively that it contained no antiquities—though he had Burckhardt's text and map to consult if he had taken the trouble to do so. Even the archaeologist who excavated them was in some doubt at first as to whether they were artificial or natural. I cannot believe that he would have had any hesitation in deciding if he had had a preliminary training in field archaeology at home; and I think this instance reinforces Dr Wheeler's argument that no one should be allowed to excavate abroad until he can write 'Passed R. B.' after his name.[2] I would remind those who protest that Sir Flinders Petrie himself, the founder of modern methods of excavation in Egypt, qualified in just this way planning the earthworks of Kent before any of us were born. He himself told me that he owed much to the early influence of F. J. C. Spurrell, one of the best Kentish field archaeologists of the nineteenth century.

Barrows are, however, only one of the many things to be found, and barrow-hunting is now somewhat of a sideline. The earlier archaeologists, many of whom were collectors first and foremost, attached a rather excessive importance to them. They have their place in the programme, but not as the first item. Nowadays we are interested in the habits and habitations of the living, rather than those of the dead. We remember that the prime human needs are those of food, clothing and shelter, and of these, two at any rate have left tangible traces on the surface. Food is grown in fields, and I have already mentioned how air-photography revealed prehistoric field-systems. It was not for the first time. Every observant countryman had long been aware of the lynchets covering the sides of the hills; more than half a century ago Thomas Hardy mentioned the ' "lanchets" or flint slopes which belted the escarpment at intervals of a dozen yards.'[3] Colt Hoare knew about them, and Skinner described and left rough plans of many, though he mistook them for the streets of prehistoric towns. Poulett Scrope and Colley March also observed them in Wilts and Dorset respectively in the nineteenth century.[4] My own interest was, I think, first aroused by books like those of Hubbard, Gomme, Seebohm and Johnston, which led me to look for such things on the hills near my home at East Woodhay; and the first lynchets I saw were those near Coombe and on Great Litchfield Down near Ladle Hill, now, alas, under plough again. Of the last I made a plan on the ground somewhere about 1910, of course before air-photographs were available.

Air-photography shows these field-systems best, and many have already been published.[5] You will see that the ground is divided up into a number of more or less rectangular divisions bounded by banks. You will also see that these banks are steeper and bigger when they run more or less parallel to the slope than they are when they run up and down it. The reason is that, though artificial in the sense that they are caused by cultivation, they are produced by natural agencies and not deliberately made. Let us reconstruct in imagination what must have happened. At some remote date a group of people living nearby must have come and marked out the ground preparatory to ploughing it. They must have removed the turf exposing the bare soil and then turned it over with the

---

[2] See Note at end of chapter.
[3] It is possible, however, that he had in mind the strip-lynchets of abandoned medieval fields
[4] *Wilts Arch. Mag.*, XII, 185–92. *Proc. Dorset Field Club*, XXIV, 67–92.
[5] See *Wessex from the Air, Antiquity*, and my Ordnance Survey publications.

plough, and this latter process would, of course, be repeated annually. Now the moment the protective mantle of turf is broken and removed, the soil is exposed to the erosive action of rain and frost. Every time rain falls the water will run off downhill, carrying some of the soil with it. That soil will be deposited as silt at the edge of the field, because the water will not run over the turf beyond, but sinks into it. There is thus a steady passage of soil downhill to the edge of the field where it stops, and in the long process of time a bank is piled up. Remember that we are concerned with centuries; the Celtic field-system lasted for about 1,000 years, and every year this process was repeated, in fact after every shower of rain. The banks or lynchets are the cumulative and visible result of the action of the natural agents of rain and frost (which loosens the soil) over a long period of time. They are always bigger on the steeper slope, but they form also more slowly on the other, for nearly every bit of ground has two directions of slope, one more steep than the other. Even on slight slopes and on ground that is almost or quite level, traces of banks can be seen; these may have been caused, or increased, by the decay of the turf bank which may have marked the bounds of each plot.

The soil that is piled up on the lower side is derived ultimately from the upper side of the field, where a negative lynchet is formed. In chalk districts, especially near the foot of the downs, you will see this happening to-day in any ploughed field; the upper side is visible from a long way as a white belt, because there the plough has eaten deep into the chalk subsoil. The lower lynchet is called 'positive'.

In the Iron Age, as now, there were tracks between the fields. They were quite narrow as a rule, and were bounded on each side by a bank which once probably had a fence or stockade. In Rumania to-day—or should I say yesterday?—the fields are enclosed in wattle fences constructed like hurdles and looking like them. The purpose, of course, is to keep the animals out. (But as anyone who has dealings with them knows, animals are experts at penetrating hedges, and pigs are particularly pertinacious; the Rumanian pigs wear spiked collars to prevent them getting through; see Plate 21). In stony country these field-lanes were bounded by stone walls, as also were the fields themselves. When the track ran along a steep slope a positive lynchet accumulated above it, and a negative one was formed below it; such tracks are called double-lynchet ways. A striking example is on Pertwood Down, Wiltshire,[6] where a Roman road runs into and for a short distance follows, a pre-existing double-lynchet way (Fig. 11). There is evidence here that the Roman road was driven right across the field-system regardless of boundaries, as we might expect; and that these boundaries were then laid out afresh terminating on the Roman road. The pre-Roman boundaries ran parallel with the double-lynchet way, and traces of them can be seen in the air-photograph which I took in July 1924.

On Farthing Down in Surrey a bivallate road leading between Celtic fields on either side was 'certainly still in use in pagan Saxon times' as a road leading to a burial-ground. The acreage of the field-plots is exceptionally large—up to a maximum of 4.2 acres.[7]

Sometimes one can even see on air-photographs—and when thus initiated on the ground also, even without air-photographs—the actual marks of ploughing. That is seen best when the plough has had to swerve aside to avoid an obstacle. On the Marlborough Downs

---

[6] *Wessex from the Air*, Plate 26. *Luftbild und Vorgeschichte*, p. 60.
[7] See Brian Hope-Taylor, 'Celtic Agriculture in Surrey', *Surrey Arch. Coll.*, L, 1949, 47–72, a model of what such a survey should be. Another is P. P. Rhodes's of the same in Berkshire, *Oxoniensia*, XV, 1–28.

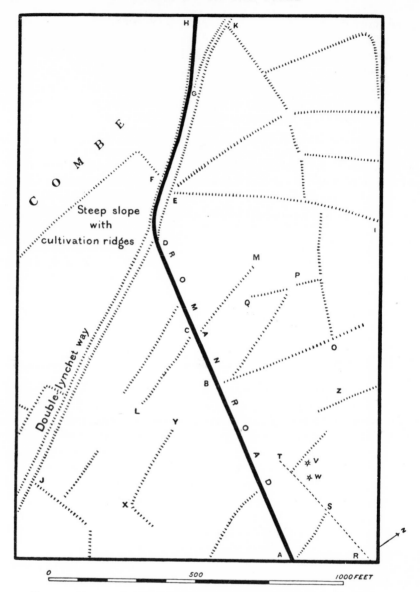

Fig. 11. Roman road following pre-existing double lynchet way over
Pertwood Down, Wilts.

such obstacles were the sarsen stones littered over the downs—natural relics of a former
geological formation. The stones are seen to lie in the middle of a cigar-shaped slip of
ground that had to be left unploughed.[8] Elsewhere it was a round barrow that was left,
as on Shillingston Hill not far from Blandford in Dorset, where a very fine area of
Celtic fields still survives intact. The effect of ploughing close round the base of a mound

[8] *Wessex from the Air*, Plate 19.

is to steepen its slope and of course obliterate its ditch, and many if not all of the barrows which are said to have no ditch are in fact merely those which have been ploughed round in Celtic or later times. Other good examples survive near Bokerley Dyke. There is a certain impressiveness in these Bronze Age barrows which were already ancient monuments in prehistoric times.

Everywhere in the chalk districts of southern England may be seen shallow round depressions like dry ponds. These are collapsed shafts which were originally not more than ten to twenty feet deep. When perfect they are called dene-holes, and have quite a big literature.[9] The primary purpose for which they were dug was to obtain chalk for marling the fields. It may at first sight seem curious that this should be necessary in chalk districts, but in fact the chalk is often covered for a depth of several feet by a reddish clay (called clay-with-flints by geologists) deficient in lime, so that marling is necessary. In days when roads were bad or non-existent and transport difficult, it was easier to obtain chalk thus than from an open pit even a short distance away. There are still dene-holes open to view beside the road from Upton to Andover and near the Devil's Jumps in east Hampshire. Not far from the former (where there are also Celtic fields) I picked up a broken sandstone rotary quern, doubtless of prehistoric age. There are others at Four Marks near Alton (*Proc. Hants Field Club*, XVI, 1945, 192–3) and at Biddesden. (See App. 1, p. 234).

We are able, for once, to explain these Celtic fields and dene-holes by reference to documentary sources; though such an explanation is not really necessary. Pliny, who wrote about A.D. 70, says of Britain: 'The chalk is dug from shafts often 100 feet deep, with narrow tops but spreading out below. The effects [of the marling] last 80 years. This practice is very common in Britain.' The widening out is a feature often observed; at the bottom lateral shafts are often dug, forming a trefoil or a cinquefoil plan (Fig. 12). One such that has collapsed is revealed by soil marks near Basingstoke (see Plate 2b). One wonders whether the 'thry scytan crundel' in the bounds of Welford, Berkshire (*Berks, Bucks and Oxon. Journ.*, XXXII, 26) may not have been one of these trefoil pits. In north and east Hampshire, where most of the chalk has a clay covering, these collapsed shafts are very common, far commoner than in Wiltshire where the clay is less universal and the normal soil is bare chalk, which would not of course need marling.

It is always nice to find evidence of relative date that is visible on the surface without the need of excavation. That is forthcoming on Milston Down, between Tidworth and Bulford, where a particularly fine Celtic field-system is crossed diagonally by a linear earthwork that is quite certainly later than the field-boundaries which it intersects obliquely.[10] The linear earthwork forms part of a network covering a large tract of country on both sides of the River Bourne; as a whole it is possibly of the Late Bronze Age and older than the Iron Age hill-fort on Quarley Hill, for the rampart of the hill-fort overlies one element of the system.[11] In this sequence the Celtic fields are the oldest item, and they must

[9] For it see Johnson, *Folk Memory*, Chapter XI and Appendix I. See also F. J. C. Spurrell on 'Dene-holes and artificial caves with vertical entrances', *Arch. Journ.*, XXXVIII, 1881, 391–409; XXXIX, 1882, 1–22. Plate I in the first part is a plan of Jordan's Wood and Plate II of dene-holes with sections. Spurrell acknowledged being helped by Flinders Petrie in making the first plan. Petrie always acknowledged his debt to Spurrell, both in conversation and in his books; he himself contributed an article to *Archaeologia Cantiana* (vol. 13) on the earthworks he planned. (The originals are now in the British Museum).

[10] The evidence will, I hope, be published eventually by the Ordnance Survey, when what was prepared as the Amesbury Sheet of the Celtic Fields Series appears. (See Fig. 15).

[11] See *Air Survey and Archaeology*, Plate X, and Professor Hawkes's excavation report in *Proc. Hants Field Club*, XIV, 1939, 136–94.

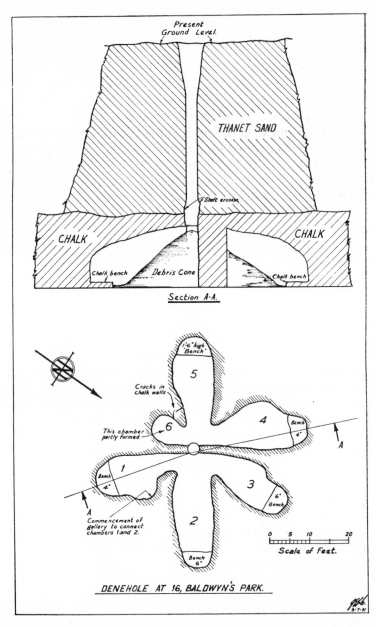

FIG. 12. Plan and section of typical denehole, Baldwyn's Park near Bexley, Kent. (Reproduced from Arch. Cant. LXIV, 154, by permission of the Editor and Mr Caiger.

be a good deal older than the linear earthwork, to allow time for the quite considerable lynchets to have formed.

Another instance of relative dating is at Soldier's Rings, South Damerham, Hampshire (formerly Wiltshire).[12] The 'rings' are actually banks laid out with that perfect straightness and symmetry that is everywhere the mark of the Roman surveyor, and there can

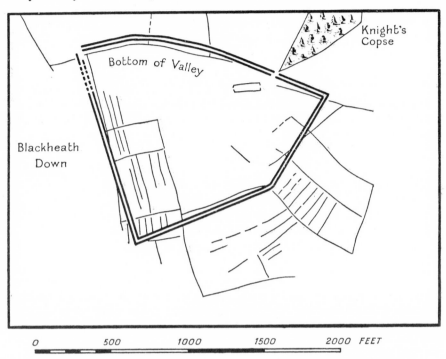

Fig. 13. Soldiers Ring, S. Damerham, Hants: a Roman earthwork superimposed on preexisting field-banks. (Reproduced by permission from *Wessex from the Air*, fig. 60)

be no doubt that they are of Roman date. They cut through portions of a typical Celtic field-system, which is therefore earlier (Fig. 13).

Both these examples show that field archaeology can sometimes date its raw material without the aid of excavation. I wish to emphasize this point because there will often be occasions when excavation is not possible. The field-worker should always be on the watch for them. When an earthwork such as a causeway-road, whether Roman or later, comes in contact with another of unknown age, it should generally be possible even from ground observation alone to say which is the older; and with the aid of an air-photograph it should nearly always be possible. A good example is seen on the Sussex Downs where the Roman road, Stane Street, cuts through an obviously older bivallate linear earthwork, obliterating it.[13] This is obvious at sight and was noticed by the Curwens on the ground before air-photography came into use in archaeology.

[12] See *Air Survey and Archaeology*, Plate IX (a shockingly bad illustration) and the diagram, Plate IXb. A much better photo is reproduced in *Wessex from the Air*, Plate 49.
[13] Curwen in *Sussex Arch. Coll.* LIX, 11, Plate III.

The chalk downs of Southern England are the chief areas where Celtic fields have survived, and it was here that they were first observed. Occasional patches occur on the Tertiary formations of the Hampshire Basin—in Cranbury Park (on Bagshot Beds) and in Nightingale Wood, Rownhams (on Bracklesham Beds). Both sites are on loamy sand, and close to hill-forts where lived the cultivators. Outside Wessex, Celtic fields occur all over the South Downs, where they have been described by Dr Cecil Curwen and Mr G. A. Holleyman;[14] and there are a few faint remains in Ashdown Forest on the highest ground of the Weald. Most surprisingly none have been found in Kent,[15] where cultivation must have been intensive and is mentioned by Julius Caesar. Their absence may be due to continuity of tillage.

An air-photograph of the chalk outlier called the Gogs near Cambridge shows plain marks of rectangular Celtic fields in ploughed land there. The vast area of the Fenland is covered with most extensive remains of cultivation during Romano-British times, nearly all revealed by air-photographs mostly unpublished. Here it would be possible to produce an accurate and nearly complete plan of large areas of cultivation, complete with diked field-roads and villages, some built of crude native bricks. In one case remains of a wooden bridge have been discovered where one of these field-roads crossed a water-channel.[16] Most of these remains appear as crop-sites or soil-sites, but there are, or were in the 1930's, a few small patches of never-ploughed meadowland where the banks and ditches have survived intact. These are eminently suitable for field archaeology, if they still survive unploughed. They have not yet been described, but must be located from air-photographs.

On the limestone formation of the Cotswolds and their southern continuation the Celtic fields were enclosed within dry stone walls, just as are the modern fields. Good examples occur on Bathampton Down and (although the aerodrome has now destroyed the latter) on Charmy Down, and there is another small patch on West Littleton Down near Bath. There is a very fine group in similar soil in Wessex on Kingston Down in the Isle of Purbeck,[17] where the lines of ploughing are plainly visible; and in the middle are the stone foundations of the farm. This is a particularly fine site for field-work, and it has not ever been done. The examination and planning of the farm itself is a crying need; I tried in vain to get it done many years ago.

On the older and harder rocks near Bristol there are some excellent and well-preserved patches especially in Ashton Park opposite the Clifton Suspension Bridge.[18] On Clifton Downs there are many traces to be seen of the stone walls of Celtic fields. Some of these were inserted (from my own field-work) when the large-scale Ordnance Maps of that area were revised in the 1930's.

A little south of Bristol on the Mendips there are several good areas, one above (north-east of) Cheddar from which place they can be seen, and another at the western end of the range on Bleadon Hill near Upton. These were marked by Colt Hoare on his map of

[14] See *Antiquity*, IX, 1935, 443–54 (Holleyman).

[15] With the possible exception of a single long lynchet on Barham Downs, for which see my field-notes printed in *Archaeologia Cantiana*, XLVI, 1934, 57–8.

[16] See air-photo in *Luftbild und Vorgeschichte*, 57.

[17] *Luftbild und Vorgeschichte*, 51; R. H. Hodgkin, *A History of the Anglo-Saxons* (Oxford, 1935), Plate 8.

[18] Planned by Mr C. W. Phillips in *Proc. Spelaeological Society* (Univ. of Bristol), IV, No. 2 (Feb., 1933), 139–50. See also his plan of earthworks (including field banks) on Walton Common near Clevedon, ib. id. Vol. IV, No. 1 (May 1931), 34–41.

the Roman road and also (independently) by Skinner who misinterpreted them as the remains of a prehistoric town.

In the west of England small cultivation patches have been observed in association with some of the hut-clusters on Dartmoor and Bodmin Moor where they are assigned to the Early Bronze Age.[19] These differ radically from the Celtic fields in plan.

A wholly new group was discovered and photographed from the air by Group Captain Livock on the Long Mynd in Shropshire. I have not seen them on the ground, but the photograph indicates a similar network to that of the Wessex areas. Speaking from memory I think they were most perfect on the southern slopes of the ridge.

There is a particularly fine group of prehistoric fields with dry stone walls and double-walled tracks on Grassington Moor, Yorkshire.[20] Here amongst the fields is a burial-cairn.

All of these areas except the Fenland contain the lynchets and stone field-walls more or less intact and visible on the surface. In the Upper Thames region there are certain crop-marks revealed by air-photography (Major Allen's chiefly) which may well represent the ditches bounding areas of cultivation. Such ditches do occasionally occur on Salisbury Plain, and would be expected to occur more commonly on the lower lands which needed drainage.

Curious evidence of early cultivation comes from the Isle of Man, Holland and Denmark; in the Isle of Man clearance of a Viking burial-mound and of the surface respectively have revealed the scratch-marks of the plough. Some of these marks cross at right angles, showing that cross ploughing was practised.[21] Prehistoric-fields have also been found in many other places in both Denmark,[22] Holland, and in Ireland at Cush, Co. Limerick.[23]

In Scotland no absolutely certain remains of prehistoric fields have been found, though such have been claimed for the cultivation banks near Torwood Lee (Selkirkshire). Similar claims have been made for the strip-cultivations near the Roman fort at House-steads on the Roman Wall. The terraces on Arthur's Seat near Edinburgh and on Shaw Hill above Culter, Lanarkshire[24] are probably later, as also are most of those which are so common in the Cheviots.[25]

Although air-photography has played a very important part in the elucidation of Celtic fields and has revealed many groups that would certainly not have been discovered by ground-observation alone, it was not responsible for their discovery, as I have already pointed out. They had long before been observed by Stukeley and Poulett Scrope in Wilt-shire, Colley March in Dorsetshire, Toms, Seebohm and others;[26] and by a curious coincidence, just at the time when I was working on them myself, preparing an account of the field-systems revealed by the Hampshire air-photographs, Dr Eliot Curwen and

[19] Curwen, *Antiquity*, I, 1927, 282 (plans).
[20] Air-photo in *Luftbild und Vorgeschichte*, 52, and others in *Yorkshire Arch. Journ.*, XXXIII, 1937, 166–74. For an account of the fields (which were marked on the 25-in. Ordnance Map before they were air-photographed) see Eliot Curwen, *Antiquity*, II, 1928, 168–72. (The structure there called a 'Circus' may be otherwise explained.)
[21] *Antiquity*, XX, 1946, 38–9, 158.
[22] *Oldtidsagre* by Gudmund Hatt, Copenhagen, 1949.
[23] *Proc. R. Irish Acad.*, XLV, 1940, 139–45; see also ib. id. LII, 1949, 61–2.
[24] *Antiquity*, XIII, 1939, Plate vii (between pp. 280 and 281).
[25] *Luftbild und Vorgeschichte*, p. 54; see also below, p. 205–6.
[26] See *William Stukeley* by Stuart Piggott, 1950, 72; *Wilts Arch. Mag.*, XII, 185–92 (Poulett Scrope); *Proc. Dorset F.C.*, XXIV, 67–92 (Colley March); *Antiquary*, 1911, 411–17 (Toms). For Lynchets in France see L. Aufrère, *Annales de Géographie*, XXXVIII, 1929, 529–60.

his son, Dr Cecil Curwen, were also working on them in Sussex. We had not at that time become personally acquainted and were ignorant of each other's work,[27] although the Curwens had already published half a dozen admirable surveys of Sussex earthworks. Someone—it must, I think, have been Dr Williams-Freeman—told me about the Curwens' work and that they were then engaged upon a survey of Celtic fields, advising me to get into touch with them. I therefore wrote to them telling them what I was doing. We found that we were both on the same track, and agreed that the best course would be to proceed independently until each had completed writing his particular article, so as to avoid complications. This we did. The Curwens published their survey of 'Sussex lynchets and their associated field-ways' in *Sussex Archaeological Collections*, Vol. LXIV (1923), and I published mine in the *Geographical Journal*, Vol. LXI (May 1923). The two articles were published almost simultaneously, and the Curwens added a footnote to theirs, after going to press, expressing their gratification at finding how closely their conclusions agreed with mine, although arrived at quite independently. The Curwens' treatment was more thorough-going than mine, entering deeply into the details of lynchet formation and the size and shape of the fields, and their relation to old field-units recorded in historical documents. They also for the first time described the difference between positive and negative lynchets, and the existence of double-lynchet-ways and other field-ways. They illustrated these features by plans and sections drawn by themselves which have since been republished many times and have become classical. Although based primarily upon surface observation and mapping, i.e. upon pure field archaeology, their observations were constantly checked and supplemented by excavation.

Their article is so closely parallel in some ways to mine that future students may find it difficult to believe that there was no collusion; but there was not! It is possible that, in our preliminary exchange of letters, one of us may have mentioned an article by some previous worker on the subject which may have been previously unknown to the other, though I cannot now remember an instance of such.[28] But that, at the most, was all, and it is negligible. The coincidence was fortuitous—one of those which not uncommonly happen when two or more people are both working on the same lines in the same field of research; and it proved to be a most fortunate one, for it laid the foundations of a life-long friendship.

NOTE ON 'PASSED R.B.'

This means 'Passed Roman Britain', i.e. that he or she has emerged satisfactorily from a course of training in the excavation of Romano-British sites. The phrase was first used by Dr Wheeler in his Inaugural Lecture, delivered on 7th October 1948, and published by the Institute of Archaeology (5th Annual Report, 1949). His thesis was that, though there still remain problems to be solved by excavation, the chief service performed by the Northern School would in future be to provide a training in method. One might add that to have been trained in the Southern School under Dr Wheeler himself would also qualify, as the careers of his pupils in Mediterranean

[27] In those pre-motor days communications were less easy and workers in one field were far less closely in touch with their fellow-workers in another than they are to-day. My own work was confined to Wessex, which has always been rather cut off from Sussex. A resident in Hampshire could extend his researches into Wilts, Berks, and Dorset more easily than into Sussex, and consequently there was more interchange between workers in these four counties than with those elsewhere.

[28] The Curwens' letters to me were destroyed, with all my other correspondence in November 1940, when the Ordnance Survey was bombed. I cannot therefore refer to them to check my memory, as I should like to have done.

H. B. Curwen

3. Quern in use about 1902 at Foula, Shetland; see pages 98ff.

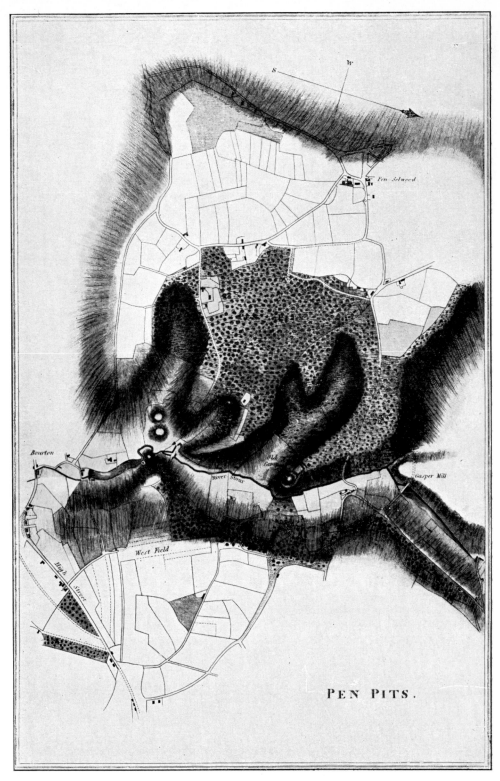

W

S

Pen Selwood

River Stour

Bourten

Gasper Mill

Old East

West Field

High Street

PEN PITS.

4. Pen Pits, after Sir Richard Colt Hoare; see page 100

and Eastern lands are showing. Though speaking of excavation, he also, I think, had in mind the sort of field archaeology that is the subject of this book. This demands an eye for country, and the observation and interpretation of all those myriad minor irregularities of the surface that are due to human, not natural, agency. Britain is an ideal country for learning this technique, and the aptitude once acquired can be applied elsewhere. It is not true that archaeology in the East (or in any other part of the world) differs in kind from archaeology in Britain or North-West Europe. There are of course differences due to climate and soil, but the principles remain the same whether one be excavating or merely observing.

One must not, however, interpret 'Passed R.B.' too rigidly. Both excavation and the interpretation of surface irregularities can of course be learnt wherever the raw materials exist and the training is available. For the latter—surface observation—what is important is that the learner should be made to realize how much there is to see when he has learnt to see it; and also to record what he sees in words, plans and photographs. The ability to do this well will only come with practice, but it may be achieved in other lands than Britain—in Africa for instance.

G

CHAPTER 9

Querns and Quern-Quarries

MODERN ARCHAEOLOGY differs from ancient not only in its methods (which have been fully discussed earlier) but also in its orientation. The old formalist archaeology dealt with all forms of culture-products alike, whether found in palaces or middens; but for the most part it studied them in a vacuum, divorced from the people who made and used them. This concentration on objects led to a sort of departmentalism; we got elaborate (and often valuable) studies of brooches, pots, swords, axes and so on, but not studies of culture-groups. A good example is the work done in Britain in the nineteenth century on barrows and bronze implements respectively, represented by the classic books of Canon Greenwell and Sir John Evans. Much of that work was excellent and is still useful, and it represents a necessary stage in the development of the science; but the division separated graves from implements, many types of which were unrepresented in the graves, and implements from pottery, nor were either related to contemporary habitations. From such separatist studies there could emerge no picture of the culture of a single region at a given period. By combining the evidence of implements, burials, pots and habitation (or at any rate occupation) sites it was possible to discover a major movement of peoples; and by a similar combination of pots and implements with geographical factors a new light was shed on the distribution of population.[1]

This interest in a group's culture as a whole has provided archaeology with *values*. The archaeologist no longer regards all his finds as of equal importance (though of course he records them); he puts more value on those of certain kinds.[2] As Tallgren said:[3] 'The essential material will consist of such objects as play a decisive part in the genesis of the culture-stage; not ornaments but the instruments of production—implements, *necessary* things; in regard to such it is their *function* which is decisive, not their *form* or analogies. In this last instance one does it violence by separating the object from the system of production of which it is the instrument and from its economic environment. One should no longer deal with it in isolation, but rather in association with its group or complex; thus, for instance, not only the sickle but also the hoe, hammer-stones, pots, the whole organic body of the craftsman's equipment.'

Querns are an excellent instance of 'necessary things', for they grind the corn, which,

---

[1] See my articles in *Ant. Journ.*, II, 1922, 27–35, and in *Geogr. Journ.*, XL (Sept. 1912), 184–203; 304–17.
[2] We may ignore for the moment objects whose importance is of another order for dating (e.g., coins), or to serve as evidence for trade (e.g., imported objects).
[3] *Antiquity*, XI, 1937, 158–9.

for an agricultural people, is the chief basis of life (Plate 3). They were virtually ignored by excavators of the old-fashioned school, even by some of the best of them. 'Truhelka, for instance, generally so scrupulous in the full publication of all his finds, does not illustrate nor even describe a single quern from Donja Dolina in Bosnia, where he found plenty.'[4] Nor was he alone; Childe criticizes also the excavators of classical and barbarian sites who have been too preoccupied with statuary and art objects to provide the historian of science with the data he craves. The classical writers, many of them living in conditions far removed from the basic realities of life, tell us little or nothing about the way in which their daily bread was prepared. Not so disdainful were the prehistoric Syrians, living nearer, both in place and (by at least a millenium) in time to the invention of agriculture. The newly-discovered epic of Ras Shamra describes the rite associated with the cult of Mot, whose body was cut up with a sickle, ground in a quern and part then eaten and part cast on the fields as grain. Similar rites are still practised.

If this were a book on general archaeology it would now be necessary to summarize our existing knowledge about querns. But it is not, and I must therefore refer readers to certain standard articles on the subject. The two which led the way were by Dr Cecil Curwen; and they were followed by Professor Gordon Childe.[5] Curwen gives at the end of his second article, some notes on the origin of the word 'quern' (Old English 'cwearn'), which means 'the grinder' and is from the same root as that word, as also is 'corn', that which is ground. He also divides them into two main types (1) saddle-querns and (2) rotary querns. Saddle-querns were of course the first and go back to a remote antiquity, and have still not been superseded in some parts of the world. The rotary quern, according to Dr Curwen, was an invention based upon the donkey-mill, but, although it is certain that it was in use several centuries B.C., neither the place nor date of its invention is yet certainly established. It was a very important invention—'the first major application of rotary motion since the invention of the potter's wheel and the lathe in the remote Oriental Copper Age. It led on directly to the invention of geared machinery and the water wheel, and so to the first employment of inanimate motive power, apart from the harnessing of winds to the sail' (Childe).

Querns, or fragments of them, have been found in many British sites; and if it be objected that they are not likely objects to be found by the field archaeologist in his rambles, I can reply that I did once find one, in three large fragments, during just such a ramble. Very appropriately it was lying on the bank of a modern field in an area which, as air-photographs showed, was covered by the lynchets of prehistoric fields.[6] Small fragments of querns may also be found fairly often on prehistoric sites, and can be recognized quite easily by the ground surface, which is also slightly curved or concave.

The stone of which querns were made varies considerably, even in Wessex. The chief rocks there used were Greensand, Tertiary heathstone and sarsen, Tertiary puddingstone

[4] Childe in *Antiquity*, XVII, 1943, 19. He published in 1904. (For Dolja there read Donja.)

[5] *Antiquity*, XI, 1937, 133–51; XV, 1941, 15–32; XVII, 1943, 19–26. For an early account of querns see *Archaeologia*, VII, 1785, 19–24. The last quoted describes the two parts of a rotary quern found about 1760 'in removing a large stone at Durwood near Hartle Moor in the Peak; they lay by the side of a large urn, half full of burnt bones.' It seems that at this date (1785) rotary hand-querns were still used in Derbyshire, the upper stone being called the 'runner' and the lower the 'ligger' (lier).

[6] The find was made beside the road from Upton to Whistler's Farm, between those places and on the boundary of the parishes of Vernham's Dean and Hurstbourne Tarrant. The fracture is an ancient one, and was repaired by binding with an iron band which has left its mark. It is the upper stone of a rotary quern of the sort of indurated sandstone called 'heathstone'. It is now in the Winchester Museum.

(conglomerate) and perhaps Oolite.[7] No study has been made of querns from a geological point of view, and one such is overdue. The enquiry should begin at both ends—a petrological examination of existing querns and fragments thereof in museums, and also of certain localities where quern-quarries are known or suspected to exist.

There are two such quarries which have been known from of old and become famous —though their fame is now forgotten.

The Pen Pits (Plate 4) cover an area of 700 acres near the point where the counties of Wiltshire, Somerset and Dorset meet, situated in the parishes of Penselwood, Somerset and Zeals, Wiltshire, and near the Upper Greensand escarpment.[8] Somewhere near this point two battles were fought, the first in A.D. 658 by Cenwealh, king of the West Saxons, who defeated the Britons there, and the second in 1016 between King Eadmund and a Danish army.[9] Now in those days battles were nearly always fought on important highways, and Penselwood is situated on one of the main natural arteries leading westwards off the chalk downs of Wiltshire into the west country. The road selected this particular spot for its exit because here the Upper Greensand and Cornbrash form a natural bridge across the clay forest belt that elsewhere forms a continuous and then almost impenetrable hedge along the western frontier of the chalk lands. That same road was also in medieval times the boundary between the forests of Gillingham and Selwood, and was called Hunting Path. Further west it is still called Hardway. It was one of the major routes of England, for eastwards it ran by Yarnbury Castle (with its great fair) and Stonehenge, falling into the Harroway at Weyhill (where was another famous fair); or it may also be regarded as going on to London. Penselwood is therefore situated at one of the gates of Wessex, and it may be suspected that it was the Britons who were attempting to enter Wessex when they encountered Cenwealh's army. That the site was regarded as important in early medieval times is proved by the existence, right in the middle of the Pen Pits, of a fine castle mound and bailey.

The road, I think, partly accounts for the Pen Pits. The Greensand rock in which they were dug does not outcrop here only, but all along the escarpment for many miles northwards. Why did they select this spot for their quarries? Obviously because it was near a thoroughfare. Querns are heavy, and there was no object in quarrying them elsewhere, when, by quarrying them beside the road, transport over rough, trackless country could be avoided. More probably the actual sequence of events was slightly different. The quarries would be initiated by those who lived by the road; a specialized industry would then grow up there because, being so easily accessible and so frequented by travellers, there was a ready-made market provided. That will acount for the extent of the workings. We shall see that the Cole Pits can be explained on similar geographical lines.

The Pen Pits appear to have been first brought to the notice of 'the curious' by he

---

[7] These rocks are listed from my own personal knowledge merely; even in Wessex other rocks such as the Purbeck and Wealden Beds must surely have been used. For a possible quern-quarry in the oolite at Cirencester see my *Long Barrows of the Cotswolds* (1925), 129. There can, however, be no *genetic* relation between the words 'quern' and 'crown', and the O.E. *crundel* has no etymological connection with O.E. *cwearn*.

[8] The Upper Greensand here forms a belt of undulating ground 3 miles wide, and the pits are confined to this formation. The Upper Greensand terminates abruptly in a fault-line which runs from Wincanton eastwards, parallel with and a little north of the modern main road, through Haywood to Bourton Bridge, where it coincides with the road. The fault is about ¼ of a mile south of Long Lane and necessarily forms the southern limit of the quarry area.

[9] See the *Anglo-Saxon Chronicle* under these years.

Hon. Daines Barrington in 1784,[10] who mentioned them (from hearsay only) as comparable with Cole's Pits. A generation later Sir Richard Colt Hoare, who lived at Stourhead close by, published a plan of the region in his *Ancient Wilts*.[11] He refers to the constant discovery in the pits of unused querns and fragments thereof, and with his natural good sense saw no mystery in them. But the obvious explanation was not good enough for a certain Victorian antiquary called Thomas Kerslake. Pit-dwellings were fashionable, and here was a veritable metropolis of them! Nennius had mentioned in his list of British towns a 'Cair Pensauelcoit' (v.l. -coin); that looks rather like a Celtic form of Selwood, with -*coit* for -*wood*[12]; therefore the Pen Pits at Penselwood were the remains of the British town. It was all so easy if one used one's imagination and ignored the facts. He produced a monograph with the usual high-sounding Victorian title,[13] begging the question at the outset; and when the Somerset Archaeological Society met there on 29th August 1878, he read extracts therefrom to the assembled party. Prebendary Scarth was inclined to agree, and so was Bishop Clifford; but the Rev. W. Hunt would not have it at all, regarding the pits as quarries dug for chert and sandstone wherewith to make grindstones and other implements. A committee was formed on the spot, but we need not linger over its reports,[14] because they were superseded by one from no less a person than General Pitt-Rivers, who was then Inspector of Ancient Monuments. One imagines that the Pen Pits controversy, in which Boyd Dawkins was also involved, had become something of a nine days' wonder; for if Kerslake was right it was a site of outstanding importance—a prehistoric town covering 700 acres! It should therefore be protected, and it seems likely that Kerslake had sent Pitt-Rivers a copy of his monograph requesting this. One can imagine the reaction of the General, who did not suffer fools gladly. In order to decide the matter it would be necessary to excavate, and he proceeded to do so. The result was published as an official report to the Board of Works.[15]

The Report first describes the site superficially, a piece of field-work. Kerslake's 'ridge' representing the defences of the 'Cair' proved to be a cultivation terrace (a lynchet) of insignificant size and no great age. A cursory inspection of the pits showed that their circular shape was largely a delusion brought about by the method of disposing of the overcast; they were not really pits, at any rate not round pits, but shallow excavations of no regular shape at all. Moreover there were no roads or paths between them as there must have been if it had been a town; as it was, the inhabitants could have had no way of reaching their homes, if they lived near the middle, except over the tops of a maze of 'pit-dwellings'. The General at once spotted the place to dig—the rampart of the medieval castle on Gasper or Gaspar Common called Castle Orchard. It stood surrounded by pits, and he decided to dig a trench right across the hill. Glazed medieval pottery was found on the old surface-line under the outer rampart (part of the bailey), proving it to be Norman. 'During the excavation of the rampart, the remains of one of the old pits with which the hill is covered was found beneath the body of the rampart, showing that it existed there,

[10] *Archaeologia*, VII, 1785, 239. Kerslake probably got his theory of a pit-dwelling metropolis from this article.
[11] Vol. I, 1812, plate opp. p. 35; reproduced here as Plate 4.
[12] For an authoritative discussion of the name see Professor Jackson in *Antiquity*, XII, 1938, 49–50.
[13] *A Primeval British Metropolis, with some notes on the ancient topography of the south-western peninsula of Britain*, by Thomas Kerslake, Bristol, 1877 [Bodleian, Gough, Adds. Somerset 8vo., 75].
[14] *Proc. Som. Arch. Soc.*, XXIV, 1879, 57–61; XXV, 1880, 7–17 (with a plan of Orchard Castle by General Pitt-Rivers).
[15] *Report on the Excavations in the Pen Pits near Penselwood, Somerset*, by Lieut.-General A. Pitt-Rivers, F.R.S., Inspector of Ancient Monuments in Great Britain, 1884.

in continuity with the others on the outside of the ditch and those which covered Gaspar Common, before the fortification was thrown up, and that it was filled up by the earth excavated from the ditch during the construction of the rampart.' In the pits themselves not a fragment of pottery was found, but they were proved to be older than a Norman castle, and it is reasonable to infer that the quarries began to be dug during the Saxon period or even earlier. I have no doubt myself that it began earlier, and that the petrological examination of querns from dated sites will one day prove this; but there is at present no evidence except that some of them are pre-Norman. The quarrying was carried out horizontally, and the General explains the method followed and the reasons for it. His excavations began on 22nd October 1883, and lasted until the 4th November. Before they began an invitation to be present was sent to all those interested, including Kerslake, but the only one who responded was the Rev. H. H. Winwood[16]. Antiquaries of the Kerslake type—now almost extinct—can never face cold facts; Kerslake is remembered only because he came within the orbit of Pitt-Rivers; and the 'primeval British mettropolis' of Cair Pensauelcoit has passed into limbo.

Cole's Pits are $1\frac{1}{2}$ miles south of the town of Faringdon in North Berkshire, and a little more than half a mile east of the village of Little Coxwell, a name often used in referring to them. They cover much less ground than the Pen Pits, occupying a field of about 1,700 by 600 feet, though they may once have been more extensive. They can never, for geographical and geological reasons, have been as numerous as the Pen Pits. The general appearance of the ground is similar, but the pits themselves are deeper, some being as much as 30 feet deep. When I visited them in 1930 there were many fragments of millstones lying about, and one nearly complete one. It was much larger in diameter than a rotary quern, and thinner, and was evidently intended for a power-driven mill. They appear, therefore, to be later in date than the Pen Pits; but they are early enough for their origin to have been unknown to antiquaries in the eighteenth century. We must not, however, rely too much on negative evidence from this source; those antiquaries loved a mystery as much as their nineteenth-century successors. Did they make searching local enquiries about the purpose of the pits? The yokels of Penselwood were shrewder than the antiquaries, and correctly guessed the nature of the pits, unaided, it seems, by traditional memories; and if Kerslake had given heed to them, he would have been saved a fall. If Cole's Pits are medieval millstone quarries, as they probably are, they would surely have been in use down to the sixteenth century at any rate; and it would be strange if that use had become totally forgotten in two centuries.

The name does not help. If it were Cole Pits one might suggest that it was given because they looked like, or were even thought to be, old surface-workings for coal, such as abound in the area south of Bristol. But that seems improbable, and it is more likely that they got their name from a person called Cole. The name is first recorded in 1687.[17]

These Cole's Pits may well have initiated that theory of pit-dwellings which has haunted

[16] I met him at Bath in 1919, not long before his death. He was obviously a good, sensible archaeologist whose geological experience had stood him in good stead. One felt that he would have been more at home amongst the archaeologists of this century than he was amongst those of the last.

[17] *Archaeologia*, VII, 237.

British archaeology down to the present times.[18] It seems to have been first put forward by the Hon. Daines Barrington in a letter to the Rev. Dr Douglas.[19] The writer of this letter had a survey of the pits made, and it was published to illustrate his article. The pits covered an area of just over 14 acres and were 273 in number. He discusses their possible origins, deciding against the quarry theory on the ground that 'not a single stone is to be found in the bottom or sides of these pits'; but that was simply because detritus and weathering has covered up the stony stratum. He also rules out fuel or mining, and concludes that it was 'a considerable city of the Britons in the time of the earliest inhabitants of this island', with a population of about 1,400 people (5 to each house). He dates it as earlier than Stonehenge, because the Britons at the time of Caesar were not sufficiently barbarous to have lived in such primitive dwellings. He then proceeds to quote examples of underground dwellings mentioned by classical writers and some contemporary ones in Kamskatka. It is interesting to find a writer in the eighteenth century postulating, on purely archaeological evidence (though wrongly interpreted), an earlier prehistoric period before that of Julius Caesar; and his anthropological parallel from Kamskatka shows that his method was sound and in advance of his times. But his observations were at fault; surely a closer inspection, even without any digging, would have revealed fragments of millstones and suggested the correct solution? But it had not yet dawned upon men's minds that excavation was a technique for solving *problems*; it was practised, but only to obtain *things* for the collector's cabinet. Excavation would have shown that the suggested explanation was untenable and the Kamskatka analogy a false one.

The geological formation is Lower Greensand; there is a good exposure of the hard reddish-yellow rock in an adjacent pit (misleadingly called 'gravel pit' on the 6-inch map, Berks 8 SW.) midway between Little Coxwell and Faringdon. This projecting tongue of Lower Greensand forms a natural bridge of hard ground across the otherwise almost continuous belt of Kimmeridge Clay which fringes the northern escarpment of the Berkshire Downs from near Swindon on the west to the Thames on the east. That bridge serves to connect the chalk downs with the Corallian ridge running from Highworth by Faringdon, Buckland and Longworth towards Oxford. A modern road still uses that natural bridge, running from the village of Fernham to that of Uffington, where the low clayey ground—the narrow western end of the wide Vale of the White Horse—is only a mile wide. The road passes under the western slope of Barrowbush Hill, and as it descends to cross the Ock at Gains Bridge it is pointing directly at the famous White Horse Hill, which it climbs, being called Broad Way between that hill and Uffington. Here, then, is another of the natural gates of Wessex. That is a geographical fact which holds good regardless of the age of Cole's Pits, whose position on the road is exactly analogous to that of Pen Pits on the Hardway or Hunting Path. Tempting though it be to suggest that querns were quarried in earlier times on the site of Cole's Pits, there is at present no evidence for it. Their proximity to the market town of Faringdon makes it more probable that they were made because there was a good sale for them in that market. (It was called Cheping Farendon in the thirteenth century). But Faringdon was a market because it was

---

[18] E.g., the Ordnance Survey pamphlet on *Field Archaeology* by the present writer (1932) calls the pits found in prehistoric villages (open and defended) 'pit-dwellings'; but they are now rightly regarded as storage-pits. The ghost was finally laid by Professor Bersu.

[19] *Archaeologia*, VII, 1785, 236: 'An account of certain remarkable pits or caverns in the earth in the County of Berks.' (Lysons wrongly gives this as in *Archaeologia*, Vol. VI.)

a great road centre; even to-day six main roads converge on it, and it is the focus of all the roads that led south-east from the Cotswolds to Wessex. Beyond Faringdon they unite into a single road that goes by Stanford in the Vale and Petwick Farm (at Challow Station) to East Challow and Wantage where it joins the Icknield Way. (A possibly older route continued on south-eastwards, passing west of East Challow, and climbing the chalk scarp at Letcombe Castle; this seems to fall into Long Lane, an old road that is certainly as old as Saxon times). At Faringdon, too, the Corallian ridgeway already mentioned meets this convergence of roads. There is little doubt, I think, that these roads are in a general way the modern representatives of much earlier and perhaps prehistoric thoroughfares.

There is evidence in support of this conclusion, and of the prehistoric use of the Fern-ham-Uffington 'bridge', from the existence of prehistoric hill-forts. There are two such near Faringdon; one is that of Badbury,[20] already well-known on an outlier of Lower Green-sand, two miles west-south-west of the town. The other was unknown until I discovered it purely by chance when I went to see Cole's Pits in 1930. As it is still undescribed[21] it may be as well to give some details of it here. It is situated on the Lower Greensand on a hill called Mount Pleasant above the park of Ringdale, midway between Little Coxwell and Fernham whose parish boundary runs through the northern part of it. The hill-fort consists of a single large rampart, well-preserved on the west side, above a patch of scrub on the steep western slope. Up this (at the north point of the park called Furze Hill) runs a hollow way leading to a gap, probably an original entrance, in the rampart. The rampart and ditch are best preserved at the north-west end where the hill is called One Tree Hill, possibly from a large plane-tree which grows on the rampart here. Another hollow leads from the camp here across Little Coxwell Furze in the direction of Gorse Farm. It would there fall into line with the present road by Tollington House to Faringdon, which is the continuation of that across the 'bridge' to Uffington. On the west and south sides the rampart has been levelled by ploughing, but by no means obliterated; and it can be fol-lowed throughout as a low mound, round to the hollow way on the west side where we began. On the west side the rampart follows the steep edge of the high ground; elsewhere it runs over the high ground of the plateau. When I visited it the northern (Little Coxwell) part was under grass, but formerly arable, the southern (Fernham) part under corn, showing some crop-marks; but as there was modern brick lying about they were probably not ancient. In this southern part I picked up the cutting edge portion of a polished flint axe.

There is a magnificent view from the site. In the south one sees the White Horse and Uffington Castle and further to the west Barbury Castle. The whole escarpment of the Berkshire Downs can be seen fading away eastwards to join the Chilterns which are probably visible on a clear day. This hill-fort on One Tree Hill must surely have been placed there with some regard to the existence of a road across the 'bridge' to Uffington Castle.

North-eastwards the plateau narrows, as shown by the 400-foot contour, and at right angles across it, running from NNW. to SSE. I thought I could detect traces of a bank,

[20] Not to be confused with Badbury Rings in Dorset.

[21] I reported it to the late Mr Harold Peake, who mentioned it in his book on 'Berkshire' (Methuen's *County Archaeo-logie*). [After writing this I have discovered that it was mentioned by Lysons, *Berkshire*, 1806, 214. He describes it as the remains of a square camp near Little Coxwell, and says that its 'double ditch' was nearly entire on the west side, but that few traces remained in other parts. The site commanded a very extensive view. The camp seems to have subsequently been ignored both by Berkshire archaeologists (few of whom were field archaeologists) and by the Ordnance Survey.]

but they were very faint and might perhaps be only the remains of a track—there is an old one running in the same direction along the line of the parish boundary which bounds Cole's Pits on the south-west; and the field in Shellingford where it meets Fernham and Little Coxwell is called Red Dyke, according to Dr Grundy.

The third quern-quarry is on Worm's Heath, in the parish of Chelsham, Surrey (20 SE.), beside the road from Croydon south-eastwards to Westerham in Kent. Unlike the other two, this site is of Tertiary age, and consists of an outlier of Oldhaven beds (i 2^1), which is a pebble bed at the top of the Reading Beds (i 2) and the bottom of the London Clay (i 3). The outlier is on a hill 750 feet above the sea and covers an area of about a mile in diameter. The 6-inch geological map describes it as follows: '30 feet dense pebbles in purple, red, orange and yellow clayey sand matrix; large mass of iron cemented pebbles in south end of pit; chalk pinnacle rises nearly to surface.' The pebbles are thoroughly rolled flints from the size of a pea to a length of several inches, mostly of a flat ovoid shape.[22] The whole of the heath is pockmarked with pits, but it is smaller than both Pen Pits and Cole's Pits. The Ordnance Survey map called it (on the 1914 edition) a 'camp', adding 'supposed British remains'. I cannot now find my authority for the fact, but I am sure that I have come across a reference to the discovery of querns here. The evidence for these pits as quern-quarries must therefore remain somewhat in doubt, though I have no doubt whatever about it myself. Rotary querns made of this pudding-stone conglomerate have been found, and I have seen them in museums, but again I cannot unfortunately quote instances.[23] The same formation occurs also in the north of the London basin, near Radlett in Hertfordshire and elsewhere; and quern-quarries should be looked for there also.

Perhaps the least-known quern-quarry is at Waverley, Surrey. Here a quern is recorded on the Ordnance Map (30 SE.) as having been found in 1895, and a visit to the spot showed many pits, much overgrown with bracken and looking ancient. The formation is that called Folkestone Sands, the uppermost division of the Lower Greensand, here containing layers of concretionary ironstone, from which the querns were made.[24] The site is only a couple of miles south of the great North Downs trackway which divides near Farnham into two branches, one the Harroway and the other the Lunway. When investigating the district I discovered two short dykes which are now marked on the 1-inch Ordnance Survey Map, but not otherwise recorded.

These quern-quarries are not a mere by-way of archaeology; they are connected with one of the vital needs of existence—food, and that is the justification for devoting a special

[22] See *History of Surrey*, by Manning and Bray, Vol. II, 1809, 422 (mention only): 'The section at Worm's Heath Surrey', by William Whitaker, *Quarterly Journal of the Geological Society*, LXXV, 1920, 7–31 (the best general account, giving references to previous literature): Report by the director, G. M. Davies, of a field meeting at Worm's Heath on 20th April, 1929, *Proc. Geol. Assocn.*, XL, 1929, 384–7 (also giving references): *The Geology of the Country around Reigate and Dorking*, by H. G. Davies and F. H. Edmunds, H.M.S.O., 1933. None of these mention querns. I am indebted to the Librarian of the Geological Survey, Exhibition Road, S.W.7, for much help in connection with these references. See also *Neolithic Man in North-east Surrey*, by Walter Johnson and William Wright (London, 1903), 32–4, with a plan of the district on p. 33. The authors mistook the quarry-pits for pit-dwellings which were then much in vogue. In spite of this and some other lapses this book and Johnson's other book, *Folk Memory* (Oxford, 1908), contain much good stuff and are still readable, for the angle of approach is a correct one.

[23] See, however, *Proc. Soc. Ant. Lond.*, 2 Ser., XXVII, 1915, 148: Fragments of querns of 'Hertfordshire conglomerate' picked up in Maiden Bower Camp, Beds., by Worthington Smith.

[24] *A Survey of the Prehistory of the Farnham District*, by various authors, published 1939 by the Surrey Arch. Soc. (Castle Arch, Guildford), pp. 4, 206 (site 7, mention only).

chapter to them. That this one happens to be rather thin is simply because the subject is new. It is only since archaeology became basic, so to speak, that we have begun to be interested in such once despised things. There must be plenty of other quern-quarries to be found by field-work, and there are certainly plenty of querns to be examined petrologically and traced to their source in exactly the same way as have the stone axes and the foreign stones of Stonehenge. A new field of research is waiting to be explored.

CHAPTER 10

Prehistoric Linear Earthworks

THE TERM 'linear earthwork' was invented quite recently, after considerable discussion, by the Earthworks Committee of the Congress of Archaeological Societies, to meet a long-felt need. It is better than the picturesque but whimsical 'wandering' or 'travelling earthworks' and far better than the older 'covered ways' derived from Colt Hoare. It covers a larger number of earthworks than the terms 'bivallate' and 'univallate', for it includes also the semi-defensive entrenchments of the Dark Ages and other periods such as Wansdyke, Offa's and Watt's Dykes and the huge Belgic banks near St Albans. It fails only in the north where linear earthworks of a certain kind are replaced by stone walls.

The commonest kind of linear earthwork in Wessex is the small ditch, with a bank on one or both sides, which is to be seen all over the chalk downs. For such Dr Williams-Freeman used, and I think invented, the term univallate and bivallate respectively. It is these banks, quite low but nearly always visible, that enable one to recognize the type and to distinguish it from ditches of other origin. These small banked ditches are easily recognized on air-photographs, and since air-photography came into use as an aid to field archaeology it has been possible to map their courses with far more accuracy and completeness than before. When this had been done over a fairly large area, and the Celtic fields in that area also mapped, the purpose of the ditches began to emerge. It was seen that some of them enclose quite large areas in which there are often no Celtic fields. One of the best examples is that on Figheldean Down,[1] where a rectangular area of never-ploughed downland about 700 by 800 yards is found surrounded on three sides by Celtic fields. Another such area is the much larger oblong one immediately north of Quarley hill-fort, about 2,500 by 1,200 yards; and there are many others. It seems reasonable to explain these enclosed areas as ranches, and the ditches which enclose them as the boundaries which, perhaps strengthened by some fencing, prevented the sheep and cattle grazing within from straying outside over the cultivated land. This hypothesis has found general acceptance,[2] and we may therefore call these bivallate and univallate ditches boundary ditches, or ranch boundaries.

It has been observed that near these boundary ditches are often found certain quadrilateral enclosures, some of which have been proved by excavation to be contemporary, in an archaeological sense. The first to be dated were those on Handley Hill and Martin

[1] *Air Survey and Archaeology*, 39, and map at end. It was this one that first suggested to me the ranch explanation. It is later (but perhaps not much later) than the adjacent Celtic fields which protrude into it in places. See the map (still unpublished) of the Celtic fields of Salisbury Plain (Amesbury Sheet). (Fig. 15).
[2] e.g., by Professor Hawkes, *Proc. Hants. Field Club*, XIV, 143, and Dr Stone, *Wilts Arch. Mag.*, XLVII, 488.

FIG. 14. Prehistoric fields and ranch-boundaries on the Hants-Wilts border. (Reproduced from *Proc. Hants Field Club* XIV, by permission of the Club and Professor Hawkes).

Down in Cranborne Chase, excavated by General Pitt-Rivers.[3] Others on Thorny Down and Boscombe Down East were excavated by Dr Stone.[4] All, with the possible exception of Handley Hill, were proved to belong to the Late Bronze Age. They were proved to be habitation-sites, but the finds suggested occupation rather as shielings than as more permanent and substantial residences. That is in perfect accord with the ranch hypothesis; and so is the discovery at Martin Down of a large pottery vessel which might

[3] *Excavations in Cranborne Chase*, IV, 185 ff.; see also my article on 'A Prehistoric Invasion of England', *Ant. Journ.*, II, 1922, 27–35.

[4] *Wilts Arch. Mag.*, XLVII, 466–89, 640–60.

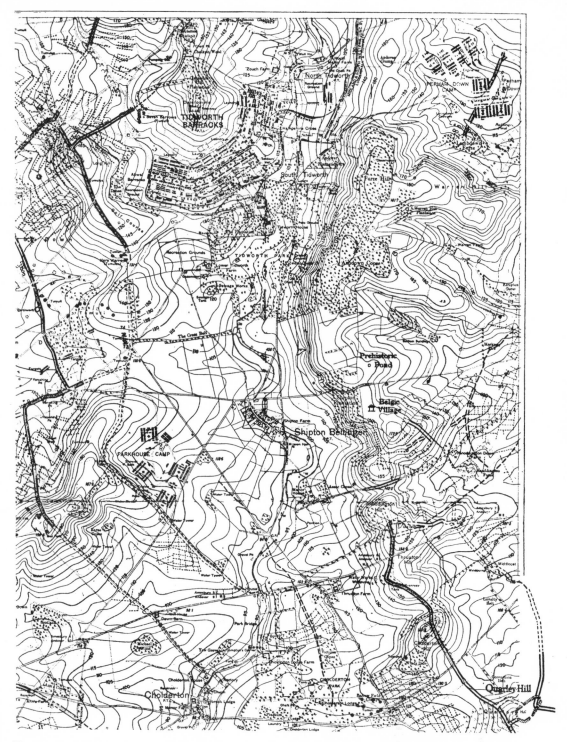

FIG. 15. Part of the O.S. map (printed but not published) of Celtic fields on the Amesbury sheet. Those on Milston Down, obliquely crossed by a ditch, are on the extreme left, just below the middle. (Reproduced with the sanction of the Controller of H. M. Stationery Office: Crown Copyright reserved).

well have been a milk-pail. When visiting the enclosure on Boscombe Down East with Dr Stone I observed that from it one commanded an uninterrupted view northwards over the whole of the ranch at whose southern corner it was placed. That would be of obvious value to the shepherds and cowherds who may have occupied it.

This system of ranches belongs, then, to the Late Bronze Age. South-east of the Bourne river the ranches run up to the watershed of the Test basin, along which runs a long boundary ditch that can be traced with a few short breaks from Snoddington Down north of Quarley to the high ground at East Winterslow, a distance of over six miles (Fig. 14). This long stretch of ditch follows for the greater part of its course the watershed between the basins of the Test and Avon; it marks the geographical boundary between Hampshire and Wiltshire, and it is not far from the actual boundary of to-day. It therefore suggests that those two counties may have had some sort of existence at any rate in this region, as early as the first half of the first millenium B.C.[5] This remarkable conclusion is strengthened by other probabilities. If we continue the line of the southernmost known portion on Roche Court Down we find that it runs into the existing county boundary between Bentley Wood and Hedgemoor Copse which continues thence almost in a straight line to the stream at West Dean. Northwards it is lost beyond Snoddington Down; but there is a strong probability that it joined up with a fragment on Pickpit Hill, which may have joined up with the ditch (more than two miles long) which runs north-eastwards by Scots Poor. Here it comes to a roughly oval area, lying within the curve of the Roman road, called Chute Causeway, which in medieval times was the Bailiwick of Hippenscombe, a forest area claimed by both Savernake (Wilts) and Chute (Hants). To attempt to trace it further as a distinct entity would be premature; that can only be done by the intensive study of the air-photographs of the region, combined of course with field-work. For there are here many disjointed fragments, and until we can see what pattern they form we cannot know which belongs to which. But it should be observed that a similar type of ditch goes along the slope of the main escarpment, which here is not so steep as usual, and bears the names of Botley Down and Rivar Down. I shall describe another and more striking example of a scarp-slope ditch further on.

The ranch system of the Hants-Wilts border seems certainly to have been initiated in the Late Bronze Age, for the reasons stated by Professor Hawkes in his excellent review of them already quoted; and as it forms a coherent system one would think that it must have been laid out as a whole at one time by groups of people acting in concert. It is difficult at any rate to think that more than a century or two at the most can lie between the earliest and latest members. If that be so, then a group of Celtic fields on Milston Down must belong either to the beginning of the Late Bronze Age or to an even earlier date. For it is obliquely traversed by one of the ditches bounding the two long 'ranches' which sprawl over the hills between Sidbury and the river at Cholderton (Fig. 15). The air-photograph illustrating this was published in 1932,[6] and there can be no doubt about the priority of fields to ditches. Changes of plan have then to be allowed for occasionally, by which agricultural land was turned over to pasture—for this ditch completely ignores the planning of the fields, and is dug ruthlessly across their delimiting banks, so that its only conceivable purpose seems to be that of a boundary to a tract of pasture land. We do not know when

[5] This has also been observed by Professor Hawkes, *Proc. Hants Field Club*, XIV, 148.
[6] Kendrick and Hawkes, *Archaeology in England and Wales*, 1914–31, 300, Plate xxiv, 1.

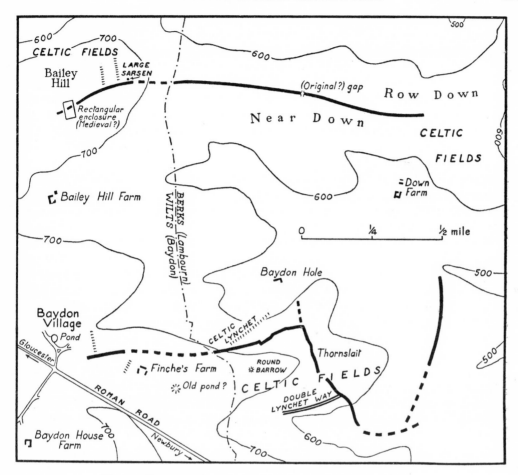

FIG. 16. Linear earthworks on the Downs round Baydon, Wilts.

Celtic fields[7] were first laid out, but there is evidence that they were in existence in the Late Bronze Age, for Dr Clay found and excavated three Late Bronze Age barrows at Marleycombe Hill in South Wilts which were demonstrably later in construction than the adjoining field lynchets.[8] A quite early date is therefore possible for the fields on Milston Down.

The general tendency, on the other hand, was in the opposite direction. More and more land was brought under cultivation during the prehistoric Iron Age, as agriculture gained at the expense of pasturage, and as the population increased proportionately. That the progress was gradual, and that there was no radical change of system is shown by the fact that when the fields impinged on an earlier ranch boundary they respected it. The property rights represented by these boundary ditches evidently persisted. That can well be seen in another part of Wessex which is also thickly covered with them, Berkshire. The best exam-

[7] For the term see note at beginning of Chapter 8.
[8] *Wilts Arch. Mag.*, XLIII, 556, quoted by Hawkes, *op. cit.* 145.

ple is near Baydon, a hill village whose origin probably goes back far into the prehistoric period. Baydon itself is in Wiltshire, but close to the Berkshire boundary (Fig. 16). It lies on high ground at the north-west end of the ridge separating the Lambourne and Kennet valleys. One of these ditches begins close to the church on the northern ridge of the village.[9] It can be seen in Hedden's Copse and Thornslait Ridge, between which and Thornslait Plantation it makes a small but characteristic right-angle bend. It then curves round to the south. There are Celtic lynchets on both sides of it and a double lynchet way south of Thornslait Plantation. But the important thing to notice is the character of the ditch itself. On the lower (north and east) side is a low bank; on the upper a lynchet, whose surface is level with the bank opposite. This can only mean that those who cultivated the ground (on the south and west) respected the ditch.

A mile north of Baydon is another ditch,[10] running east and west; it begins to be observable in Bailey Hill Copse on Bailey Hill and can be traced without a break for 1¼ miles until it disappears east of Near Down.

On Bailey Hill where, though not marked on the map, it is very well preserved,[11] some very fine lynchets impinge at right angles on its north side. On Near Down there is a gap where apparently other ditches left it running north and south respectively. This, and the existence of the ditch by Dean Stubbing Copse already mentioned, suggests that the Bailey Hill ditch had other ranch boundaries running from it like those on the Hants and Wilts border. There is another point of resemblance, for the boundary between Wilts and Hants, which runs due north across Bailey Hill, itself follows a prehistoric boundary ditch which is plainly visible as it approaches Lambourn Corner. At that point it turns sharp west.[12] It seems likely that the prehistoric boundary continued northwards along the line of the Ashbury-Lambourn boundary, for fragments of ditch that appear to be of the same character are marked on the map on or close to the boundary as far as Knighton Bushes.

There is another boundary ditch, called East Ditch, north of Lambourn (Fig. 17). Its northern end is on the parish boundary, and it runs in a southerly direction, making one triangular and several right angle bends; it passes west of Sheepdrove Farm and the Beeches, ending on Ewe Hill, where a very fine Celtic lynchet ends against its east side. In a valley west of the Beeches are some old chalkpits (marked on Berks 19 SE.) which are later than East Ditch, but look very old and may be either flint-mines or (much more probably) marl-pits, possibly contemporary with the Celtic fields. The ditch is about a

[9] Its course for the 700 yards between the village and the county boundary is not marked, but I identified it on the ground in 1931, and joined it up to the portion marked on the map (Berks 25 NW.) in the copse called Thornslait Ridge. The 'Site of ditch' between Dean Stubbing Copse and the road to the NW. is wrong; south of the road the ditch turns east, and joins the ditch (marked on the map) between that and Lodge Copse. This continued north across the road, passing immediately east of the tumulus, beyond which its course is shown for over a quarter of a mile on an air-photo.

[10] A short part of it is marked by hachures on Near Down, but it is not named. The rest of it as here described I identified on the ground and inserted on the map (Berks 25 N.-W.) in 1931.

[11] My remarks, though in the present tense, refer to 1931. Here and also elsewhere the past tense may now be applicable, for much of the downs is being ploughed up, and prehistoric earthworks obliterated.

[12] This spot abounds in prehistoric remains. At Lambourn Corner is a fine flat-bottomed earthwork of the 'circus' type, round whose edge bends the parish boundary of Ashbury to meet the county boundary on the south side of the 'circus'. Four hundred feet north of the meeting-point is a well-preserved hut-circle near which the map records the discovery of an 'iron chain and coins'. In Fognam Clump is a round barrow with the remains of a peristalith of sarsen stones; and Fognam Down is covered with Celtic lynchets which formed the subject of one of Major Allen's best air-photos. The earthwork surrounding Upper Wood is medieval, and cuts through the Celtic fields; it is not prehistoric, as Grundy and Peake imagined. The wood was enclosed by Glastonbury Abbey, which held the Manor of Ashbury. The Rev. Charles Overy has shown that Grundy's identification of the Saxon bounds of Ashbury are quite wrong; the bounds as always, circulate clockwise.

FIG. 17. East Ditch on the Lambourn Downs, Berks.

mile and a half long, and may be the Grynesdiche (an error for Grymesdiche?) near Gare, a field-name in Bockhampton mentioned in the Cartulary of St Frideswide.[13] Bockhampton Down to the east is covered with Celtic fields and there is a contemporary road east of Sheepdrove Farm, 800 feet long. East Ditch is about a mile east of the famous Lambourn Seven Barrows.

The right-angle bends mentioned above are exactly paralleled by similar bends made by existing parish boundaries when they thread their way between the arable fields of two adjacent communities. That some of these are very ancient is proved by Saxon boundaries given in charters, which in such cases mention *hlinc* and *andheafda* (lynchet and headland). By analogy the bends of prehistoric boundary-ditches should originate from the same cause. Confirmatory evidence such as lynchets resting against the boundary-ditch at the bends is not, however, always forthcoming.

There are more boundary-ditches marked on the map on the cultivated country further east and south-east; one runs from Warren Down southwards towards East Garston. In fact these boundary-ditches occur not only on the open downlands, where they are easy to understand and interpret, but also in fragments throughout those parts of Wessex which are now and have for long ages been under cultivation. In Haylen Wood, eleven miles east of Winchester in the angle between the Fareham and Petersfield roads, is a ditch of precisely the same kind as that already described near Baydon, with a lynchet on the upper side and a bank on the lower.[14] There are very many ditches in the cultivated areas which are revealed as crop-marks on air-photos; and they are generally associated with Celtic

[13] II, 315 (*Oxford Hist. Soc.*, XXXI, 1896).
[14] Unfortunately my 6-inch map (Hants 52 SW.) with its field-notes was lost at the Ordnance Survey, and I cannot now give exact details; but I remember noting the resemblance at the time and recorded it on the Berkshire Sheets. In his *Field Archaeology* (p. 292) Dr Williams-Freeman describes this as a boundary-ditch whose dimensions suggest that it may have also had a defensive character. It can be traced for two miles.

H

fields. It would be rash to claim that all such were originally ranch-boundaries; ditches like this may well have continued to be made throughout what may be called the Archaic Period of cultivation,[15] and for more than one purpose. But it seems established that an elaborate network of ranch-boundaries was laid out early in the period, and gradually swamped (but not obliterated) by the rising tide of cultivation.

There is one ditch which can only be the boundary of a large area and that is the Grim's Ditch which runs for some ten miles along the escarpment of the Berkshire Downs, from Lattin Down 2½ miles south-east of Wantage to the steep-sided coombes running down to the Thames north of Streatley (Fig. 18). It has been curiously overlooked, and I do not know of any references to it in archaeological literature, though doubtless there are such. In 1930 I walked the whole length of it and noted its features on the maps, subsequently observing the west end of it from the air in June of the same year. The overhead view showed that it followed the parish boundary between Charlton and West Lockinge as marked on the map (Berks 20 NE.), but left it nearly at a right angle and not as there marked. Close by on Lattin Down are some old claypits where a hoard of bronze axes of the Late Bronze Age was found in 1872. Proceeding eastwards it meets the West and East Lockinge parish boundary, follows it for 100 yards and then leaves it again at right angles. These sharp changes of direction are characteristic of all these boundary ditches; they are not necessarily all of the same origin. Where there are many close together they must surely represent the zigzags of a boundary between cultivation plots; such are the zigzags of East Ditch north of the Beeches. Precisely similar zigzags occur on the same parish boundary as that here followed by Grim's Ditch about ¾ of a mile further north where the boundary threads its way between the arable fields of the two Lockinges; and that boundary is certainly of relatively late formation, representing a subdivision of a large early unit of Lockinge into East and West. But this creates a difficulty; if it be late, how account for the fact that Grim's Ditch interrupts its course to follow it for 100 yards? I cannot believe that the boundary is as old as Grim's Ditch; and it is almost equally difficult to believe that those who laid out the boundary would have selected a short and then insignificant deviation in an obsolete boundary bank.

Grim's Ditch continues along the escarpment which between here and Scutchamer Knob is a gentle slope varying between one in seven and one in twelve. For most of the way is consists of a ditch with a bank on the lower (north) side, but at the Covered Yard[16] a bank is faintly discernible on both sides. It can be followed the whole way to below Scutchamer Knob with only very small breaks, the gaps left on the map being represented by a band of greener grass. The escarpment is scored at regular intervals by deep hollow tracks leading from the downs to the villages on the streams to the north. Below Scutchamer Knob it is well preserved and runs parallel to an old track called Reading Way, whose old tracks are first visible south of East Ginge, continuing along the south side of Downs House Park and falling into the Ridgeway on Roden Downs.[17] East of Downs House Park the course of Grim's Ditch is less straight, for it follows the irregularities of the

---

[15] This term covers the period from about 1000 B.C. to about A.D. 500 during which there was no radical change in the agricultural pattern. It was preceded by the Middle Bronze Age—a Dark Age—and followed by the Saxon period, introducing the system which lasted through out the Middle Ages down to the enclosures, when the modern period began.

[16] Here in 1898 was found a Roman brooch which in 1930 was in the possession of Mr A. Thomas Loyd of Lockinge House. See Hallam, *History of East Lockinge*, 96.

[17] About half a mile west of the point called 'thære flodan aet Swin weges slo aet thære wege gelaeton' of the Blewbury bounds: Birch, *Cart. Sax.*, II, 801 (A.D. 944). Reading Way may well be as old as the Lockinge group of villages.

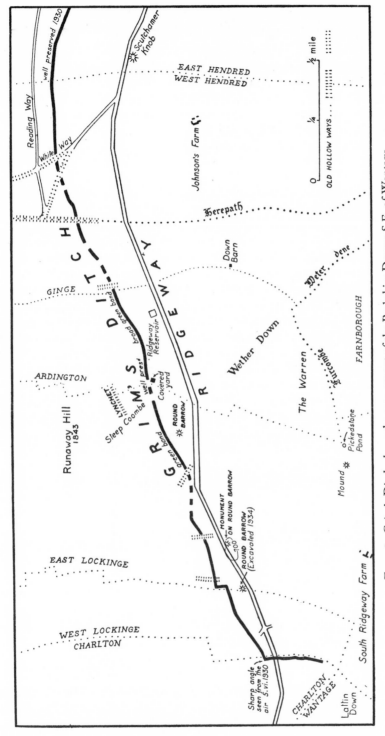

FIG. 18. Grim's Ditch along the escarpment of the Berkshire Downs S.E. of Wantage.

escarpment. As far as the Newbury and Oxford road at Kate's Gore its course is marked on the map, coinciding with the southern boundary of Chilton parish. Beyond Kate's Gore there is a gap of half a mile where it is interrupted by some old enclosures, but it is recognizable again on the northern edge of the map (Berks 21 NW.) and is well preserved, with a bank on the north, as far as Fox Barrow (21 SW.), the *Foxes beorge* of Saxon times.[18] The barrow has been dug into on the south-west side, revealing a small sarsen stone; it appears to be earlier than Grim's Ditch.

I followed the ditch on foot across Churn Plain and Aston Upthorpe Downs, but my 6-inch sheet (21 SE.) with field-notes was lost at the Ordnance Survey. I remember that it was plainly visible in one form or another throughout, and even if it has since been levelled by cultivation, its course can easily be recovered by air-photography. There can be no doubt that it eventually joined up with a ditch called Devil's Ditch on Moulsford Downs (22 SW.). That too has its bank on the east and north-east side. Its western end is visible beyond the point marked on the map, running north-west across Unhill Wood.[19] It is not visible in Unhill Bottom, but the high ground above is called *Grim gelege* (the track of Grim) in the Saxon bounds of Cholsey.[20] The name Devil's Ditch is, here as elsewhere, the Christianized form of Grim's Ditch, for the Christian priests used the word as a term of abuse for the pagan deities, much as to-day Communists use the word 'capitalist', and vice versa. On the long ridge of Thurle Down are many Celtic fields and Grim's Ditch lies out on its northern slope, two miles from the Thames, above a dry valley called Trencher Catberry. It may well have continued, or had its counterpart, on the Chiltern escarpment, for there is a similar ditch (formerly called 'Danish Entrenchment' on the Ordnance Maps) on the northern slope of Swyncombe Hill, two miles east of Ewelme; it ends on Postwell Hill, having a total length of a little over a mile (Oxon 50 NW.).

I have described this Grim's Ditch in some detail, partly because it is a little-known representative of its class, that of scarpside boundary ditches, partly because it will, I suspect, when correlated with the fragmentary ditches and Celtic fields of the chalk hinterland, help considerably towards the construction of a map of the area in prehistoric times. For it belongs quite clearly to the chalk lands on the south, and must have been made by the people living there, not by the people living below the escarpment on the north. It seems to have been a major ranch boundary like that on the Hants and Wilts watershed. There must have been minor ranch boundaries running off it southwards, and there are in fact two such still visible on the Sheep and Cow Downs south-west of Chilton (21 NW.) This conclusion is reinforced by the southern turn at its western end on Lattin Down; there is no trace of a continuation westwards along the escarpment, or northwards along the parish boundary, and a course like this, combined with the abrupt change of direction, indicates unmistakeably that it was an area of the downs that was enclosed. It cannot be interpreted as a southern boundary of the cultivated lands to the north both for this reason and because it runs well beyond and south of their southern limits, and never did so bound

---

[18] See Birch, *Cart. Sax.*, II, No. 801 (A.D. 944): bounds of Bleoburh (Blewbury) and Grundy in *Berks, Bucks and Oxon Journal*, XXVII, 203. The Saxon bounds followed the ditch without naming it. But Dr Grundy suggests that the *Draegeles baec* along which the boundary of 944 went after Fox Barrow, may be Grim's Ditch, and I agree with him. *Draegele* is unknown to the dictionary.

[19] Here I noticed on the surface many white quartzite pebbles, an extension beyond the Thames of the glacial drift of the Chilterns.

[20] Birch, *Cart. Sax.*, No. 565: see Grundy in *B.B.O.*, XXVIII, 1924, 69, and Forsberg, *Contribution, etc.*, 1950, 76–7. I should put *Grim gelege* a little further north than Dr Grundy, on the down called the Fair Mile.

them. It belongs, in fact, to a group of upland settlements of which Farnborough and East Ilsley are the modern survivors. This is the region where upland settlements, probably of prehistoric origin, survive; further south are others—Peasmore, Chaddeleworth, Leckhampstead, South Fawley, Beedon and Chieveley. Continuous occupation has obliterated the early remains; but one such, which was abandoned, has survived on Roden Downs, where a Romano-British farm has recently been destroyed by ploughing.[21]

It is of course a far cry from Romano-British times to the Late Bronze Age, when, as we have seen, both ranches and arable fields were laid out. But it is no further than from Romano-British times to the enclosures which ended the medieval system, and in both the Archaic and Medieval systems there was no radical change or break of continuity.

In dealing with these boundary ditches so far I have tried to confine myself to those whose *sole* purpose appears to have been to delimit areas. It has been claimed, however, that some of them were used as roads, and this purpose is claimed in particular for 'Crossdykes', leading from the head of one coombe to the head of another, and for the multiple ditches of Cranborne Chase and Sussex.[22] The claim is based upon the flat, well-trodden character of the bottom of the ditch, as revealed by excavation. It is reinforced by the excavation of a ditch at Winterbourne Dauntsey which Dr Stone found not only to be shallow and broad-bottomed, but also to have had a stockade of posts set in round holes along both its berms (Fig. 19).[23] The ditch was dated by pottery to the Early Iron Age. Professor Hawkes calls attention to the age-long association of boundaries and roads, and suggests that ditches primarily designed for boundaries may have been followed by travellers. The white chalk would have been a good guide. Even to-day sheep and cattle tend to follow them, and I found a sheep-track following the almost ploughed-out remnants of one of the Old Ditches on Salisbury Plain for nearly a mile.

It is obviously impossible here to give a complete enumeration of all the boundary ditches and their stone equivalents on the Highland Zone; I can only mention a few and indicate the chief areas where they occur. West of the area mapped by Professor Hawkes (my Fig. 14, borrowed from him) they abound on Salisbury Plain, several distinct ones bearing the name of Old Ditch, which goes back to Saxon times. The longest continuous length is that of the western Old Ditch running for $4\frac{1}{2}$ miles from the prehistoric settlement of Knook Castle (Wilts 52 SE.) to beyond Warminster Down. Eastwards it runs for two miles along the top of Breakheart Hill north of Chitterne. The total length, therefore

[21] See *Trans. Newbury & District Field Club*, IX, 1948, 10 ff.: summary in *J.R.S.*, XXXVII, 1946, 144 (published November 1949).

[22] See Hawkes, op. sit. 145–6 and references there given to R. C. C. Clay, *Antiquity*, I, 61–5; Curwen, *Sussex Arch. Coll.*, LXIX, 35–75; *Prehistoric Sussex*, 113–16; Williams-Freeman, *Antiquity*, VI, 24–34. For Cranborne Chase see Heywood Sumner, *Earthworks of C.C.*, 35–7 and Plate xvi.

[23] *Wilts. Arch. Mag.* XLVI, 448 (Plate 4 reproduced here as fig. 19), 450–3. The existence of stockades consisting of a single line of large posts (doubtless reinforced) is proved by George Allen's air-photos ($\frac{8}{108}$ to $\frac{8}{117}$) at Northfield Farm on the Thames opposite Burcot (Berks 11 SW.). One of the air-photos first appeared in *Oxoniensia*, vol. 5, plate xx, and then subsequently in the Ashmolean *Guide to an exhibition of air-photos*, 1948, Plate xvi. It is to be noticed that the line of post-holes is continued beyond the arable as a low bank (not to be confused with a modern cart-track crossing it obliquely). Remains of Celtic fields and a Romano-British settlement exist in the fields west of the farm, having been detected in 1898 by Professors Haverfield and Myres by means of crop-marks observed on the ground (see *Antiquity*, VII, 295). No doubt the stockade belonged to this settlement. For the objects found here see Peake's *Berkshire* (Methuen's County Archaeologies), p. 248. They are now in the Reading Museum. Close to the stockade is a rectangular enclosure with a gap in the middle of one side, of a type usually associated in Oxfordshire with Roman houses. There are also some barrow-circles.

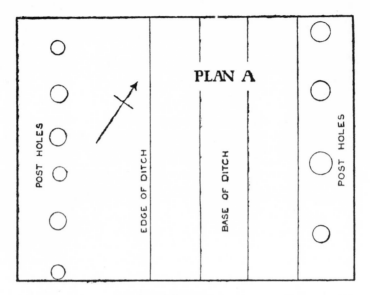

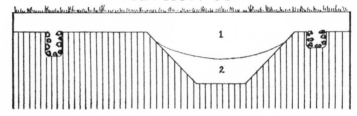

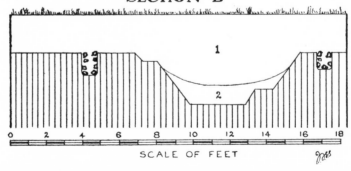

FIG. 19. Early Iron Age boundary-ditch at Winterbourne Dauntsey, Wilts (after J. F. S. Stone) showing post-holes of stockade. (Reproduced by permission from *Wilts Arch. Mag.*, XLVI, 448, Plate 4).

would be 6½ miles, plus an unknown distance at each end; but there is such a marked change of alignment at Knook that I should hesitate to call the two parts one ditch. In the western part the bank is on the south or lower side of the ditch, and although zigzags occur they are rare. There is a square enclosure (the sides 26 yards) close to the ditch at the north end of Bishopstrow Down, and there is also a silted-up ditch that may be contemporary and represent a ranch based on Old Ditch. Except near Knook there are no Celtic fields associated with this ditch.

There is another Old Ditch south-west of Tilshead Lodge (Wilts 53 NW.) which utilizes a very long Long Barrow conveniently aligned on its course. Further east is another long stretch which runs north-east over Orcheston Down for two miles to join at right angles another of about the same length.

Further to the north-east there is quite a complex of ditches west of Casterley, a Late Iron Age defended settlement; one of them can be followed right up to the ramparts of the village. South of Casterley runs a long and well-preserved ditch (called *Eald dic* in the Saxon bounds of Enford (A.D. 934),[24] associated in places with Celtic fields. It is not of the usual type, but consists of a low bank between two ditches. The ditch can be traced on air-photographs for more than half a mile beyond its end on the map (47 SW.)[25]

Further east still across the Avon, is the ditch-system radiating from Sidbury. There are four in all (though one stops short one third of a mile south of the hill-fort). That which runs northwards is double, consisting in one place of two banks with a ditch on the west side of each. This line forms a major boundary from which subsidiary ditches run off east and west, bounding ranches. That on the west, south of Weather Hill Firs, is complete, forming a curved rectangle, so to speak, half a mile long from east to west and 300 yards wide. The one opposite is wider, nearly a quarter of a mile across, and the sides are straighter. It encloses the well-known group of Early Bronze Age barrows on Snail Down.[26]

I have described the boundary ditches of Salisbury Plain and the Berkshire Downs at considerable length because, with the exception of Professor Hawkes' often-quoted article, there is no adequate modern account of them. Moreover it was on Salisbury Plain that they were first studied by Sir Richard Colt Hoare and later by the Cunningtons and Mr Percy Farrer, whose interest in them was passed on to Dr Williams-Freeman, from whom it was passed on in turn to Professor Hawkes and myself. It was these ditches' tiresome habit of vanishing into a cornfield that first caused Dr Williams-Freeman and me to hanker after an overhead view that we foresaw would reveal them there. So, apart from their intrinsic merits, which are great, they have a place in the history of field archaeology. They also have a future, for they are abundant, indestructible, and concerned with a fundamental element of prehistoric life—food-production.

Outside Wiltshire boundary ditches occur in Cranborne Chase where one such now

[24] Birch, *Cart. Sax.*, No. 705.

[25] Although I walked this ditch in January 1935, I was then interested in other matters, and beyond its size remember nothing except that it was a very cold day! The statement above is from my note in *Antiquity*, IX, 1935, 90, where the adjacent Celtic and strip fields are described and illustrated by a map.

[26] For the major boundary see my *Air Survey and Archaeology*, 1928, 5; also a short description in an old book called *A Description of Stonehenge, Abury etc.*, p. 73, where it is said to be 'traced almost to the verge of the plain.' (The book is anonymous and contains a lot of rubbish about 'the learning and discipline of the Druids', but also some valuable observations about 'the Antiquities on Salisbury Plain'. It bears no date, but was published in 1776. There is a copy in the library of the Wiltshire Archaeological Society at Devizes).

called Grim's Ditch[27] encloses an area of sixteen square miles.[28] It is called *Strete Dich* in the bounds of Damerham.[29] They are common on the Dorset Downs, but usually in the form of short fragments only, the earlier ones having perhaps been obliterated by the intensive Iron Age cultivation of that region. They may also be found in nearly every part of the chalk region of Hants; one climbs the steep eastern slope of Beacon Hill, Highclere; another is associated with the unfinished hill-fort and field-system (now ploughed out) on Ladle Hill and Great Litchfield Down opposite Beacon Hill. There is one at least[30] on the downs between Kingsclere and Whitchurch and another (called Devil's Ditch) north-east of Wonston.

All the ditches hitherto mentioned are in the chalk region of Wessex; they are confined to it, and almost unknown in the Tertiary country. Nor, with one important exception, are they known in the chalk regions outside Wessex. There are, it is true, some short lengths of ditch in Sussex, but no ranches, either because they were never made or because subsequent prehistoric cultivation obliterated them. There are none on the North Downs of Kent and Surrey nor in East Anglia and Lincolnshire. But the chalk wolds of the East Riding of Yorkshire are covered with an intricate maze of ditches, both single and multiple, which have not been studied or excavated by modern methods. When the first large-scale Ordnance Survey Maps were published in the middle of the nineteenth century, the wolds had only just been enclosed and turned into arable fields, and the earthworks on them were still plainly visible and were marked on those maps. They must now be visible as crop-sites. It is possible that they may have been first introduced by the Late Bronze Age invaders, one of whose settlements has been discovered at Scarborough.[31]

Outside the chalk areas, in stony country, boundary-ditches occur, together with long lines of decayed walling. In the absence of excavation their age must remain uncertain, and some of them may be medieval; but most of them probably belong to that same Archaic culture as the Wessex boundary ditches. The boundary walls have survived only where large blocks of stone lying on the surface were set up as 'grounders', as to-day in Cornwall[32] and Scilly. These form a strong support for the smaller stones built in between them, so that a wall so built will stand much longer than one of small stones only—unless it is of great thickness. Remains of such walls reinforced by 'grounders' may be seen on Dartmoor and in Cornwall,[33] and also on the mountains of North Wales.[34] Remains of them will probably be found on all the rocky uplands of Britain when they are looked for. On Dartmoor an 'ancient bank' is marked on the Ordnance Map (Devon 98 SW.) running across Cudlipptown Down from the Petertavy Brook in the south to a 'camp' at White Tor on the top of a hill 1,527 feet high. North of the 'camp' is another similar bank (not named on the map, but marked by a double dotted line) forming for part of its course the eastern side of an 'enclosure'. There are other 'enclosures', a 'pound' with hut-circles, an elongated cairn and a cist in the immediate neighbourhood. The fact that the bank runs from a hill-fort to a river suggests that it may be a ranch-boundary like the

[27] The name was applied to Bokerley Dyke in 1618.
[28] See the detailed description (with map) by C. M. Piggott in *Antiquity*, XVIII, 1944, 65–71; air-photo of it in same, V, 1931, Plate vi (pp. 450–1).
[29] Birch, *Cart. Sax.*, II, 817, A.D. 940–46.
[30] Photographed by George Allen.
[31] *Archaeologia*, LXXVII, 1927, 179–200.
[32] *Antiquity*, X, 1936, 162, Plate ii (Zennor).
[33] *Antiquity*, X, 1936, 168, Plate vi (Mulfra Hill, Madron).
[34] *Arch. Camb.*, 6 Ser., XX, 1920, 117, 124 (plan, Pen Dinas, between pp. 128 and 129).

Wessex ones. South of Belstone Tor, in the parish of that name (Devon 77 SW.) is marked 'the Irishman's Wall' running in three very straight sections westwards from the Taw to the East Okement river. It is not marked as an antiquity, and its straightness suggests a more recent origin. I have not seen these two Dartmoor sites.

It seems probable that the Black Dyke of Northumberland is such a prehistoric ranch boundary.[35] It runs north and south between the North and South Tyne for a distance of thirteen miles; the ditch is on the west and is six feet deep in places. The dyke is 'intermittent in character, for it takes advantage of natural features, especially crags and morasses', some of the latter having formerly been lakes and often containing a remnant of water still, even after draining. The use of such bogs and lakes is characteristic of two other linear earthworks, one near Melrose[36] and the other in Ireland—the famous Black Pig's Dyke which runs right across the island (Plate 14).[37] A precisely similar device was independently invented by English sheep-ranchers in Tierra del Fuego in 1894. 'Will, with his Yahgan lad, Teddy . . . had divided Gable Island into three parts. By taking advantage of certain lakes and running fences from one to the other, they had effected a great saving in time and material. The lakes, of course, when frozen and covered with a little snow, were no barrier to sheep, but during that period of the year barriers were not much needed.' Corrals were also made for gathering the sheep at shearing time.[38] In timbered regions trees were felled to form an *abattis*—a procedure that has been suggested to explain the gaps in British linear earthworks of another kind such as Wansdyke.

The Black Dyke is said to be 'obliterated by the Vallum and the Roman Wall', and so to be older than those works. As the author of the description cited remarks, excavation at the point of contact between the Black Dyke and the Vallum—a very simple and easy operation—would determine the relative age beyond question, and is much to be desired.

There are several other linear earthworks of similar character in the Border Counties. One, called Heriot's Dyke, runs over the moors north of Greenlaw in Berwickshire. The best known is that called the Catrail[39] which consists of two quite distinct earthworks— a short one about five miles long between Galashiels and Selkirk, and a much longer one of about eleven miles crossing the moors south-west of Hawick. This latter one seems to have the same sort of geographical relationship to the Teviot and its tributaries as the Northumberland Black Dyke has to the two Tynes and their tributaries. They seem to be designed against animals rather than men. I do not believe that any of them were simply political (tribal) boundaries and no more; the labour of making them must have been considerable and the objective a practical one.

The linear earthwork near Melrose is between three and five miles long. When I wrote an account of it in 1936 I suggested that it might be a defensive frontier made by the inhabitants of the fort on Eildon Hill. In the light of Mr Lucas Bridge's experiences it now

[35] For an excellent detailed description of its course, illustrated by maps, see 'The Black Dyke in Northumberland', by G. R. B. Spain, *Archaeologia Aeliana*, 3 Ser., XIX, 1922, 121–68. The writer explains its purpose as military, but even if one does not accept this, one is grateful for the descriptive portion which forms the bulk of the article, and is of permanent value.

[36] *Antiquity*, X, 1936, 346–9.

[37] See Kane's articles in *Proc. R. Irish Acad.* xxvii (1909) and xxxiii (1917), but they are confused and not based on field-work.

[38] *Uttermost Part of the Earth*, by E. Lucas Bridges, (Hodder & Stroughton, and Readers' Union), 1948, 183. In another part of the same country the author managed and fenced farms totalling about 254,000 acres, divided into fields of which the largest was about 90,000 acres (p. 486). This most readable book contains much that is of interest to the student of prehistoric conditions in Europe. But it is also very much more than that, and will live to become a classic.

[39] See 'The so-called Catrail', by J. H. Craw, *Proc. Soc. Ant. Scot.*, LVIII, 1924, 40–44.

seems equally probable that it may have been designed to restrict the movements of sheep.
Whatever its purpose it seems to have been made by people living to the north-east of it.

A linear earthwork called the Deil's Jingle runs for a mile in the loop of the White Esk
south of the Roman fort of Raeburnfoot. It starts on the east bank on Bank Head Hill, opposite Castle O'er, crosses the Langholm road and continues north-eastwards towards the
Meggat Water. I followed it for some distance northwards beyond the road and it showed
no signs of ending when I had to leave it. The line is continued on the map by a parish
boundary that runs over Shiel Moss to Muckle Knowe; if this marks its further course the
Deil's Jingle would cut off a large tract in the fork between the White Esk and the Meggat
Water. The region was one still devoted to sheep-rearing before it was invaded by the
Forestry Department, and the earthwork may well have been a ranch-boundary.

There are many linear earthworks in the south-western counties of Scotland. Several
are marked on the Ordnance Maps. They run for the most part along the sides of valleys,
and are less inaccessible than those just described in the Border District. Their purpose
will never be discovered until someone walks along them, inserting his observations on the
6-inch map and filling in the gaps. I suspect that there are far more in existence than the
few already marked, and that many of them will be, or already have been, revealed by
air-photography.

One called the Celtic or Deil's Dyke follows the slopes of the hills on the east side of
the Nith between Thornhill and Durisdeer. Going up the Kirkburn it then turns across it
and the Carron Water, and thence over to the Enterkin Burn. Further to the north-west
there is a stretch of about five miles in the parish of Sanquhar over the moors at 800–1,000
feet, south of the Nith. It seems to be well preserved (to judge from the map). There is
another Deil's Dyke in the parish of Minnigaff, Kirkcudbrightshire, on the moor of Dran-
nandow in the same parish (3½ miles). Here and in the parish of Mochrum the map marks
many 'old fences'; they may of course be quite modern, but they would be worth examining. There are some fragments called Deil's Dyke near Lake Ochiltree in Wigtonshire.
There is a 'ditch' at Kirkcowan, and a Deil's Dyke running north-eastwards from the east
shore of Loch Ryan for a mile and a half, ending at the ancient site called Shinriggie. [40]

The list given above is by no means complete. The omissions are obviously necessary
in a book of this kind which is intended rather to guide field-workers to promising fields of
research than to provide encyclopedic information. Partly for the same reason I have not
described the character of the linear earthworks. Some of them change their character in
their course; the Melrose earthwork has one, two and three ditches in different parts of its
short length, and the Black Pig's Dyke has the ditch sometimes on the north and sometimes
on the south. These variations may have been intentional and made to suit the topography
or needs of the builders; they can hardly indicate any differences in function. While, therefore, all such structural features should be noted in the field, and their probable causes investigated, they cannot serve as a basis for classification according to presumed function. A
single-ditched linear earthwork that suddenly acquires two other ditches did not at the
same time change its function, but only its tactics.

---

[40] Since I wrote this Angus Graham's account of the Deil's Dyke in Galloway has been published, too late for more than
a reference added on page-proofs. See *Proc. Soc. Ant. Scot.*, LXXXIII, 174–85.

CHAPTER 11

Ponds

BEHIND THE technical expression 'linear earthworks' lies much of the pastoral and agricultural prehistory of Wessex, as we have just seen; they are closely connected with food supply. Equally important on these dry Wessex Downs was water for man and beast. In pre-Roman times wells of the modern type were not dug;[1] so that prehistoric man had to depend on streams, springs and ponds. Many of his ponds still survive, and some are still in use. In studying them the student who is primarily concerned with the Archaic régime can best reach them on stepping-stones provided by an intermediate period, the Anglo-Saxon; for in the bounds of land units written down in eighth, the ninth and tenth centuries ponds are often mentioned as bound-marks. I have collected some of the evidence from these bounds and from place-names in general, in an Appendix (2).

The Anglo-Saxons had many names for ponds, giving a different name to each distinct type. The word of most general connotation was *mere*, which was also applied to natural lakes, e.g. Grasmere, Windermere, and ev·n occasionally to the sea (Mersea, Margate). Indeed, these meanings are the only ones recognized by Ekwall[2] and place-name students in general, although the meaning 'pond' is, as will be seen, both more common and proven up to the hilt. In composition *mere* is often confused with *mōr*, 'moor, waste upland, fen', so that we get in modern spelling the forms Cranmore, Peasemore, Rockmoor. In the absence of early forms it is sometimes impossible to be certain that the second element is not in fact *mor*, for ponds on moors might be called after the moor.[3] But that the normal meaning of *mere* in Wessex was 'pond' can be proved by the identification of some *mere*-names with ponds that still exist. Thus Rockmoor Pond still exists at the present[4] meeting-place of the counties of Hants, Wilts and Berks, and the parishes of Vernham's Dean, Linkenholt, Buttermere and Combe. In A.D. 863 it was called *throcmere*,[5] in 961 *th(o)rocmere*[6]

---

[1] Two wells in the chalk were found in the Romano-British village of Woodcuts by General Pitt-Rivers (*Excavations*, I, 1887, 27–8, Plate v). Both were dry and their bottoms considerably (12 to 33 feet) above the existing water-level in adjacent wells. One (136 feet deep) is dated by Prof. Hawkes (*Arch. Journ.*, CIV, 45) to c. A.D. 150–175; the other 188 feet deep with a Romano-British bucket on the bottom, proving use, is assigned to his Phase III of the village which falls within the fourth century.

[2] *Oxford Dictionary of English Place-names*, 1936, 307, s.v. *mere*.

[3] Blackmoor, Hants, was a pond so called (called 'stagnum' and spelt 'Blackemere' in the tenth century); Blackmoor, Dorset, a royal forest, was a moor (Blakemor, A.D. 1205); see Ekwall, s.v.

[4] The county boundary was altered in living memory by the transference of Combe from Hants to Berks.

[5] Birch, *Cart. Sax.*, 508 (bounds of Buttermere).

[6] Birch, *Cart. Sax.*, 1080 (bounds of Hurstbourne Tarrant, including Vernham's Dean).

and in 1410 Trokkemere.[7] The identification is quite certain, and the pond when I last saw and photographed it some forty years ago was a pleasant spot, overhung with trees and overgrown with flowering frog-bit. It is encircled by a high artificial bank.

Another *mere* whose identification with an existing pond is certain is the *risc mære* of A.D. 909 in the bounds of Bradley.[8] This is now called Rushmoor Pond (Plate 7), and lies at the junction of five roads and of the parishes of Bradley, Wield and Bentworth (Hants 34 NE.). The name, whose meaning is obvious, is quite common; there are five other examples given in my list, most of which are the names of ponds which still exist.

The list of *meres* in Appendix 2 will, I think, provide conclusive proof that *mere* was applied in pre- and post-Conquest times to ponds. I call special attention to the position of some of them, on the highest points in their neighbourhood. If further evidence should be asked for, I might well reply by another question—if these *meres* are not ponds, what are they? There are now practically no natural lakes in the south of England,[9] the nearest approach to lakes being those small shallow expanses of water that accumulate after rain on the heather-covered gravel plateaux of the Tertiary country, such as Ocknell and Janesmoor ponds in the New Forest; and these have no bank round them. It would be impossible to find a more unlikely (and geographically impossible) position for a lake than the tops of these chalk ridges, as Ekwall recognized.

At the north-west corner of Conholt Park is a large round pond called Ashmore Pond. It lies a few yards south of Chute Causeway, the great curve made by the Roman road (Winchester–Marlborough) round the steep-sided coombs of Hippenscombe. In A.D. 1300 it was called Asshemere[10], and formed one of the bound-marks of the Bailiwick of Hippenscombe in Savernake Forest. The name means the pond of the ash tree, and occurs again in Ashmore, Dorset, where in the middle of the village is another of these big round embanked ponds. They exist also in the villages of Buttermere and Dummer, both well attested *mere* names; the pond at Buttermere has the name 'Buttermere Pond' on the map. We may safely conclude that these three villages owe their names to the ponds which still exist there. It should be of interest to the people of Buttermere to know that their pond is certainly more than 1,000 years old and possibly twice as much. But there are many others which, though not so well attested, may well be just as old. When we come to look at these upland villages we find that nearly every one of them has just such a pond in it. So too, of course, do many other non-upland villages; but they do not have *mere*-names; in other words, it was the pond which was there first and gave its name to the village. That being so, a reasonable probability is established that these ponds are of pre-Saxon origin. To prove this it is necessary to show that such ponds are found in Romano-British villages.

[7] *Proc. Hants Field Club*, IX, 267 (Perambulation of Vernham's Dean; sixteenth century copy at Winchester College). The first part seems to be OE. *throc*, a piece of timber on which the ploughshare is fixed; hence by transference of meaning, the trestles of a wooden bridge, as in Drockbridge. But it is extremely hard to see how such a word can be applied to a pond. Professor Ekwall (who does not recognize that *mere* also means 'pond') suggests (p. 444) that the meaning of our Rockmoor may be a 'lake with trestles for the support of a bridge, e.g., one for washing'. It is conceivable that such a wooden structure might have been made to facilitate access to the water, especially if the margin was clayey. Those who have tried to get fresh clear water from such ponds, especially where used by sheep and cattle, know how difficult it is to do so without some such aid.

[8] Birch, *Cart. Sax.*, II, 625, A.D. 909.

[9] There are of course a few natural lakes still surviving in valleys, such as that in the Test valley near Marsh Court, opposite Mottisfont; and even here a partly artificial origin is not to be ruled out. But in a state of nature there were probably a few such existing in the valleys of these chalk streams, as there are to-day in the valleys of the Somme and Marne and elsewhere in France.

[10] Crawford, *Andover District*, 82.

Those who are familiar with them—and there are (or were until recently) scores of them on the downs in the same state as when they were abandoned some 1600 years ago—will often have seen in them round and oval banked depressions, some of which were certainly ponds.[11] A good example is to be seen in the Romano-British village, a large one, of Knook, by the hill-fort there (Wilts 52 NE.). Another on Twyford Down near St Catherine's Hill, Winchester, has been proved by excavation to be Belgic (Iron cAge C, say about the beginning of the Christian Era or a little earlier).[12]

Two other good examples of these ponds may be mentioned. One is on Chettle Down near Farnham, Dorset (15 NW.). It lies on a plateau surrounded by the lynchets of prehistoric fields, through which a sunken field-track approaches it. In 1924–5 trenches were dug in it by the late Mr H. S. Toms, one of General Pitt-Rivers' former assistants; on a layer of chalk mud was found some Romano-British pottery, charcoal and burnt flints, and he concluded that 'for a long period in ancient times the Chettle Down depression served as a cattle pond', and was periodically cleaned out. Mr Toms' account was published in the Proceedings of the Dorset Natural History and Archaeological Society (Vol. LI, 1930, 194–203). Mr Toms was a pioneer in the study of these ancient ponds, in Cranborne Chase and in Sussex. The other pond is on Fognam Down, Ashbury, Berks (19 SW.), south of Ashdown Park and only a few yards south-west of the road from Lambourn to Ashbury. It too is surrounded on all sides by remains of prehistoric cultivation, some of the fields near the modern road still having rows of sarsens along them. A sunken field-track approaches it from the south, indicated on the map by the boundary between Wilts and Berks which follows it, turning west at the pond. This turn, and the fact that the boundary between Lambourn and Ashbury parishes comes up to and goes round the pond, shows that whoever laid out these boundaries recognized the pond as a landmark. Possibly it was then still functioning; it is now dry.

Ringmere[13] Pond on Bell Hill, Dorset (23 NE.) is another good example. The ancient settlement lies on the down to the east, in the midst of its fields; it also has a 'circus', but as I have not seen it I can say nothing about it. The pond is close to the boundary between the parishes of Okeford Fitzpaine and Turnworth and stands near the edge of the escarpment, at a height of 830 feet above the sea.

It is therefore suggested that these upland villages have either been continuously occupied since pre-Saxon times, or that they were re-occupied, after abandonment for a period, by early Saxon settlers. (That the upland regions of Hants and Berks were fairly thickly populated in pre-Saxon times is proved by the large areas covered by Celtic fields, mostly now again under plough, but all still visible on air-photographs.)[14] If one makes a list of the upland villages, using as a criterion whether the houses round the church are on the top of a hill[15]—an objective test—one finds that most of them fall outside the River Basin groups.[16] What is the significance of this? It means that, when the first Saxon settlers

[11] Such is probably the true nature of some of Hadrian Allcroft's 'circuses'. See his article on 'The Circus in Britain', *Arch. Journ.*, LXXIX, 1922, 173–215. But there remain some which, tested by the Curwens' excavations, were pronounced quite definitely NOT to be ponds (e.g., that at Binderton *Sussex Arch. Coll.*, LXVI, 163–71).

[12] *Proc. Hants Field Club*, XIII, 1936, 194–5.

[13] As spelt on Isaac Taylor's Map of Dorset, 1765. The spelling of the present Ordnance Maps is Ringmoor, an instance of the very common confusion between *mere* and *mor*. As *mere* is now obsolete and *moor* is not, the tendency for *mere* to be replaced by *moor* is accentuated.

[14] Air-photography, however, does not work after several centuries of ploughing over Celtic field-lynchets.

[15] i.e. not at the head of a dry valley.

[16] See my *Andover District*, 1922, Appendix C.

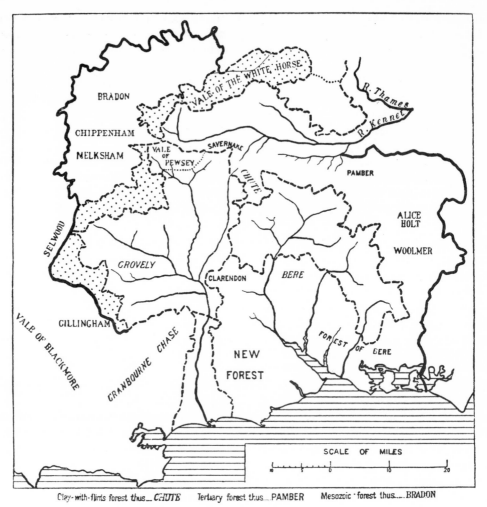

FIG. 20. Types and groups of settlements. (Reproduced by permission from Crawford's *The Andover District*, p. 50).

had chosen sites for their homes in the villages and laid out their boundaries, certain areas were left over, not included within these boundaries. The two biggest groups are those in Berkshire between the Thames and the Lambourne (with Baydon just beyond), and those in Hampshire between the Upper Test and the Weald between Alton and Petersfield (Fig. 20). This latter lies between the River Basin groups of the Test, Micheldever, Itchen and Meon valleys on the west and the chalk escarpment of the Weald on the east. Those villages lucky enough to be within this area were not absorbed (and presumably extinguished) by the River Basin groups, that is, by the normal Saxon settlements, and thus have survived to the present day. That will explain why they only have survived and not those which existed just as thickly on the ground in Dorset, Salisbury Plain and the Marlborough Downs. Salisbury Plain is divided up into fairly equal wedges by the permanent rivers meeting at Salisbury and Wilton, with the Till dividing the largest wedge into two convenient halves. The valley-settlements were therefore near enough together to have a common frontier down the middle of the intervening wedge. They thus squeezed out and obliterated any earlier upland settlements there may have been—and archaeological evidence shows that there were many. Thus on the Groveley ridge, between the Wylye and the Nadder, nearly every spur had its occupants, but not a single upland village has survived.[17]

This discussion started with ponds; and that it could do so and lead to such far-reaching conclusions is evidence of the importance of common things, especially those which (like water) are a fundamental need of existence. The objection may be raised that these upland *meres* were quite inadequate to supply a community with water, and that in any case the people must have been fools not to use other sources. Primitive people never act like fools, and the reply is that in some cases they certainly did make use of other sources, both better in quality and more abundant and dependable than *meres*. These were what the Saxons called *seaths*, spring-ponds, of which several can be identified.[18] A spring-pond is simply a large, deep hole dug in the bottom of a dry valley to tap the underground water which was often not far below the surface. One of the best examples is on Salisbury Plain, at the meeting-point of the parishes of Everley, Fittleton and Enford; it was called Igean seath in the bounds of Enford (A.D. 934),[19] Comesdeane Well (A.D. 1591)[20], and Sadler's Pit twenty years ago. It lies in the bottom of a dry valley, immediately below Coombe Down, on which is a large Romano-British settlement, surreounded by its fields. That the *seath* was used by the settlers is proved by the existence of a wide and deeply cut track, testifying prolonged use, leading to it from the village down the side of the hill.[21] Like so many of these spring-ponds its true nature has been forgotten, and both it and another half a mile further up the valley to the north-west are called 'Old chalk pit' on the map. (People do not dig chalk-pits in the bottoms of valleys but in the sides.)

There is (or was) a huge spring-pond near Winchester in King's Worthy, half a mile north-east of Hookpit Farm, not far from the head of a side valley which ends southwards on the Itchen at King's Worthy village. Here again there was a Romano-British settlement on the hill immediately above to the south, surrounded by fields; and from it a hollow way runs down to the pond. I visited the site in November 1922, before it was submerged by bungalows and prefabs, and found the head of a Romano-British bone pin on the site of the settlement.

Another spring-pond lies in a ploughed field near the head of the Somborne Valley; it is called *deopan delle* in the Saxon bounds of Crawley, and the name survives as Dibdel, applied to the two adjacent fields.[22] There is another in a side valley half a mile to the south. The Saxon name is unusual, for *del* means chalk-pit, the name often applied by the Ordnance Survey to spring-ponds; it merely means that they did not trouble (in either case) to find out its exact nature and called it simply 'pit', which of course it is.

[17] For a fuller treatment of this area and Cranborne Chase see my article 'Our Debt to Rome?' in *Antiquity*, II, 1928, 173–88.
[18] For an excellent account (with plan) of a spring-pond on Rockbourne Down, Hants, near a Roman dwelling, see Heywood Sumner's *Excavations on Rockbourne Down*, 1914, 7–12 [Bodleian ref. G.A. Hants 8° 226 (9)].
[19] Birch, *Cart. Sax.*, II, 705.
[20] *Wilts Arc. Mag.*, VI, 194 (Survey of Everley in the 2nd Book of D. of L. Surveys in the P.R.O.).
[21] See my air-photo and account in *Wessex from the Air*, Plate 22.
[22] Names found on the Tithe-map by Dr Grundy, *Arch. Journ.*, LXXXI, 1924, 44.

The digging of a spring-pond implies a certain elementary knowledge of the behaviour of streams in the chalk country. These chalk streams rise in the bottoms of their valleys, but at different points in different seasons. The source at one time may be a mile or two, and even more, above the source at another. There is a normal seasonal fluctuation, the streams usually reaching their highest point about May or June, when the previous winter's rain has had time to percolate—a process taking about six months. After periods of excessive rain the source mounts far up the valley, and the river flows for some weeks along the normally dry upper portion. Conversely a prolonged drought lowers the source and dries up the upper reaches of a normally perennial stream. After the dry summer of 1921 I saw the bed of the Kennet quite dry just above Marlborough; and after the wet winter of 1936 I saw a spring-pond full of water at Cold Henley. It was in a valley that is usually dry for a mile further down; it is called Winterdane on the Award Map of Whitchurch, and is the *wintres dæne*[23] of the Saxon bounds of the same in A.D. 909. A strong stream flowed down the bottom of the ploughed field and across the Whitchurch–Kingsclere road at Cold Henley. The usual source seems (from the map) to be at a point just north of where it is crossed by the old road called the Harroway, at about 270 feet above O.D. The spring-pond is on the 300-foot contour line, so that even if the water-table stood formerly at the same level it would only be necessary to dig down 30 feet to tap it.[24] But Pitt-Rivers' dry well at Woodcuts shows that the water-table stood higher in Romano-British times.

There is a fine spring-pond on the bounds of Everley and Pewsey called *Ceolbrihtes seath* in the bounds of Everley (A.D. 940), and perhaps 'Carrell pit' in the bounds of 1591. It lies at the bottom of a valley near its head, and is a deep embanked pit rather like *Igean seath*.

The word *seath* is the same as the modern 'seethe' and implies something which boils up. It was not therefore necessarily confined to spring-ponds, but might be used of any source that welled up strongly, though for such the word *æwielm* or *æwiell* was more usual. The source of the stream which rises at Sydmonton and flows north by Ecchinswell to join the Enborne near Headley, is called *Ceacgan seath* in the bounds of Burghclere of 943.[25]

There are two other words used by the Saxons to describe ponds. One is *sol*, which Ekwall defines as a 'muddy place, wallowing place for animals'. He cites *heortsol* (hart's soil) as an example, to which I would add *bulloces sole* (A.D. 900) on the parish boundary of (and near) Woodmancott, midway between Winchester and Basingstoke, Hants.[26] Sole Pond, formed above and by the causeway of the Roman road (Gloucester–Silchester) in Welford, Berks, is probably another example.[27] A third may be Bullock's Hole Farm near Salisbury on the Avon Valley. An early reference may be the 'stagnum quendam cuius vocabulum est *ceabban solo*' in the bounds of Crux Easton (A.D. 796).[28] The word is still in use occasionally as 'soil', and occurs frequently in early books on hunting.[29] The

---

[23] The name is presumably equivalent to *winter burna*, which is usually interpreted as meaning 'stream that flows in winter only'; but in fact such intermittent streams never do this.

[24] Actually a foot or two less, for the table rises as it approaches the higher ground.

[25] Birch, *Cart. Sax.*, II, 787; *Andover District*, 77.

[26] Birch, *Cart. Sax.*, II, 596 (Myceld=fer, including a very large area).

[27] *Man and his Past*, 1921, 180.   [28] Birch, *Cart. Sax.*, I, 282; *Andover District*, 68.

[29] See, for instances, the *Master of the Game*, by Edward, second duke of York; the oldest English book on hunting; ed. by W. A. Baillie-Grohman, 1904 [Bod., 1898, b 3].

5a. (*above*) Sheep-tracks near Cowthalley Castle, Lanarkshire
5b. (*below*) Buffalo paths (revealed by snow) at Gratton Coulee, near Wainwright, Alberta,
52° 48′ N, 110° 45′ W.; see pages 60, 214

6a. (*above*) The road at Atmur showing deeply-trodden tracks made by camels and donkeys; see page 61

6b. (*below*) The road south of Shereik, an example of a hollow way actually in use, and still forming. Here it is crossing the bed of a wadi; see page 58

word occurs also in the place-names Bradsole, Kent (broad soil), Grazeley, Berks (badger's soil), Sollom, Lancs, (doubtful) and Soyland, Yorks (soil-land).[30]

The other pond-word is *pōl*, a common element in place-names, denoting a pool, a deep place on a river and also a tidal stream. The best example of its meaning is one which is also an outstanding example of the value of field-work for the study of place-names. I have already published a full account in *Antiquity*.[31] The site is exactly five miles south-west of Carfax (Oxford), on a stream that forms the boundary between the parishes of Appleton and Bessels Leigh. Here in a wood called Lower England's Copse I found the *styrian pol* mentioned in the bounds of Besselsleigh (A.D. 959) and Eaton (*æt Cumenoran* A.D. 968). The expression means the 'pool of the sturgeon', but *styria* is also used of other fish, and it may mean no more than 'fish-pond'. The pool consists of a rectangular trough 160 feet long by 30 feet wide, fed by an intake from a reservoir (now dry) behind a small artificial dam. The chief interest lies in the documentation of a field-site, which is rarely possible, and in the fact that it can be assigned to the pre-Conquest period, which is particularly poor in earthworks of any kind. The connotation of Old English *pōl* is also enriched; to Ekwall's definition we can now add '(fish)pond'.

There are two words, 'flash' and 'plash', which are also pond-names. 'Flash' goes back only to the Middle English period, but 'plash' is the Old English *plæsc* which is found in the place-names Plaish, Plash and Melplash. Both words seem to have the same meaning, of a 'shallow piece of standing water'. In the New Forest the name 'flash' is given to those very shallow ponds that form themselves, through the action of wind-driven wavelets, on the often waterlogged plateau gravels. Ocknell Pond, Janesmoor and Flash Pond on Beaulieu Heath are examples. There is a pond at Aldershot called Rushmoor Flash. On the Bath road in Savernake Forest just east of the third milestone from Marlborough, is a pond called Flashetts, which may be a diminutive (and unrecorded) form. 'Plaish' is the name of some houses on the Lukely Brook, Carisbrooke.

That concludes the survey of ponds and their names. For completeness I add a few paragraphs on other Old English water-names. They are of interest to the field archaeologist when studying the topography of a region that is fortunate enough to contain Saxon boundaries—a prolific source of objects of interest in the field. The subject is of course fully dealt with in the standard book, Ekwall's *English River-names*, in the introductions to the English Place-name Society's county volumes, and in the Society's Introductory Volume on the chief elements in English place-names. I shall therefore confine my remarks to minor names and some wrong notions about some of them.

The Old English word *well* (also spelt *wiell*, *wæll*) meant both a spring and a stream, and it is often very difficult to keep the two meanings apart. Wells in the modern sense, deep shafts from which water was drawn in a bucket, were probably rare in Saxon times. The sense of 'spring' is obviously that meant in such names as Seven Wells.

Old English *flōde* is defined by Ekwall as meaning 'a channel, perhaps also an intermittent spring'; Dr Grundy has, however, I think, made out his case for the meaning 'intermittent stream'.[32] A typical example, though the name is not known to be applied to it, is the inter-

[30] For further remarks on *sol* see my article in *Arch. Journ.*, LXXVIII, 35.

[31] See *Antiquity*, IV, 1930, 480–3 (a Saxon Fish-pond near Oxford), and Birch, *Cart. Sax.*, No. 977, 1221 (Aelfthrithe dic).

[32] See, for example, his remarks on two Berkshire examples, *maer floda* and *cytel floda* (boundary spring and kettle spring) on the bounds of Farnborough, Berks, in *Berks, Bucks and Oxon. Arch. Journ.*, XXIX, 1925, 102–3.

mittent stream along Winterdene which (as described above) occasionally rises in the spring
pond at Cold Henley. That pond is in a side valley whose head is at Ashley Warren Farm,
three miles to the north. The main valley which it joins at Cold Henley is that followed
by the Newbury–Winchester road through the village of Litchfield. Where that valley
widens out into the plain near Beacon Hill are the Seven Barrows—actually ten or more
—some of which belong to the Early Bronze Age. Here in the winter of 1872–3 'a spring
burst forth and turned the turnpike into a river course as far as Litchfield'.[33] Now it is
just here that occurs the bound-mark *botnes floda* (bottom's flood) in the bounds of Burghclere.[34] Here, therefore, if the identification is correct, is an excellent example of the meaning 'intermittent stream'. The root meaning of *floda* is that which flows or fluctuates, and
appears in 'flood-tide' and in the modern 'flood' which implies an exceptional rise of water.

Old English *fleot* is a kindred word, applied to tidal estuaries and rivers up which the
tide flows. It is now 'fleet', and there are many examples of the name all round the coast,
e.g. Ebbsfleet (Kent), Shoesfleet[35] (now Palmer's Brook, south-east of Barton, Isle of
Wight), Pukefluut and Tintelesfluut[36] on the Medina estuary near Werrar Farm.

Old English *lacu* means a stream, not a lake. There are many inland examples of its use,
generally applied to quite small streams. Ignorance of the true meaning has led to erroneous
identifications with mill-ponds and fish-ponds. The Ordnance Map marks Ruscombe Lake
(Berks 30 SE.) as a district name applied to a low marshy tract; actually it is the name of the
stream there. The stream forming the boundary between the parishes of Longworth and
Charney Bassett is called *gemaer lac* (boundary stream) in a Saxon charter. The word
'lake' was in use locally to describe streams down to the days when schools obliterated
such usages. In the harbours of Langstone, Portsmouth, Lymington and Newtown the
tidal creeks are called 'lakes', where we should have expected them to be called 'fleets'.

Old English *rith*, *rithig* means a small stream and occurs often in composition, e.g. in
the place-names Meldreth, Shepreth, Hendred, Childrey, Shottery, Peckham Rye. The
longer form *rithig* occurs in Cropredy and Fulready. *Rith* too is applied to tidal creeks
in the harbours of Langstone and Chichester (Binners Rithe, Fowley Rithe, Nore Rithe,
Mill Rithe).

The word 'pond' itself only appears in Old English in composition, the commonest
form being *pund-fald*, a pin-fold or penning in which animals were herded or kept from
straying. Its application to water only became common after the Norman Conquest when
water was *pounded* behind dams to form mill-ponds or fish-ponds. But it *was* used in this
sense in Old English. An example occurs in the Wylye Valley above Wilton. The Saxon
bounds of South Newton[37] mention two bound-marks, *pynding forda* and *pynding mersc*
which Dr Grundy correctly locates, the latter at a point just under half a mile due south
of South Newton Church. His identification is confirmed by an old map of about 1800
of the parish of South Newton Without which gives the name Pin Marsh to a parcel of
water meadows exactly at this point. Now it so happens that this is exactly where the
theoretical line of the Roman road from the Groveley ridge to Old Sarum *should* cross the
Wylye Valley. When searching (unsuccessfully) for traces of it (and before I had come

[33] J. Stevens, *History of St Mary Bourne*, 69, note 1.
[34] Birch, *Cart. Sax.*, II, 787.
[35] Cal. Inq. Misc. III, No. 64, A.D. 1355, V. C. H. Hants v, 183.
[36] Hist. MSS. Comm., 4th Report, 454 (bounds of Werrore).
[37] Birch, *Cart. Sax.*, 782, A.D. 934.

across the old map), I found a flint causeway a quarter of a mile long extending right across the valley from the parish boundary and road (*portweg* in the bounds) to the road at spot-level 187 on the east side, forming a sort of low dam. This is undoubtedly the origin of the name *pynding*, but whether the causeway is that of the Roman road or one made in Saxon times for some utilitarian purpose I do not know. The marsh on the old map occurs *below* the dam, and South Newton Mill above it. Here, then, we have an instance showing how the word 'pond' developed from Old English *pund* as the name of 'a small body of still water of artificial formation' (O.E.D.). Ponds are water-pounds.

CHAPTER 12

Camps

I HAVE HEADED this chapter 'Camps' because that is the name which appears on the Ordnance Maps and is still used quite often in conversation. But it is a legacy of the older archaeologists who regarded them as merely temporary refuges, and it would be a good thing if we could give up using it. We cannot do so unless we can find a better word to take its place, and that so far has not been done. On the Ordnance Maps 'camp' is applied to earthworks of many different kinds, from Maiden Castle, down to such tiny earthworks as Lidbury and those on Aughton Down and Martin Down, whose only common attribute is that their banks and ditches enclose an area. When I went to the Ordnance Survey in 1920 I had to decide whether to retain the word 'camp' or abolish it, and I decided to retain it, for there was no substitute available.[1] As implying settlement (albeit temporary) it was more definite than 'earthwork', the only other possible word, which does not. The essence of that which we wish to connote is 'habitation plus defence'. The Saxons called such places, whether still inhabited or deserted, 'burh', and sometimes 'eorth-burh', earth-bury, and this would not be a bad term to adopt, though only applicable in stoneless regions, and not everywhere even there. Perhaps the Old English words 'fastness' and 'stronghold' come nearest to covering all the various sites, but even these words are not universally applicable, and they suggest the work of armies or armed bands rather than of tillers of the soil. Having thus explained its inadequacy, I shall therefore call these defended habitations 'camps'; the word may be unsatisfactory, but it does at any rate convey a meaning to most people who have used the Ordnance Maps in the field.

Camps[2] were classified by the Earthworks Committee as being of three kinds—promontory, contour and plateau. The distinction between them is of course merely superficial, and with the progress of knowledge it has lost whatever use it may once have had, except that between promontory and other camps. Nor was the distinction drawn between contour and plateau camps ever at all clear. Moreover, since the Earthworks Committee drew up its scheme of classification, a wholly new type has been recognized—that of the causewayed neolithic camps. There was a time when all camps were regarded as 'neolithic', but that was when the term had only the vaguest connotation, covering the then dimly-

[1] 'Hill-fort' would do for many 'camps', but not for those on low ground, such as the Dyke Hills at Dorchester-on-Thames or Tournerbury on the coast of Hayling Island. 'Fort' alone is far too military. 'Ringwall', the German word, would hardly do, for a wall in English does not suggest earth, but rather bricks and stones; nor could it be used of rectangular enclosures or promontory forts.

[2] A useful general account of Iron Age camps is that by Christopher Hawkes in *Antiquity*, Vol. V, 1931, 60–97. Neolithic camps were first described by Dr Cecil Curwen in *Antiquity*, Vol. IV, 1930, 22–54. Both articles are fully illustrated by plans and photographs. I have drawn largely upon them in the present chapter.

perceived period before the Romans. Then in 1908 and 1909 Mr and Mrs Cunnington carried out excavations at Knap Hill, Wiltshire, between Marlborough and Devizes. 'They were struck with the fact that the rampart, which is deficient on the steepest side of the hill, is interrupted by at least six gaps, opposite each of which the ditch is broken by a causeway of undisturbed chalk—evidently an intentional feature. . . . In the filling of the ditch they found a strange, new type of pottery together with evidence of local flint-knapping, pieces of sarsen, and other relics of occupation.' They concluded that the pottery 'cannot be of later date than the Bronze Age, and it is quite likely that [it is] neolithic'.

Then a similar causewayed camp was discovered on Windmill Hill near Avebury. The history of its discovery has not been recorded, nor unfortunately has Mr Alexander Keiller ever published any account of his extensive excavations there. Attention was first drawn to the site by the Rev. H. G. O. Kendall,[3] then rector of the adjacent parish of Winterbourne Bassett. He was an enthusiastic 'flinter', and one of his best hunting-grounds was the ploughed slope of Windmill Hill. Eventually he began to dig there and wrote[4] to me, saying he had found neolithic pottery. Knowing that his knowledge of pottery was not so good as of flints, I was sceptical; it was then common to dub all prehistoric pottery 'neolithic'. He asked me to help him with the survey of the section of the ditch which he had dug, and having previously promised to do so I proceeded, rather reluctantly, to Winterbourne Bassett, bicycling the seven miles from Marlborough loaded with a level and staff. The moment I arrived I was taken into his study, where he showed me pieces of pottery which, to my surprise, obviously resembled those from Knap Hill. I immediately recognized them as being neolithic, for there were obvious resemblances to the few fragments of neolithic pottery then known, which included some sherds I had myself found in 1914 on the old surface under a long barrow at Wexcombe.[5] The next morning we went to the hill, and I had the good luck to be present when Mr Kendall, who was doing his own digging, found a large fragment of neolithic pottery right on the bottom of the ditch, below the rapid chalk silting. This was conclusive proof of the neolithic age of the camp.

When Mr Kendall began to dig, only one rampart had been recognized. He soon detected obvious traces of another one, inside the first and concentric with it, but separated by a considerable space. He showed it to me, and we found that this too was interrupted by causeways. We retired to the top of one of the barrows to eat our lunch, and while we were contemplating the scene Mr Kendall spotted yet a third innermost circle. We found that it too was causewayed. Altogether it was a good day's work.

The history of how Windmill Hill emerged from complete obscurity to become the classic type-site of the Neolithic A period has been told, because it shows what can be achieved by field-work. It was 'flinting'—a branch of field archaeology—that took Mr Kendall there; and although excavation developed later, it was surface observation that revealed its characteristic features, the causeways. The later history is not relevant, but may be told in a few words, and is not, I think, on record. An infamous proposal was made by some big business concern to erect a forest of radio masts on Windmill Hill and the

---

[3] He published accounts of his flint-finds in the *Proceedings of the Prehistoric Society of East Anglia*.
[4] I gave his letters, which now have some historic interest, to Mr Keiller.
[5] Now in Devizes Museum, Newbury Museum and in the Harvard University Museum. The excavations were carried out in co-operation with Professor E. A. Hooton of the Peabody Museum, but were interrupted by the outbreak of war in 1914. My notes and records were unfortunately all destroyed by bombing in November 1940, and no published record of the dig can now be composed except from memory. There is a brief note in *Wilts Arch. Mag.*, XLIX, Dec. 1940, 165.

environs, and the whole area was actually pegged out. The news was released, as such news always is, just before the August holidays, when parliament was about to rise; I did what I could to raise protests, but the local society ratted, and it was difficult. The scheme was eventually dropped, not on grounds of amenity or archaeology, but because the R.A.F objected to high masts near their aerodromes on Salisbury Plain. But I wanted to be sure that such a threat should not occur again, and I persuaded Mr Keiller to buy the hill.

The discovery at Windmill Hill of a second example of a causeway-camp and of a type of contemporary pottery that had already been found at the first (Knap Hill) naturally made one look for others. I managed to get an air-photograph taken in 1925 of the Trundle near Goodwood and the result showed very plain remains of a faint inner rampart and also traces of another which had been obliterated by the outer one except at one point. I sent the air-photo to Dr Cecil Curwen, expressing the opinion that the older circles, if excavated, would prove to belong to the neolithic period like those at Windmill Hill. In order to test this Dr Curwen began to excavate there, proving that this opinion was correct. He continued his excavations during 1928, exposing the causeways and finding much neolithic pottery.[6]

From the point of view of field archaeology, these causeway-camps are particularly interesting, because they are recognizable on the surface without excavation. The interrupted ditch, with the opposing gaps in the bank, can be seen without any difficulty; the only point to determine is whether the causeways are genuine or merely the result of some later attempt to fill in the ditch. That too can be discovered without excavation, as it was at the Trundle by the device of 'bosing', which must now be described.[7]

'Bosing' is a method of percussion; the ground is hit with a rammer or with the central (socketed) portion of an iron pick held vertically. When the ground hit is undisturbed the sound is a 'thud'; when it consists of the loose material filling of a ditch or pit it is a 'thoomp'. The 'boser', says Dr Curwen, 'can easily be made of a narrow cylindrical tin filled with about 8 lb. of lead, a short piece of iron piping being embedded in the lead to serve as a socket for the handle. This is an improvement on a navvy's rammer, as the latter has a wide base; the narrower the base, the more concentrated is the blow, and the clearer is the percussion note obtained, especially on a sloping surface. The ideal would be to have a hemispherical base, but this is not easily obtained.' Though so far tested chiefly in chalk districts, the method will probably work in other, especially rocky, regions. The field-worker will find a 'boser' invaluable. The sling can easily be made from a loop of 4-inch webbing with a leather socket for the base of the tool. 'In using this instrument the handle should not be gripped by the hand at the actual moment of impact with the ground, as that jars the arm and damps the vibrations. The boser should either be allowed to drop from the hand or else be thrown down with a flick of the wrist and caught again on the rebound. The resulting vibration is appreciated not only by the ear as a 'thud' or 'thoomp', but by the feet as well. The method is useless on cultivated ground, as the boser simply sinks into the mould without producing any vibration; and it is also defeated if the undisturbed chalk is covered by a *deep* layer of mould under the grass, as this itself yields a booming note.'

[6] Reports in *Sussex Aich. Coll.*, LXX, 33–85; LXXII, 100–49.
[7] See Crawford, *Man and his Past*, 1921, 214; *Antiquity*, II, 1928, 258; IV, 1930, 30–1. The term, introduced by Dr Cecil Curwen, is derived, according to him, from a northern Irish provincialism, bose, an adjective meaning 'hollow-sounding'. The quotation is from Dr Curwen's article on Neolithic camps in the last reference.

Though first practised by General Pitt-Rivers and his staff, bosing was in actual fact the invention of one of the diggers employed by him.[8] It was used over the ground near Wor Barrow to try to discover traces of habitation where the surface of the ground was perfectly smooth, without any depression or even discoloration of the grass. By beating with the flat surface of a pick, a filled-in ditch, which the General named the Angle Ditch, was found and excavated. The General records that the discovery was made by the deeper sound given by the blows of the pick over spots in which the ground was comparatively loose below, as it always is in chalk soil where a filled-in ditch exists, and he added that the method, though applicable to grass-grown downland, was useless on cultivated ground. When I was digging the Roundwood barrows in 1920[9] I had in my tent a set of his *Excavations in Cranborne Chase* and I decided to test the method. There is no reference to bosing in my report, because the ditch of the disc-barrow on which I made the experiment was found first by observation of the growth of the grass over it. But the following year I was able with Mr Hooley to construct a plan of the complex of ditches, wholly invisible on the surface, at Worthy Down. When compared with the results of excavation there was little to alter.[10] The method employed was to run a line of bosings across the ground, and when the sound indicated that one was crossing a ditch, a peg was inserted on each side to mark the limits of the 'thoomp' and the presumed edges of the ditch. The process was repeated further on until the whole course of the ditch was thus demarcated. Pits were similarly located by two traverses across each, at right angles to each other.

Bosing was used extensively by Colonel Hawley at Stonehenge, and later by Mr Alexander Keiller, who had a special boser made for use at Windmill Hill.

This excursus on bosing arose from its close connection with the causeway-camps whose interruptions can so well be tested thereby. The purpose of these remains, however, obscure. It seems curious to make an enclosure whose object must have been protection, and to leave so many gaps in it by which an enemy (human or animal) could enter. Some light was thrown on the problem by Dr Curwen's second season of excavations at the Trundle in 1930. He found that round the margin of the pits forming the second neolithic ditch (whose plan was spiral) were shallow post-holes, two on each side and one at each end. These holes were not deep enough to have held a stockade, but might well have been intended for roof-supports, and he concluded that 'the pits were dwellings, and the holes are contemporary with them, and probably formed part of some scheme for roofing them with long ridge-roofs.'[11] Similar holes have been found in Yorkshire and in Germany, associated with neolithic pottery. The outermost and innermost ditches showed no such post-holes, and were therefore presumably for defence only. The problem of the causeways, which occur in *all* the ditches, still remains therefore. A possible explanation is suggested by a photograph of the camp of the Beni Mguild tribe in Morocco,[12] noticed by Dr Curwen.

[8] According to my recollection of a conversation on this subject with Mr H. S. Toms. One of the General's assistants, Mr St George Gray, in a letter dated 20 Jan. 1949, replying to one of mine, stated: 'I did not know that any special workman in the General's employ was responsible for the idea, and for the tool; my recollection is that we occasionally used a pick-axe for the purpose, and I have done that myself in connection with the Angle Ditch close to Wor Barrow.' I have also to thank Mr St George Gray for kindly sending me typed extracts from the General's *Excavations in Cranborne Chase* (vol. IV, 59, 102), where he refers to this method. There is also a short allusion in the General's Presidential Address to the Archaeological Institute at Dorchester in 1897 (*Arch. Journ.*, LIV, 322.).

[9] See *Proc. Hants Field Club*, IX (2), 189–209.

[10] *Antiquity*, II, 1928, 258. For Mr Hooley's excavations see *Proc. Hants Field Club*, X, 1929, 178–92.

[11] *Sussex Arch. Coll.*, LXXII, 108–9.

[12] *Antiquity*, VII, 1933, 344–5, Plate iv. See also XI, 1937, 210–12, referring to similar prehistoric dispositions of huts in the province of Kiev, U.S.S.R., and Gordon Childe, *Proc. Preh. Soc.*, 1949, 186 (Kolomoschina). See Figs. 21 and 22 here.

The tents are arranged in a circle in the middle of which the flocks and herds are kept, to protect them from raiders and from straying. The space between each tent is filled with thorny brush. It had already been suggested by the Abbé Breuil that the people of Windmill Hill lived in the ditches there, thus accounting for the very abundant remains that the excavators found in those ditches. This explanation seems on the whole to satisfy the

FIG. 21. Reconstruction of a Tripolje neolithic village. (Reproduced by permission from 33 Bericht d. Röm-Germ. Komm., Abb. 6, p. 39).

conditions best. It agrees with the presumption, supported by evidence, that the neolithic people of Britain were chiefly pastoral.

Causeway-camps as a distinct type had not been recognized when the Earthworks Committee drew up their classification, which was a premature effort. Classification is the last, not the first, act when you are marshalling a large number of facts. You cannot classify until you have come to know at least the majority of the items, and in those days I am quite sure that no single person or committee had the requisite knowledge. But their group called promontory-forts was a useful one. Fundamentally, of course, a promontory-fort is merely a camp that is incomplete, relying upon some natural feature such as a precipice, a steep slope, water or swamp on one or more of its sides. Such camps are very common all over the world, often consisting of no more than a rampart and ditch across the neck of a spur. Good typical examples of important camps that are promontory-forts are Hengistbury Head and the Dyke-hills, Dorchester (Oxon). In the rocky Highland Zone, and especially in Scotland, there are an immense number of minor examples; and the cliff-castles of Cornwall belong to the same type.

Further, it was impossible really to know the camps until a fairly large number of them had been subjected to fairly complete excavation. When the Earthworks Committee began to operate very few camps had even been dug into, much less properly excavated.[13]

[13] The work of the Cunningtons excepted, of course; but it began a little after this. Dymond's work at Worlebury was chiefly survey, though very well done. Pitt-Rivers excavated Winkelbury Camp in Cranborne Chase and Cissbury and Highdown in Sussex. For the first see *Excavations in Cranborne Chase*, and for the other two *Archaeologia*, XLII, 53–76; *Journ. Anthr. Inst.*, V, 357–89. He also excavated at Caburn, Sussex, in 1877–8 (*Arch.*, XLVI, 423–95) and at the medieval hill-fort of Caesar's Camp near Folkestone (*Arch.*, XLVII, 429–65).

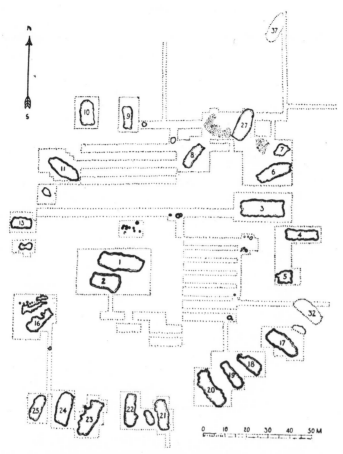

FIG. 22. Plan of a Tripolje neolithic village (fig. 21). (Reproduced by permission from Childe, *Prehistoric Migrations in Europe*, fig. 81.)

Now that this defect has been to some extent made good, certain types begin to emerge. At one end are the imposing oppida of Hertfordshire and Dorset—Wheathampstead, Prae Wood, Braughing, Maiden Castle—which were certainly tribal centres; to this group belong also the pre-Roman predecessors of certain towns whose names indicate as much, such as Sorbiodunum (Old Sarum) where great ramparts still remain. Not much different except perhaps politically are many other big camps like Hod Hill, Hambledon, Badbury and scores of others. All these were the defended habitations of large communities; their interior was a mass of huts, and in size, though hardly in function, they must have resembled small towns. But in fact they were probably no more than large, self-sufficient villages.[14] Next come those single-ramparted camps of which Little Woodbury near Salisbury may be regarded as the type, although its rampart has long been ploughed flat. These were simply farms standing in the midst of their fields, which here began immediately

[14] I agree with Childe, as against Wheeler, in making this distinction, and regarding e.g. Maiden Castle as a large village, not a town.

beyond the rampart. Air-photography has revealed many crop-sites that probably belong to this class, which on *a priori* grounds may be assumed to have been more numerous than the first. It may also be conjectured that the Rounds (or stone-walled enclosures) of Cornwall were defended farms whose stone-walled fields, often megalithic, still survive.[15] Traditionally the land was full of giants, living in castles and rich in pastoral wealth. Excavation has proved that Woodbury began in the Iron Age A, to which period such camps may provisionally be assigned.

At the other end of the series come the raths which are so common in Ireland. Professor Bersu's excavation of raths in the Isle of Man have shown that these were simply defended houses, the Dark Age equivalent of the moated homestead. There are no raths in England, but a sophisticated version may perhaps be seen in those Roman villas which, in the Oxford district, stood within a rectangular enclosure, though here the defence motive is less obvious. In the north of England and in Wales, where hostile raids were a constant menace, the few Roman villas that are known were all quite strongly defended by a rectangular earthwork.

Although it is convenient for purposes of classification to draw a distinction between the big camps, often on hill-tops, like Maiden Castle, and the little ones like Woodbury, it must not be forgotten that, socially regarded, the former is merely a larger edition of the latter. No doubt the increase in size involved all sorts of other differences in social and perhaps also in political organization within the community; but both were essentially defended settlements—fortified villages and farms. How and where the idea of such fortification originated is a fascinating problem which can only be touched on here. To search for a single origin is probably as incorrect as to look for a single ancestor. Yet there may be some sort of line of descent theoretically discernible, even if it be not possible to prove such by rigid scientific methods. We have already seen that the best analogy for the causewayed camps was found in the zareebas of nomads. Surely it is on *a priori* grounds probable that, in Europe at any rate, the earliest agriculturists would form their permanent settlements on the same lines as the temporary ones of their nomadic predecessors. Lehner long ago drew attention to the resemblance between the German causeway-camps and the neolithic Greek towns of Sesklo and Dimini, pointing out that the concentric walls pierced by radial alleys corresponded to the causeways of the earthen forts.[16] It is moreover to be observed that some of the early prehistoric forts of Central Europe, such as that on the Wittnauerhorn,[17] seem to use a ring of huts as the line of defence rather than a specially built rampart; and in many of our ramparted camps the huts follow the line of the rampart—though this may also be explained otherwise.[18] That is also the rule in the early Christian cashels, like Bangor (N. Ireland), which were simply hill-forts of a later age. That the device is of great antiquity is proved by its use in one of the oldest hill-forts known, at Mersin in Cilicia, the port of Tarsus.[19] Here

[15] See my article on 'The Work of Giants', which embodied a good deal of field-work, *Antiquity*, X, 1936, 162–74. This article was partly an expansion, with the added benefit of fourteen more years' experience of field-work, of an article I contributed to the *Wiltshire Gazette*, 13th November 1924.

[16] Cited by Curwen, *Sussex Arch. Coll.*, LXXII, 74.

[17] See *Antiquity*, XX, 1946, 4–8. Also at Sudbrook Camp, Monmouthshire, timber huts of the first century B.C. were arranged round the inside of the rampart, 'leaving the centre of the enclosure free for the disposal of stores or the corralling of cattle'. *Arch. Camb.*, XCIV, 1939, 55.

[18] Ib. id., XII, 1937, 210–11.

[19] *Antiquity*, XIII, 1939, 238–9, Plate ii. For city-walls in the Fertile Crescent and in Iraq see Mallowan, *Iraq*, VIII, 1946, 118–19.

the houses on level xvi, assigned by the discoverer to the middle of the fourth millenium B.C., were built in a row behind the town wall, which was five feet thick, and their flat roofs would have formed a continuous defensive platform. We may see exactly the same thing to-day in Tunisia, where the vault-towns like Medinine (Plate 12) and the adjacent villages are laid out in rectangles facing inwards, the backs of the vaults forming a continuous line of masonry just like a city wall. So too the Tripolitanian *kasrs* or fortified granaries perched on hilltops are defended by a surrounding wall of houses; the *kasrs* are certainly a very ancient institution, being mentioned by Diodorus Siculus.[20] In the Aures mountains of Algeria the same feature recurs; the town of Ouled Mansour is a promontory-fort, and that portion which faces the *col* of approach 'is defended by a lofty wall of stone—in reality the back of a number of its dwellings—which spans the spur from cliff to cliff and is penetrated by but one narrow gateway.[21] Does it not seem probable that the first city-wall may have been merely a reinforcement of the backs of a ring of houses? Such a re-inforcement would naturally be the last act in laying out a new site; the first would be the construction of dwellings; and even when, later, the idea of a wall or rampart as a separate entity had developed, it might still not be built until the builders had made huts to live in during the construction.[22] Even as late as our Middle Ages town walls were not built until long afterwards. Southampton had none for over 200 years after the town was established on its present site.[23] It required the stimulus of a destructive French raid to force the authorities to do what they should have done long before, and the same is prob-ably true of some prehistoric camps, whose ramparts were certainly strengthened when the menace of hostile invasion appeared.

The earthen ramparts which are now the first thing we think of when we speak of camps were often in their original state stone walls with a rubble core, and what we now see is but the grass-covered remnants of that core. Excavation, and even careful surface observation sometimes reveals on each side the protruding tops of a row of stones. Such protrusions can be seen, for instance, at Uffington Castle, close to the famous White Horse, and at Alfred's Castle not far away, where the walls were built of sarsen, the only stone available in this otherwise stoneless region. At Maiden Castle (Plate 8) the walls, quite un-suspected before digging, were of a size and excellence that was most impressive, and the stone had had to be quarried and transported several miles. Similar walls were revealed in the ramparts of Charlbury (Dorset),[24] Corley (Warwickshire),[25] Winterbourne (near Bristol) and several other places. It is certain that all camps in stony country will be found, on examination, to have had similar walls; and it should be one of the normal tasks of the field archaeologists to look for such when visiting them. Even in stoneless country, blocks of hard chalk may have been built up on the outer side; there is a hint of this at Ladle Hill. Where no possibility of using stone existed the rampart may have been held up by a struc-ture of hurdling and timber, as at Hollingbury in Sussex and perhaps at Blewburton, Berks. The gates of some camps—always the most vulnerable point—were certainly con-structed of timber, and very solidly constructed too, as the huge holes for the gate-posts testify.

[20] III, 49, 3. See Despois, *Le Djebel Nefousa*, 182, 201.
[21] *Antiquity*, I, 1927, 392, Plate iii.
[22] The evidence of Ladle Hill, an unfinished camp, is against this.
[23] There was an earlier earthen rampart that may have been made at or soon after its establishment.
[24] *Ant. Journ.*, XXIII, 1943, 98–121.   [25] *Trans. Birmingham Arch. Soc.*, LII, 1930 ,282–7.

British camps, therefore, accepting the existing nomenclature, fall roughly into two classes—neolithic causeway camps and Iron Age defended farms and villages; while in the Highland Zone and in Ireland are a multitude of defended sites (often labelled 'fort' on the maps) where there stood a single house only. Between the causeway camps and the others is a gap that has not yet been bridged. With the single exception of Rams Hill in Berks[26] no habitation-site of the Middle Bronze Age is known. It has been suggested[27] that the latter was a dry period when life on the chalk downs became difficult and the once forested lowlands less formidable. There are certainly many Middle Bronze Age finds from the Midland counties, but there are nearly, or quite as many from the barrows on the downs. Probably the predominantly pastoral regime of the earlier period continued until the Late Bronze Age and subsequent invaders introduced an improved agriculture. The unsettled conditions made it necessary to erect defences round places of temporary or permanent habitation. The first was usually a wooden palisade. Later an earthen bank was thrown up. From these early beginnings came eventually the massive defences of the typical later Iron Age hill-forts. The beach-head defences on Bindon Hill consisting of a long linear earthwork along the brow of the hill and an unfinished rampart across the western end, above the harbour of Lulworth Cove, show that about 400 B.C. the invaders brought with them into this island an already well-developed art of military defence. No doubt the art was soon learned by the islanders, so that it is not necessary to regard the earliest defences of such sites as Quarley as made by the invaders, but rather as made against them.[28]

But we must beware of allowing our legitimate interest in the defences to occupy too much of our attention. Now they are often the sole visible remains, but they were only the protective shell, the clothes, so to speak, of the community that lived within. In studying the armour we must not forget the man inside it. The itinerant merchant trading his goods and approaching one of these defended villages that we call 'camps', sees as he threads his way through the surrounding fields, a forest of conical thatched roofs crowning the hill-top. He comes to the huge wooden gateway and passes through it into a collection of dwellings with narrow streets[29] unmetalled but clearly defined, the whole resembling per-haps one of our older villages of mud-walled thatched cottages. Arriving in the early afternoon he finds the place occupied chiefly by children and dogs, with an occasional wandering goat and a few chickens strolling about. Most of the inhabitants are at work in the fields, but one or two women may be seen returning from the water-hole or river, and perhaps a mule or pony similarly employed and in the charge of a child. A little business may be done in trinkets and with the blacksmith; the evening will probably be employed in that time-honoured ritual of all commercial travellers—the promotion of 'good-will'. His visit may last several days; time is of little account in primitive communities whose life is strenuous but unhurried. He retires to sleep in a guest-house (if there is such) or in the dwelling of a customer where he is wakened at dawn by the booming of a rotary-

---

[26] *Ant. Journ.*, XX, 1940, 465–85; *Antiquity*, II, 1928, 217–18.

[27] By Dr Wheeler; but neither he nor I can remember where.

[28] The evidence is derived from excavations such as those conducted by Professor and Mrs Hawkes at St Catherine's Hill, Quarley and Balksbury in Hants, Dr Wheeler at Maiden Castle, Dorset, and Mr Collins at Blewbury (*Antiquity*, XXIII, 1949, 208–11). The early excavations of the Society of Antiquaries, directed by Mr J. P. Bushe-Fox, at Hengistbury Head, near Christchurch, Hants, revealed important evidence, but the defences were not excavated. Earlier still was the work of the Cunningtons at Casterley in Wilts.

[29] For such see my air-photo of Hod Hill, *Wessex from the Air*, Plate i, now obliterated forever by agricultural vandals.

quern next door. He spends the next day in breaking down the sales-resistance of his customers—perhaps more feigned than real and the recognized opening move of the buyer. His goods will of course vary with time and place; normally they will consist of such portable objects as cannot readily be made locally, for lack of access to the raw materials. Such things as flints for strike-a-lights, and tinder, will find a ready market in the flintless Cotswolds; whereas querns (roughed out only perhaps) will sell best in the chalk regions of Wessex. The bronze tinker will do a brisk trade in horse-furniture and tools, and occupy his spare time repairing cauldrons. We may be sure that those early forerunners of the vendors of patent medicines—the sellers of charms—will be seen, though such are more likely to be permanent residents than itinerant tradesmen. The community makes most of its necessary goods itself. There is no sale for pots or woven fabrics or corn, nor are there any shops. One or two men may specialize in such matters as the sharpening and repair of tools, primitive surgery and dentistry, and carpentry; but for the most part the men and women make for themselves all the chief necessities of their daily life.

This reconstruction of life in a prehistoric Iron Age village is not purely imaginary; it is based upon the actual findings of excavation and upon the observation of similar conditions to-day. I have stayed in a hill-top village in Algeria that differed in no essential features from such prehistoric settlements as Maiden Castle. Such, for instance, is the village of Ouled Mansour in the Aures mountains which must be very like Badbury in Dorset (Fig. 23) about the year A.D. 100, except that the French have not yet made a road there, whereas an important Roman road passed by Badbury. The resemblance is very close, for just as at Badbury a settlement sprang up under the *pax Romana*, outside the ramparts, so at Ouled Mansour a number of houses have been built, since the French occupation of Algeria, outside the compact village and among the gardens in the valley beneath.[30] The time-traveller who goes back on a holiday to the prehistoric life of the Aures district can still hear the booming of the rotary quern and see the unfinished product being trimmed down ready for use. When I was at Ouled Mansour in 1928, by a lucky chance I came upon the quern-dresser[31] at exactly the same spot as he appears in the illustration, similarly employed. It was almost as if I had been able to see and converse with an ancient Briton, and I could not resist the temptation to tell him that I had seen his picture in a book. His reaction was characteristic and enlightening; mere literary fame had no attractions for him at all unless it also carried with it some more tangible reward. Primitive man is a realist; he lives in a world of his own whose values are concrete. The outer world means nothing to him; why should it? His reply to such foolish remarks as mine is, 'What of it?' If one could have told the Piltdown man that he was destined to be world-famous thousands of years after his death, and to be housed in a glass case in a palatial building, he would surely have made the same sensible reply, if he could speak.

From the foregoing remarks it will have become evident that our British camps, and that special variety of them called promontory-forts, are not confined to prehistoric times or to this island. The need of protection is as universal as its cause—the desire of plunder. This is not the place for a general survey which would require a large book. I will mention

[30] See *Among the Hill-Forts of Algeria*, by M. W. Hilton-Simpson, 1921, 141; and the same author's article in *Antiquity*, I, 1927, 389–401.
[31] *Antiquity*, I, Plate vii, opposite p. 400.

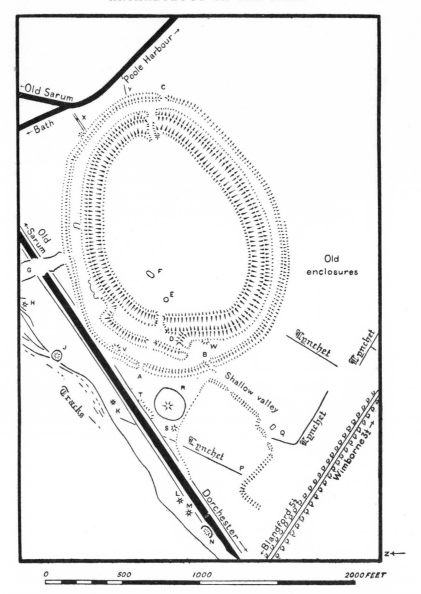

Fig. 23. Badbury Rings, Dorset, an Iron Age hill-fort with later open settlement outside on the south. (Reproduced by permission from *Wessex from the Air*, fig. 7.)

just a few areas where they have been observed and where field-work (and even more, excavation) is required to supplement and amplify the record.

In Italy a whole new series of neolithic or Early Bronze Age villages has been brought to light by air-photography and the vigilance of Mr John Bradford.[32] The ramparts are often multiple—or strictly speaking one should say the ditches, for they alone show; and

[32] For references see p. 50.

the interior is covered with hut-circles. These are crop-sites and likely therefore to yield little more to the field-worker than potsherds and appreciation of their topographical position. But careful excavation on modern lines—and the adjectives are important in Italy—will transfigure the prehistoric period to which they belong, which at present is little more than an arid playground of the typologist.

The Iberian peninsula, and Portugal and Galicia in particular, is said to contain many hill-forts, some of outstanding perfection. But the modern Iberians have so far not produced any descriptions of them that can be compared with ours; it is practically a virgin field. When Mr Hemp and I were having our holidays in Majorca, his practised eye soon detected remains of stone-built ramparts on the hills, where none had been observed before, and he has found them also in France and Spain.

France abounds in hill-forts, some of them described by Caesar, but since Napoleon III's work little has been published, and the excavation of one of them (Peu Richard) was a travesty of method. There is as yet no field archaeology in France.

There are hill-forts in Soviet Armenia. I saw one of these from a bus as we were going from Erivan to Akstafa on the Baku-Tiflis railway; it was, I should say from memory, twenty miles or less north of Erivan, on the east side of the road. Where there is one such, there must be many more.

The latest discovery of defended villages comes from Siam, which on air-photographs look surprisingly like our British camps.[33] None as yet have been visited on the ground, nor is their date known. Another virgin field. One wonders what may one day be revealed in China.

Africa, south of the Sahara, has so far yielded nothing except modern hill-forts, though the *ambas* of Ethiopa, so often mentioned in the Annals of that country, must have been hill-forts. Some of them may have had wooden stockades, and others depended chiefly or wholly upon their inaccessibility, like Debra Damo, which can still only be reached on a rope. But the eye of the practised field archaeologist will assuredly one day find many. Indeed one such is plainly visible (though unobserved by the author) on Plate xvi of Archbishop Mathew's *Ethiopia* (1947). It seems to consist of a single rampart of earth with an outer loop on the right, surrounding the 'palace of John IV'[34] at Macalle, which is obviously later as it encroaches upon the rampart on the left. The old Ghibbi at Addis Ababa shown on the same plate, has two concentric walls some distance apart. And was Barara, the ancient capital, a hill-fort? Surely it must have been, and if so some traces should still be visible if not obliterated by later work.

There are, however, some excellent examples of modern hill-forts on the bank of the Shari river south of Lake Chad, in the extreme northern part of French (formerly German) Cameroon.[35] One superb air-photograph (Plate 19) shows the Kotoko village of Divel surrounded by an elongated wall of sinuous outline, the whole pear-shaped and with seven V-shaped re-entrants at whose apexes are gaps serving as entrances. Measurements are not given, nor is there a description of the huts which cluster in one part, leaving more than half the interior unoccupied. Water is obtained from artificial reservoirs immediately below the wall on the outside, where a streamlet has been dammed. Tracks lead from the gates

---

[33] *Antiquity*, XXIV, 1950, 30–6.
[34] The title of the illustration is wrong. The building is now ruined; it was built as a house (and monument to himself) by Dedjajmach Abraha about forty years ago. I am indebted to Mr Derek Matthew for kindly pointing out these facts.
[35] *La découverte aérienne du monde*, ed. Paul Chombart de Lauwe; Horizons de France, Paris, 1948, plate on pp. 184–5.

through the surrounding scrub. The plan has a remarkable, if merely superficial, resemblance to the famous Welsh hill-fort on Tre'r Ceiri.

There are even hill-forts to be found in the deserts of Arabia. One such is in the basalt country of Transjordan, Latitude 31° 48′ 20″ N., Longitude 37° 30′ 30″ E.,[36] and it too closely resembles Tre'r Ceiri in plan. So far as I know it has never been visited or described; its age is quite unknown, and it can only be described from the air-photograph. The site is a flat-topped hill, round whose edge a stone wall has been built, the inner row of uprights being plainly visible in one part. Nearly the whole of the interior is covered with large kraal-like circles of stones, and much smaller ones which seem to be the remains of huts. Below the hill at the bottom of the photograph is a mass of stone kraals. One is always loath to make sensational claims, and particularly (as here) on imperfect evidence; the site should be visited on the ground first. There may be some commonplace explanation of the apparent facts; but appearances suggest permanent habitation, and that is definitely ruled out under the present climatic conditions. Can it belong to an earlier climatic epoch? Once the stones were arranged, the forces of nature here would do nothing to disarrange them, and the usual destructive agents, such as use of ancient sites as quarries for other buildings, are absent.

[36] Air-photograph in *Antiquity*, I, 1927, Plate ii, opp. p. 201, on which a plan of Tre'r Ceiri is reproduced.

7. Rushmore Pond, Bradley, North Hampshire; see page 124

8. The walls of Maiden Castle, Dorset; see page 139

CHAPTER 13

Huts and Houses

DURING RECENT decades archaeologists have become progressively more interested in the living than in the dead, in houses than in tombs. In the nineteenth century, when collectors dominated archaeology, the chief subjects of excavation were those which most easily enriched their cabinets; hence the orgy of premature 'barrow-opening'. The only habitations explored with equal fervour were the Swiss lake-dwellings which, for special reasons, also yielded an abundant harvest. To-day a more balanced outlook has been achieved, and we value finds not so much intrinsically but as evidence. Our aim is the reconstruction of past life, and since that centres on the house, we are particularly interested in houses, and regard finds as subsidiary. That does not mean that they are unimportant—far from it—but simply that their importance is relative, not absolute. They serve a double purpose, of dating the structure, and of indicating the manner of living. The former aspect needs no elaboration; pottery, coins (when available) and any other objects whose date has already been established are used to date the house, with due regard of course to stratification and relative position. The latter aspect—the function of finds in providing evidence of the manner of living—is exemplified in every excavation report, where the rôles of hunting, collecting, fishing, agriculture and industry are assessed by expert examination of the objects found and of their relative proportions. By such means we are gradually accumulating knowledge which one day will enable us to produce a pedigree of regional house-types.

This new point of view represents an immense broadening of outlook which, once attained, enables us to see the old habitation-remains in an entirely new light. We no longer regard them from the outside, as archaeologists, but from the inside, from the point of view of the people who made them and lived in them. Formerly we classified habitations as hut-circles, pit-dwellings, brochs, forts and the like. Now we realize that it is our business to get behind the outward form to the function. When we do so, we are able to see an inner resemblance between two habitation-sites that under the older classificatory system would have nothing in common. To take an example. No two sites could be less like each other outwardly than Little Woodbury in Wiltshire and Clettraval in the Outer Hebrides. Yet both were farms; and if we make due allowance for climate and geography, fundamental resemblances emerge. These resemblances may be due to the fact that the Hebridean settlers were culturally akin to those who occupied Wessex at about the same time.[1]

---

[1] See Sir Lindsay Scott's article on the aisled round house, *Proc. Preh. Soc. N.S.*, XIV, 1948, 46–125.

This change of view from the old formalism to the new functionalism may probably be attributed to the impact of anthropology upon archaeology, and so we are back once more to General Pitt-Rivers who, starting as an anthropologist, gave new life to archaeology by his excavations in Cranborne Chase. It was he who revealed and brought to life the prehistoric and Romano-British farms there. The archaeologists of Victorian England had lost touch with the realities of primitive life, with which they had little or no concern. Living like the lilies of the field in a world of ease and plenty, they forgot that their prehistoric ancestors had had not only to toil and spin, but also to plough, sow, reap and build.

What, it may be asked, have all these historical and theoretical matters to do with field archaeology? The answer is that what the observer sees is what he is interested in, and that is to a large extent determined by his own cultural background, which includes his archaeological and anthropological training. What he sees is what he has learned to see. The collector on a ramble over the downs will see the barrows and flints, but ignore the linear earthworks and lynchets. Of course there are many exceptions, but I think the statement is a valid explanation of the fact that the Victorian period in England was one when field archaeology as now understood was regarded as less important than it is to-day. All that we can see and much more was there for them to see too, and some of it was in fact seen and recorded during the seventeenth, eighteenth, and early nineteenth centuries.[2]

The subject of early British houses is so vast that one hardly knows where to begin. In a book designed primarily to assist the field-worker to recognize and understand what he sees in his rambles, there would be no object in beginning with the Mesolithic scratch-holes and crannogs[3] which are not visible on the surface. Next in order of time come the neolithic causeway camps which have already been dealt with. They contain, however, no remains of huts or houses, unless the ditches are to be regarded as the remains of habitations. An exception is Hembury hill-fort in Devon where remains of a curvilinear hut were found on the inner edge of the rampart. At Haldon near Exeter remains of a rectangular hut have been found.[4]

At Skara Brae in the Orkneys are the remains of a group of houses which, thanks to a protecting mantle of sand, are more perfectly preserved than any others in Britain.[5] They were uncovered, under the supervision of Professor Gordon Childe, by the Ancient Monuments Branch of the Office of Works.[6] The whole complex might be described either as a cluster of six one-roomed houses or as a single six-roomed house.[7] The rooms or houses are parallelograms with rounded corners, varying in size from 21 x 20 to 15 x 11 feet internally. On each side is a bed, the larger—probably the man's—on the right; in the middle is a hearth, at the end opposite the door a dresser, and in the far corner on the left a cell or alcove. In the wall above the beds are niches, probably cupboards.

---

[2] These matters are dealt with also in Chapter 21 (end).

[3] For those at Farnham see *Antiquity*, XI, 1937, 476–8 (Plates v, vi), and *Proc. Arch. Soc. N.S.*, V, 1939, 61–118; for Star Carr, near Flixton in Yorkshire (a crannog), see *Antiquity*, XXIII, 1949, 207–8, and the preliminary report in *Proc. Preh. Soc. N.S.*, XV, 1949, 52–69. See also *Antiquity*, XI, 1937, 210–12.

[4] *Proc. Devon Arch. Exploration Society* (Exeter), II, 161 (Hembury); ib. id., 249–51 (Haldon).

[5] Probably the next best preserved (though barely half as old) are the hermits' huts on Skelig Michael off the coast of Kerry.

[6] See *Skara Brae*, by V. Gordon Childe (1931). For another example see *Proc. Soc. Ant. Scot.*, LXXIII, 6–31.

[7] Childe, *Scotland before the Scots*, 1946, 32.

On Dartmoor[8] and Bodmin Moor hut-circles may be seen in large numbers. Excavation suggests that many of those on Dartmoor belong to the Early Bronze Age. They are always round, and associated with them one often finds small lynchetted cultivation-plots.

But it is not possible in a book of this kind to give even an outline of the chief house-types from the neolithic period to the Dark Ages—and to write a proper account one should not even stop there. The subject demands a book to itself, indeed several books, for the cottage of medieval and post-medieval times is itself a vast subject. One can only refer briefly, as I have done, to a few of the earliest known examples of British houses and then suggest some of the things which it is important to observe. I am fully conscious of the inadequacy of this treatment of so important a subject, and advise professional archaeologists not to read the rest of the chapter. It is not intended for them, but for those who are beginners.

Hut-circles are extremely common; the rambler is bound to come across them, whether on the moors of Scotland, the mountains of Wales or (less often) on the chalk downs. He will naturally want to know how to recognize them and how to distinguish them from other circles. That is not always as easy as it might seem. There are two sorts of round earthen bank found in southern England, both of which might easily be mistaken for hut-circles. One is a type of burial-mound made in the Early Bronze Age which is called a disc-barrow. It consists of a very small mound of earth seldom more than a foot high, surrounded at a distance of several yards by an *unbroken* circular ditch whose bank is nearly always on the outside. Disc-barrows are not usually found in isolation, and it is usual to find other ordinary barrows close by. When ploughed over, the bank, in chalk country (where they are commonest) shows up as a ring of lighter coloured soil. The diameter of a disc-barrow is much greater than that of any hut-circle. The other circles that might be (and often are) mistaken for hut-circles are the circular banks made round clumps of trees, especially firs and pines, during the eighteenth and nineteenth centuries. They may be of any diameter, but are sometimes about the size of a large hut-circle. Good examples are to be seen round the pines that are planted on some of the Hampshire and Surrey commons. When the trees have gone they look just like hut-circles, but they may be distinguished by having no entrance gap. There is also often the decayed stump of a tree still left. These tree-circles are not unlike disc-barrows, but they always have their ditches *out*side their banks. A very distinguished archaeologist once made a plan of a tree-circle in Kent under the impression that it was a disc-barrow.

The true hut-circle consists of a small ring of fairly large stones mixed with smaller ones and often covered by an earthen bank and overgrown with grass, so that the stones are not visible. In country where stone occurs they are found in hundreds, and can nearly always be identified (unless they have been tampered with) by the entrance-gap which breaks the ring. This ring is of course the remains of the low wall, probably no more than two or three feet high, on which the roof rested. That wall may have been made entirely of stone or of stone and mud or turf mixed, or of mud or turf without any stone—in which case the surviving ring will be so slight as to be hardly noticeable. When in Darfur I came across a group of huts that had been inhabited by nomad cultivators the year before (1949). They were already in every stage of decay and made an interesting study (Plate 9). Every stage from the hut with its roof to the hut-circle was plainly visible.

[8] See Brailsford in *Antiquity*, XII, 1938, 452–5.

In another village not far away, larger and permanently inhabited, I found and photographed examples of similar huts still in use. It was interesting to observe that in a region where, as here, stones, mud and straw were all equally available in any quantity, all were used, together with light timber, for hut-construction. It was also to be observed that there was often no central supporting pole for the roof, which was supported by an ingenious arrangement of wooden branches. In our colder and wetter climate a heavier roof would be desirable, one covered, perhaps, with turf sods; the Dartmoor huts generally had a socketed stone for their central pole.

Many of the Sudanese huts are built entirely of wood and straw, and are very inflammable in that dry, hot climate. They must often have been burnt down in the past, as they are to-day. Here, current observation interpolates a warning to excavators who may be a little too ready to interpret a conflagration as the act of an enemy, and a major disaster. It is often nothing of the kind, and it is quite common. Every hut has a hearth, and one wonders that the roof is not set on fire far more often. In one hut, where walls were of straw only, a mud fire-back had been roughly plastered over the wall behind the fire. When I was at Abu Geili near Sennar in 1914 half the village was burnt down one day; the scene revealed impressed me vividly, and I mentioned it in a book[9] to illustrate a similar context to the present. By a very curious coincidence, when I revisited Abu Geili last year (1950), I came across the site of a burnt-out hut, and took a photograph of it (Plate 23a). There was nothing left but a ring of ashes and an old tin plate, part of a petrol-tin. What would the excavator make of such a curious feature? Would he fall back on that unfailing source—a religious motive?—the ritual circle of ashes endowed with some magical significance? The true explanation might well escape him, for the contents of the hut (if any) had all been removed, and the post-holes might have been so slight as to escape notice in that soil. He might argue, on negative evidence, that it could not represent a hut, but he would be quite wrong.

There is another aspect of these African huts which the prehistorian should study. They fall into two distinct classes: (1) those grouped together in permanent villages, and (2) those occupied only when cultivating the adjacent plots. The former are agricultural villages, and the latter, though also agricultural of course, are the homes of nomads who depend primarily upon their flocks and herds for a living. Yet excavation would reveal no difference between the huts of either, and the finds would prove contemporaneity. Could the excavator discover the real situation? It is doubtful whether he could do so directly by his digging, though he might by inference from the topographical situation. The villages beside the wadis are permanent, and usually larger, and their associated cultivation-plots are larger and more permanent also; but these would probably have been obliterated by subsequent continuous use. The fences round the plots are of dead thorn-bushes which would leave no trace. The African conditions are those typical of marginal regions where rainfall is sporadic and uncertain, and cultivation consequently intermittent (Plate 22). But surely we should find a similar semi-nomadic regime of desultory cultivation amongst a people in a transitional stage between a pastoral and an agricultural life? That may have been the state of British society in the Neolithic and Early Bronze Ages, and we may have to allow also for the difference of the climate then. A diminution of rainfall would favour pasturage at the expense of agriculture in all limestone districts.

[9] *Man and his Past*, 62.

The best support for the roof of a round hut is a low wall of stone or mud or a mixture of both, or, in Europe where it is available, one of turf. In Africa the stalks of grass or millet (dhurra) are also used. The wild grass there has stalks as thick as those of corn, and stronger. Wattle-and-daub hurdling is also used. The straw of corn may have been used in prehistoric Britain and wattle-and-daub certainly was. The hut-walls of stone and mud will survive as rings of stone and earth, those of wattle-and-daub may leave a slight trace (for the daub is imperishable). But those of straw will leave no visible trace on the surface. It is therefore in stony regions that hut-circles will be most commonly found. Wessex is for the most part a stoneless region; flint is almost the only stone (except in districts where sarsens occur), and it does not seem to have been much used by prehistoric man, who probably developed better substitutes. In those parts of Wessex, especially in Dorset, where suitable stone is readily accessible it was of course used. There are some excellent specimens of stone hut-circles in the hill-fort of Chalbury near Weymouth,[10] and a good isolated example about two miles east of the hill-fort of Eggardon, in Compton Valence parish (Dorset 39 NW.).

Besides hut-circles one finds also hut-platforms. These are shelves levelled out on sloping ground for the accommodation of buildings. They have only been recently recognized as a distinct type, and are commoner than is yet realized. The purpose of the levelling was to secure a horizontal floor and also to economize in building, by using the back and sides for walls. Examples occur in the hill-fort of Hambledon, Dorset, where they are arranged in a row along the edge of a steep slope.[11] The consequent plan was presumably more or less rectangular. There may be many others of prehistoric date, but most of the sites so far recorded belong to the Dark Ages. The classic examples are those on Margam Mountain discovered and first described by Sir Cyril and Lady Fox;[12] here the platform is much broader, somewhat like a tennis-court made on a sloping ground. The material excavated on the upper side was tipped on the lower side. The buildings had dry stone walls, and there were also remains of what seemed to be barns. The site is beside a ridgeway whose age is suggested by an inscribed memorial-stone of the fifth century A.D. The post-Roman date of the buildings was subsequently proved by excavation.

Mr W. J. Hemp has observed similar sites in Wales, where the buildings must have been smaller. His trained observation and experience enabled him to find a very close parallel in the Alps at a height of about 6,500 feet.[13] Near La Grave (Hautes Alpes) can be seen the foundations of a house of several rooms, with a dry-stone field-wall running up to it on both sides; it was built on a platform just like the Welsh ones, with a talus-slope on the lower side, and was probably a summer shieling or hafod. There are other similar sites in the neighbourhood. What is most needed is excavation to determine the age.

The Alpine châlet with its veranda on piles may well be a modification of this type. Wood is usually abundant in the lower Alpine regions, and with the Swiss pile-dwellings so near one would expect that prehistoric houses of the châlet type would be found.

No one could be more conscious than I am of the inadequacy of the above paragraphs. My excuse is that any adequate treatment would not only fill a book, but also be beyond my capacity to write. Such a book should be written, but it should be by one who has

---

[10] *Ant. Journ.*, XXLII, 1943, 98–121.

[11] *Wessex from the Air*, Plate 2.

[12] *Antiquity*, VIII, 1934, 395–413.

[13] *Antiquity*, XIII, 1939, 89–92.

excavated prehistoric houses himself—one can easily think of several archaeologists well qualified for the task. All I can do here is to call attention to some of the published descriptions.

The standard book is by Professor F. Oelmann of Bonn.[14] British and Irish prehistoric and Dark Age houses have been excavated and described by Sir Lindsay Scott and Professor Gerhard Bersu, and the latter has also much experience of European houses. To the examples of early houses quoted at the beginning of this chapter should be added those of Lough Gur in Country Limerick, excavated by Professor O'Riordain.[15] The ancient villages of Northumberland have been studied by Mr A. H. A. Hogg, now Secretary of the Welsh Commission.[16] Mr C. W. Phillips, Archaeology Officer of the Ordnance Survey, excavated a Dark Age house-site in Anglesey.[17] Many house-plans have been recovered from within the ramparts of hill-forts and similar defended sites, of which Little Woodbury, with its large round wooden house is a good and classic example.[18] One could prolong the list indefinitely.

[14] *Haus und Hof in Alterthum*, I, 1927 (only volume published).
[15] *Journ. R. Soc. Ant. Ireland*, 1949, 126–45; *Proc. R. Ir. Acad.*, LII, C. No. 3.
[16] *Antiquity*, XVII, 1943, 136–47; XIX, 1945, 80–4.
[17] The excavation of a hut-group at Pant-y-Saer in the parish of Mathafarn-Eithaf, Anglesey, by C. W. Phillips, *Arch. Camb.*, LXXXIX, 1934, 1–36; XXV, 1951, 174–86.
[18] *Proc. Preh. Soc. N.S.*, VI, 1940, 78–92.

CHAPTER 14

Caves, Houses and Tombs

IN A RECENT article[1] Professor Gordon Childe has reviewed the problems that arise when we attempt to classify megaliths and explain their distribution. He shows that the word 'megalith' is not in archaeological usage applied to all structures built of big stones, but only to those 'which we presume were erected for some superstitious, ritual or religious end'. Discussing those of them which were used for burials, he shows that, if we admit (as bases of classification) 'associated traits' such as collective burial and similarity of plan, we are bound to include within the 'megalithic' complex both rock-cut tombs (or artificial burial-caves) and those built above ground of small, not big, stones. So too, it might be added, are we bound to include in one and the same category both long barrows of earth and long cairns with burial-chambers of stones, both large and small. And there is the obvious and well-known genetic relationship between Woodhenge and Stonehenge. This complex, which extends discontinuously from Ireland and the Orkneys to India, has, however, certain traits, such as collective burial and port-holes, which point unmistakably (as Dr Wheeler pointed out long ago)[2] to 'a commonalty of religious ideas over a wide area'. As he admirably expresses it: 'Essentially the fundamental *religious concept* was the only really important factor. To us, the only important—because the only surviving—factor is the *form of expression* which in various times and places that concept took.'

But how did it all begin? Surely the long barrows and long cairns are merely above-ground replicas of earlier artificial caves? That may be typologically true, even though examples of both sometimes occur in one and the same group of monuments. But the theoretical typological evolution is confused, and sometimes apparently reversed by collateral influences. There is at least one certain instance of an artificial burial-cave (in Majorca) over which some kind of a long cairn was built, above ground.[3] Now this strongly suggests that the artificial burial-cave was here regarded as a substitute for the more orthodox cairn above ground. The cairn in this case was a sort of vestigial relic without function and of (presumably) ritual significance only.

The plan of the earliest long cairns, the *allées couvertes* or passage-graves, does most plainly recall the plan of a cave. We know that in the Palaeolithic period people were buried in the caves in which they lived; what more natural than to suppose that the passage-grave was an attempt to reproduce above ground the chief features of such caves? It might be argued that a cave is so simple a thing that it can hardly be said to have a plan

---

[1] *Ancient India*, No. 4 (1947–8), 4–13.   [2] *European Civilization*, ed. Ed. Eyre, Oxford, Vol. ii, 1935, 182–3.
[3] See *Archaeologia*. LXXVI, 1927, 139–41 (Cave 14, Son Caulellas).

at all. That is not so. Inhabited natural caves have at least three functional parts. The first, which may be called the forecourt, is the ground outside immediately in front of the entrance, where, because the inside is dark, the inhabitants sit about in fine weather, performing various tasks. For this reason it is sometimes roughly paved and enclosed. The second, which may be called the mouth or entrance, is usually barred by a rough stone wall[4] with a gap in it. The third, the cave itself, consists of the front part, which is light and used for work, and the back part, which is dark and used for sleeping, washing and storage. In long cairns the corresponding forecourt is the part between the curved horns flanking the entrance,[5] the mouth or entrance is the portal, and the cave itself is represented by the passage and burial-chambers. These, it may be observed, are often at the end nearest the portal, leaving the rest (corresponding to the back of the cave) a shapeless mass of stones. Is it fanciful to see in this an echo of the light and dark parts of the cave? However this may be, prolonged observation of caves and cave-dwellers, and also of long cairns, convinces me that there *is* a genetic relation between the two. I remember many years ago coming upon some cave-dwellers in the island of Gran Canaria. It was a lovely morning in May, and they were sitting in the forecourt, the father of the family in the middle. All around were the sheep and goats with tinkling bells browsing on the aromatic flowering shrubs that scented the whole air. I was hungry and thirsty, as I had slept out in the open, on a rock in a neighbouring gorge, and they gave me some milk and cheese. The whole cave was full of cheeses and receptacles for milk. It was the sort of scene one might have encountered at the dawn of history. The earlier inhabitants, the Guanches, lived in caves, both natural and artificial and also buried their dead in them.[6]

There is one feature, however, common to both long cairns and rock-cut tombs but not normally found in natural caves, and that is the side-chambers. It is the presence of these in long cairns that makes me think that the long cairn is derived rather from an artificial than from a natural cave; for artificial caves nearly always had these obviously convenient annexes hewn out in their sides. There is also a chronological difficulty in supposing any *direct* connection between the long cairns and the Late Palaeolithic caves. How can we fill the gap of so many millennia? I suggest some such stages as the following. At some date at the end of the Late Palaeolithic period or just after it, some people who lived in caves and buried in them, and who were, so to speak, traditionally cave-minded to a very high degree, migrated to a caveless region and proceeded to make artificial caves both for living purposes and for burial. At some later stage, some of these people, or others to whom the custom had spread, moved into a region where the ground was too hard to dig artificial caves, and made replicas of them above ground, the long cairns and passage-graves. But these people seem to have retained a lively recollection of the 'points' of an artificial cave, for when they settled in regions where the ground was diggable but also stony, they made both burial-chambers above ground and artificial burial-caves below it.

---

[4] e.g., the entrances of the inhabited caves in the Wadi Qubhudh in the Hadhramaut 'are built up with loose stones, and only a small gap left for man and beast to enter', *Geogr. Journ.*, LXXXVIII, 1936, 539. Similar walls have been observed in ancient caves in Wales and Scotland.

[5] For a possible forecourt to an earthen long barrow see *Wessex from the Air*, 232. The object consists of a raised and ditched platform, set at a short distance beyond the east end. It is merely a guess that it had any connection with the barrow.

[6] E. A. Hooton, *The Ancient Inhabitants of the Canary Islands* (Harvard African Studies, VII, 1925), 57. R. Verneau *Archives des Missions scientifiques et litteraires*, Paris, 1887, ser. 3, vol. 13, pp. 557–817; caves, 739–41. The sophisticated caves of Atalaya are, if I remember right, at any rate partly and probably wholly artificial; they have glass windows.

The close resemblance even down to such details as the side-shelves with pot-holes, between the artificial burial-caves of Majorca and the modern bear-pit caves (to be described below) of Matmata suggests that the Majorca cave-makers got their ideas from some ancestral bear-pit tradition located somewhere in the western Mediterranean region.

It is not likely that the story of evolution was quite as simple and diagrammatic as I have made it out to be. For one thing, everyone did not live in caves. Huts with dry stone walls were built above ground in the earliest Neolithic period and even before; and once that began, the houses of the dead would tend to follow suit. The easiest hut to build is a round, not a long, one; and from the hut may have come the tholos-tombs. The architecture of the living may thus have strongly influenced that of the dead. But, when due allowance is made for such deflections, I still think that the evolution sketched above may be an approximation to the actual one. The persistence of the passage-grave over so wide an area must surely have been due to some religious ritual that was deeply rooted; the houses of the dead were originally modelled on those of the living, and for countless generations men had lived and buried in caves. Religious conservatism clung to the model of a dwelling long after it had ceased to be used in any particular region, even though that model may have been modified by later types of dwelling that had come into fashion. We see the same conservatism to-day when most (but not all) churches are built in a Gothic style once normal for all houses but now dead for several centuries.

In the above outline I have as far as possible purposely avoided mentioning particular geographical regions because that would require a detailed analysis of plans and associated objects for which there is no room here. But such an analysis must eventually be undertaken, and it will have to cover the chief megalithic groups round the shores of the Mediterranean and in western France. It will have to take account not only of burial-places, but also of contemporary dwellings, and of the nature of the subsoil, whether resistant (as granite and other igneous rocks) or diggable (as limestone and loess). Perhaps it will be necessary to cover an even wider area, for the existence of burial-caves in the chalk regions of France and their absence in those of England is a fact that demands some explanation.

In the winter of 1930–1 I spent a holiday in Tunisia, and visited the underground village of Matmata, twenty-seven miles south of Gabes. Previous holidays in Majorca with my friend Mr W. J. Hemp had aroused a great interest in the artificial Bronze Age burial-caves of that island; and the discovery of a living community that still made and inhabited artificial caves was most opportune. Here was the chance of studying at first hand the habits of troglodytes. I gave a short account in *Antiquity*,[7] summarizing my observations and calling attention to certain suggested resemblances of plan to the caves of Majorca and to other prehistoric monuments. My hope of being able to revisit the region and produce a fuller account of the caves, illustrated by measured plans, has not been fulfilled; and it seems desirable now to make the best use possible of the rough diagrams I then drew, in the hope that someone else may be stimulated to go there and make better ones (Figs. 24 and 25).

The first sight[8] of the 'town' of Matmata is a strange one, for one sees no houses! The

[7] V, 1931, 1–4.
[8] For the convenience of those who do not possess *Antiquity* for March 1931, I quote with a few alterations part of what I wrote in it. I do not know whether Matmata still looks the same, or whether more houses above ground have been built; possibly not.

people live underground like rabbits, in rooms excavated in the rubbly loose soil and opening out on a central courtyard like a bear-pit. Entrance to this bear-pit is by a narrow
passage or tunnel with side-chambers for stabling donkeys and camels and for the storage
of fuel. There are openings all round the bear-pit, each closed by a wooden door; these are
the living-rooms—long, barrel-vaulted excavations, along whose sides are shelves or
ledges for storage-jars and sometimes wider ones for beds. Across the end is another shelf
for smaller jars. These shelves have shallow cup-shaped depressions for the pots to stand
in. The fact that the Bronze Age burial-caves of Majorca have similar shelves with shallow
saucer-shaped depressions cut in them is proof of the great antiquity of the tradition
represented by these modern bear-pits. Above the end-shelf is a kind of 'dresser', like
those which used to be so common in English farm-kitchens, on which are displayed the
flotsam and jetsam of western civilization, together with the finer products of their own
culture, such as glazed plates. Facing the entrance is a loom, on which a *burnous* is being
woven (Plate 11 and Fig. 25); beyond it is the bed, a structure of hard clay raised three feet
above the ground on clay legs. The loom is separated from the bed by a raised sill in the
floor, demarcating the light part of the cave from the darker interior.

I visited and made rough diagrams of three typical bear-pits. The first (Fig. 24) visited
1st January, 1931, was at Sauanif near Tijma on the outskirts of Matmata, and was inhabited by Ahmed ben el Haj Mahmoud. I was told that the whole complex was made
about 1923 by three men in three and a half months. The entrance was by a trench cut in
the side of the hill; the first part of the trench was open, the rest a tunnel entered by a doorway with a stone threshold. Just before reaching the doorway were two rectangular side-
chambers; that on the left contained a wheel-barrow, two palm-logs, two baskets for holding water-pots and some straw; it had a barrel-shaped roof. The chamber on the right
contained wood for fuel. Inside the door were two more side-chambers, containing a
camel and a donkey respectively. The tunnel narrowed and then emerged into the bear-pit.
Opening out on the left was the kitchen with a hearth on the floor; next to it was the
women's room and one for the dog, neither of which could be entered. On the opposite
side of the pit were the two principal rooms, A and B. Room A had the usual loom and
bed. Along the right-hand side ran a shelf with seven depressions. Beginning at the entrance
end, the first depression contained an empty pot, the second one dates, the third olives,
the fourth olive-oil, the fifth was empty, the sixth had a basket with barley, the seventh a
jar of chaff. Across the end was a shelf two feet wide on which were thirty pots. On the
wall above were fastened bottles, pots, pictures and plates. In the left-hand corner was
the bath-chamber, in which (as always) was a bucket-shaped hole to contain the water.
The shelf on the left of the cave was one foot six inches wide and had two wooden (clothes?)
chests standing on it. The room narrowed slightly in the centre, between the bed and the
loom. Room B was entered by two descending steps in front of a wooden door, turning in a
socket-hole. The room then opened out by recesses; in front (as always) was the loom;
in the corner on the right was a big vessel for oil or corn, placed at the end of a shelf
six inches wide. Then came the sill, where the sides of the cave narrowed, and immediately
beyond it the bed. On the farther end of the right-hand shelf was a pile of wood, and across
the end a shelf one foot six inches wide with pots (one an amphora) standing in holes.   In
the left corner was a side-chamber for a bath.

The second dwelling was at Matmata itself and was said to have been made for the

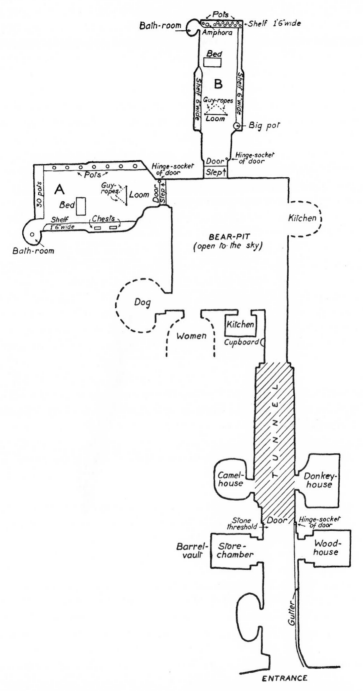

Fɪɢ. 24. Rough diagram of habitation at Sauanif near Matmata, S. Tunisia.

'ancien sheikh Ferjany' and his brother Senussi 220 years ago. I have no complete plan, as, if I remember right, objections were raised after I had begun to make notes—always a procedure that arouses suspicion; but I was able to make a detailed measured plan of one of the principal rooms (Fig. 25). The entrance was by a tunnel through the side of the hill, and a most interesting feature was observed there. The slope of the hill for a short distance on either side of the tunnel entrance was reinforced by a retaining wall of dry stones curving inwards towards the entrance. This very strongly recalled the horns that flank the chambered cairns everywhere from Sardinia to Caithness and the megalithic walls flanking the portals of the Maltese 'temples', so-called. If it served a useful purpose it may have been to prevent erosion, which would eventually wash away the sides and encroach on the habitations; unfortunately I did not ascertain its purpose by enquiry. The arrangements of the principal room can best be seen from the plan (Fig. 25), which does not show the sill in the floor dividing the cave into two halves. Note the hens' nests; they were cut in the vertical face of the dresser, and round the opening of one were cut ten small ventilation-holes—an obvious necessity during the heat of summer. On the wall above the dresser were fixed six shallow glazed bowls, five glass bottles, a pair of old opera-glasses, some jars, an old lantern, two old mirrors, the lid of a square biscuit-tin, an empty picture-frame and a hand-mirror frame without a glass.

The third dwelling (also at Matmata itself) was that of Haj Mahmud. My 'plan' of this is too sketchy to reproduce. It shows a long approach, all of it I think in the form of a tunnel. First comes a pair of side-chambers, one for the donkey and the other (opposite) for its fodder. Then came two steps leading into an expansion of the passage occupied by a camel and the wood-fuel. The passage then contracted again and led out into the bear-pit. On the wall of the bear-pit were carved representations of hands and feet and of a fir-cone. These had some magical purpose and are a common feature throughout the region. On the right was the kitchen, at the back of which was a side-shelf with pots and pans. Next to it, also on the right, was a side-chamber used as a fowl-house, with smaller side-chambers. Then came the women's room and another, and opposite the entrance the main room. Here the back-room was in the corner on the left of the doorway. The loom and bed occupied the usual positions; there were the shelves along each side, that on the left being a foot only above the level of the floor; and at the end was a shelf three feet wide.

I also made a sketch-plan of a room in the dwelling where we found a negress making pots by the primitive coil-method. The finished pots stood out to dry in the middle of the open bear-pit, which (if I remember right) was much smaller than the others. The principal room had two detached bed-shelves, two feet above the ground, on the right-hand side, and on the left, beyond which was a pot-shelf, one foot above the floor. The place usually occupied by the bathroom on the left of the dresser was a cupboard of about the same size, perhaps a little smaller. At the end was a shelf about a foot wide with one row of pot-holes, and above it, in the end-wall, was an end-chamber used for sleeping in during the winter (when the nights are very cold) whose sill was four feet above the floor. In the side was cut a small niche for a lamp—not, I suspect, for reading in bed, but to give warmth.

The nucleus, the primary unit, of the bear-pit is the long room such as that shown in Fig. 25. (One may conjecture that originally it stood alone, facing directly towards the

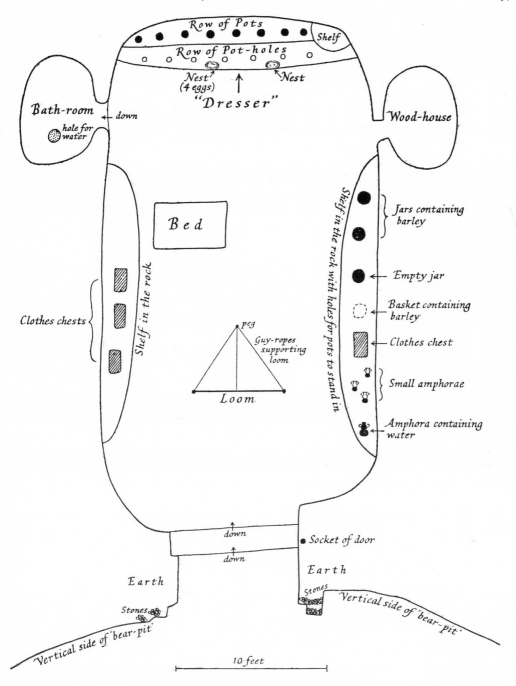

FIG. 25. Cave-room at Matmata, S. Tunisia.

open, without any bear-pit or passage of access; that would be when the natural-cave-dwellers made the first artificial cave.) The next stage is when the cave-makers come to the surface and build houses above ground. By all the rules of typological evolution these houses should resemble the older subterranean ones, and that is exactly what they do. There are many examples all round Matmata. The old town of Medinine (Plate 12), about thirty miles south-east of Matmata consists entirely of rows of barrel-shaped vaults, sometimes with a second and third storey built on the top of the first, which are simply stone-built versions of the long rooms of the bear-pits. Even the superimposition is paralleled, for in some of the bear-pits there are rooms excavated higher up in the sides whose floors are on a level with or above the roofs of the ground-storey rooms. Architecturally they are about the most primitive kind of building that can be imagined. The roofs, though now reinforced by concrete, were doubtless originally of corbelled stones. There is a doorway at the end of each, but no other openings of any kind. Access to the upper floor is sometimes provided by an external stone stairway, sometimes presumably by ladders only.

The town-plan of Medinine consists of huge rectangles whose sides are formed by these rows of superimposed vaults. They are used as granaries for storing the produce of the fields, and Medinine is said to be but one of many such granary-towns. That may be true to-day, but one suspects that originally the inhabitants also lived in vaults, and that their present exclusive use for storage is a recent development, due to the improvement in housing that has come with the French occupation. Certain it is that the village of Metameur a mile or so from the modern town of Medinine, consists of a single such rectangle, whose vaults are lived in. The whole unit is designed to provide protection against marauders. It is a sort of walled town whose walls are the backs of the vaults.

The vault is the normal house-type of the whole of this region. When flying from Gabes to Tripoli in 1938 I observed several farms on the coast between Gabes and Ben Gardane (which is another vault-town) that consisted simply of an agglomeration of vaults. The style is accretive, and vaults are added to each other exactly like the cells in a honeycomb. The nucleus of the town of Houmt Souk, the market of the island of Jerba, consists of vaults, as can be seen most plainly when one flies over it. The modern town has many houses of the ordinary flat-roofed kind, but the centre of the town is the market-place, which was no doubt originally a vault-rectangle just like those of Medinine and the adjacent villages.

The geographical extent of the bear-pit villages and of their above-ground counterparts is considerable. There is an extensive literature on the subject of troglodytes in North Africa, but many of the descriptions lack precision and are tantalizingly silent on just those points that are important. It is seldom stated whether the habitations are natural caves or artificial ones, whether they open on to a central bear-pit or straight out of the hillside. No room plans are given, for such plans of the settlements as have been published are on far too small a scale, and in other respects fail to inspire confidence. In these matters it is the precise details, the close-up view, that is all-important. Troglodytes have been reported as far east as Cyrenaica, where Oric Bates[9] writes of whole communities living in

---

[9] *The Eastern Libyans*, 1914, 168, quoting H. Vischer, *Across the Sahara*, 38 ff.; he mentions in particular Gebel el Ahdar and Gebel Gharyan. The habitations at Garian, fifty miles south of Tripoli, are true bear-pits, as is evident from an illustration of one that was published in the *Völkischer Beobachter*, 4th April 1937, accompanying an article by Rudolf Jacobs describing them. (I am indebted to Professor Bersu for kindly sending me the newspaper in question).

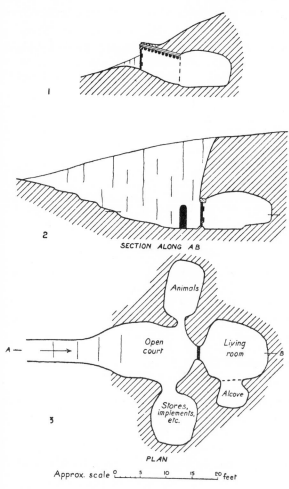

SECTION ALONG A B

Animals

Open court

Living room

Alcove

Stores, implements, etc.

PLAN

Approx. scale 0 5 10 15 20 feet

FIG. 26. 1. Er Rehibat; Despois, type 1. 2 and 3. Nalout; Despois type 2. (After Despois, fig. 15.)

artificial caverns. Jean Despois[10] writes about troglodytes in Tripoli. Tilho mentioned their existence in Tibesti (crater of Koussi).[11] There are bear-pit villages south of Matmata, along the Tripoli frontier, and also all over Tripoli itself. As we shall see, more important in connection with 'megalithic' origins is the existence of what seems, to judge from the cursory description, to be a bear-pit village in southern Spain at Guadix, outside Santiago. Here in a region of Pliocene conglomerate, where the soil is both coherent and easy to excavate, are habitations hollowed out in the ground and visible only from their whitewashed chimneys. There are more than 3,000 inhabitants. The illustration given is so minute[12] (2 x 2¾ inches) and indistinct that it would be hazardous to base much upon it, but it does show a more or less flat expanse of ground, not a steep slope, so that presumably access was by means of bear-pits.

In his book on Djebel Nefousa M. Jean Despois has given a full account of the troglodytes of the Tripoli region. They are found in that ridge or scarp of land extending from Garian (50 miles due south of Tripoli) on the east to the Tunisian frontier beyond Nalut in the west, a stretch of 140 miles. At the frontier the high ground bends northwards, ending 100 miles further on at Matmata. The Tripoli part of this ridge is the troglodyte region *par excellence*; and it is also that of vaulted buildings (*ghorfas*) and fortified granaries (*kasrs*). M. Despois does not regard the *ghorfas* as derived from the artificial caves, a theory propounded by M. Aug. Bernard[13] and, independently, by the present writer; but his argument does not appear convincing. He groups the caves into four main types: (1) horizontal; (2) sunken with small forecourt; (3) sunken, with large forecourt; (4) mixed type containing both caves and *ghorfas*. The first unit (Fig. 26, 1) consists of between two

[10] *Le Djebel Nefousa (Tripolitaine)*; étude géographique: Larose, Paris, 1935. [Review in *Amer. Geogr. Review*, July 1935, 496].   [11] J. Tilho: *Du lac Tchad aux montagnes de Tibesti*, 38.
[12] J. Brunhes, *La Géographie humaine*, 3rd ed., Paris, 1925, I, 107 (text): II, figs. 22–4. Fig. 23 shows the flat part, the others a steep hill. One wonders what purpose is served by such general statements devoid of all content, especially when illustrated only by bad half-tones.
[13] *Enquête sur l'habitation rurale des indigènes de la Tunisie*, Tunis, 1924, 59; see also his 'Les troglodytes du Matmata', *Bull. de la Soc. Normande de Géographie*, 1907. I have not been able to consult either of these.

and four cave-rooms excavated in the side of a hill; the excavated material is spread out in front to form a level platform, the forecourt, round which is a wall of stone or, in stone-less country, a *tabia* of earth set with branches of the jujube tree. The plan given by M. Despois shows two habitation-rooms close by a door, and a coach-house (remise) or stable for animals without one. The floors of the rooms are often a little below the level

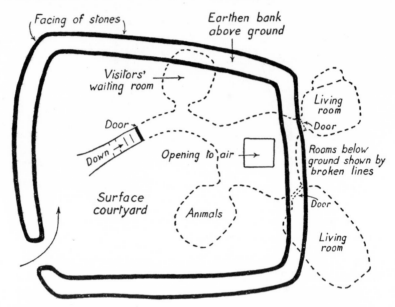

FIG. 27. Nalout; Despois, type 2 (variant). (After Despois, fig. 16.)

of the forecourt. The inhabited rooms often have secondary alcoves in their sides, used for sleeping in. Holes in the sides are made for cupboards, and sticks are also inserted for hanging things on. Sometimes there is a small underground granary entered by a door at the end of the cave.

The second unit, which might also be called the Nalut type, is found where the ground is flat, without a convenient hillside to dig into. The rooms open out of a court which is merely an expansion of the sloping ramp leading down to them. M. Despois contrasts this unhygienic plan with the much better one of Matmata and Garian, where an airy, open court (bear-pit) is approached by a narrow passage or tunnel. The ramp is roughly stepped, and is only 3½ metres wide at the lower or inner end. The rooms form a trefoil plan, and those of one of the groups planned (Fig. 26, 2 and 3) are round or oval and not so long as those of the first type, possibly because of lack of ventilation. A bed of hard rock is chosen for the roof, a feature recalling the exactly similar natural roof of the prehistoric cave, the Grotte des Fées near Arles. In rainy weather the water runs down the ramp and turns the court into a regular cesspit. Another group, planned (Fig. 27) but inadequately described in the text, is also of trefoil plan with a roughly rectangular interior court, apparently half covered in and half open to the air. There is a waiting-room for visitors opening out of the passage, which is closed by a door at the bottom of the stairway. Except that the court is much smaller, this plan resembles that of some of the bear-pits, and one of the

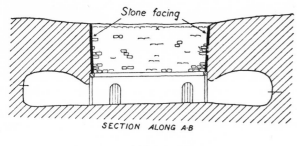

SECTION ALONG A·B

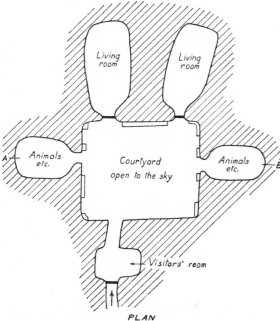

PLAN

FIG. 28. Ez Zintan; Despois, type 3. (After Despois, fig. 17.)

three rooms is twice as long as it is broad. The ground above is surrounded by a thick wall consisting of earth piled up between two retaining walls of stone. In this outer court are the camels and *petit bétail*; but others —donkeys, horses and cows—shelter below.

The third unit is that of Garian and Matmata already described above. M. Despois gives a plan of one such at Ez Zintan (Lat. 32° Long. 12° 15′) about midway between Garian and Nalut (Fig. 28). The walls of the bear-pit here are partially reinforced with a stone revetment, especially at the entrances of the rooms; this feature is important because, if my theory of development is correct, the reinforcement in these places is the typological ancestor of the horns which flank the entrance of the chambered cairns, and also of the curved façade of the Balearic nevatas and Maltese 'temples'. Here in the soft earth of Tripoli there is a good structural reason for such reinforcement—to protect the sides of the entrance from crumbling and erosion.

The fourth unit is a mixture of the second and third with the above-ground *ghorfas*. The two styles may be combined in many ways. Houses are built *over* caves, which then serve as basements or stables. It sometimes happens that ruined villages, whose caves of course have escaped destruction, are rebuilt and the caves put to use again. This type Despois calls that of superposition. There is another type, which he calls that of lateral association, where both caves and built rooms are grouped round a central court (Despois' Fig. 18). In such cases the caves are usually relegated to the use of stables, store-sheds (remises) and kitchens, and the built structures are used for habitation; but the reverse also occurs. The buildings are simply flat earthen roofs resting on supports of stone, with transverse beams of palm or olive wood. Many of the poorer villages consist simply of one or two such rooms attached to one or two caves. The granary here is built over a room which may be either free-standing or backed against the natural earth; it is always vaulted, to ensure protection against the percolation of rain-water, and always well constructed. For the housing of food supplies demands more precautions than that of the family. So too in the Aures mountains the granary is always the most

L

important and often the most conspicuous building in the village, and has a special guardian who holds the keys.

The tendency in Tripoli, according to Despois, is to revert from built houses to caves, which are cheaper to make and keep up, and are also cooler in summer and warmer in winter. The climatic factor is important here; the heat in summer is very great, and the highest temperature ever recorded on the earth's surface (136° F.) was at Azizia near Garian on 13th September 1922. Political factors are also involved. The central *kasr*-granary was a necessity in disturbed conditions; now each family can safely have its own separate granary. An exactly parallel development has occurred in the Butana (between the Atbara and the Blue Nile) where nomad groups once large, can now safely revert to much smaller units.

That underground habitation in North Africa is of old standing is suggested by the statement of Herodotus that the Garamantes, who lived thirty days' journey from the Lotophagi, hunted the Ethiopian troglodytes in four-horse chariots. The Garamantes are to be located in the oases of Fezzan whose chief centre is now Mourzouk; and the Loto-phagi are certainly to be put somewhere north of them. There is no clue to the location of the Ethiopian troglodytes, but no part of anything that Herodotus could call Ethiopia is less than 1,400 miles from Mourzouk, and between them lies a vast and almost waterless desert. The Ethiopian troglodytes of other classical authors lived on the Red Sea coast, and there are not and never have been troglodytes of any kind in the Sudanese portion of the Nile valley. The only troglodytes the Garamantes can have chased were those within a reasonable distance of the Fezzan, whether to the north or south of it. The evidence does not allow of any closer identification, but it does justify a claim that troglodytic habits in some part of North Africa are as old as the days of Herodotus.[14]

Archaeological evidence of ancient bear-pit settlements is unlikely to be easily forth-coming. Such a settlement once abandoned would rapidly become obliterated, leaving nothing but at the most a few circular depressions over the bear-pits and low mounds representing the excavated soil. Excavation would be extremely difficult in view of the depth of the rooms; but it might well be very profitable. Air-photography might well reveal some such sites, if undertaken at the right time of day (early morning or late even-ing). The whole matter is admirably suited to field-exploration, and may be commended to the notice of the students of the British School at Rome, who have already done so much good work in North Africa.

What bearing have these bear-pit habitations upon the problem of megaliths? Any arguments based upon the modern habitations must of necessity be by analogy only and to that extent inconclusive; but they need not for that reason be unsound. For example, the modern reed-huts of lower Mesopotamia have been used to illustrate the remains of similar ancient constructions unearthed by archaeologists in the same region. They represent an age-old tradition that is just as much a response to the local environment as are the bear-pit villages. When, therefore, we find, as in Malta and Gozo,[15] megalithic buildings whose plan has many resemblances to the plan of the bear-pits, it is surely legitimate to ask whether those buildings may not be stone reproductions of underground prototypes.

[14] I wish to thank Professor G. F. Forsey for kindly verifying the remarks of Herodotus about the Garamantes.
[15] See *Antiquity*, IV, 1930, 55–79; 'The prehistoric remains of the Maltese Islands' ,by Sir T. Zammit.

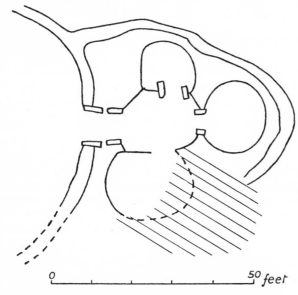

FIG. 29. Plan of Ta Hajrat, Malta, after Zammit.

The essential plan of such mega-lithic groups as Ixxaghra ta Cordin, Tarxien, Mnaidra, Ta Hajrat (Mjar) and Borg-in-Nadur in Malta and of the Jigantea in Gozo, is that of a forecourt or enclosure, from whose interior opens out a series of chambers or rooms. At Borg-in-Nadur the enclo-sure is still complete, though betray-ing signs of remodelling. Is is not possible that there were similar enclo-sures at all the sites? That the fore-courts are merely the imperfect sur-vivals of such? What is called the 'entrance' of the enclosure at Borg-in-Nadur[16] looks suspiciously like the portal of a group of rooms (now vanished) opposite those still extant. The enclosure would thus correspond exactly to the bear-pit from whose side walls the rooms open out. However this may be, an actual bear-pit plan does occur in the Hypogeum of Hal Saflieni near Valletta, on the lowest storey.[17] Now the Hypogeum was certainly used for collective burial; indeed, if such is the hallmark of a 'megalith', it is the world's classic example, for no less than about 7,000 persons are said to have been buried there,[18] and I have seen myself a huge pit there entirely filled with human bones. It certainly belongs to the same culture as the megalithic monuments on the islands. These I still firmly believe—*solus contra mundum*—to be burial-places. Owing to the fact that there has been no scientific excavation of these monuments, neither their date nor their purpose has been determined. Several of them when first found were covered by mounds and were cleared without any regard to method. Tarxien 'was completely buried under field-soil until 1914'; Hajar Kim's uprights protruded from a mound; Ta Hajrat (Mjar) was covered by a 'mound of earth through which blocks of stone emerged' before it was excavated in 1925–7 (Fig. 29)[19]. I believe that they were roofed, perhaps by corbelling, and covered in by the masons, that they were in fact simply tombs comparable with Antequera, Gavr Inis, New Grange and Maes Howe. Burials have actually been found in some, in stone cists; but the fact has, for various reasons, not been sufficiently emphasized. Moreover, to support the mound or cairn there was a retaining peristalith, still extant at Ta Hajrat (Mjar) and Mnaidra,[20] and of which there are evident traces on the plans of the other sites. The southern of the two complexes at Mnaidra is, in fact, nothing but a rather compressed horned cairn from which the covering has been removed; it could

---

[16] Ib. id., Fig. 8, p. 76.   [17] Ib. id., Fig. 5, p. 70 (dotted lines on south part).   [18] Ib. id., p. 71.

[19] After Zammit's plan in *Bulletin of the Valetta Museum*, I, 1, 1929, opp. p. 6.

[20] The plan of Mnaidra (*Antiquity*, IV, Fig. 6, p. 73) shows part of a peristalith round the southern rooms, but none round the northern. An air-photo (Pl. 13) shows the plainest possible remains of a wall of big stones completely enclosing the northern rooms on three sides (on the fourth they impinged on the southern rooms). This wall must be quite plainly visible on the ground.

be paralleled with examples from Sardinia and (less closely, but still legitimately) from the Cotswolds and Caithness.

If my contention be admitted, we have in the Hypogeum and the megaliths of the Maltese islands exactly the same conjunction of contemporary but disparate structural devices as in France, Spain and Algeria,[21] and in the Balearic islands *par excellence*, namely the artificial burial-cave and the above-ground burial-chamber. That some megalithic burial-chambers are the above-ground counterparts of artificial burial-caves was conclusively demonstrated long ago by Mr W. J. Hemp, in his studies of Balearic and southern French tombs. My thesis is that both megaliths and burial-caves probably go back to a type of habitation still extant in the traditional style represented by the Tunisian bear-pits, and that these could ultimately be carried back, if the links were not missing, to the caves of the late palaeolithic period. The problem of typological development is complicated, I suspect, by the influence on tombs of the contemporary house-plan in every period and stage, accounting perhaps for tholos-tombs.[22]

Evidence is not wholly lacking that some of the earliest above-ground habitations in the Mediterranean region may have been modelled on the bear-pit plan. Clusters of huts disposed round a circular court-yard occur in the neolithic period in Italy.[23] At a later date some of the artificial burial-caves of Palestine and Syria are grouped round a central area open to the sun.[24] But up to the present, apparently, no example of any ancestral bear-pit, whether for living or dead, has been discovered anywhere except at Hal Saflieni. Surely there must be examples in some of the limestone regions of Spain or North Africa? These are more promising than those in softer formations, where unfortunately they are most likely to have been made and where the idea may well have originated.

In conclusion my argument may be summarized briefly. The earliest known burials are those of the Palaeolithic period, which were in habitation-caves. This custom of house- (or rather home-) burial, which still survives in remote places, is therefore firmly grounded in antiquity; and when, for whatever reason, special burial-places were made, they imitated the contemporary house or home. Religious conservatism retained obsolete house-plans for graves, but admitted modifications due to the influence of contemporary house-plans. The earliest post-palaeolithic tombs were artificial caves, modelled on living-caves. Migration to regions of hard rock necessitated substituting above-ground structures (megalithic and other burial-chambers) whose plan followed that of the artificial caves. But in regions where the rock could be dug, both types occur mixed. It is probable that a special type of habitation (the bear-pit), consisting of caves (rooms) opening on to a central open court developed at a very early date, probably in the western Mediterranean, in a region of soft earth, not rock. From this may have come the Maltese megalithic monuments, which are simply tombs. There is throughout a strong lateral influence from contemporary house-types.

[21] At Roknia near Constantine there is a large cemetery *consisting both of 'dolmens' and rock-cut tombs*. The 'dolmens' are well known; the rock-cut tombs less so, though they can be seen from the train-window on the main line.

[22] Implicit in the theory is a North African origin for many western megalithic tomb-plans. One must not attempt to push the theory too far, but North African connections during the neolithic period have been claimed by an Italian archaeologist who re-excavated the famous Ligurian cave of Arene Candide; in fact, he claimed that the Italian neolithic was of North African origin. See *Gli Scavi nella caverna delle Arene Candide*, by Luigi Bernardo Brea, published as a monograph in 1946 by the Istituto di Studi Liguri, Bordighera. (Reviews in *Proc. Preh. Soc.*, 1949, 196–7, by Gordon Childe, and in *L'Anthropologie*, LIII, July 1949, 258).

[23] Peet, *Stone and Bronze Ages in Italy and Sicily*, 90, 92. cf. *Bull. Pal.*, III, 1.

[24] *P.E.F. Annual*, 1912–13, II, Plate vii.

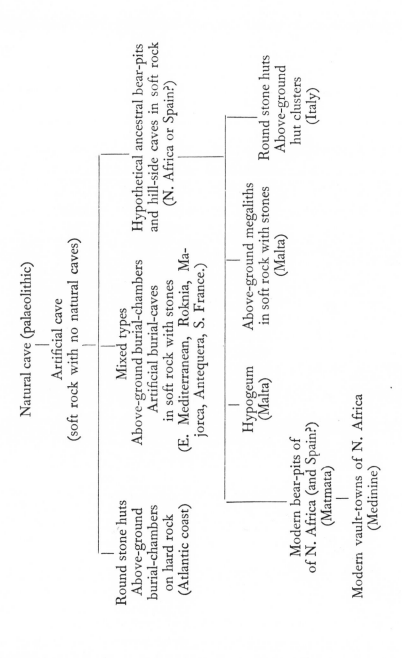

CHAPTER 15

Megalithic Monuments

THIS BOOK IS intended to answer questions, and its plan must therefore conform, not so much to the facts themselves as classified by archaeologists but rather to the same facts as they appear to the questioner. It may often happen that an interest in archaeology is first aroused by the sight of some mighty monument, or by mounds and banks obviously unrelated to the present regime of the countryside, and recognized as belonging to an older world. It was in this way that archaeology began, and the individual often recapitulates the history of the subject just as the organism does that of the species. The sight of mysterious monuments such as burial-chambers (once called dolmens), barrows, stone circles and 'camps' is a challenge to the enquiring mind. Thus did Avebury, Stonehenge and the lesser earthen monuments impinge upon the minds of Aubrey, Stukeley and Colt Hoare and produce the famous and still flourishing school of Wessex field archaeologists. It is quite natural that the earliest attempts at classification should be based upon such monuments, which were the first things to be noticed; so that in the earlier books we find prehistoric cultures named after them—hence come such obsolete terms as *civilisation lacustre* or *des palafittes, cultures des tumuli,* the mound-builders of Ohio and, lastly the word 'megalith' itself. Such systems of nomenclature must ultimately be superseded, for they do not correspond closely enough to the facts. There was not one but a series of lake-dwelling cultures, spread out over many centuries, nor were they the only habitations, and people made burial-mounds in many periods from the Neolithic to the Saxon. Nor are megalithic monuments restricted to a single age or area. These things loom large in our vision because they have survived; they were, however, single units or traits of the culture to which they belonged. The megalith-builders not only made things like Stonehenge, Avebury and stone circles and burial-chambers, but also things of earth and timber. You cannot call Woodhenge or the earthen circles of Durrington, Marden and Thornborough 'megaliths', though they belong to the same culture; therefore the heading of this chapter is incorrect, for in it these earthen monuments will also be briefly mentioned. I have used it because, though unscientific, it is convenient and no other single term covers the monuments described. Nor could it; we do not now think in terms of such things at all, for we know that, granted some general affinity, even so small an area as the British Isles never at any period had a single culture in the true sense, but rather a number of regional ones, constantly fluctuating. To hold this Protean thing called 'culture' at all in our minds we must keep it, like the Greek giant, in close contact with the earth.

When, therefore, we are asked such questions as 'What are standing stones?' we can only reply that the question, put in that form, is unanswerable—or answerable only at very great length. It would be as difficult to answer a Martian's question: 'What are wheels?' Questioner and questioned have little common ground. The questioner rarely realizes the vast extent of time covered by human activities, or even, very often, that time is an essential element in such matters at all; that before he can understand the reply to his question he must learn to *think in time*. To the question implicit in the heading of this chapter, namely 'What are megalithic monuments?' there is therefore no simple answer, if one excludes the one that they are structures of large stones, which is mere tautology. An adequate reply would comprise nothing less than a book dealing with all the regional groups of megaliths, from Scotland to India and Easter Island, and from the European Stone Age down to the nineteenth century in Assam. Such a book has been written[1] and it is still useful for reference; but we do not now think about the past in that way. We have learnt to go behind the monuments to the people who made them and their whole cultures, and having done so we have discovered that the older systems of classification are inadequate; so they have just faded away. They belong, like the questioner, to an early stage in the discipline of archaeology. Nevertheless I shall, after covering myself by the foregoing explanation, attempt to answer the question in the questioner's terms.

Megalithic monuments consist of standing stones (single or in rows), stone circles and rings, and burial-chambers in long or round mounds or cairns.

Standing stones, single or in groups, are found all over the Old World from Scotland to Abyssinia; they range from the beginning of the second millennium B.C. to modern times. In Britain their erection is best evidenced in the early Dark Ages (say *c.* A.D. 400–800). Everywhere their purpose was to mark the grave of an important person; they were in fact simply tombstones. That this was their purpose in the earliest times has not been proved, nor do I know of any *isolated* standing stones which have been proved to have been set up during the Early Bronze Age; but there are many such in the neighbourhood of other megalithic monuments (e.g. the stone circles of Scotland and Cornwall) which are generally regarded as being contemporary with them. Their sepulchral nature may be inferred from the fact that the stones set up in rows and circles frequently had burials at their foot. The fact that burials occur at the foot of a standing stone does not of course prove that the stone and the burial were contemporary, but surely it is legitimate to infer that the stone was regarded as the monument of the dead man. Certainly the standing stones of the Dark Ages were such, for many of them bear inscriptions, in Latin or Ogam, recording his name. My own belief is that most of our British standing stones belong in fact to the Dark Ages, or that they were not originally isolated but formed part of some monument whose other parts have been removed.

In the south of France the standing stones are shaped into the resemblance of a human figure, the so-called 'dolmen-idol', whose distribution extends as far south as Morocco and possibly as far east as Troy. The sepulchral character of the 'dolmen-idol' is proved by its occurrence, carved in chalk, in the certainly sepulchral caves of the Marne district. In Southern Abyssinia are whole groups of such 'dolmen-idols'. The age of these is quite unknown, but even if it be not as great as that of the European examples—and it may be—

[1]*Rude Stone Monuments in all Countries*, by James Ferguson, 1872.

there must surely be some cultural connection therewith. There is a group of standing stones, which I have seen, near Tshumen in Bulgaria.

Where found in association, standing stones are more often arranged in rows. The classic instance is at Karnac in Brittany, where there are many rows running parallel to each other. Single rows are rare, but instances occur at Trelleck in Monmouthshire (Harold's Stones), near Rothbury in Northumberland (the Five Kings), and near Borough-bridge in Yorkshire (the Devil's Arrows). A peculiar feature of the Devil's Arrows is that the tops are grooved, and this has sometimes been regarded as done intentionally. That is not so; the grooves are simply the effect of long-continued weathering which has worn away the softer strata of the sedimentary rock of which the stones are formed. A similar grooving occurs elsewhere, e.g. at the Queen Stone, Goodrich (Herefordshire), and the Devil's Thumb and Finger (Shropshire); and there are traces of it on some of the uprights at Stonehenge.

Single rows of standing stones also occur on Dartmoor (where small, double rows also occur). Here a warning should be given. Ancient field-walls were often, especially in the west of England, built with large stones set some distance apart, the intervening spaces being built up with smaller stones. When the wall became derelict, the smaller stones collapsed, leaving only the big ones standing, and these have sometimes been mistaken for stone rows of a ritual nature. Such walls are still being built in the Scilly Islands. When derelict the walls may be recognized by the pile of smaller stones that can usually be detected, forming a low bank.

Ritual stone-rows are sometimes associated with burial-cairns, and I suspect that the curious contemporary causeway of small stones that forms a sort of tail to the megalithic burial-mound of Bryn yr Hen Bobl in Anglesey is in fact some sort of echo of a substitute for a stone row. Burials were found in it.[2]

But more common than single rows are the double ones, usually called avenues. The classic example is at Avebury where the avenue is over a mile long. Burials have been found at the foot of some of the stones, establishing their sepulchral character. Of course the burial was in these cases subsequent to the erection of the stone, but even so the association of ideas is surely evident. Although the stone was not set up to mark a grave it did in fact do so and may therefore be regarded as a tombstone. There are stone avenues at the stone circles of Callanish in the Outer Hebrides. The avenue at Stonehenge consists of earthen banks and ditches; whether there were ever any settings of stones or of timber uprights along it is unknown, but could easily be ascertained by excavation. Probably there were not, for if there had been the holes would almost certainly have been revealed (as part of the avenue itself was) by air-photography.

Stone circles are the best known of these stone-settings and need no lengthy description here. They are probably the most familiar of all kinds of field monuments; and as this book is designed rather as a guide to explorers than as a summary of knowledge, certain aspects only will be dealt with. Roughly speaking there are two kinds of stone circles—large ones with free standing stones and lines of small ones that formed the peristalith of a burial-cairn. The latter is often confused with the former, especially when the stones of the cairn have been removed; but it is not of course a stone circle at all *sensu stricto* but merely the remains of a wall supporting the stones of a cairn. These cairn-circles are far commoner

[2] W. J. Hemp, *Archaeologia*, LXXXV, 1936, 253–92.

9a. & b. How a hut circle is formed (Darfur); see page 227

10. Pimperne Long Barrow, Dorset; see page 171

11. Underground room at Matmata, South Tunisia; see page 154

12. (*above*) Medenine, South Tunisia; general view of square; see page 158
13. (*below*) Mnaidra, Malta; see page 163

than stone circles proper, just as there are more graves than churches. They usually have a small central cist formed of slabs of stone. The big circles, of which Stonehenge and Avebury are the classic examples, are often described as temples, that is to say, places of communal gathering for some religious purpose, and we can accept this description as being probably correct. But they are also closely associated with burial. When inspecting a stone circle the central part should be examined carefully for any remains of a burial-chamber or cist or even for slight disturbance of the ground that may be all that remains of such. Megalithic structures of the 'dolmen' type occur inside the circles at Avebury, Stanton Drew and Cairnpapple, and in the great circle at Armagh in Ireland. It should be observed whether there is a bank and ditch round the circle, and if so whether the ditch is on the inner or outer side. It should also be observed whether the stones are smoother on the circle side (facing the centre) than on the outer, and whether there are any traces of cupmarks or other carvings. If stones are missing, the stone-holes are often visible. It is unlikely that (apart from cupmarks) there will be any signs of artificial dressing, but they should be looked for.

Besides stone circles there are a certain number of circular earthworks which have an internal ditch, and are therefore certainly not defensive. At first sight they may be mistaken for camps, and have been, for when they are in the midst of cultivation, the ditch is filled in and less easy to detect. It is never quite obliterated, however, and when it was on the inner side, the rampart on this side is generally steeper, and the ground at its foot rather lower, than on the outer side. A good example is Durrington Walls,[3] a mile and a half north of Amesbury, Wilts. The area enclosed is a coombe on the west bank of the Salisbury Avon, and for this reason alone the earthwork should never have been mistaken, as it was, for a defensive structure. Its diameter varies from 1300 to 1160 feet, which is slightly more than that of the great enclosure at Avebury, whose average diameter is 1,130 feet. Woodhenge is only 80 yards away on the south. There are no remains of standing stones, nor of holes in which such stones, or timber uprights may have stood. But there has been no attempt to find them by excavation, and although, if they had existed, one could have expected them to have been revealed by air-photography, their existence cannot be ruled out. A characteristic feature is the presence of two gaps in the rampart, opposite each other.

Other similar enclosures exist at Marden in the Vale of Pewsey and at Maumbury and Conquer Barrow outside Dorchester, Dorset.[4] There is another, consisting of two concentric circles with two opposed gaps, outside Dorchester, Oxon. The 'camp' revealed by air-photography at Upper Heyford, Oxon., may be another such; and also that at Eubury near Stow-on-the-Wold in the Cotswolds. It should be observed that all these six circles occur close to the banks of streams.

There are also other circular enclosures of a ritual character which usually occur in groups. Examples are found at Knowlton in Dorset, Priddy on the Mendips and at Thornborough and Hutton Moor in Yorkshire.[5] A large group in the Upper Thames basin was found by George Allen. One of the circles at Knowlton is simply an enlarged version

[3] See *Antiquity*, III, 1929, 49–59 (description with plans and air-photos).
[4] Both these were accidentally overlooked by me (though I knew them well) and omitted from the *Map of Neolithic Wessex*, published by the Ordnance Survey in 1932.
[5] The chief facts are recorded in the Ordnance Survey maps covering the area. The standard account is that by Dr Grahame Clark in *Proc. Preh. Soc.*, N.S., II, 1936, 1–51.

of a disc-barrow or bell-barrow, thus emphasizing the sepulchral nature of this kind of monument.

All these ritual circles, however one may classify them, were probably constructed for similar or cognate purposes. We can only guess at the reasons which may have dictated the building of a small wooden circle in one case and a large earthen enclosure in the other. That different purposes were served is pretty clear from the fact that both at Dorchester (Oxon) and Durrington, the two types occur side by side and appear to belong to the same culture.

Since the preceding paragraphs were written the whole subject of 'henge monuments' has been discussed at length by R. J. C. Atkinson in Chapter VIII of his *First Report on the Excavations at Dorchester, Oxon* (Ashmolean Museum, 1951.) He accepts the Piggotts' division into two groups, with a single entrance and with double opposed ones. Stuart Piggott has now added to them yet another type consisting of circular arrangements of pits. He quotes[6] an example from Dorchester, Oxon, and regards the Aubrey Holes at Stonehenge—the earliest part of the monument—as another. The whole subject has now become complicated in proportion to the increase of evidence from excavation. The 'henges' seem definitely to belong to a late Neolithic, pre-Beaker culture.

These remarks about circles and 'henges' have been introduced chiefly in order to dispose of a group of monuments that the field archaeologist will constantly come across in his rambles. It is necessarily superficial and unsatisfactory because it attempts to cover a vast field in a few pages. My intention has been merely to record the existence of these monuments, which no book on field archaeology could omit. Having done so, and indicated in footnotes where fuller information can be obtained, I can now pass on to consider the second group, burial-chambers.

The word 'burial-chamber' was adopted by the Ordnance Survey and subsequently by other official bodies, to describe the remains of megalithic tombs to which an earlier generation had given the pseudo-antique names of 'dolmen' and 'cromlech'. In my book on the *Long Barrows of the Cotswolds* I showed that the free-standing 'dolmen' was a myth, and that it was simply the surviving remains of chambers of vanished burial-mounds or cairns. This discovery, opposed by some when first made, has now been generally accepted and been found true of the 'dolmens' in other lands, e.g. in Sardinia.[7] The 'dolmens' are, in Childe's words, 'just the most stubborn remnants of more complex structures'. They were more stubborn because heavier and therefore more difficult to move than the smaller stones of which the 'complex structures' were composed. Farmers could use these smaller stones to build field-walls with, but the megalithic ones were useless for that purpose and therefore left alone. Careful observation, however, and the record of early drawings, shows in most instances a scatter of smaller stones still surviving round the foot of the megaliths, remnants of the cairn in which they were once buried. In visiting a 'dolmen' these stones should always be looked for. Good examples of typical 'dolmens' that are still half-buried in their cairns (both long ones) may be seen at Egryn (Carneddau Hengwm) and Dyffryn in Merionethshire.[8]

---

[6] *Aspects of Archaeology*, 279.

[7] See Gordon Childe in *Ancient India*, No. 4, 1947–8, 7. For a useful set of plans (of the usual sketchy and diagrammatic Mediterranean type, but all we have) see *Il Convegno Archeologico in Sardegna*, Giugno, 1926, 2nd edn., Reggio nell' Emilia, 1929.

[8] See my plans in *Archaeologia Cambrensis*, 6 S., XX, 1920, 129–33. Since 1920 many others have, of course, been recognized and planned.

The importance of this discovery lay in the fact that two types of monument—the 'dolmen' and the burial-mound or cairn, whether long or round—that previously had been regarded as distinct were thus shown to be the same. To publish the plan of a 'dolmen' without including its cairn (when present, or without recording the remnants when such are visible) would be like publishing the plan of a porch and omitting the house. Consciousness of this fact has not yet spread to Mediterranean lands, where there is a fine field for research in making proper plans of megalithic remains. It is eminently a subject for the field archaeologist, who can do this work with nothing but a tape-measure.[9]

In the south of England (east of Devon and Cornwall) the covering mound was invariably long and is called a Long Barrow (Plate 10). In stony regions it was a cairn, elsewhere an earthen mound. The burial-chambers consisted of a mixture of megaliths and small stones, and the whole was surrounded by a retaining wall of dry stone. No mortar was used (so far as we know) in Wessex, where the flat Oolitic stones could easily be made into good walls, as they are to-day. But in the Scilly Isles and in North Wales traces of a mud mortar have been found between the stones. In the Marlborough region, where huge sarsen stones occur, these were used for the burial-chambers; and at West Kennet, where is the longest long barrow known (340 feet) Oolitic stones were also used in a mound of earth. These must have been fetched from the nearest outcrop about five miles to the west. Elsewhere in the stoneless regions of Wessex and in Lincolnshire it would be reasonable to suppose that wooden chambers or enclosures were built for the dead, but there is no evidence of it.[10] The earth for the mound was obtained from a quarry-ditch on each side which was only very rarely continued round the ends. The mound was higher and broader at the east end.

Some evidence of development can be traced in the plan. The earliest, typologically, have a megalithic portal at the east end, flanked by the incurving ends of the surrounding retaining-wall. A passage led from the portal down the middle of the cairn, out of which opened chambers of round or polygonal shape. Later it was found more convenient to make the entrances to the chambers in the sides of the cairn. The passage was then discontinued, but the the portal at the east end was retained, though merely a dummy. I called these two types the true and false passage-grave types respectively.

The entrances were often formed of two stones set together in whose sides a notch had been cut, but occasionally a single slab was perforated by a hole. This hole, unlike the notches, was not big enough to admit a human body, and is thought to have had a ritual significance. The port-hole occurs in every region where megaliths are found, and it has a large literature. It is found in Britain, in the Mediterranean, in the Caucasus and in India.

A peculiar variety of the long barrow is that to which I gave the name Bank Barrow.[11] This type came to light in Dorset, in 1937, where Dr Wheeler found and excavated one within the ramparts of Maiden Castle. It was 1,700 feet long, and the mound passed over the silted-up ditch of the Neolithic causeway-camp, thus proving that the barrow was much later in date. During 1938 I happened to be doing some field-work in Schleswig-Holstein and found similar bank barrows there, 380, 450 and 600 metres in length.

---

[9] In some cases, however, e.g., at the Grotte des Fées near Arles, some preliminary clearance of rubbish and vegetation would greatly help.

[10] See Stuart Piggott in *Proc. Preh. Soc. N.S.*, I, 1935, 122–6: ib. id. *N.S.*, III, 1937, 5 (turf enclosure, Holdenhurst).

[11] See *Antiquity*, XII, 1938, 228–32.

The 'megalithic' group of monuments, therefore, includes many which are built of small, not large, stones, and some built of wood; in Mediterranean lands it must also cover rock-cut tombs. (This matter of nomenclature is discussed at the beginning of the next chapter). Strictly speaking one should call the mounds in which the burial-chambers were covered with small stones 'long cairns', reserving the term 'long barrow' for those of earth.[12] When I went to the Ordnance Survey in 1920, I was faced with this problem of nomenclature at the outset, and had to produce a system that could be used throughout Great Britain. The term 'long barrow' was obviously unsuitable in Scotland, where the covering is exclusively of stone and where the word 'barrow' is not used. I therefore adopted the term 'long cairn' for all such. But, as always with attempts at standardization, difficulties at once arose. The Cotswold examples were really cairns; since, however, many of them already possessed ancient names like Ganborough, Longborough,[13] Lamborough, Woodbarrow, which could not and should not be changed—Longborough is the name of a parish—and since they were already known as long barrows and included some of the classical examples of the type, familiar to all archaeologists since Thurnam's famous monograph in *Archaeologia* (Vol. 42), I decided that logic must be sacrificed to custom and convenience, and retained the term 'long barrow'.

In parts of Britain, particularly in the west and north, i.e. in the Highland Zone, another type of burial-cairn occurs which is round or oval. The typology is difficult and somewhat controversial, and need not be discussed here.[14] The facts are undisputed. There are many examples of round cairns covering megalithic burial-chambers in the Scilly Isles, and it is, in my opinion, certain that the majority at least of the Cornish burial-chambers (so-called 'dolmens') originally stood in round or oval cairns. (There are, however, at least two undoubted long cairns or long barrows in Cornwall). In Wales both long and round cairns are found,[15] the round predominating in the north-west and south-west, and the Brecknockshire group consisting exclusively of long cairns. In Ireland the most famous round cairn is that at New Grange, seventy miles north-west of Dublin; some of the great boulders of the cairn-circle round it are ornamented with elaborate incised spirals and other patterns. The burial-chamber itself is cruciform; it has long ago been robbed of its contents. In Northern Ireland are many long ('segmented') cairns, which have been well excavated and planned by the active group of archaeologists in that country.[16] South-west Scotland contains some round cairns and many long ones, long ago explored by Dr Bryce and described in a series of classic articles.[17] The cairns of the Outer Hebrides are also round

[12] The term 'long barrow' seems to be a modern re-invention. It was, however, used in Saxon times. There are several references to long barrows in Saxon Charters. A 'langan hlaew' in the bounds of Tackley, Oxon, is called Long Banck on a map of Whitehill Farm (1605) and is still plainly to be seen (*Antiquity*, IV, 1930, 358). The bounds of Wonston, Hants (Birch, *Cart. Sax.*, 604, A.D. 904), mention a 'barrow between the two long barrows'. The (round) barrow and one of the long ones were rediscovered by Mr G. C. Dunning (*Antiquaries Journal*, XXVI, 1946, 185–6; see also, *A Contribution to a Dictionary of Old English Place-names*, by Rune Forsberg, Uppsala, 1950, 202–3).

[13] The Saxon word *beorh* usually becomes 'barrow' in Middle and Modern English, and the Saxon word *burh, burg*, dative *byr(i)g*, a fortified place, usually becomes 'borough' or '-bury'. But by a confusion of sound 'borough', as in this instance, represents the Saxon suffix *beorh*.

[14] See 'The Long Barrow in Western Europe', by Glyn E. Daniel, in *The Early Cultures of Northwest Europe* (ed. Sir Cyril Fox and Bruce Dickins), 1950, 3–20, and books and articles there referred to. See also *Proc. Preh. Soc., N.S.*, II, 1936, 213.

[15] For South Wales see W. F. Grimes, Ordnance Survey Map of S. Wales, showing the distribution of Long Barrows and Megaliths (1936); for the Brecknockshire group see my book, *Long Barrows of the Cotswolds* (Bellows, Gloucester, 1925), 53–66, and Grimes in *A Hundred Years of Welsh Archaeology* (Bellows, Gloucester, n.d., but 1950), 36–9.

[16] See articles in the *Ulster Journal of Archaeology*, recent numbers.

[17] *Proc. Soc. Ant. Scot.*, XXXVI, 1902, 74–181; XXXVII, 1903, 36–67 (Arran); XXXVIII, 1904, 17–81 (Bute).

and some have been excavated by Sir Lindsay Scott.[18] One of the most famous of all megalithic monuments is the Mound of Maes Howe in Orkney, robbed by Vikings who left an inscription there in runic characters. There are also long cairns there. Caithness and the north-eastern coastal region is the land of Horned (Long) Cairns, but some are almost equal-sided. Aberdeenshire is a county of stone circles, peculiar in having a re-cumbent stone in the periphery. Long cairns are almost non-existent on the east coast south of the Moray Firth, but one or two isolated examples do occur. Going south to Lincolnshire we find a large and important group of long barrows on the Wolds. East Anglia contains only one long barrow. There is a small group in Kent, of which Kit's Coty House, a 'dolmen' at the east end of a long barrow, and Coldrum which is somewhat similar, are the best known instances. There are a little over half a dozen long barrows on the Sussex Downs.

A distribution-map of these monuments shows that they do not occur evenly throughout the country, but are concentrated into groups; that is due to special conditions of soil, vegetation and water-supply. A detailed description of their distribution would take several pages. The largest group is that on the chalk downs of Wessex. For the field archaeologist the point to notice is that a long barrow or long cairn, or a ritual circle of stone or earth, that is reported in any place far distant from one of the recognized groups should only be accepted as a genuine example if its character is quite certain and confirmed by the exist-ence of several of the characteristic features. Some long mounds at first supposed to have been long barrows have proved on further investigation to be something else; pillow-mounds, actually rabbit-warrens, have been mistaken for long barrows,[19] and it is not easy at first sight to distinguish a long-disused rifle-butt from one such. Pillow-mounds usually occur in number close together (which long barrows rarely do), and lack big side-ditches. But it is still possible that a few small groups of long barrows exist undetected. The Brecknockshire group in the Black Mountains and the Lincolnshire group had both escaped notice, though in both areas some of the long barrows were already marked, and obvious as such, on the Ordnance maps. The groups of earthen circles, probably ritual, in the Upper Thames region were completely unknown and unsuspected (though many are visible on the ground) till discovered by air-observation by George Allen, and the same is true of the crop-sites at Dorchester, Oxon. Isolated but genuine long barrows do occur —near Christchurch, Hants, near Northampton, near Farnham, Surrey and at Gourdon near Stonehaven. There is a little-known small group of monuments near Muckleston in West Staffordshire, east of Market Drayton. The best example has a perforated stone and is called the 'Devil's Ring and Finger'. No field archaeologist has explored the district, and there may well be others awaiting discovery.[20] It would be easy to make plans of the existing remains, and I would suggest this as a task for any reader of this book who has the means of doing so.

This rapid and imperfect survey will at any rate serve to indicate what is meant by megalithic monuments and where some of them are to be found. It is not the purpose of

[18] See articles in the *Proceedings of the Prehistoric Society*, recent numbers.

[19] In *Wessex from the Air* (18–24); stimulated by the discovery of a fine group (Plate xxvii), I devoted more space than they deserved to these rabbit-warrens of quite recent origin; subsequent research by myself and others, set them in their proper place; see *Antiquity*, II, 1928, 205–6; IV, 1930, 199.

[20] My notes on these were lost during the war, nor have I seen the monuments. Doubt has been cast on their authen-ticity recently, but the perforated stone demands an explanation, and its name suggests antiquity. See my note in *Ant Journ.*, IV, 1924, 405–6; and Glyn Daniel, *Prehistoric Chamber Tombs*, 1950, 45–6.

this book to do more than draw attention to the chief things that a person interested in
archaeology will meet with in rambling over the countryside. If he wants to know more
he must consult some of the excellent books now available on British prehistory, and the
more detailed descriptions in the articles referred to in the footnotes.

There is one final matter that cannot be passed over in silence. How were the great
stones and wooden tree-trunks erected? Archaeology can tell us something; excavation
has revealed the sliding-grooves made for the timber uprights of Woodhenge, and the
graze-marks on the (opposite) sides of the post-holes made by the upright as it was lowered
into the hole. Modern analogy from the Naga region of Assam, where megalithic monuments are still erected, or were until recently, shows how the big stones were packed for
transport, and man-handled.[21] The rest is at best informed speculation. We know neither
the route by which the foreign stones of Stonehenge were transported from Pembrokeshire, nor the method of transport. Nor do we know how the lintels were raised and placed
across the trilithons. There are many possible solutions; all are pure guess-work. The
archaeologist does not waste his time guessing; there are many problems which can be
solved but only by hard work, in field and library. Knowledge is not advanced by idle
theorizing.

It has been suggested that the foregoing account is incomplete without some mention
of those far commoner things—round barrows. Perhaps it is; but for several reasons I
do not propose to deal here with round barrows. The chief reason is that they have been
described far more thoroughly by Mr L. V. Grinsell, both in a book[22] devoted to the
subject and in detailed county surveys published in the proceedings of the respective
county archaeological societies. Round barrows are of course far commoner than long
ones—indeed in Wessex they are the commonest of all field monuments. Bell-barrows (a
fine one at the edge of Stonehenge) and disc barrows belong to the Early (or Middle)
Bronze Age. A low, saucer-like type may have been introduced by the Late Bronze Age
invaders. The Romanized Britons built barrows too, usually recognizable at sight by the
steepness of their sides; the Six Hills at Stevenage are such, and can be seen from the
train on the main eastern route to Scotland. There are others beside the Roman road at
Badbury Rings (Dorset). Saxon barrows are of several kinds; big single barrows like
that covering the chief's grave at Taplow Court, or the Asthall barrow (Oxon), and
probably *Cwichelmeshlaew* on the Berkshire Downs above Didcot; or groups of small ones
over single graves such as occur in Kent on Barham Downs and in Surrey on Farthing
Down near Croydon. Christianity put an end to barrow-burial—unless the Sutton
Hoo ship-barrow was erected by Christians.

[21] See *Antiquity*, III, 1929, 324–388 (J. H. Hutton: 'Assam Megaliths').
[22] *Ancient Burial-mounds of England*, 2nd edn., 1953 (Methuen). See also my article on Barrows in *Antiquity*, I, 419–34;
Dunning and Jessup on Roman Barrows, ib. id., X, 37–53 (XII, 103).

CHAPTER 16

Roman Earthworks

THE ROMANS INVADED Britain in the first century A.D. Their armies swept swiftly over the whole of the Lowland Zone, but encountered some opposition from the tougher inhabitants of Wales and Scotland. They came as conquerors and exploiters, like the Normans, not as settlers, like the prehistoric and Anglo-Saxon invaders. They did not therefore disrupt the Archaic agricultural system, which persisted throughout the occupation. There are, however, a few examples of intrusion into the agricultural areas of Wessex. Two farms of the Roman period have been proved by excavation, one on Rockbourne Down, Hants,[1] and another on Roden Down, Berks.[2] The enclosure-banks of these farms have the straightness and regularity that in all periods (including the present) distinguishes the work of the professional surveyor from that of the peasant. I remember the banks on Roden Down before they were destroyed by the plough; they were so well made and well preserved that I put them down as comparatively modern and not perhaps earlier than the later medieval period. They were, in fact, so regarded by the Ordnance surveyors, who marked them on the 6-inch map with the same symbols as modern field boundaries and not as antiquities.

A similar perfection is shown by the banks of what must surely be another Roman farm called Soldier's Ring, not far from the one at Rockbourne.[3] This has not been proved by excavation, but the banks are demonstrably later than the Celtic fields which they over-run and ignore.

There must be many other such farms. When taking the photographs published in *Wessex from the Air* I found at least two others on Salisbury Plain which seem to be of similar origin, and from their shape I called them 'Kites'. Until they have been excavated, proof of age is lacking; and although a medieval date is not impossible, I still prefer to regard them as Roman. Quite possibly they may be the farms of retired soldiers, which would account for the military precision of their design.

The most familiar Roman intrusions are of course the so-called Roman villas, which were farms or large country houses.[4] Their distribution, shown for the first time on the Ordnance Survey Map of Roman Britain, proves that they occupied the areas then still

---

[1] Excavated by Heywood Sumner; see his *Excavations on Rockbourne Down, Hampshire*, 1914 [Bodl. G. A. Hants, 89 226 (9)].

[2] See above, p. 117.

[3] *Air Survey and Archaeology*, 1928, Plate 9; *Wessex from the Air*, Plate 49. See also Fig. 13, p. 93 above.

[4] For the most part self-sufficient, even probably the fulling-mill at Chedworth. See Haverfield and Macdonald, *Roman Occupation of Britain*, 1924, 230, for these fulling establishments.

less thickly populated and available therefore for agricultural exploitation. Such were the chalk lands of Hampshire, where a covering of clay supported a heavier growth of vegetation than the light soil of Salisbury Plain. That does not imply that Hampshire was unoccupied or that the whole of Salisbury Plain was cultivated. We know that large areas of the Hampshire chalk-lands were covered by Celtic fields, and that some of the cowdowns and sheepdowns of Wiltshire remained unploughed down to the present day. It means that the Romans or Romanized Britons, with their better tools and technique, were able to deal more effectively than their predecessors with the clay scrublands and forest. Unfortunately we still know little of the field-systems associated with the villas.

We do, however, know something of the fences round the villas. I call them 'fences' because that word seems the best to describe what we know of only as crop-marks in air-photographs. Until George Allen discovered and photographed several examples in Oxfordshire they were unknown. His photographs show that the villas stood in a rectangular enclosure, of which the ditch only remains. The best example is at Ditchley, which he made famous as the finest example of a house-plan completely revealed by air-photography, and whose fame was enhanced by the excavations of Mr Ralegh Radford.[5] There is another example (unexcavated) at Callow Hill not far off, and several other probable ones in the neighbourhood. In no single instance have the banks survived, so that in a book which deals as this does, mainly with remains visible on the surface, and how to recognize them, a bare enumeration must suffice.

Roman villas are rare in the north of England, and there are none north of Hadrian's Wall. A single example that has been found in Yorkshire stands within defences that seem to have been of a more formidable kind and designed as a protection against raiders. A similar measure of protection was taken about A.D. 300 to defend the Roman house at Ely near Cardiff, which recalls the moated homesteads of the Middle Ages.[6]

Besides remains directly connected with houses, there still survive a certain number of Roman engineering works. The great sea-bank on the Monmouthshire shore of the Severn estuary seems to have been made by the Roman army, for near Goldcliff, three miles south of Caerleon, an inscribed centurial stone was found, recording that 'the company of Statorius Maximus of the first cohort of the 2nd Augustan Legion' (built so many feet of this sea-wall).[7] This being so, a Roman origin is possible, though unproven, for sea-banks elsewhere, as in Kent (e.g. near Ebbsfleet) and in the great expanses of the Fenland, where the Cambridgeshire portion of the sixty-mile long Car Dyke has recently been proved by Dr Grahame Clark to be a Roman canal.[8] The Fens abound in evidence of Roman engineering, which include innumerable fields with their accompanying drainage-ditches, and field-roads between drainage-ditches. Along one such road the remains of a wooden bridge have been found[9] and there must have been very many others. But until the field-systems of the Fens have been reduced to order by the publication of maps based on air-photographs, and some of the remains tested by excavation, it would be premature to enlarge upon them. Most of them, moreover, are merely crop-sites, and the few vestiges

[5] *Oxoniensia*, I, 1936, 24–69.
[6] Wheeler, *Prehistoric and Roman Wales*, 1925, 258, Fig. 106 (plan).
[7] Ib. id., p. 228, Fig. 98.
[8] *Antiquaries Journal*, XXIX, 1949, 145–63.
[9] *Luftbild und Vorgeschichte*, 57 (Rookery Farm, Cambridgeshire). See also *Geogr. Journ.*, LXXXII, 1933, 434–41, 'A Roman bridge in the Fens'. It is at Nordelph, near the Old Bedford River (Norfolk 68 *S.E.*).

that still survived intact under grass in 1939 have probably now been consumed by the omnivorous plough.[10]

Aqueducts are, in Europe, amongst the most outstanding of Roman remains. No such examples occur in Britain, but there are many minor works. One supplied the Roman town of Durnovaria (Dorchester, Dorset) with water from a spring near Maiden Newton, seven miles to the north-west. It consisted of a trench along the hillside superficially resembling the scarp-side Grim's Ditch along the Berkshire Downs. Under Poundbury, just outside Dorchester, it is still well preserved, and was excavated in 1939.[11] A similar aqueduct (whose earthwork no longer survives) supplied the Roman town of Lindum (Lincoln), being made for some distance along the Roman road approaching the town from the north-east.[12] There are others in the north, near and south of the Roman Wall. Their superficial appearance, when they survive intact, hardly needs description; they should be easy to trace, for they necessarily follow the contour line pretty closely, so that their course may be plotted ahead with some confidence.[13]

Roman barrows[14] may be distinguished superficially from those of other periods by their steep conical shape and from the presence in some of them of a small bank round the bottom. The best examples are those at Badbury Rings (Dorset), the Six Hills, Stevenage (Herts), and the huge Bartlow Hills (Cambridgeshire). They have been fully dealt with by Dunning and Jessup, to whose article readers are referred.

Britain even contains examples of Roman theatres, the best known being the amphi-theatre at Caerleon and the theatre at St Albans. Probably there was one outside every town; they still survive outside Richborough, Dorchester (Maumbury Ring), Cirencester (the Bullring) and Silchester, and the Roman fort at Tomen-y-Muir in Merionethshire. It is even possible that the Britons may have adopted them from the Romans, for there are certain theatre-like earthworks at several of the Wessex village-sites. This explanation was put forward by Hadrian Allcroft, who elaborated it in an article[15] full of interesting speculations and illustrated by some plans. Some of the alleged structures (which he called 'circuses') are demonstrably spring-ponds; and it is notoriously difficult to prove the nature of use by purely archaeological methods. But others may well be what he claims they are.

Roman military earthworks and stone defences are a subject in themselves, for which the reader is referred to books dealing specifically with Roman archaeology, and to articles about particular sites.[16] Here a brief enumeration of the chief kinds must suffice.

In Britain the most important military establishment was the legionary fortress of which three are known, at Isca Silurum (Caerleon in Monmouthshire), Deva (Chester) and Eburacum (York). There were, however, military headquarters that must have approxi-mated to this status at Gloucester and Castor (Northants)[17] and at Inchtuthil in Perthshire. When conducting a campaign the army entrenched itself each night in a marching-camp of large extent, but of no great strength, so far as the dimensions of the rampart were

[10] A good example of Roman work is revealed by an air-photograph of Welney Washes, published in *Luftbild und Vorgeschichte*, 1938, 58. [11] *Antiquaries Journal*, XX, 1940, 435–9. [12] *Arch. Journal*, CIII, 1947, 36–7.
[13] On the water-supply of Roman forts see Richmond, 'The water-supply of the Roman fort at Lyne' (Peeblesshire), *P.S.A.S.*, LXXV, 1940–1, 39–43, and references there to other sources.
[14] *Antiquity*, X, 1936, 37–53; see also XII, 103. [15] *Arch. Journ.*, LXXIX, 1922, 173–215.
[16] For instance, R. G. Collingwood's *Archaeology of Roman Britain* (Methuen, 1930), and the books mentioned in my pamphlet on *Field Archaeology*, published by the Stationery Office for the Ordnance Survey in 1932, but now out of print. For Scotland, see my *Topography of Roman Scotland north of the Antonine Wall* (Cambridge, 1949,.) and the plans and references there given.
[17] For Gloucester, see *Journ. Roman Studies*, XXXII, 1942, 39–52; XXXIII, 1943, 15–28; for Castor, see *Antiquity*, XIII, 1939, 178–90; 455–8.

M

concerned. The banks may often be recognized by their straightness (though they are not always straight) and symmetry, and by the small bank and ditch (called a *tutulus*) made in front of the entrances (usually four or six) as an added protection. Sometimes instead of a detached *tutulus*, the entrance was defended by curved banks (called *claviculae*) resting on the rampart-ends. The camps were carefully sited and sometimes (as at Battledykes, Oathlaw) deliberately included an eminence that could serve as a look-out. At Little Clyde near Crawford (Lanarkshire) a streamlet is crossed, presumably to provide a water supply. Along Strathmore the marching-camps are set at the distance of a day's march apart. Marching-camps were the first defences to be built in an invaded territory; and when the invasion was successful, it would be natural to place the permanent forts on the same sites. This was done at Richborough (Kent), where the Claudian camp has been found beneath the later occupation remains. At Ardoch (Perthshire) the famous fort, one of the best-preserved in Britain, was preceded by several marching-camps. If we could clear away the overlying Roman and medieval remains, I expect we should find military forts, and per-haps also some marching-camps, beneath the sites of many of the Roman towns which, like Winchester and Silchester, were the radiating points of roads certainly laid out at an early stage in the conquest of Britain.

To an early stage in the conquest must also belong some of the signal-stations. In Scotland (where the best group is that along the Gask ridge in Perthshire) these consist of round, ditched platforms about fifty feet in diameter, on which were built wooden towers. They were placed a mile or two apart so as to be mutually intervisible; and sig-nalling was by means of lighted torches fixed to posts thrust through an aperture, and also by beacons, whose pile of fuel is shown on Trajan's column in Rome.[18] Other signal-stations of the Gask type were found by the writer (in a reconnaissance flight in 1939) along the Roman road from Birrens to Little Clyde, in the neighbourhood of the latter. They were visible only (as shadow-sites) when the sun was low and form an excellent subject for air-discovery; for the small circular ditch shows up very well as a shadow-site, and should be equally plain as a crop-site, resembling a barrow-circle with a gap. Until recently none were known south of Hadrian's Wall; but recent excavations at Willoughby-on-the-Wolds have revealed what may be the remains of one such on the Foss-way, which is exactly where a line of signal-stations would most be expected if (as Colling-wood thought) it formed a temporary frontier during the Roman Conquest. It is certain that there must be others, probably along the whole length of the road from Exeter to Lincoln. All should be recoverable by air-photography except in built-up regions.

The round signal-stations were not the only ones. There were others of a slightly larger and more elaborate type, represented by Kaims Castle and another, both near Ardoch. Others, of a not dissimilar plan but of much later date (early fourth century), were built along the Yorkshire coast as a defence against the early Saxon raiders.[19]

---

[18] See *The Roman Wall in Scotland* (2nd ed., 1934), by Sir George Macdonald, Plate lx (opp. p. 356), and the adjacent text for fuller details of signalling methods. See also Collingwood's *Archaeology of Roman Britain* (1930) Chapter 4; Signal Stations and Light-houses; and Sir George Macdonald's 'Die Küstenverteidigung Britanniens gegen das Ende der Römi-schen Herrschaft', published in *Funfundzwanzig Jahre Römisch-Germanische Kommission*, Berlin, 1929, 107-13, containing maps, plans and illustrations. See also *Aspects of Archaeology*, 1951, 293–302.

[19] See J. P. Bushe-Fox, *Journ. Roman Studies*, XXII, 1932, 60–72, and earlier F. J. Haverfield, *J.R.S.*, II, 1912, 201–14. Besides these in Yorkshire another has been found and proved by excavation on the N. Devon coast at Old Burrow, and a second (not excavated) identified by field-work. There must be others along the north coast of Somerset and Devon, and possibly on the south coast also. If so, they could most easily be rediscovered by air-reconnaissance, for their plan is unmistakable and uniform. It is possible that some may already be marked on the map with an incorrect description.

Amongst the most interesting of the remains belonging to an early stage in the conquest of a territory are the siege-works. The most famous example in Britain is at Burnswark near Lockerbie in Dumfriesshire. There on a flat-topped hill that is a landmark for miles around is a native hill-fort whose slight—and perhaps slighted—defences would not suggest that it was of much importance. On the slopes north and south of it are two Roman camps.[20] That on the south is the best-preserved, and is remarkable for the great size of the traverse-banks protecting the entrances facing the hill; it has been suggested that they were the stations of siege-engines. Birrenswark stands on guard on the main entrance to Scotland on the west coast, and it must, for this reason, have been chosen by the natives for their decisive but unsuccessful stand.

There is also evidence of Roman earthwork, presumably connected with a siege, at the hill-fort of Woden Law in the Cheviots. There on the gentle southern slope is a long straight rampart of unmistakably Roman character, ending in the air at each end, with its ditch on the side towards the hill-fort. Apart therefore from the character of the earth-work, which is quite unlike that of the hill-fort, it is obvious, when one sees it, that it was made by an attacking force.[21]

Roman siege-works are known from other parts of the empire. Those round Numantia in Spain were studied by Schulten,[22] who used a bad Spanish air-photograph. Masada on the Dead Sea where Titus besieged the Jewish rebels in A.D. 71 has been described by Professor Hawkes.[23] The remains of the Roman forts on its slopes, connected by an en-circling vallum, are amongst the best-preserved examples of such known. Some seventy miles west of Mosul (Nineveh) in the Syrian desert are the romantic ruins of Hatra, the caravan city four times besieged (by Trajan, Severus and Ardashir). There too not only is the line of circumvallation visible throughout, but also the platforms on which the siege-engines were mounted.

Such platforms occur also within the fort at Bremenium (Northumberland) where they were made in the third century and used of course for defence. They were built immediately behind the Severan fort-wall, and the vertical backs were of squared masonry standing on a plinth. The core was composed of rubble set in tough, resilient clay, and the whole edifice had a diameter of thirty-two feet from the fort wall. Such stone platforms were the permanent equivalents of the long platforms (*tribunalia*) upon which *ballistae* are shown, mounted for siege operations on Trajan's column; but those at Bremenium were probably not *ballistae* but *onagri*, which discharged a large globular stone weighing about a hundredweight. (Two of these are preserved on the gable of Rochester (Northumberland) school porch).[24]

Caesar's siege-works in Gaul were explored by Napoleon III, and the results published in two sumptuous volumes.[25] One could wish that they might be brought up to date by

---

[20] For air-photos, see *Antiquity*, XIII, 1939, 280–1; also *The Roman Occupation of S.W. Scotland*, ed. S. N. Miller, 1953, Plates 36 and 37.

[21] I observed these facts on the ground in the 1930's, and reported them at the time in a letter to Sir George Macdonald, who passed it on to the Secretary of the Royal Commission on Ancient Monuments (Scotland) for filing. The earth-work has recently been investigated again. It was air-observation that first drew my attention to it in 1928. It is now considered to have been made for training or practice purposes, not for actual siege-operations.

[22] For Schulten's publications on Numantia, see Déchelette, *Manuel*, Vol. 5 (Arch. gallo-romaine), 1931, 221, note 2. Schulten's plan of the site is reproduced on p. 222, Fig. 30.   [23] *Antiquity*, III, 1929, 195–213.

[24] Richmond, 'The Romans in Redesdale', *Hist. of Northumberland*, XV, 1940, 98.

[25] *Histoire de Jules César*, I (1865), II (1866) (Bodleian reference 221 h 148); there is another volume called *Cartes du tome premier* (Bodleian, History d 146). See also a book with the same title by his archaeological supervisor, Col. Stoffel, 2 vols. of text and one of plates, Paris, 1887.

air-photography, which would surely reveal much that escaped the French excavators of the mid-nineteenth century, when excavation everywhere was in its infancy.

The central item, so to speak, in Roman military defences, was the permanent fort. This was an earthwork of square or oblong shape, whose distinguishing feature (important for the field-worker) is its rounded corners. (Marching-camps were similarly distinguished). By this means it is often possible to tell a Roman fort at sight from a medieval or Bronze Age enclosure. The rounding was intentional to give room for more defenders at a weak point. Forts were carefully sited, and after some experience of them in the field, it is possible, when exploring new country, to decide beforehand which are the most promising places to search. The favourite position was on elevated ground that was not commanded by higher ground[26] and was also near a river. The Roman fort at Fendoch, rediscovered by Prof. Richmond, is typically situated near the Almond, but well away from the mountains to the north and south. The entrances of the forts were not, like those of marching-camps, defended by traverses. The ramparts were of stone, earth or turf, and the buildings within of stone or wood, as also were the gates.[27] With the internal arrangements we are not here concerned; but it should be mentioned that all Roman forts had bath-houses, usually situated just outside. Occasionally (as at Carpow) the bath-houses have been found before the fort; and in military regions the discovery of baths is a clue to the presence of a fort near by.

As I have said above, Roman forts can be distinguished by their rounded corners. That was a differentiating feature that was not observed by some of the early pioneers in field archaeology, with the result that many square or oblong earthworks, mostly medieval (such as those at Ardargie and Fortingall), were wrongly set down as Roman. There is seldom much difficulty in recognizing a rampart of Roman construction even on the ground, and from the air it is usually quite unmistakable.

Roman forts are of course commonest in the military parts of the province—Wales and Britain north of Hadrian's Wall. In the Lowland Zone the conquest forts are probably masked by later accretions. One, however, has survived more or less intact, in the north-west corner of the Iron Age fort of Hod Hill, Dorset.[28] Another of an abnormal type still exists at Ashley, beside the Roman road from Winchester to Salisbury. Its age was proven by the discovery of a Roman entrenching tool on the bottom of the ditch, thus settling in Dr Williams-Freeman's favour a long, friendly argument which we had about its age. There are other Roman forts (unexcavated) at Easton Grey near Malmesbury on the Foss-way and at Greensforge, south-west of Birmingham, on a newly-discovered Roman road from Droitwich to Wroxeter.

Excavation is of course the only method of reconstructing the history of a fort, but

[26] In reviewing my book on Roman Scotland in *Antiquity*, XXIII, 1949, 108, Prof. Richmond rightly criticises my hypothetical fort at Stirling on these grounds. Air-photography now supports his contention.

[27] For details of a wooden fort see Prof. Richmond on his excavation of Fendoch, and a short account based on that (with his plan) in my *Topography of Roman Scotland*, 45–7.

[28] This was perfect and unploughed in 1860, with all its internal arrangements plainly visible on the surface. In that year they were destroyed by ploughing. Now the plough is again at work and has already obliterated that half of the hill-fort which had escaped the earlier ploughing; and if measures of protection are not soon taken it will destroy the Roman defences upon which it is already encroaching. The ploughing (at first confined to the previously ploughed area) was reported at the time to the Chief Inspector of Ancient Monuments, and action was taken to see that the rest was not ploughed, but it was without effect. The *whole* interior of the hill-fort is now under plough, and a ragged barbed wire fence now runs along the crest of the rampart. This vandalism is a typical example of what is occurring all over the country. As I write this note I am informed that 'Oliver's Battery', a hill-fort near Alresford, has been recently levelled by the plough.

superficial observation can profit by the lessons of such excavation as has been carried out. It has been established, for instance, that what might appear to be a later annexe is sometimes the disused portion of an older fort, abandoned when its area was reduced. Thus, at Castell Collen in Radnorshire an earlier oblong fort was replaced early in the second century by a square one.[29] The same thing may have occurred at Ardoch. These abandoned portions look like annexes, and indeed are often indistinguishable from them on the surface; for such annexes contemporary with or later than the smaller square fort do occur, as at Gellygaer in Glamorganshire and Blakehope near Elishaw in Northumberland,[30] and in many other places.

Roman forts are seldom simple or of one period only. I have already mentioned their association with early marching-camps. That is established; but not all such were in fact strictly marching-camps. Some were what are called labour-camps, the dwelling-place of those who built the fort. A good example occurs at Chew Green,[31] a perfectly preserved complex site on the Border beside Dere Street, admirably elucidated by air-photography and Prof. Richmond.

Besides the normal permanent forts there were others, smaller in size, that have recently been revealed by air-photography. Such are those at Dalmakethar and Redshaw Burn on the western Roman route into Scotland.[32] Other examples occur at Tassiesholm (now renamed Milton) and Durisdeer. As seen on the air-photographs the two former have a single entrance only, on the side nearest the road; at Dalmakethar there is something which looks like an external *clavicula* protecting the entrance, and at Redshaw Burn there is a bank and ditch nearly the length of the fort in front of the entrance, between it and the road. The rampart-ends at the entrance are not symmetrically placed, but the bank of one ends opposite the ditch of the other, necessitating a sideways approach favourable for the defence. Many of these smaller forts or fortlets are placed at the crossing-places of ravines and streams, and one of their purposes may have been to protect a wooden bridge across them. Being set back a little distance from the road, they easily escape the observation of those who are walking along the road; both I and others had missed the fortlet at Redshaw Burn, though we had often walked close by it. Since air-photography called attention to their existence in 1939 I have not had an opportunity of walking again along the line of some of the Scottish roads where others may be awaiting discovery. The most promising stretches are those over open moorland, such as on the Durisdeer road, and the places to be examined most closely are the crossings of ravines.

No account of Roman military defences would be complete without at least a passing reference to those of stone (other than forts) though they lie beyond the scope of this book. They consist of town walls, forts of the Saxon Shore, and the great frontier wall of Hadrian from the Tyne to the Solway.[33] Remains of the Roman wall still exist round many towns (Canterbury, Colchester, Gloucester, Chester, London and many others).[34] They are more visible and better preserved round towns that ceased to exist,

---

[29] Wheeler, *Preh. and Roman Wales*, 230, Fig. 100, giving other instances.

[30] Wheeler, *Preh. and Roman Wales*, Fig. 100; Richmond, 'The Romans in Redesdale', *History of Northumberland*, XV, 1940, Fig. 5, 71.   [31] Richmond, *op. cit.*, 74, Fig. 9 (plan), plates opp. pp. 63 and 76 (air-photo).

[32] *Antiquity*, XIII, 1939, 282, Plate ii, where these small forts are discussed and other examples cited. See also S. N. Miller (title on p. 274 below), where full descriptions and plans of these forts are given.

[33] The Antonine Wall from the Forth to the Clyde was of turf. It has been dealt with in Sir George Macdonald's *magnum opus*, *The Roman Wall in Scotland*, 2nd ed., 1934 (Oxford).

[34] For their relative sizes in Roman times see the diagram in Haverfield and Macdonald's *Roman Occupation of Britain*, 1924, 217, Fig. 50.

such as Silchester, Verulamium (St Albans), Wroxeter and Kenchester. At Silchester the stonewalls were not built until the third century.[35] The forts of the Saxon Shore, extending from Branodunum (Brancaster) in Norfolk to Portchester (Hants) were constructed during the fourth century as a protection against the raids of Saxon pirates. They were under the command of an officer called the Count of the Saxon Shore, and a list of them with their names and garrisons is preserved in the fourth-century Notitia Dignitatum. All are marked on the Ordnance Survey Map of Roman Britain. Besides those in the Notitia Dignitatum there is another, found in or before 1927 at Carisbrooke Castle in the Isle of Wight.[36] There is no doubt from the character of the construction, and the bastions, that this is Roman work. Though standing near the head of the Medina estuary, it can hardly be called a shore-fort; but it is placed in the geographical centre of the island, at a point from which troops could quickly be despatched to any point on the shore where a landing was made or threatened. There is another fort built about A.D. 300 on a first-century site at Cardiff, marking 'the westerly limit of the system represented by Portchester, Richborough and the other coastal forts of south-eastern England.'[37]

To the period of the Saxon Shore forts may belong those enigmatic walls at Caister-on-the-Wolds and Horncastle (Lincolnshire). Nothing is known about them, though they were observed by Stukeley long ago. Lincolnshire has a barren archaeological history, though rich in remains, and it presents a fine opportunity to the field archaeologist.[38]

Hadrian's Wall and its accompanying turf vallum is a subject in itself (and one admirably suited to the hiking field archaeologist). For the former reason, however, it is unsuitable for treatment here. Much more work has been done upon it than upon any object of like size in Britain, not even excepting that other wall in Scotland. But it is not the most promising field for making new discoveries by surface observation. On the other hand, the beginner could not do better than walk along its length—in itself a pleasant undertaking—as a preliminary to the study of some of its literature.[39] Having done so, he can then study that literature at leisure—and walk it again in the light thereof. He will not understand what he reads until he knows the ground, and he cannot understand what he sees without reading about the excavations.

There is perhaps more scope for new superficial discoveries on the line of the Scottish Wall where there may still be a few crumbs left after the feast, especially between the forts —there are hints of such in Sir George Macdonald's *Roman Wall in Scotland* (2nd ed., 1934).[40] There is also the problem of the southern road and where it reached the wall. But for the most part the walls are training grounds rather than fields of discovery.

[35] For Silchester dates see 'Excavations at Silchester, 1938–9', by M. Aylwin Cotton, *Archaeologia*, XCII, 1947, 121–67.
[36] *Antiquity*, I, 1927, 476 (illus.).   [37] Wheeler, *Preh. and Roman Wales*, 1925, 235.
[38] Who will begin by consulting C. W. Phillips' admirable catalogue of sites of finds in *Arch. Journ.*, XC, 1934, 106–49; XCI, 1935, 97–187, and the Lincoln volume (CIII) of the same journal, published in November 1947.
[39] The best accounts are the following: 1. *Handbook to the Roman Wall*, by J. C. Bruce, 10th ed., edited by Ian Richmond, 1947 (Harold Hill & Sons, 62 Northumberland Street, Newcastle-upon-Tyne). Full bibliography. 2. *Hadrian's Wall: a History of the Problem*, by R. G. Collingwood; *Journ. Roman Studies*, XI, 1921, 37 ff.: *Hadrian's Wall, 1921–30*, by the same, ibid., XXI, 1931, 36–64. 3. *The Turf Wall of Hadrian, 1895–1935*, by F. G. Simpson and Ian Richmond, ibid., XXV, 1935, 1 ff. 4. *A Short Guide to the Roman Wall*, by R. G. Collingwood, revised by Ian Richmond, 1948 (Harold Hill & Sons,). 5. *Hadrian's Wall, 1939–49*, by Ian Richmond, *Journ. Roman Studies*, XL, 1950, 43–56. 6. *Hadrian's Wall*, 1938, by the same; *Arch. Aeliana*, 2 S. XVI, 264 ff. 7. *The Building of Hadrian's Wall*, by C. E. Stevens: being the third Horsley Memorial Lecture, delivered 24th October 1947. (Soc. of Antiquaries of Newcastle-upon-Tyne, 1948, 3s.) 8. *The Centenary Pilgrimage of Hadrian's Wall*, 4th–9th July 1949, by Eric Birley, published by the Society of Antiquaries of Newcastle-upon-Tyne; excellent bibliography. I have to thank Miss M. V. Taylor, C.B.E., F.S.A., for kindly supplying these references.
[40] e.g., beacon-platforms, for which see his book.

CHAPTER 17

Defensive Linear Earthworks

THE CUSTOM OF demarcating a frontier by constructing along it a barrier of earth, stone, brick or barbed wire is one that goes back to a remote antiquity. Such barriers, whether military or political or both, differ from the linear earthworks already described in being directed against men, not animals; but it is not always possible to distinguish between them. Some medieval enclosure banks round parks and woods, which were certainly made to keep animals in or out, are as big as those whose purpose was purely military; those made by the Bishop of Winchester at Hursley (Fig 34) and Avington are examples, and there is another at Bramshill Park in the north of Hampshire whose age and purpose is still uncertain. The first (A) version of Bokerley Dyke in Cranborne Chase has been claimed as perhaps a game-enclosure of Romano-British date, the rest of whose area was formed of a timber abattis.[1] But there are others whose military-political purpose is patent and universally admitted, such as Offa's Dyke, Wansdyke, the Cambridgeshire dykes and those in country round certain Belgic and Roman towns such as Chichester, Silchester, Cirencester and Colchester.

The idea of making such barriers may have been suggested by the walls of cities; the oldest instance seems to be the Great Wall of China, a land of walled cities, which was completed in the third century B.C. But it was the Romans who developed the art to its fullest extent, probably quite independently; the idea of connecting a line of forts by a wall is not one that needs much originality. Although called military, such defended frontiers may often have served also as customs barriers to canalize trade. Alvarez describes[2] certain 'gates' at a place on the frontier of the provinces of Amara and Shoa in Ethiopia where dues were paid. The gates were kept shut, but he does not describe them. They were placed on the chief route of the country, at the top of a pass. There is no mention of any wall of earth or stone, nor may such have been needed; but it is not unlikely that in our less rugged land some of the shorter dykes may have served a similar purpose.

The purpose of these barriers being to obstruct or canalize, they had to rest their flanks on some natural obstacle that was either insuperable or so difficult and dangerous to use that it could be regarded in practice as insuperable. The sea was the best, for early armies never used it; and against sea raiders no land defences were possible.[3] The principle is still

---

[1] Christopher Hawkes, *Arch. Journ.*, CIV, 1948, 70–2. Professor Hawkes is persuasive, but I am not convinced.
[2] *Narrative of the Portuguese Embassy to Abyssinia* (1520–7), by Father Francesco Alvarez: Hakluyt Society, 64, 1881, 160–1.
[3] For politically unorganized people the Romans organized a system of coastal defence which seems to have answered the purpose.

valid and was used in both the two great wars of modern times. The Maginot line was a
waste of time and labour not only because, ignoring this principle, it stopped short of the
sea, but also because it trusted too much to the natural obstacle of a river valley, where it
was penetrated. The lines of Alamein could be held because their flanks rested on the sea
and on a formidable combination of precipice, marsh and desert. The Roman walls in
Britain ran from sea to sea and so in effect does the Danish Dannewerk, an old frontier
that cuts off the Danish peninsula from Germany. Starting at the earthen rampart of the
Viking town of Haddeby on an inlet of the Schleswig estuary, it ends in a swamp near the
sea at the town of Hollingstedt. It is about nine miles long and is also called Margarethen
Wall; it faces southwards and was begun in the ninth century and reconstructed at various
later dates. In the thirteenth century part of it was built in yellow bricks of extremely
modern appearance by a Danish king who had been to Lombardy and seen them made
there (Plate 16). Between one and two miles to the south is another defensive line
called Kograben or Churgraben running from the head of the same inlet (here called
Selker Noor) and converging towards the Dannewerk at its middle in the neighbourhood
of Kurburg. Unlike the Dannewerk it runs dead straight for the whole of its course. It
should be noted that the Dannewerk has a gap of nearly half a mile near its eastern end,
where it uses the head of a marshy inlet, in just the same way as the Black Pig's Dyke
in Ireland and the Melrose Dyke used lakes.

It is quite possible that the Dannewerk, some of the longer British Dykes (Wansdyke
and Offa's Dyke, for instance), and the Black Pig's Dyke in Ireland (Plate 14) may have
been conscious imitations of the Roman frontier-defences, which must have been well
known throughout the barbarian world. But there is no real need to postulate this knowledge. Tacitus[4] tells us that the Angrivarii used some such earthen ramparts to delimit their
territory long before any of the Roman *limites* were constructed; and in Britain they were
certainly made in pre-Roman times. The Devil's Dyke near St. Albans is a most formidable
affair, surpassing in dimensions all other such dykes; and it has been proved by excavation
to be pre-Roman. Nevertheless these pre-Roman dykes (which have a character of their
own) are exceptional; most of the defensive linear earthworks here mentioned are either
late Roman or post-Roman.

A large group in Central Europe still awaits dating by the modern technique of excavation. Most of its members seem to be designed to obstruct an enemy coming from the
east; and it is a good guess that it was the barbarians of the great Russian plains—the curse
of Europe in all ages. Their course is marked on the old Austro-Hungarian military maps,
from which I compiled a descriptive note. The accompanying diagram (Fig. 30), reproduced by kind permission of the Royal Geographical Society, and the Editor of the
Geographical Journal where it was first published (December 1950, p. 219) gives a general
idea of their location; field-work is needed for more.

The best known group is that in Cambridgeshire, running across the open chalk belt
from bush to fen—which must have been used from the earliest prehistoric times. The
traffic eventually formed a definite track-way which was used in Saxon and medieval times
and is now known as the Icknield Way.[5] The dykes were a barrier erected across this
track-way; they run from the forest scrub or bush country at the south-east to the fenland

---

[4] *Annales*, II, 19. The original passage is quoted in *Antiquity*, IV, 1930, 315. The earthwork seems to have rested its
flanks on a morass, though Tacitus does not actually say so.   [5] See p. 79.

14. The Black Pig's Dyke, Lattone, Co. Leitrim; see page 184

15. Farms and fields of medieval aspect, Kisumu, Kenya (page 229)

16a. (*above*) Waldemars-Mauer, part of the Dannewerk, a defensive frontier in Schleswig of the
eleventh century, built of yellow brick
16b. (*below*) Detail of the Dannewerk showing brick construction; see page 184

marshes on the north-west. That is a feature of other dykes crossing the chalk belt further
to the south-west. Thus the Oxfordshire Grim's Ditch is a barrier thrown across the
Icknield Way and the Chiltern ridgeway in the great loop of the Thames between Walling-

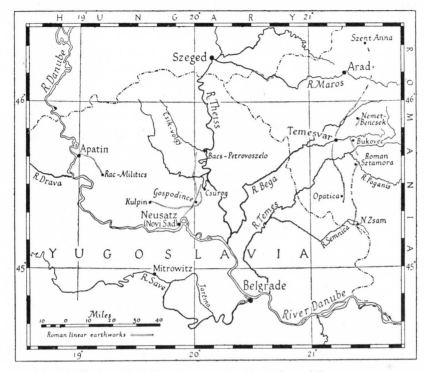

FIG. 30. Defensive linear earthworks in Central Europe.

ford and Henley.[6] The west end rests on a large spring-pond in Mongewell, 600 yards
from the river; the east end at present ends in forest country on the top of the Chilterns.
So too the Aldworth Grim's Ditch in Berks on the other (west) side of the Thames runs
across and was certainly designed to obstruct the Berkshire ridgeway; and an isolated
ditch continuing its line south of Streatley was probably built across the Roman road
(not now to be traced here) from Dorchester to Silchester. The Devil's Dyke east of Andover bars a gap between woodlands north and south (later the Bailiwick of Finkley in
Chute Forest and the copses of Harewood) through which ran a Roman road and the
Harroway—an old road from Kent and London to the west.[7] There is just such another
gap between the woods of Cranborne Chase and the Tertiary country on the borders of
Wilts and Dorset, and it is blocked by Bokerley Dyke. Further still to the south-west,
between Blandford and Dorchester, is the least well-known of such dykes, called Comb's
Ditch, running from Whatcombe Down (Dorset 33 NW.) on the north-west, across the
main road between Salisbury, Blandford and Dorchester, to Charlton Down and Great
College Wood on the south-east (Dorset 33 NE.).

[6] See *Antiquity*, V, 1931, 163–4, and map opp. p. 168.
[7] See pp. 79, 100 (the Hardway and Pen Pits).

Most of the other dykes have obvious relations to important thoroughfares, as has often been pointed out. Some of these thoroughfares are ridgeways, others Roman roads. The Grey Ditch (Derbyshire) bars the way above Bathamgate, and the Silchester dykes are obviously directed against traffic (or invaders) coming along Roman roads from the north-west and north. The Strong Ditch (*faestan dic*) in Joyden's Wood (Kent) must have continued northwards across the Roman road from London to Canterbury, and that on Hartford Bridge Flats crossed a well attested *herepath* from London to Basingstoke and the west of England. Sir Cyril Fox has pointed out the function of the cross-dykes on the ridges leading across the Welsh Marches.[8] Three of the four short dykes in the south-east corner of the New Forest (Hatchet, Dibden and Beaulieu road) cross ridges at narrow points and are obviously connected with some threat from the Solent; the two southern ones face northwards and must therefore have been made by the authors of the threat. One is tempted to suggest Cerdic and his West Saxons, though if so he could not have landed at Totton, as I once claimed.[9]

Other dykes were built to defend towns. The great series outside Colchester has been proved to be pre-Roman (Belgic), but not all of it is of the same date. Another set of dykes outside Chichester has not been excavated, but I suspect it too to be pre-Roman, in spite of the straightness of the alignments. The Silchester dykes obviously also defended Silchester. The Bagendon dykes still await excavation, and indeed description,[10] but must surely be closely connected with Cirencester, and probably with the battle of Deorham (Dyrham, north of Bath) in 577 which led to the capture of Cirencester. The great ramparts of Stanwick (Co. Durham) are hardly linear earthworks, and so are not included in the list (Appendix III), but must surely be compared with the similar defences of pre-Roman age at Colchester. Nor, indeed, are they earthworks at all, but stone walls. In writing about linear defences one is beset by the same problems of terminology as in writing about barrows and cairns.

There are some linear earthworks which were designed to defend a beach-head. The bank on Bindon Hill is of this nature, as Dr Mortimer Wheeler perceived before his excavations proved that he was right. The Giant's Hedge on the south Cornish coast is over seven miles long; its ends rest on the estuaries of Fowey and Looe, and thus cut off and isolated a quite considerable tract of country. Bolster Bank on the north coast near St Agnes does the same but for a much smaller area. The Danes' Dyke on Flamborough Head looks on the map more like a beach-head affair than a fort, though the area is again very small and the name itself suggests use at any rate by a Dane or Norseman (Flein's burg).[11]

The most famous beach-head defences are the great walls which run across the isthmus west of Constantinople, between the Black Sea and the Mediterranean. The Asiatics who captured this European beach-head thereby came near to overrunning the whole continent and did overrun the Balkans.

There is a defensive linear earthwork called Le Hague Dicke running across the Joburg peninsula, near Cherbourg.

---

[8] See *Bulletin of the Board of Celtic Studies*, VIII, 282, and *Arch. Camb.*, XCIV, 41.

[9] *Cerdices ora* would then be at or near Calshot. There were two landings there, separated by nineteen years. But one cannot pursue the matter further in a footnote. See *Antiquity*, XXVI, 1952, No. 104.

[10] I have examined them all in the field, but not written them up. They are very curious; one dyke ends 'in the air'.

[11] Pitt-Rivers excavated there in 1879; see *Journ. Anthr. Inst.*, XI, 455-70.

Defensive linear earthworks are found in Pakistan where, as here, they run between two natural obstacles.[12]

Enough has been said to indicate the many facets of these most fascinating earthworks, so far as Britain is concerned. There is still much to be done; many have never been walked along and surveyed, and until then, even though their course may be marked (probably incompletely) in the Ordnance Maps, it cannot be said that their character is known. Even some described long ago need re-investigation in the light of what we have learnt in recent years. The Scots Dyke, Becca Banks and other northern linear earthworks need this surveying.[13] The true nature of the mysterious Danes' Pad in the Poulton-le-Fylde district needs to be ascertained by digging, and the whole of its course carefully walked and checked on the map.

I have not attempted here, or in the list in Appendix III, to describe all the many short cross-ridge dykes that are so common on the chalk downs. They are not all of the same character, some being bivallates. Nor have I included the examples in the Cheviots, at Woden's Law, where there are several close together across a narrow col between the heads of two steep coombes, and across the drovers' road from Hounam to Harbottle. (Wallace's trench seems to be another of these, but I have not seen it). Nor have I included those which I believe to be Roman, near the marching-camps at Glenmailen and Raedykes.

There are many defended frontiers in Europe and Asia, and so far as I am aware none of them has been properly, and some not at all, surveyed and described. The Central European lines are now almost as inaccessible as the Chinese Wall. Derbend where the Caucasus meets the Caspian, is one of the great Iron Gates of the world, capable of holding back the hordes of a whole continent. Its wall, from sea to mountains, though short, would be well worth studying in close detail. On the other side of the Caspian, Alexander's Wall, fortunately just on the right side of the Iron Curtain, has recently been photographed from the air, but the results are only such as to make one want more air-photos, and also a ground survey.[14] Only two, apart from Roman *limites*, appear to be still open for examination—the Median Wall and Shebib's Wall. The Median Wall runs from the Tigris twenty miles westward into the desert,[15] but nothing whatever is known about it. Shebib's Wall[16] runs north and south in the Kingdom of Jordan, from a point between Ma'an and Petra to near Daouq, where is a Roman settlement. It may belong to the tenth century A.D. It is rather a boundary than a line of defence, and I mention it here more because of its relative accessibility than for its importance.

[12] *Five Thousand Years of Pakistan*, by R. E. M. Wheeler, 1950, 129–30.

[13] Although I have walked all these in order to get them correctly marked on the Dark Ages Map, and have recorded my observations on the 6-inch maps (now at the Ordnance Survey), I did not attempt any proper survey of them.

[14] See, for this and Derbend and the legend of Gog and Magog associated therewith, *Alexander's Gate*, by A. R. Anderson, Monograph 5 of the Medieval Academy of America, Cambridge, Mass., 1932.

[15] Air-photo in *Geogr. Journal*, LXXIII, June 1929, opp. p. 506.

[16] *Antiquity*, XXII, 1948, 151–4.

CHAPTER 18

Medieval Castle Mounds and Parks

THE IDENTIFICATION OF certain types of earthwork as medieval is a recent achievement, brought about by the impact of field archaeology on history. Prehistorians in the course of their field-work found mounds, banks and ditches which, from their associations or from explicit documentary evidence, could only be regarded as medieval. It is some measure of the bookishness of medievalists that only in the present century was it established that castle mounds were Norman, not Saxon. The proof, when it came, was historical, not archaeological, for the medievalists could not even date their own pottery until Dr Wheeler and his former pupil Mr Dunning came and helped them out; and in such a sorry state of affairs even excavation cannot produce results. It is rather to such common but minor earthworks as park-banks and those which enclose fields and copses that I wish to direct attention, for these, long familiar to the field archaeologist, are still beneath the historian's horizon. But first a few words must be said about castle mounds and castles.

The custom of building castles on mounds came to England from Normandy with William the Conqueror. One such is actually represented on the Bayeux tapestry and has often been reproduced. A twelfth-century[1] chronicler has left an admirable though verbose description of a castle mound at Morchem (near Dixmude in Flanders). It is described as a *munitio* near the *atrium* of the church. 'For it was the custom of the rich men and nobles to heap up a mound (*aggerem*) of earth as high as they could, and to dig round it a ditch (*fossam*) as wide and deep as possible, and to set round it a wall (*vallo*) of wooden planks, firmly set, in place of a wall (*muri*), with towers when possible. In the middle they would build a house (*domum*) or fort (*arcem*) to command the whole, in such a manner that its gateway could only be approached by a bridge starting from the (outer) edge of the ditch and supported by pairs of piers, and thus leading upwards across the ditch to the threshold at the top of the mound.' Clark also quotes Suger's twelfth-century definition of *motam*: 'A hill or tumulus on which a castle was built. Once castles were built only on the highest ground; but in Flanders, a low, flat land, mounds (*motis*) were made by piling up heaps of earth from all sides so that forts (*arces*) might be placed on them.'

From this it would appear that the mound may have arisen as a special adaptation to the

---

[1] The passage occurs in the life of a certain John, Bishop of Thérouanne, who died in A.D. 1130 and was canonized. His life is published in *Acta Sanctorum* for 27th January. My extract is taken from the appendix to an article on 'Earthworks', by George T. Clark (*Arch. Journ.*, XXXVIII, 1881, 40–1): in translating I have slightly condensed the original text. The account seems to imply a bailey as well, for the towers could hardly be set round the central building, itself merely a large wooden tower. Clark does not state when the life was composed. His article contains much useful information, but is an attempt to prove that all British castle mounds were pre-Norman, which we now know to be quite wrong.

terrain of the Low Countries. That seems to agree with the facts. The castle mound was not, in England, the only type of fort; instead of a mound there was sometimes a small circular earthwork or ring; attached to this (as also to the mounds) was a much larger earthwork called the bailey. The typical plan was that of the old-fashioned loaf of bread (now extinct) with a small round top and a big flat bottom. Now the ring, the core of the defence, occurs without the bailey in certain ninth-century forts of Saxon construction between the Elbe and the Baltic (e.g. at Stade). It looks as if the mound may have been developed in the Low Countries as a local variation of the ring. However this may be, the origins of our medieval fortification are to be looked for somewhere in that part of the continent.

Both mound-and-bailey and ring-and-bailey forts are quite common in England. But there are also many mounds that were certainly thrown up for castles but have no bailey attached. They are seldom of any great size and usually unmentioned in documents, and for these reasons it is thought that they were thrown up by robber chieftains during the unsettled (and largely undocumented) times of the twelfth century.[2] It is often difficult to be sure that such mounds are not prehistoric or later burial-mounds (barrows); there is one which was both.[3] When a causeway is left across the surrounding ditch, and the top is flat, a castle mound may be suspected. These mounds occur all over England, but are particularly common (and hard to diagnose) on the Welsh Marches.

The mound-and-bailey castles ranged from royal castles, such as Windsor, to quite small affairs. The royal castles were important administrative centres; the forest dues were, for instance, paid to them (e.g. those of Savernake to the Constable of Marlborough Castle). It was in these royal castles—called 'the king's houses'—that the king stayed during his progress through the kingdom. Except when situated in a town, these castles all had a park attached to them. The park was often elliptical or oval in shape, with the castle at one of the narrow ends. Such an arrangement occurs at Devizes (Fig. 31) and Odiham, and in many bishop's castles such as Farnham and Merdon (Fig. 34). Parks are always to be looked for in the vicinity of castles; they were not, of course, primarily pleasure parks, any more than hunting (which took place in them) was merely a country gentleman's hobby. They were enclosures for storing live meat in the form of deer and other animals; and they were also a source of timber for building purposes and for fuel. Not only the king but also the bishops and the great feudal lords and the abbots of monasteries, who were also of course great feudal lords, also had parks attached thereto (e.g. Titchfield). There are a great many parks without castles, and there may be some castles (other than those in towns and adulterine ones) without parks; but field-work and old maps would probably reveal many missing ones.

The economic function of parks is well brought out by Dr Williams-Freeman in the prelude to his description of John of Gaunt's deer-park near King's Somborne, Hampshire.[4] 'All the winter's meat was killed at Martinmas, cut into strips called "collops", salted and laid down . . . and the necessary stock for breeding was turned out to lead a half-starved existence on the common lands. There were no roots to feed them on, and no

[2] Technically called 'adulterine' castles.
[3] In Rug Park, Corwen: see R. Comm. Anct. Monts. Report, Merioneth, No. 38 (parish of Corwen, Lat. 52° 59′ 1″, Long. 3° 24′ 20″; Mer. 7. S.-E.). A fuller account appears in the *Bulletin of the Board of Celtic Studies*, by Mr W. J. Hemp, to whom I am indebted for the above facts.
[4] *Field Archaeology of Hampshire*, 1915, 224–5.

potatoes to feed their owners. A diet
of salted meat with only water-cress,
pot-herbs, and perhaps a little cab-
bage for fresh vegetables, produced,
as might be expected, much illness.
. . . Scurvy and leprosy—loose terms
of course, including nearly all skin
diseases—were the scourges of all
classes, and fresh fish was as great a
necessity for a rich man's house as
was the deer which he enclosed in his
park.' As we shall see, fish-ponds are
to be found in or near most parks,
and also near all moated homesteads
and manor houses. The Serpentine in
Hyde Park was originally a string of
fish-ponds and was altered to its
present form by Queen Caroline.[5]

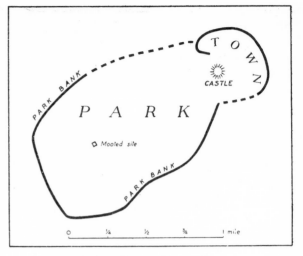

FIG. 31. Devizes Park, Wilts.

Parks had to have some form of bank or fence round them to keep the deer and other animals from straying. Since all deer were the king's, special licence had to be obtained for enclosing a park. Many such licences are preserved in the Patent and Close Rolls, beginning in the early thirteenth century. In granting the licence it was stated that the enclosure might take the form of a live or dead hedge with a foss. It is with the last that field archaeology is concerned, for these great banks and ditches still survive in consider-able numbers and in a good state of preservation. By field-work, that is to say by going out with a large-scale Ordnance Map and walking the boundary, the course followed by the park-bank can often be recovered; to do so may involve two or three days' work, but when it has been done, one unit in the medieval system has been restored to knowledge. That is surely worth doing.

A good example of a large twelfth-century park is that which was attached to the castle of New Buckenham in Norfolk (96 NW. and adjacent sheets). The castle itself is said to have been built by William d'Albini in the mid-twelfth century;[6] it is of the ring-and-bailey type, the ring consisting of an earthen bank whose top is still thirty feet above the bottom of the encircling ditch. Inside are the remains of a flint-built tower (wall nine feet thick) and of another wall. The ring has an internal diameter of over 300 feet. Attached to its eastern side is a bailey,[7] whose earthen bank encloses an area not much larger than that of the ring. From the north-eastern part of this bailey starts a bank and ditch, going north-eastwards and traceable for about seven miles; the bank is missing for considerable stretches where the ditch only can be seen, sometimes on the *inner* side only. The first part coincides with the parish boundary between Old and New Buckenham and then between the former and Carleton Rode. On sheet 86 SW. (edition of 1907) it is called here 'Double Bank'. At the junction of the three parishes of Old Buckenham, Besthorpe

---

[5] *Archaeologia*, VII, 127.
[6] Harrod, *Castles and Convents of Norfolk*, 213; *Norfolk Archaeology*, XI, 137; P. Westgate, *Buckenham Castle*, 1937; Blomfield, *History of Norfolk*, I, 383.
[7] Not marked on the Ordnance Map.

and Carleton Rode it ceases to coincide with any parish boundary, but is continued by a long line of continuous field-boundary where the ditch only is visible. At the western edge of the sheet it coincides again with a parish boundary (Old Buckenham and Besthorpe) and under the name of Bunn's Bank continues westwards to just beyond the road from Attleborough to Old Buckenham, beyond which I could not trace it. Bunn's Bank is in places eight and twelve feet above the bottom of its ditch, which is on the inner (south) side. The existence of a park here is evidenced by the name Park Farm nearly two miles north of New Buckenham. If it was enclosed as early as the mid-twelfth century, no record of the fact is likely to survive.

One of the earliest mentions[8] of a park is in A.D. 1071-82 at Wickhambreux in Kent, four miles east of Canterbury. The area included was not less than twenty-five acres, and a Saxon version of the grant appended to it translates the Latin *parcus* by *deorfald*. This suggests that the *deor falds* of the pre-Conquest charters were in fact parks. The OE. Chronicle (*sub anno* 1123) calls Woodstock Park *der fald*.

So far I have not attempted to define a park, regarding it for the moment as topographically resembling the modern parks which still survive, such as Richmond Park, Regent's Park or Woodstock Park. Many medieval parks were of course not unlike some modern parks both in size and general appearance. Parts of the parks at Hamstead Marshall, near Newbury (Fig. 32), and Cornbury in Wychwood Forest (Oxon) probably look much the same to-day as they did when they were first enclosed. But the records show that the term 'park' covered a very wide range; it seems, in fact, to have denoted any area of more than 30 acres that was enclosed with a bank or pale. In 1270, for instance, it is stated that the wood of 'la Cufold' which Peter de Coudray was given licence to enclose and make into a park was of more than 30 acres in extent.[9] The word originally meant 'enclosure', being derived from the Old English *pearruc, pearroc*, a diminutive form (like 'bullock') of an Old English substantive *spar*,[10] a beam. *Pearroc* became 'paddock'; the word 'park' is a French form of spelling. Etymologically, therefore, a park meant no more than an enclosure, and it was frequently used in that sense in field names. Nearly every parish had at least one field called '——— Park', 'the Old (or New) Park' and such like. But parallel with this usage was that with which we are concerned here, denoting much larger areas. Even so the range of size was very great. At one end of the scale are such uninhabited enclosures as the wood of Horsleye in Crux Easton (Hants 8 SE.) which John de Drokenesford was licensed to enclose and make into a park in 1292.[11] This is now Easton Park Wood, a triangular enclosure whose greatest (south) side is exactly one mile long. There are many others to be found in Hampshire, some with the enclosure-bank still well preserved. They were simple enclosures differing only in size from the smaller ones such as woods and fields, and having no castle or fish-ponds attached to them. At the other end of the scale are such huge enclosures as the royal parks of Clarendon (3 miles in diameter) and Windsor, and the bishop's parks of Waltham, Hants (2 miles by 1 mile), Avington (about the same) and Merdon or Hursley ($1\frac{1}{2}$ by $\frac{3}{4}$ of a mile). The park of Odiham, attached to the royal castle there, was $1\frac{1}{4}$ by $\frac{3}{4}$ of a mile, and that of Devizes a mile by $\frac{3}{4}$ of a mile. Between these extremes of size were many parks enclosed by

[8] *Book of Seals* (Oxford, 1950), No. 431.
[9] Calendar of Charter Rolls (P.R.O.), II, 133.
[10] Inferred from the OE. verb *sparran*, to enclose, lock, fasten.
[11] Calendar of Patent Rolls (P.R.O.), 20 Edw. I, 470; see also my *Andover District* (Oxford, 1922), 63.

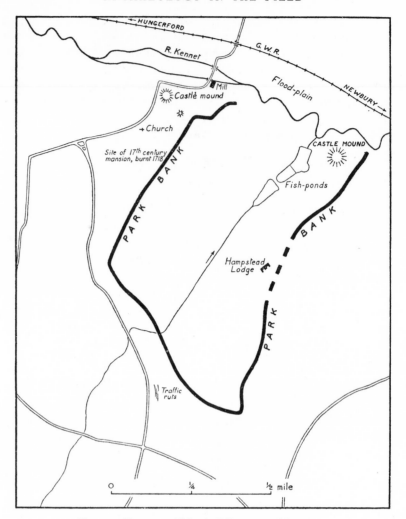

FIG. 32. Hampstead Marshall Park, near Newbury.

feudal lords. The park of Hampstead Marshall (Berks 42 NE. and Fig. 32) is a quadrilateral area whose longest (east) side is a mile in length and whose width is about half a mile. The bank is still well preserved on three sides except for a short gap where the east side has been destroyed by the grounds of Hampstead Lodge; the fourth (north) side does not seem to have had a bank, but to have used the River Kennet instead. There are three castle mounds there and some large fish-ponds in the middle.[12] Parks thus enclosed seem never to have included, at the time of their enclosure, any arable land; to do so would have been uneconomical. The state of the land enclosed is often described in the licence; thus in 1328 Robert de Sancto Manefeo was permitted to enclose at Heckfield, Hants, 5 acres of meadow,

[12] For an interpretation of the history of the castle-mounds, see J. L. N. Myres, *Trans. Newbury District Field Club*, VI, 1932, 114–26. I traced the bank of this park on the ground, inserting it on the 6-inch map, some forty years ago; it was this and the park banks of Highclere and Adbury (also traced then) that first aroused my interest in the subject.

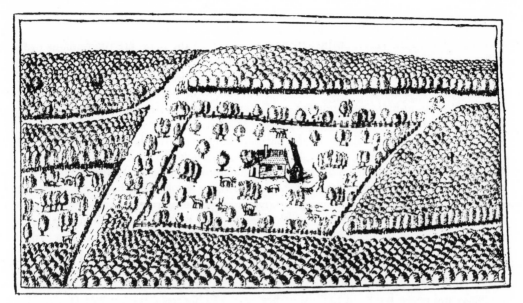

FIG. 33. Grovely Lodge in its wooden pale, 1589. From a contemporary drawing.

15 acres of pasture, 40 acres of wood and 30 acres of moor in his manor and to make a park thereof.[13]

Thus we may conclude from the evidence of specific records[14] that a medieval park was simply an area over 30 acres in size which was surrounded by a bank or pale to keep the deer from straying out or in. In the case of woods the purpose obviously was to protect the young trees and undergrowth from being nibbled by the deer. Since deer were royal property, such restriction of their feeding was illegal unless a royal licence had been obtained, and provision was sometimes made in the licence for the free ingress and egress of the deer, by deer-leaps or otherwise.

Forest lodges also stood in park-like enclosures. Thus Bagden (now Savernake) Lodge in Savernake Forest stood within a roughly circular enclosure of about a mile in diameter (see Fig. 43). Where the boundary crossed Showell's Bottom, half a mile south-west of Savernake Lodge (Wilts 36 NE.)[15] it consists of a deep ditch between two banks; further east it consists of a bank with a large ditch on the south (outer) side and faint traces of another on the inside. The earthwork can be traced almost continuously throughout its course. There are remains of two such enclosure-banks round the lodge of Lyndhurst in the New Forest. The name 'lodge' is common and it will often be found that the farm or site to which it is applied stands within a park; the word meant, originally, an arbour or bower, and denoted a temporary structure erected for the convenience of hunters (it is cognate with the words 'leaf' and 'lobby'). Grovely Lodge in Grovely Forest (Wilts) is shown in a contemporary illustration surrounded by a rectangular wooden pale (Fig. 33).

A typical deer-park is that called John of Gaunt's deer-park in King's Somborne,

[13] V.C.H., *Hants*, IV, 45.
[14] Of which samples only out of hundreds are quoted here.
[15] Marked there on the 1900 edition by hachures indicating a bank only.

N

Hants (39 NE., SE.). The enclosure is a little over a mile in length from north to south and a little over half a mile in width; it takes in portions of the valleys of the Test and Somborne, and in the latter, at the extreme south end of the park, are the remains of fish-ponds. Dr Williams-Freeman has described the remains of the bank, which is best pre-served along the south side of the park, where it runs beside the Horsebridge road and is 12 feet high.[16] The ditch was on the outside. A fact to be noticed is that the bank is well preserved for about half a mile where it runs between the present main stream of the Test and a branch, east of the village of Houghton. It is possible, therefore, that a similar bank may have formed the fourth side of the park at Hampstead Marshall; but there the valley is much swampier than here, and might have been a sufficient obstacle.

It was probably the ambition of every lord of a manor to have a park; but certain onerous conditions had to be fulfilled even before the enclosure-bank could be begun. There had to be waste available on the manor and no overriding customary rights attached thereto;[17] and there had also to be no conflict with the claims of the Crown—or, more probably, someone who could be bribed to overlook or reduce them. After the king the bishops, especially the Bishop of Winchester, were possibly the greatest holders of parks. Of the Bishop of Winchester's Hampshire manors those of Hursley, Bitterne, Marwell, Bishop's Sutton, Highclere, Bishopstoke, Fareham and Farnham certainly all had parks attached. The park- and copse-banks of the bishop are on a very big scale; the bank of Hursley Park which is still in existence in Ampfield Wood (though not marked on the map, Hants 40 SW., SE.) is a colossal one, about a mile long here[18] with a broad flat top—the whole more like Ackling Dyke than anything else (Fig. 34). Branching off from it is another called Port-land Bank more than a mile long, running west to Hawker's Fir Hill and turning north-wards at Claypit Hill. The labour involved in making these enclosure-banks must have been tremendous, but in assessing it one must remember that the bishop had command of as much forced labour as a modern Communist Commissar. There are several other detached fragments of huge banks in the same neighbourhood (in Hocombe Upper Plantation and on Cranbury Common); they are probably the remains of copse-banks. The interpretation of these banks can only be made after prolonged study of the topo-graphy by field-work and of the estate maps and other records. There has been much record work, but hardly any field-work.

These park-banks, then, were no minor earthworks but amongst the biggest of their kind, rivalling the defensive linear earthworks like Offa's Dyke and Wansdyke, and often equal to them in size. Indeed, they have been confused with them; the bank round Saver-nake Lodge was mistaken for Wansdyke by Albany Major; and I am still in some doubt myself about a bank that I discovered on the north-east side of Bramshill Park (Hants 12 NW.). It runs for about a mile along the south-west side of the wood called Eversley Upper Common, parallel with a straight track for most of the way.[19] The southern end

---

[16] *Field Archaeology*, 1911, 224–6. The bank looks higher than it is by reason of the steep slope on which it stands; but it is a formidable one even on the flat ground beside the Test.

[17] Exceptions, however, are recorded. In 1403, at least a century after Highclere Park (Fig. 36) had been enclosed, the rector of the adjoining parish (Burghclere) received compensation for the inclusion of arable land within the park. The arable was not his, and there is no mention of compensation for those who lost the fruits of their labour. But their loss deprived him of his unearned increment of a tenth thereof, and it was for this that he claimed compensation. See *V.C.H. Hants*, IV, 1911, 285–6, quoting the original source in Wykeham's Register, Hants Record Society, II, 554.

[18] It can still be traced almost without a break, except where the war-camp has obliterated it in the west.

[19] Where the bank and ditch are crossed by the 300-foot contour; that contour reveals them by performing a remarkable double bend.

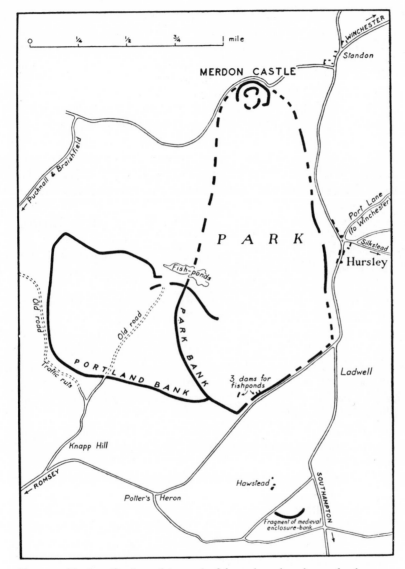

FIG. 34. Merdon Castle and its park, fishponds and enclosure banks; now Hursley Park, between Winchester and Romsey, Hants.

rests on the head of a small stream running southwards into the River Hart, and the northern end curves right round and also ends in low ground just north of the fishpond. The overall width is 16 yards, the ditch is on the north-eastern side, and the general appearance is defensive; but Bramshill Park is an old one, and the bank seems on Isaac Taylor's map of Hampshire (1759) to be regarded as the boundary of the park. Enclosure banks should enclose—not end 'in the air'; but there are authentic examples of park banks that do not go all round the parks. That of Adbury, for instance, in the parish of

Burghclere (Hants 3 SW.) runs from the small stream on the west which, lower down, is the boundary between Newtown and Burghclere, to the next on the east, a bigger one, one branch of which rises at Hockley's Hole. The Pyott's Hill intrenchment which puzzled Williams-Freeman, is simply the bank of Basing Park. It runs from just above the Lower Mill on the Loddon over Pyott's Hill to Petty's Brook at Broad Bridge, a total length of about a mile. The bank is quite plain throughout; where visible the ditch is on the west (i.e. the outer) side. It thus cuts off a triangular area bounded on two sides (north and south-east) by rivers and on the third by itself. Within this area is only one building—Basing Lodge Farm, doubtless the successor of the park lodge. There is also a decoy pond and some fishponds, but I have not seen them and on the map they do not look ancient. Close to what was once the southern end of the park is a small castle mound and bailey called Oliver's Battery.[20] There are other examples of parks formed on the same principles as promontory forts.

There is evidently another park that uses a river for one side at Sonning. I have not seen this, but on the 6-inch map (Berks 30 SW.) the 200-foot contour turns and runs northward for a third of a mile beside Sonning Lane, evidently following the bank on the east side of Holme Park, inside which the Ordnance Map marks the site of the residence (called 'palace') of the bishops of Salisbury.

Before leaving the subject two other parks may be mentioned. One is that called Harbin's Park in Cranborne Chase, in the parish of Tarrant Gunville (Dorset 14 NE.). I have not seen it, but the Ordnance Map shows it as a wood bounded on all sides by a bank with a ditch on the inside. The wood is about half a mile across. The other is Cerne Park (Dorset 31 NW.) on the downs a mile west of Cerne Abbas. The area enclosed is a chalk combe, and is about half a mile long by a third of a mile wide. Both these parks have straight sides. Not having seen either I will not attempt to guess their age, and no documentary evidence is forthcoming.

Readers may well ask themselves two questions: (1) How can I recognize park- and copse-banks, and distinguish them from others? (2) What further research is needed, and how can I start doing some?

Unfortunately there is no way by which an isolated fragment of a park-bank—or of almost any bank—can be recognized at sight. The only way to explain it—and that sometimes fails—is to follow it across country and insert the course on a map. This may take several days. The park-bank of Savernake (Bagden) Lodge is in one place a bivallate, and most bivallates are prehistoric ranch-boundaries (Fig. 43). But when traced further it turns into a normal bank with a big outer ditch. Seen where it crosses Showell Bottom, however, it would puzzle anyone and defy an explanation. There are, however, one or two things which seem to be characteristic of a park-bank. There is a tendency for them to be in rough general conformity with the adjacent field-system; the boundary of Odiham Park, for instance, is marked throughout its whole course by a continuous line of field-boundaries, and the park was spotted there by me before I verified the existence of the bank on the ground. Old trees often grow along them; there are some very old yews on the bank of John of Gaunt's deer-park.

The second question, what further research is needed, is more easy to answer positively. Virtually nothing has been done. The Public Record Office has practically excluded from

[20] For these see Williams-Freeman, *Field Archaeology*, 1915, 312–13, 396 (Pyott's Hill), 311–12, 393 (Oliver's Battery).

its publications (which are of the highest order of scholarship) all purely topographical material. If that is because they are regarded as of local rather than national importance, the answer is that a nation consists of many localities. The real reason is that the study of English history has acquired an overwhelmingly legal aspect, to the exclusion of much else. It is really time that some of the topographical surveys were published. The P.R.O. has not even published the great roll of Forest Perambulations of 28 Edw. I (Pat. Roll 6A), whose national importance can hardly be questioned.[21] There are, of course, many other documentary sources to be consulted especially in the archives of big estates. Old cadastral maps, when available, are the best source of all. But the final test of all documentary sources is in the field. Go and walk along what looks, on the map, like the boundary of a park, and mark it in. That is the answer to the second part of the question.

[21] This matter was discussed in recent numbers of *Archives*.

CHAPTER 19

Medieval Cultivation-Banks

IT IS A COMMON misconception to regard medieval cultivation-banks, better known as strip-lynchets, as having been deliberately made. That is not so; they are natural formations initiated by man, i.e. by cultivation, and they have come into existence in exactly the same way as prehistoric lynchets (see Chapter 8). Soil tends to move downhill in all periods. The plan or pattern formed by these lynchets is a function of that of the field-system, which in turn is, at least in part, a function of the agricultural implements used, whether digging stick, hoe or plough. There are also different types of plough; there is no need to discuss them here and there is an abundant literature on the subject.[1] It is enough to say that medieval fields were cultivated by ploughs which did not differ in any essential feature from the modern horse-drawn one. The ideal unit of the medieval system was a square field, called a furlong or shot, whose sides were 220 yards long, divided into ten 1-acre strips. This ideal field is rarely if ever found owing to changes made during its life of perhaps half a millenium or even more. The acre strips were the unit of ownership and were often divided into two half-acre strips, and one person held several such strips scattered about in the different furlongs. The strips were separated from each other by small grass banks called balks (Plate 17), and in documents and local parlance the strips were called lands, a word that was sometimes confused with 'lawn'. Further than this we need not go; the evidence is available in a multitude of old estate plans and local surveys, the latter covering the whole medieval and post-medieval period down to the enclosures, when the medieval cultivation system, came to an end. It is better to study these records, especially the contemporary plans, than to confuse one's mind by reading the arguments of clean-booted historians. Fortunately, however, these historians are at last beginning to return to the methods of Seebohm, who began it all, and to study the fields themselves and use the air-photographs which have now been available for a generation—in other words, to do field-work. The medieval field-system can only be understood by a combined study of documents and the visible remains in the field. The student must be at home in both spheres, and whether he is called a field archaeologist or historian is a matter of words; he must be both.

It may be said without exaggeration that field-works caused by agriculture are by far the commonest of all such remains. It is therefore important to be able to recognize and

---

[1] Dr E. Cecil Curwen, 'Prehistoric Agriculture in Britain', *Antiquity*, I, 1927, 261–89 (bibliography); 'Ancient Cultivations', id., VI, 1932, 389–406; 'Early Agriculture in Denmark', id., XII, 1938, 135–53; see also his *Air Photography and the Evolution of the Cornfield*, 2nd ed., 1938, and *Proc. Preh. Soc.*, IV, 1938, 27; J. B. P. Kerslake, 'Plough Coulters from Silchester', *Ant. Journ.*, XIII, 1933, 455–63; F. G. Payne, 'The Plough in Ancient Britain', *Arch. Journ.*, CIV, 1948, 82–111 (supplying also references since 1927).

(when possible) date them, not only for their own sake, but because they may sometimes be juxtaposed to other remains which it is desired to date. There is not the slightest difficulty in recognizing at sight a group of fossilized medieval fields. On steep hill-sides the strips have become level terraces, and the appearance is exactly that of a flight of steps. Somewhere close by there will always be found traces (in what was the next furlong) of another 'bundle' of strips or lands running at right angles. Such may be seen at Bishopstone, Wilts, not far west of the White Horse at Uffington, and at the foot of the chalk scarps everywhere, from the Wash to the Channel and from the Chilterns to the Straits of Dover. There are some good examples on both sides of the Vale of Pewsey, especially near Pewsey itself and at Bratton. A little south of the Vale, at Brunton near Collingbourne Kingston, is an excellent example of a series of terraces on a hillside. Perhaps the best group of all is that north of Mere (Wilts 63 NW.) between Wincanton and Salisbury. But there are hundreds all over the country. Some of the best are marked on the 1-inch Ordnance Map, and called 'strip-lynchets'.

It must not, of course, be imagined that in any district the strip-lynchets were the only fields cultivated; they are merely those portions of the village field-system which happened to be on a steep slope. Elsewhere the visible surface remains may—and in chalk regions almost everywhere will—have vanished. The strips were separated by small banks called balks which were soon obliterated by the ploughs of the succeeding system. But on clay lands, such as the Vale of the White Horse, the low lands round Oxford, much of the Midlands, Shropshire, and the Gloucestershire shore of the Severn Estuary and many other regions, the lands seem to have been separated not by balks but by a deep furrow acting as a drain, and the lands themselves were piled up so as to look like the causeways of Roman roads. Exactly how this came about is not known; that is one of the problems we may hope will be solved by historians, for it seems doubtful whether a trench dug through such a land would do so. Huge areas remained under grass until the recent war, embalmed as it were for study. Many of these areas must now be ploughed up, but it takes many years of ploughing to obliterate them. Such areas when air-photographed enable us to reconstruct the field-system at the time of the enclosures with extraordinary accuracy and completeness, as Mr M. W. Beresford has shown.[2] But even after a hundred years or more of ploughing the deep separating furrow shows as a thin dark line, and the lands themselves are faintly visible.

Even in chalk regions the ridge-and-furrow sometimes survives under favourable conditions. There is a group in the copse on Castle Hill, one of the Wittenham Clumps, Berks.[3] The ridges average 7 feet in width and are about 8 inches in height, from crown of ridge to bottom of furrow. They are clearly older than the beech trees, since they come up to and pass through the roots of the trees: when was the clump planted? Quite recently I noticed a similar collection of ridge-ends preserved in a narrow copse beside the Southampton road at the Horns, Nursling. (The soil here is clay, not chalk.) They probably represent remains of medieval cultivation at Rownhams. Air-photos show many such survivals

---

[2] 'Ridge and Furrow and the Open Field', *Economic History Review*, 2 Ser., vol. I, No. 1, 1948, 34–45. I did the same for strip-lynchets myself many years ago; see *Wessex from the Air*, Plates 28 and 29, and the Ordnance Survey Professional Paper on 'The Strip-map of Litlington, Cambs.' See also Beresford's article on 'Mapping the Medieval Landscape' in *Antiquity*, XXIV, 1950, 114–18.

[3] I observed them many years ago but made no notes, and wish to thank Mr P. P. Rhodes for most kindly visiting the site and taking the measurements given. I have quoted what follows from his notes.

in Tertiary country. Although no evidence exists on the subject, I have the impression that the older ridges are usually narrower than the later ones.

Between the furlongs ran field-ways giving access to them. For various reasons these tended to rise, partly I suspect because the plough, in turning, cast the soil towards them, partly because they may have been the dumping-ground of weeds. This is a matter on which one would like to have expert opinion. Whatever the cause, the fact is that, wherever a medieval field-system existed, there one is sure to find these long raised causeways (Plate 18). They were like the paths between allotments, but on a much bigger scale. Some still carry roads; the Icknield Way between Harwell and Wantage is such a field-way; and all over this part of the Vale of the White Horse one may see in the ploughed fields long low causeways that are the last vestiges of others. There are some that can be seen from the train near Culham and Didcot. They are not confined to clay-lands, but are found also on stony land, e.g. near Castor, Northants, and sometimes even on the chalk, as at Litlington, Cambs. They are liable to be mistaken for Roman roads, but can be easily distinguished from such because they never occur singly, but always in groups. Field-work also shows that their surface is not, as a rule, stony.

The topographical study of the medieval field-systems offers many fascinating subjects for research for anyone who can master the techniques required. It is necessary to be able to handle maps old and new, to be able to use and interpret air-photographs, to be familiar with medieval surveys, and it would also be desirable to be able to use the land-boundaries of Anglo-Saxon Charters. It goes without saying that a fairly intimate knowledge of the country, based on field-work, is also indispensable; such can be acquired *pari passu* with work on the other lines mentioned. One thus equipped could do a most valuable piece of research by taking a manageable area such as Berkshire north of the chalk escarpment—the Vale of the White Horse and a bit beyond it on the north—or even a portion of that region. The splendid new series of 1:25000 Ordnance Maps provide exactly the base-maps required. On them would be plotted, from old cadastral plans and air-photos, the outlines of the medieval field-system and the chief roads. Next would be plotted the bound-marks of such Anglo-Saxon charters as may be available—and there are a good few here. That would be made all the easier by the preliminary work in the medieval period, which will have brought to light many old field-names to assist identification. One result would be to show, by the character of the Anglo-Saxon terms used, how far the medieval system may have had its roots in the Anglo-Saxon. Another would be to see, also from these terms, tested by examination on the ground, whether the real nature of the Celtic fields on the chalk downs just south of the scarp was then recognized. In the bounds of Ashbury there is a possible hint that it was.[4] I would particularly commend this suggested piece of research to scholars resident at Oxford because there exist there so many of the facilities required. The prime requisite—old cadastral plans—must surely exist in the archives of the colleges who own land there. (An atlas of such was published in the

---

[4] The work done by the late Dr Grundy and published in the *Berkshire Archaeological Journal*, vols. 27–32, should be used with great caution. He collected many valuable clues from the Tithe-maps, thus saving future workers much laborious work. But his identifications are by no means as certain as one might imagine from the assurance with which they are stated. He made many errors, one of the chief ones being that he made the bounds of Ashbury circulate anti-clockwise instead of clockwise, as the Rev Charles Overy has shown in an unpublished paper. But his chief shortcoming was that he did practically no field-work. That was all the more regrettable because he had a really good eye for topography. He helped to explain the meaning of some of the terms used; but some of his explanations are not accepted by scholars with a much greater knowledge than his of the Anglo-Saxon language.

17. (*above*) Turf balk between strips, South Uist; see page 198
18. (*below*) Sinuous headland between rows of parallel strips, South Uist

19. The hill-fort of Divel, Cameroons; see page 143

20. Granary, Dissa, Blue Nile Province

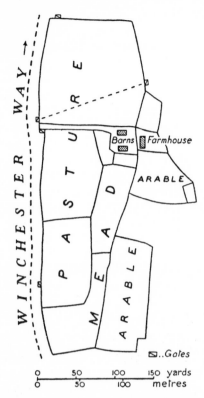

FIG. 35. Copy of a plan (A.D. 1611) of Padwell Farm, later called Bevois Mount, now part of Southampton. (By permission of the Queen's College, Oxford, owners of the original plan, by Allen of Chichester). 'Winchester Way' is now The Avenue.

1880's by the Oxford Historical Society, but I do not think it included any in this region.) The Royal Air Force library of air-photographs is not too far distant at Danesfield near Medmenham. The books are all in the Bodleian Library, and transport to all parts of this region for field-work is easy. It may well be that, in doing the field-work required for identifying the Saxon bounds, many new discoveries will be made. In a very cursory attempt in the same region I was thus led to making two such—a pre-Conquest fish-pond and a linear earthwork (Aelfthrithe dic).[5] If so little could produce so much, systematic work would certainly produce much more.

Parenthetically I would emphasize the apparatus of research needed for work of the kind just described. Apart from access to books, one must have a room to work in and somewhere (preferably a large table and not the floor) to spread maps on. One will also need drawing-paper, pens and ink. The old plans must be copied photographically; one cannot work from them direct, nor is it desirable that one should. Air-photographs must be bought, often in duplicate—a matt copy being required for making notes upon in the field. Photostats of old documents other than maps may also be required, to save time. How does it save time? Because you can transcribe photostats at home in the evenings and on Sundays, and you can't get at the originals then. There are also the costs of transport; and the student's own living expenses. That is why historical and topographical work can't be done without money, and why it needs much more money than such medieval studies as theology or metaphysics. You don't need any apparatus for the study of God or of the supernatural, except perhaps the books of your predecessors, of which there are plenty at Oxford.

Besides the arable fields of the nucleated medieval village there must also have been some arable attached to houses that were not situated in villages. These houses were simply farms, for otherwise they could not have had the means of existence; but their economic character is often obscured by the legal phraseology used to describe them. There are hundreds of them, and together they must have covered a large part of the total area of the country; yet their system of food-production was certainly different from that of the nucleated village. There is no unit of common fields or of strip-cultivation. Probably the fields consisted of closes, i.e. 'parks' in the original sense of the word, divided by hedges and ditches and devoted to pasture and arable, with copses for fuel and timber, and some-

[5] See p. 240

times a fishpond. Take, for instance, the farm of Padwell (Fig. 35), now part of the town of Southampton.[6] This never consisted of more than a single group of farm buildings; a hall and chamber are mentioned in 1326, a cow-house in 1310, and the 'old and new granges' in 1322. The lands of the farm were surrounded by banks and hedges. The granges imply corn-growing; there were meadows where hay was grown; there were two acres of draget in 1326; and there is mention of cheese, butter and a fish-pond. Seventeenth-century surveys estimated the extent of the whole farm at between thirty-six and forty-six acres. They mention several closes, a 'parrock' of three acres, a hopyard and an orchard. Or take the farm of Hickley near Southampton, another Godshouse holding. Amongst its products were poultry, sheep and cows, draught oxen and beasts, mead and wax, furze and turf (for fuel), cider, timber for building; and there was a dairy-maid. Padwell was a mixed farm and Hickley a dairy farm. Their products were probably typical of hundreds of others that existed throughout the Middle Ages (and before), but which were worked by a small, self-sufficient community of a few persons only. Such communities must have made up a considerable part of the population. They were probably pioneer foundations on land that had to be cleared of trees and scrub before they could be brought under cultivation; and therefore mostly of more recent origin than the village communities of the earliest Saxons. They went on being formed down to modern times,[7] and represent probably the natural expansion of the population.

It may seem that all this discussion of medieval agriculture has little connection with field-work. It seems desirable, however, to introduce it because the field-worker does often meet with the works of these medieval farmers. Many of the larger banks round fields and woods are probably due to them, and some of the fish-ponds. Of their arable fields the remains are less certain, except where they can be identified by old maps. Probably most of those fields remain to-day unaltered, and it may be suggested that when such fields occur on sloping ground and have a big lynchet on the lower side that must have taken many years of ploughing to form, those fields may reasonably be regarded as of medieval origin. I have elsewhere suggested that many of the older stone walls round Cornish fields may even date back earlier still; and they are often accompanied by big lynchets. Of the actual ploughing there is less evidence; but there are to be found occasional patches of ridge and furrow, in localities where the common fields of a village community can be ruled out, which are probably to be so identified. Naturally what we now see may not be medieval; it will be the state of the field as it was left when last under plough. But the fact that many such patches conform generally to the existing lay-out of the fields, when that lay-out is certainly several centuries old at least, confirms the theory that they represent the arable of medieval farms. Such a patch occurs, for instance, at Whitway in Burghclere, in that part of Highclere Park which lies *outside* the original park bank, between it and the main road at Whitway; it is now within the park, and it may well be the arable taken in by the Bishop of Winchester in 1403[8] (Fig. 36). Another patch is in a field called Burgage one-third of a mile north of Ibworth, Hants (10 SW.), in the angle of a lane

---

[6] This was acquired by Godshouse, Southampton, at the end of the twelfth century and passed with the other holdings to Queen's College, Oxford, in 1443. In 1734 it was sold to the Earl of Peterborough and renamed Bevois Mount. It lay on the east side of the Avenue, between Highfield and St Mary's. The details following above are taken from the 6th Report of the Historical Manuscripts Commission (1877).

[7] Crabwood Farm, near Southampton, for instance, was enclosed from the waste of the Manor of Millbrook in the eighteenth century; the turf that then covered the heathy ground was used to make a bank round it which still exists in places.   [8] See above, p. 194, note 17

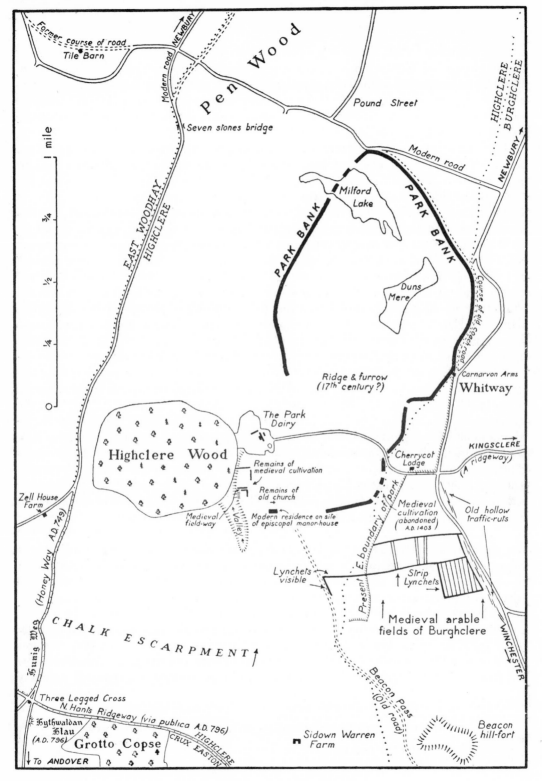

Fig. 36. Highclere Park, near Newbury.

leading to Ewhurst Park. There is a moated site about one-third of a mile to the west of it,[9] by Hopgarden Copse, but it is in the next parish (Kingsclere) and is therefore unlikely to be connected with the cultivation. Another patch is on the top of the downs above Sydmonton (Hants 9 SW.).[10] All these are suspect not so much from the character of their ridge-and-furrow as from their isolated position, far away from any possible area of common (village) fields.

There are, however, a few other instances of ridge-and-furrow that may be presumed to have belonged to the common fields of a village community. Such an instance occurs at Sydmonton, but right down beside some fish-ponds[11] in a valley (Hants 9 NW.). On the opposite side of the valley are strip-lynchets, and there are others further up it facing Sydmonton Court. The village has been swept away to make room for the park; but it is an ancient manor and the three groups of strip-lynchets are evidence of occupation.

The grid of these just described fields is a much closer one than that of the common fields in the Vale of the White Horse and the Midlands; the width of the ridge is much less. The distinction may be due to soil or it may mark a difference in age. I am not prepared to say that any of the examples cited are medieval, though I suspect it; but I think they are all probably earlier than the great outbreak of ploughing that took place during the Napoleonic wars.[12] But even this is not proven; nothing in connection with them is proven except their existence. They are a subject for research. The solution will probably come from a combined study of air-photographs and old cadastral maps.

A few words must be said of cultivation-terraces in the north. There are several fine groups in the valleys on the north sides of the Cheviots. They are not unlike the medieval village fields of southern England in their general arrangement, and are probably of the same age, continuing in use perhaps down to the eighteenth century. I have only seen air-photographs of them, however, and have not walked over them. It seems certain that they represent the fields of a community of some size, not merely of a single farm. It seems difficult to dissociate these terraces from certain other groups such as those at Romanno, Dunsyre and Culter. At each of these three places there is a well-marked group of terraces which, in the south of England, would be called strip-lynchets. These groups do not occur in isolation; the slopes of the hills round also bear marks of cultivation in the form of lynchets and boundary banks or walls. One group of terraces that was once claimed to be contemporary with the broch at Torwoodlee near Galashiels has a series of cultivation-ridges (rigs) running off from it at right angles over the lower and flatter ground (best preserved in a wood). A little cultivation would have obliterated these rigs and we should have only the terraces left, at any rate to ground observation. Precisely the same association occurs below Arthur's Seat at Edinburgh, where rigs run off at right angles to the terraces over the lower ground; but Mr Stevenson claims that here the rigs override and partially obliterate some of the lower terraces and must therefore be later.[13] The same features occur again at Housesteads where there is a fine set of terraces and rigs immediately below the Roman fort on Hadrian's Wall. But, as Mr Percy Hedley has shown,[14] precisely

[9] Ordnance Survey (Arch. Branch), Film 79, No. 9763.
[10] Ordnance Survey (Arch. Branch), Ladle Hill, 2153.
[11] Probably not very old.
[12] The ridges of Napoleonic and early nineteenth century ploughing are much wider and flatter, resembling the modern ones.
[13] *Proc. Soc. Ant. Scot.*, LXXXI, 1949, 158–70.
[14] *Antiquity*, V, 1931, 351–4.

similar terraces and rigs occur elsewhere all over Northumberland, some of which at least
are certainly medieval. The argument that they must be contemporary with a hill-fort or
Roman fort because they occur near it is unconvincing.[15] Strip-lynchets occur immediately
outside and between the ramparts of hill-forts at Battlesbury, Cadbury, and Blewburton
Hill, but they are certainly all medieval, originating no earlier than the Saxon period at
the earliest. The presence of a fine group of strip-lynchets on the northern slopes of
Cademuir Hill is certainly suggestive, expecially as they are well over 1,000 feet above
sea level. On the other hand, they are only two miles distant from the town of Peebles
and easily accessible from it; and a writer of 1689 has said: "Tis almost incredible how
much of the mountain they plough where the declensions—I had almost said precipices—
are such that, to our thinking, it puts them to greater difficulty and charge to carry out
their work than they need be at in draining the valleys.'[16] The terraces on the slopes of
the Hounam Valley are not far from the fort on Hounam Law, but they are much nearer
the valley bottom and more accessible from it, and in my opinion are certainly medieval.
Association of this vague and merely topographical nature proves nothing at all; it would
be difficult to find a site in the lowlands that was *not* near a hill-fort. There is, however,
none on the hill on which the Culter terraces are situated. It should also be stated that many
of the so-called hill-forts were very small affairs—mere homesteads that could hardly
have held enough labourers to cover the ground with lynchets, nor is it at all certain that
agriculture was their chief occupation; in the lowlands they probably lived far more on
mutton and milk. The climate of Scotland during the Iron Age was wetter even than now,
and corn is unlikely to have been grown then in such situations.

If it be argued that both rigs and the accompanying strip-lynchets are of pre-medieval
date, that would prove too much. We should be driven to conclude that there was no
arable during the later periods, or that all traces have vanished.

There are examples of rigs north of the Forth. I quoted three instances in another
context,[17]—at Guynd and in Drumshed Wood near Fordoun, where they are bounded
by an obviously medieval or later dyke, and in Tollmuir Wood between Finavon and
Nether Careston, where the ridges are sixteen yards wide and exactly a furlong in length.
In all these places the cultivation is on flat ground, where strip-lynchets cannot form; and
at Guynd and Drumshed the adjacent slopes are too short and steep for any cultivation.

Since I wrote the above Mr Stevenson and I have been over the ground together. The
rigs and terraces are in Queen's Park and the rigs extend also over the adjacent low ground
round Duddingston Loch, as the air-photograph (Plate XIX in his article) shows. They
are all within an easy walk of Prince's Street, Edinburgh, and the best light for seeing
them is during the evening in May or June. Mr Stevenson's case is that the terraces, which
run parallel with the contours, are older than the rigs, which run at right angles to
them. 'Ideas on drainage must have differed in the two cases.' He considers that the 'earlier
remains [i.e. the terraces and associated curvilinear habitation-sites] may be vaguely dubbed
medieval', referring to certain 'scooped enclosures' of similar character in the parish of
Manor, Peebleshire,[18] which he has planned and excavated. I still, however, am not convinced that there is any difference in age between the rigs and the terraces, both of which

[15] I doubt whether this thesis has any adherents to-day.
[16] Thomas Morer: see *Early Travellers in Scotland*, ed. by David Douglas, 1891, 267.
[17] *Topography of Roman Scotland*, 1949, 107.
[18] *Proc. Soc. Ant. Scot.*, LXXV, 1940–1, 106–8.

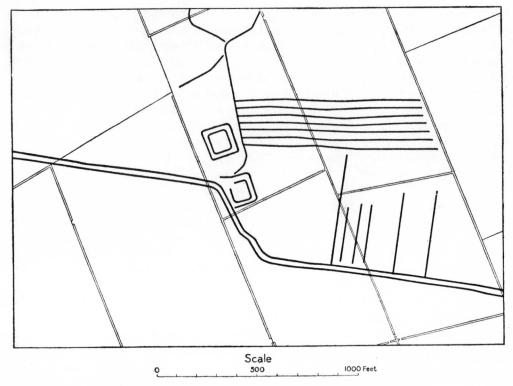

Scale

0   500   1000 Feet

FIG. 37. Diagram to show possible strip-cultivation in the Fens.

seem to me to belong to one and the same system of cultivation. This difference of opinion concerns only the rigs, for we both agree that the terraces are medieval.

Mr Stevenson and I are agreed about the age of the terraces, and neither of us would claim that such were of prehistoric or Roman age, I imagine. It has been claimed that the terraces at Housesteads were made by the occupants of the adjacent Roman fort. I am now convinced that there *was* strip-cultivation in prehistoric or Romano-British times; but I am not prepared to admit that the Housesteads terraces are of that age. The weight of evidence seems to me to be overwhelmingly in favour of a medieval date, and the onus of proof to lie on those who deny it.[19]

Evidence suggestive of strip-cultivation in Romano-British times comes from the Fens on the Cambridgeshire and Lincolnshire border. It was taken from an air-photograph (now destroyed) by Mr C. W. Phillips, to whom I am indebted for the diagram (redrawn as Fig. 37) and all the facts relating thereto. The diagram shows a local road of Romano-British origin which, when examined on the ground, shows clear traces of side-ditches and a slight convexity in the middle, though there are no traces of road-metal. Roads like this correspond exactly to the modern unmetalled Fen droveways. Although the course of the road here and elsewhere is generally straight it will be seen that it makes a sudden

[19] For other accounts of lynchets in Scotland see *Proc. Soc. Ant. Scot.*, I, 1854, 127–33; LXII, 1928, 107–20; LXV, 1931, 388–98; LXXIII, 1939, 289–315.

deviation to pass round some rectangular markings. Ground inspection here has revealed a scatter of Romano-British potsherds, and one may well infer that these markings indicate the site of buildings of the same period. Associated with these sites in the angle of the bend are several roughly parallel dark lines which clearly have no connection with the modern cultivation. Since they must be associated both with the Romano-British road and the habitation-sites beside it, they can only represent the cultivation system belonging thereto, and their character seems to indicate strip-cultivation. The site is on the south-western extremity of a large system of Romano-British fields stretching towards and across the old L.N.E.R main line and Holbeach Drove Common.

CHAPTER 20

Field Archaeology in Other Lands

FIELD ARCHAEOLOGY is an essentially English form of sport. It has developed in this island to a greater extent than elsewhere for three reasons; we have the raw materials in greater abundance and better preservation than other countries; we also have maps on a large enough scale (1:25,000, 1:10,560, 1:2,500) to annotate in the field; and in the past persons of means, leisure and intelligence have made their homes not in towns but in the country. The maps we shall always have, but the older generation of field archaeologists is rapidly dying out, and the earthworks are being destroyed at a greater rate than at any previous time. If something is not done soon[1] there will be very few left, in a decade or so, and field archaeologists will be driven into exile by the vandals of their own nation. Anticipating this event I propose to write a few notes on the possibilities of such field work abroad, ignoring (of necessity) all practical difficulties. Where there's a will, ways and means can be found of overcoming them.[2]

The student who decides to use his or her vacation doing field-work on the continent of Europe should choose the ground carefully, and buy and study a set of large-scale maps before he or she leaves England. For adequate study recent maps on a scale of at least 1:20,000 or 1:25,000 are essential; but one of the most promising regions, France, has no maps on a larger scale than 1:50,000, and that for parts of the country only. For the country as a whole the 1:80,000 map is the only one available. Practically no field-work in the British sense of the word has ever been done in France; and in such a tempting virgin field one could probably do preliminary research work on the scale of 1:80,000. Even on that map, for instance, it is possible to trace the course of certain Roman roads that survive as foot-paths, field-ways or continuous lines of hedge. During the 1914-18 war I saw several from the air; I remember two in particular, one near Estrées-Blanches, and the other (which enabled me to locate my position when temporarily lost) running due south from Cassel. By walking along them one could probably trace the continuation beyond the points where they cease to appear on the map. In such regions as the Puy de Dôme in the Jura and Vosges there must be moors and stretches of mountain that never

---

[1] The Chief Inspector of Ancient Monuments (Ministry of Works) has pretty full powers of protection, but has only quite recently begun to use them against ploughing, which is responsible for the bulk of the destruction. Often all that is required is to put up a fence round the object; it is not *necessary* (even though it may often be desirable) to prohibit ploughing the whole field or area.

[2] Germany in April 1938 was not an ideal country for a foreigner to explore on foot, making annotations on a map. But by taking the obvious precautions beforehand I was able to do so without any molestation and in a region not far from a frontier. The experiences of escaping prisoners of war suggest that the field archaeologist's best defences are an air of self-confidence combined with a command of the language and of bluff. The local archaeologists must also of course be appeased.

21a. (*above*) A 'dead' hedge of wattle in the Carpathians
21b. (*below*) Pig with spiked collar to stop him pushing through the wattle hedge

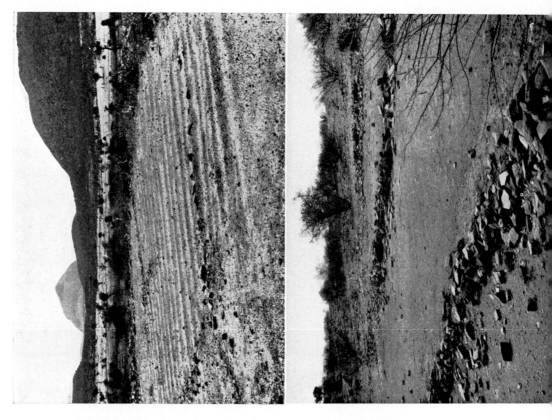

22a, b, c. Nomad cultivations at Darfur (*above*), at Ourei, Darfur (*top right*), and between Kutum and Ain Farah, Darfur (*bottom right*); see page 226

have been cultivated; and at crucial points such as passes and fords one should be able to find remains of the causeway. There must be similar, if fewer, opportunities in Switzerland and in the Alps for the application of a technique of field-work that has not yet been used there. The usual objections raised should be courteously ignored; they are usually made by people who do not realize that there is such a thing as a technique of field-work. Information that the course of a Roman road or linear earthwork is (a) well-known, or (b) lost beyond recovery, should therefore be received with polite scepticism. I do not know whether anyone has ever taken the trouble to walk across the St Gotthard pass along the *old* track, mapping its course and describing its behaviour; it would make an excellent subject for an article. One can see most of it from the train. Has anyone walked along the historic pack-horse road from Venice to Augsburg, along which went the kegs of marinated eels from the great Comacchio fisheries?[3] I am quite sure that no one except the Englishman Dr Thomas Ashby has walked the roads that led to Rome itself; and there are hundreds of miles of others. Continental archaeology has been dominated for decades by another kind of archaeology which is more at home in museums than in the open air, and out-door work has been confined largely to excavation. One of the first bits of field-work I ever did was to walk right round Rome looking at the walls. It was a wonderful experience, but I was then too ignorant to profit fully by it. Prof. Ian Richmond did the same and produced the standard book on the walls,[4] Dr Mortimer Wheeler did the same for Arles.[5] There are still hundreds of towns left for future workers. Such pastimes are far more fun than rubber-necking round the ruins of a Roman temple or villa without any particular objective; the difference is like that between giving a lecture and having to listen to one.

The tracing of Roman roads on the ground (aided whenever possible by air-photography) has the great merit that it will contribute valuable information to the International Map of the Roman Empire (*Tabula Imperii Romani*) which is now being re-started (by the Society of Antiquaries) after a compulsory pause of a decade. The field-worker can therefore be sure that his work will be used and published in map form; and for his descriptive matter, if he has the knack of making it short and readable, there is always *Antiquity*.

For those who prefer linear earthworks there is one close at hand running across the Cherbourg peninsula, and there must be many others. I should be very surprised if any plan of its course has been made since it was marked on the 1:80,000 map, or if any detailed description of its course has ever been published. Even if it has it will be buried in a publication that can only be seen (if at all) in one or two national libraries.

Prehistoric fields can be seen in Denmark and here they have been studied and splendidly planned by Dr Gudmund Hatt whose *magnum opus* on them has recently been published.[6] Those in Holland can be studied in the equally excellent publications of Professor van Giffen.[7] There are others in the Vosges, described by Mr C. E. Stevens and others.[8] Again there must be many others in other countries still awaiting discovery.

[3] *Fishing in Many Waters*, by James Hornell, 1950, 162.   [4] *The City Wall of Imperial Rome*, Oxford, 1930.
[5] 'The Roman Town-Walls of Arles', *Journal of Roman Studies*, XVI, 1926, 174–93.
[6] *Oldtidsagre*, Copenhagen (Munksgaard), 1949.   [7] See Appendix 8.
[8] *Revue Archéologique*, 65, IX, 1937, 26–37. For earlier descriptions see the Roman volume of Déchelette's *Manuel*, composed after his death by A. Grenier (*Manuel d'Archéologie Gallo-romaine*, 1934, 742–52) and the references there quoted. Grenier reproduces on p. 744 (Fig. 251) a plan by T. Welter of ancient fields, called *rotteln*, 'sur les sommets et les flancs des montagnes vosgiennes'.
O

In Mediterranean lands there is much to be done under the pleasantest of conditions. Maps are usually poor and on a small scale, but, as in France, the field of research is so wide and untilled that much may be accomplished in spite of this drawback. That is particularly true in the case of megalithic monuments. There are many that are not marked on the map at all, for continental cartographers have had no Roy nor Mudge to teach them their duty in archaeological matters. Some that are marked there have never been properly planned—the famous Grotte des Fées, for instance,[9] and many others mentioned in the early volumes of *Matériaux* and in the works of Cartailhac. Some of them are in such a state of neglect that they cannot be properly planned without a little preliminary tidying up with the reaping-hook and spade. But that is just the sort of work that even a beginner can do without much risk of harm to the monument; and he is not likely to meet with difficulties from the local antiquaries if he is tactful. Sardinia is full of long cairns, all of them in need of planning by someone who is up to date in these matters; even a casual inspection by one such person revealed important new facts.[10] There are plenty of others in the Balearic islands, where the need is urgent, or greater.[11] The island of Pantellaria used once to be regarded as a sort of inaccessible paradise of prehistoric monuments; it may be so still, but the matter is worth investigation.

The Iberian peninsula probably contains more neglected field archaeology than all the rest of Europe put together. Recent Spanish publications show that the making of plans is still in a rudimentary stage, many of them being inferior to those of Stukeley in the eighteenth century. In the current number of an official archaeological journal the plans have no scale.[12] Such omissions and shortcomings are not mere casual slips; they reveal a fundamental weakness.

Portugal too is full of neglected opportunities. There are some fine hill-forts, but no one knows what to do with them. Perhaps it is as well that they should be left alone until there is, but there would be no harm in planning and contouring them, and photographing the walls and gates—one has a carved stone lintel, I believe—before the peasants pull them to pieces. What can be achieved where archaeologists trained here in modern methods apply those methods elsewhere has been shown by British students in Tripolitania, where they are tidying up the mess left unrecorded by Italian archaeologists. The first-fruits are now beginning to be published; in *Archaeologia*, Volume 93, is a fine account of the Hunting-baths at Lepcis Magna. These were uncovered and restored by the Italians in 1932-3, but 'the only contemporary account of the excavation is that contained in the brief weekly reports compiled by the technical foreman in charge of the work'. The only record of the 'buildings as they were at the time of their discovery is contained in a small, but valuable, collection of photographs in the archives of the Superintendency'. The so-

---

[9] See Hemp in *Archaeologia*, LXXVI, 1927, 150–58, where the only existing plan of it and also of the Grotte Bounias (with important additions) are reproduced.

[10] Gordon Childe in *Antiquity*, XIII, 1939, 376. The 'dolmen' of Birori, near Macomer, a typical example, is recognized at sight to be merely the burial-chamber of a *tomba di giganti*, remains of whose façade were not observed by the Italians who planned it (*Bull. Pal. It.*, XXXII, 1906, 268). But Duncan Mackenzie was equally blind, and it was not until pre-historians trained in the British school of field archaeology inspected it that its true nature was seen and demonstrated. There must be many others that have been planned with the same incompleteness.

[11] See *Archaeologia*, LXXVI, 1927, 121–60: 'Some Rock-cut Tombs and Habitation Caves in Mallorca', by W. J. Hemp; also the same author's articles on Balearic megaliths in *Ant. Journ.*, XII, 1932, 127–33; XIII, 1933, 33–47; XIV, 1934, 277–81 (Long cairn in Eastern Provence); *Proc. Preh. Soc.*, 1935, 108–14 (Pedigree of long barrows and chambered cairns).

[12] See e.g., *Archivo Español de Arqueología*, No. 74, 1949, pp. 4 (unintelligible plan), 37 (Fig. 21), 38, 89, (plan of Tamuda): the oblique air-photograph of Tamuda (size of photo 5 × 3½ inches, size of town on it 1¼ × 1 inches) is quite useless.

called archaeologists let loose by the Italian Fascist government on its North African possessions did no more than act as the advance agents of Italian tourism. That is the besetting sin of State Archaeology; the money for the work is supplied by treasuries whose only interest is in the tourist. Money for publication of results is more difficult to obtain; moreover, the compilation of a report, and the survey and the drawing of plans which that involves, is a far more laborious and less interesting task than watching others removing sand or soil from buried ruins. The archaeologist is thus encouraged to go on 'directing excavations' year after year, until arrears of publications pile up and overwhelm him. That has been going on all over Italy—at Ostia and Herculaneum and many other sites. The visiting archaeologist was forbidden to take photographs or to publish them if permission is granted, for fear of anticipating a report which never appears. Yet such photographs might record details of great value. Archaeologists should accept state aid only if publication, whether by the state or by private bodies, is envisaged beforehand and promptly carried out at regular intervals.

The backwardness of Italian archaeology is shown also by its neglect of air-photography. Ever since I first demonstrated its possibilities more than a quarter of a century ago, first the late Dr Thomas Ashby, for so long Director of the British School at Rome, and then others have repeatedly urged Italian archaeologists to make use of it in Italy, but without the slightest effect.[13] Every sort of excuse was made for doing nothing; the soil was unsuitable because under cultivation; or archaeologists moaned that they could do nothing because they were forbidden to fly and take their own air-photos. (Some of the best discoveries have been made by British archaeologists who have used discarded R.A.F photos, without themselves leaving the ground). Yet Mr John Bradford has published[14] air-photographs taken in Italy by the R.A.F revealing a wealth of prehistoric, classical and medieval sites that has never been surpassed, and hardly even rivalled elsewhere! And he has followed this up by going to Italy and proving his case by excavation. There is an amusing side to these discoveries; they are crop-sites. The cultivation of the soil, so far from being (as alleged) an obstacle to discovery, was in fact its cause. Without cultivation many of these sites would not be visible.

One reason for this backwardness may be the failure to understand the fundamental importance of maps and plans[15] in modern archaeology. Indeed one might almost say that the ultimate (but not of course the only) aim of field-work and excavation is to produce maps and plans; the excavator does not just illustrate his report with a plan; it is in order to be able to draw a plan that he excavates. The text and illustrations are necessary to explain the plan; they are a kind of greatly expanded 'table of reference', for which there is not room on the margin of the plan itself. That is because plans (and sections and distribution maps) are a clearer and more accurate way of publishing observed facts than a mere verbal description alone. The plan, section and model are a diagrammatic representation *in parvo* of the thing itself. Vertical air-photographs are plans, and their great value was recognized at once in England because here archaeologists were already well

[13] An exception must be made in the case of Professor Lugli, who did his best to use the technique and published some air-photographs of a site on the Bay of Naples.

[14] *Antiquity*, XX, 1946, 191–200 (Apulia); XXI, 1947, 74–83 (Etruria); 197–204 (centuriation; see corrigenda xxii, 46); XXII, 58–72 (miscellaneous).

[15] And, of course, sections, but not in this context. Sections are merely plans on a vertical plane. Models are merely plans in three instead of two dimensions, and are even better therefore.

grounded in the importance of plans. This has not yet been recognized in many other countries because their archaeologists are not so grounded. They still put second things, such as *objets d'art*, inscriptions and tourist attractions, first.

It is obviously impossible, within the limits of a chapter, to survey the whole world and its possibilities for field archaeology. A few samples only can be taken, keeping so far as possible within the compass of the writer's experience and reading. The system of Roman frontier-defences in Dacia (Roumania) has never been properly investigated; it is one which would well repay work, both on the ground and from the air.[16] (I was shown some air-photos of a part near Constanza by the late Professor Wiegand, but could not then obtain publication of them; they are still in existence; I have recently seen them again, and I hope it may be possible to publish them). It was the eastern end of the European frontier of the Roman Empire, formed further west by the Danube and the Rhine, and is the least known of the great frontier defences (*Limes*, plural *Limites*), just as the central portion—the German Limes bridging the gap between the Danube and the Rhine—is the best known, thanks to the publications of the Limes-Kommission. Air-photography has recently revealed much of the Roman frontier-defences in North Africa and Syria, and it could easily do the same for the Dacian frontier. It is tantalising to think that in Roumania a few flights with a camera could have recorded the essential facts for a negligible cost between the wars.

Although I have never visited either of them, I feel sure that there must be a wealth of field archaeology in the large Mediterranean islands of Sardinia and Crete. Sardinia has already been mentioned as abounding in megalithic remains, which include habitations (*nuraghi* groups) as well as tombs. But there must also have been fields and roads, suscept-ible of study on modern geographical lines with due regard to geology and soils. In Crete we know there were well-made roads during the Minoan periods, because Sir Arthur Evans has found and described bits of them; but has anyone traced their course or mapped it as one traces a Roman road in Scotland, for instance? Here is a chance for someone, particularly if he can unearth the air-photographs taken during the war and said still to be surviving in a dump somewhere in the Middle East, unused and uncared for by their guardians but inaccessible to those who could so greatly profit by them.

The field archaeology of deserts might seem unpromising; actually the semi-deserts round the edge of the Fertile Crescent are some of the richest remaining unexplored areas. But their exploration requires motor transport and air-photographs. Although the major sites (such as Mshetta and Kasr Amr) have been adequately surveyed and others recon-noitred,[17] there probably remain others to be found or planned. Excavation is needed, but it is practically impossible for lack of labour. But it should be possible to complete the preliminary survey of such a thing as Shebib's Wall.[18] Those curious stone walls

---

[16] The only accounts of this and some of the adjacent systems which I have been able to find (partly through the kind help of Miss M. V. Taylor, C.B.E.) are these:

1. Gr. Tocilesco: *Fouilles et recherches arch. en Roumanie*, Bucarest, 1900, 115–237.

2. Carl Schuchhardt: 'Die sog. Trajans-wälle in der Dobrudsche': *Preuss. Akad. d. Wiss.*, Jahrg. 1918 (*Phil.-Hist.*, Klasse No. 12).

3. C. Uhlig: 'Die Wälle in Bessarabien', *Praeh. Zeitschrift*, XIX, 1928, 185–250.

4. Georges Cantacuzène: The Roman defences of the Lower Danube: *Aegyptus*, IX, 1928; summary in *Rev. Arch.*, XXVIII, 1928, 144.

5. 'The northern Roman limes', *Bull. Acad. Roum.*, XV.

[17] See references quoted in my article on 'Air Photographs of the Middle East', *Geographical Journal*, LXXIII (June 1929), 497–512.   [18] *Antiquity*, XXII, 1948, 151–4.

converging on stone enclosures known as the Works of the Old Men that are found all over the Syrian desert east and north-east of the Kingdom of Jordan are still undated and for the most part unsurveyed.[19] There is also an opportunity for a monograph (like Dr Hatt's on prehistoric Danish fields) on the field-systems of the desert margin. Those of the Negeb were revealed by the first air-photographs ever published;[20] others are to be seen on the excellent but much too small air-photographs in Dr Glueck's survey of Trans-jordan,[21] and in air-photographs of Umm al Jamal.[22] The field-walls of the Roman town of Bosrah can be seen from the top of the volcano of Umm Keiss. There are many lyn-chetted fields and ruined walls round the nuraghi-like towers in the Amman region;[23] they are associated with megalithic burial-chambers. It is possible that some of these fields may have remained under cultivation down to modern times and may even yet be cultivated; but no one has ever troubled to find out this simple fact, because no one who has 'passed R.B.', in Dr Wheeler's telling phrase, has yet gone out East to look at them. Yet the study of ancient field-systems is at least as important in the Fertile Crescent, where agriculture began, as in Europe. Are there any such ancient fields to be found further to the north-east, round the sites of the earliest self-sufficient villages, such as Tell Hassuna, for instance? Has anyone ever looked for them?

When flying along the Syrian coast south of Beirut on the way to Cyprus I saw a whole series of obviously very ancient field-walls on the steep sides of the hills above the coast; but it was not possible to see whether they were those of existing or of abandoned fields. All that was clear was that they were certainly the result of centuries of use, for they were strongly lynchetted. In such ancient homes of civilization the existing fields may be prehistoric.

In few other lands are the possibilities of field-work greater than in Iraq. Here air-photo-graphy is an essential aid. From a series of air-photographs taken along the great derelict Nahrwan canal above Baghdad a most valuable map could be constructed, showing the ancient towns and their remains with which its banks are studded. The ancient irrigation system is completely revealed by air-photography. The exact plan, accurate on a scale of 1:5,000, of the vast ruin-field of Samarra (Eski Baghdad), sixty miles above modern Baghdad, could be plotted and compared with Jakut's detailed contemporary description. The materials, in the form of air-photographic negatives are available in the British Museum, where I deposited them more than twenty years ago. The great linear defence called the Median Wall,[24] between the Tigris and the desert was last mentioned in print by Captain Felix Jones in 1857.[25] There are medieval *cities* whose complete plan could be plotted given air-photographs.[26] The total cost of this suggested programme of work in Iraq and its publication would be much less than the cost of building a single large aeroplane, and not much more than the cost of two or three fully equipped archaeological

[19] *Antiquity*, I, 1927, 197–203; III, 1929, 389–407; both articles fully illustrated by air-photographs and diagrams.

[20] M. Wiegand, *Wissenschaftl. Veröffentl. d. Deutsch-Türkischen Denkmalschutzkommandos*, Heft I (Berlin, 1920), Sinai.

[21] Nelson Glueck, 'Explorations in Eastern Palestine' III (*Annual of the American Schools of Oriental Research*, XVIII–XIX, 1937–9), Newhaven, Conn., 1939.

[22] *Antiquity*, XI, 1937, 456–60 (field-walls on Plate i).

[23] *Antiquity*, III, 1929, 342–3 (field-walls on Plates iv, v); XII, 1938, 93.

[24] An oblique air-photograph is published in my article in *Geographical Journal*, LXIII, opposite p. 506.

[25] *Memoirs*: selections from the records of the Bombay Government, No. XLII (New Series), Bombay, 1857. The original report was called 'Narrative of a Journey undertaken in April 1848'. For him, see Seton Lloyd, *Foundations in the Dust*, 1947, 157–61.

[26] For one such, see *Geographical Journal*, LXXIII, plate opposite p. 506.

expeditions. The results in new knowledge would be quite out of proportion to the cost. But of course the work would not all be done as a single undertaking, but split up into several smaller ones. What can be done by even a single such expedition has been shown by Erich Schmidt's *Flights over Ancient Cities of Iran*, made in 1935-7.[27] Ancient cities hitherto almost unknown were found and photographed, and the great frontier-defence called Alexander's Barrier (Sadd-i-Sikandar) or the Red Snake (Qizil Yilan), stretching over 100 miles from the Caspian to the mountains, was photographed from end to end.

I commend these suggestions, not for the first time, to the Oriental Institute of Chicago, which was responsible for the last-mentioned undertaking. Further east I shall not venture now; the field is too vast and too unknown, and is for the time being inaccessible to European and American archaeologists. What a promising field it is can be seen from Major Williams-Hunt's article on irregular earthworks in Eastern Siam[28] revealed by air-photographs taken during the war. These have not yet been seen on the ground and nothing at all is known about them.

This rapid world-tour ends where so many others begin—in America (Africa is dealt with in Appendix 5 and in Chapter 22). If it is rash (even with outside help) to write about field archaeology in Africa on the basis of a few months there, it would be foolish to attempt to describe the remains likely to be awaiting the investigator in the New World, where I have unfortunately never set foot. All I can do is to throw out a few suggestions based on reading, and hope that American field archaeologists will be indulgent. Nothing can be so infuriating to the dirt archaeologist as advice from a colleague in an arm-chair.

One of the things that badly needs doing is to photograph from the air and then follow on foot and map the course of those age-old wild animal tracks described by Mr F. G. Roe (Plate 5b).[29] Why select these when there is such a wealth of other material? Because they may well be the archetypes of all roads everywhere. As I have said above,[30] animals ridden or driven by men may well have had a hand—or rather hoof—in determining the exact course of early trade-routes. If it is found, as I expect it will be, that these Canadian animal tracks obey the same rules as 'ancient British track-ways' like the Icknield way and the Ridgeway, our respect for animals should be increased. One who had a profound and practical knowledge of the nature of cattle, Mr Lucas Bridges,[31] put them above horses in the scale of intelligence; and the buffaloes who made the deep trails in Canada may have been just as intelligent as the half-wild cattle of Tierra del Fuego. There must have been countless trails like these in Europe during the Old Stone Age. The hunters must have known them well and used them.

Air-photography has not as yet been much used in America for archaeological discovery. I do not know of any published illustration of a crop-site anywhere in that continent. But they are there, for Dr St Joseph, who has flown across the United States, tells me he has seen some. Here is an opportunity for someone.

The European's interest in American archaeology is naturally coloured to some extent by his home interests. He wants to know, for instance, whether hill-forts like those he knows here were independently invented there. If they exist there at all, they *must* have been independently invented; for it is quite certain that, whatever the exact date of man's first entry into the American continent, it was several millennia before the first European

[27] Special publication of the Oriental Institute of Chicago, 1946; see *Antiquity*, XX, 1946, 170–1.
[28] *Antiquity*, XXIV, 1950, 30–6.   [29] *Antiquity*, III, 299–311.   [30] See p. 60.
[31] *The Uttermost Part of the Earth* (Hodder & Stoughton, and Readers' Union, 1948).

or Asiatic hill-fort was made. They exist in Mexico,[32] and South America contains many.[33] In north-west Argentina there are fortified villages on the hill-tops which seem to have been refuges, since there are contemporary ones down below in pleasanter situations. Much the same occurs in Peru where the habit of building them began in pre-Inca times. There is one such at Pisac in the Urubamba valley; but the classical example is Saccsahuaman, overlooking Cuzco, which was a veritable Maiden Castle. It is regarded as a potential refuge and ceremonial centre and not as a fort erected to defend Cuzco itself. There is a famous hill-fort called Paramonga in the Central Coast area of Peru. One of the best-preserved of these pre-colonial hill-forts is that called La Fortaleza, which consists of three terrace-like platforms enclosed by a high wall and approached by narrow passage-ways commanded by ramparts and watch-towers. It is close to the sea, on a spur projecting into flat alluvial ground now under cultivation. It is one of the eight that are believed to have marked the southern limit of the kingdom of the great Chimú. La Fortaleza is in Lat. 10° 50′ S. (approximately), near the town of Supé, about 120 miles north of Lima. An excellent oblique air-photo of it has been published.[34]

There are even linear earthworks—or rather stoneworks—in Peru. One, the Great Wall, runs from the coast between 8° and 9° south near Chimbote and follows the Santa River inland for at least 40 miles. It was discovered from the air by Lieut. George R. Johnson and photographed by the Shippee-Johnson Peruvian expedition in 1931. One of the air-photographs shows it running along the edge of a steep escarpment just as Hadrian's Wall does in some places, but without its towers and forts. There are forts associated with it, however, but without a map showing the exact relationship one must beware of assuming contemporaneity. The forts are said to be 'of adobe construction', but look on the photograph (Fig. 8) more like rough stonework. The wall itself, when visited on the ground, was seen to be made of rough stones set in adobe cement and 'well chinked with small rocks', so that it could not be climbed. Originally it was estimated to have been 'about twelve or fifteen feet thick at the base, and [it] was built to taper upward to an average height of twelve or fifteen feet'. It was clearly 'erected as a defensive barrier', and it is thought that there may be others like it. A date somewhere between the thirteenth and fifteenth centuries seems not improbable.

The discoverers were surprised that it should have been left for them to make a new discovery of such evident importance 'in a region whose ruins have been for more than seventy-five years the subject of frequent and careful explorations by a long list of noted archaeologists'. It shows that there is ample scope for field-work in Peru, for the wall itself and the forts are still unmapped.[35]

Perhaps the most striking resemblance between the field archaeology of the New and Old Worlds is found in the stupendous causeway-roads of Yucatan in Mexico.[36] They

[32] See Pedro Armillas, 'Fortalezas Mexicanas' in *Cuadernos Americanos*, vol. 5 (Sept.–Oct. 1948), 143–63; mentioned in *American Journal of Archaeology*, vol. 53 (2), April–June, 1949, 208. Professor Armillas reproduces air-photos of these hill-forts there, and in *Antiquity*, XXV, 77–86.

[33] I am indebted to Mr G. H. S. Bushnell, Curator of the Museum of Archaeology, Cambridge, for some of the information which follows, and some of the references.

[34] *Peru from the Air*, by Lieutenant George R. Johnson (Amer. Geographical Society, 1930), 73.

[35] The quotations above are from Mr Robert Shippee's article on 'The Great Wall of Peru', *Geographical Review* (New York), January 1932, 1–29. Many other fine air-photographs of ancient Peruvian sites are there published. Air-photographs of the Great Wall were also published in the *Illustrated London News* for 14th May 1932.

[36] *Antiquity*, IX, 1935, 67–73 (Plates i–iii): 'The Ancient Maya Causeways of Yucatan', by Marshall H. Saville. Bibliography of nine items.

are greater in size than the Roman roads which they resemble both in their straightness and in some features of their structure. They were already in decay at the end of the six-teenth century when Bishop Landa stated that 'there was once a very handsome causeway from the city of Tiho to that of Ytzamal', but even then there were 'signs' of it only, im-plying that it was then disused and an antiquity. One such road near Coba involved 'the quarrying, transport, facing, and building in, of nearly a million tons of stone. . . . On each side of the road were great quarries [another resemblance to Roman roads] from which the stone used in its construction had been taken. Holes were apparently sunk round the great blocks, in which they built fires, and then pouring water into the red-hot holes, caused the rocks to split, so that slabs of it could be easily dug out.[37] The sides [of the causeway] were built of great blocks of cut stone weighing hundreds of pounds; the central part was filled in with unhewn blocks of limestone, and the top covered with rubble, which, as indicated by the traces of it which remain here and there, was once cemented over.'

The greatest of these roads known at present, called by Dr Gann[38] the Camino Real de Occidente, runs due west from Coba to Yaxhuana, a distance of exactly 100 kilometres (62 miles). It was first traversed from end to end in 1933. For more than two thirds of the distance the road runs absolutely straight. An interesting discovery was an immense stone cylinder on one section of the causeway, 4 metres long, 70 centimetres in diameter and weighing approximately 5 tons. The explorer, rightly I think, assumes that it was used as a road roller for levelling the top layer of plaster which once covered the surface.[39] The maximum height of the causeway is 2.50 metres and the average height 0.75 metres, the average width between 9 and 10 metres. The sides of the causeway are made of roughly squared stones, and it is suggested that these sides as well as the road surface itself were originally covered with plaster or rude cement; but of this there are traces on the road surface only.

Coba was one of the most important of the Maya cities of Yucatan and there are the remains of no less than sixteen roads in its vicinity, some quite short. One such runs south-westwards from Coba to another ruined city called Kucican, 10 miles away. 'Near Kucican there are various passages made under the road [which] would permit travellers to go from one side of the road to the other without having to climb over [the causeway].'

Mr Marshall H. Saville's article in *Antiquity* (from which the above quotations are taken) is illustrated by three photographs showing the built-up side or retaining wall of the cause-way, the cylindrical stone roller and a view of the roads from the air. The last photograph, taken near Coba, shows an immense area completely covered by dense forest with a string of small lakes in the distance. One road is seen running towards the spectator across the middle of the picture; another is seen crossing it at an angle of about 45°. The course of the raised causeways is revealed by marks or lines across the top of the forest. These appear to be caused by the fact that the trees growing on the causeway are naturally taller than the others by the height of the causeway itself, so that they cast a shadow— or, more exactly, are darker on the side away from the sun. The same phenomenon was observed and photographed by the late Major Allen where the Wychwood Grim's Ditch goes through a wood near Tomlin's Gate in Kiddington, Oxon.

[37] A similar technique was used according to Stukeley (*Abury*, 1743, 25) to split the sarsens of the Avebury stone circle; see his sketch reproduced in Dr Grahame Clark's *Prehistoric England*, Fig. 103 (and p. 110). The natives of French Guinea still use the same method to destroy rocks in the construction of roads.

[38] *Ancient Cities and Modern Tribes*, 1926.   [39] Marshall H. Saville in *Antiquity*, IX, 1935, 72–3.

The whole region covered by these roads is still imperfectly explored, and was formerly considered unsafe for travellers by reason of the attitude of the inhabitants. Some of the causeways and cities of which the chief show place is Chichen Itza were photographed from the air by Colonel Lindberg, and it is obvious that there is a considerable future here for air exploration and photography. It will, however, need to be done by someone with experience in this technique, for the tree-top lines are rather faint. The shadow by which the causeways are revealed is precisely similar to the shadow seen on certain crop-sites when the corn grows higher over a silted-up ditch. In such cases the best results are obtained by taking a photograph into the sun, not necessarily directly but at an angle. The camera then faces the darker side of the line and records it by contrast with the rest of the surface. Yucatan is extremely flat (which may account for the straightness of the roads), so that in one respect conditions are favourable for air-photography; but the forest carpet restricts its possibilities and makes flying, especially at low altitudes, somewhat risky.

Peru, already mentioned, is plainly a much more promising field for air-archaeology than these forest-covered plains. Lieutenant Johnson has published two striking air-photographs (pp. 12, 13) of 'palaces'—probably walled towns—at Chan Chan in the Chimu valley. Besides the main enclosure, which is rectangular (1,600 by 1,100 feet), and outside it are seen others, also rectangular, with roads between them, some enclosing gardens and fields. The whole complex is pre-Inca, and is evidence that the culture had reached a high degree of organization and skill. Incidentally—a point not noticed by the author—the photographs show that both the main enclosure-walls were constructed after the smaller ones, which they intersect. Vertical air-photographs taken in a low light would reveal the complete plan of these settlements, and it is very much to be desired that they should be taken while there is yet the opportunity. Modern 'development' may obliterate them at any time without warning.

This rapid survey is obviously most incomplete. Huge areas of the earth's surface—Central and Eastern Asia, Australasia and the whole Pacific region—have hardly even been mentioned, and many large countries dismissed in a paragraph or two. That is inevitable in a book which covers so wide a field, far greater than one man can possibly cover. The examples selected, however, may serve to show that field archaeology, hitherto practised chiefly in one or two European countries, is equally practicable in many others. Combined with air-photography whenever possible, field archaeology can achieve valuable and substantial results. It is not, of course, a substitute for excavation, but a valuable preliminary; it is the reconnaissance that precedes the main attack. And just as the success of the battle may depend upon the knowledge obtained before it, so may the results of the excavations depend upon a preliminary field survey. That survey may enable the best site to be chosen for excavation (just as a reconnaissance decides the field of battle); but the survey is well worth doing for its own sake, even where no excavation is contemplated. Air-photography is now recognized as an almost essential preliminary measure before digging; its practical use, and the economy effected, were demonstrated at the Roman villa near Ditchley and at Caister-by-Norwich.[40]

---

[40] For Ditchley, see *Oxoniensia*, I, 1936, 24–69. At Caister (still unpublished) air-photographs revealed the blocks or *insulae* of the town, so that one could be chosen for operations. The air-photograph of Caister was published in *Antiquity*, III, 1929, 182–7, where it is described by Dr Mortimer Wheeler.

CHAPTER 21

Archaeology and Anthropology

THROUGHOUT THIS BOOK I have referred several times to the help that an archaeologist can get from the study of living cultures, which is a branch of anthropology. Between the two disciplines there should be a close liaison, but, while personal relations are usually most friendly, there is need, I think, for a fuller appreciation by anthropologists of the various ways in which they can help archaeologists. There is no need to discuss the extent in theory, of either branch of science; in theory, of course, anthropology claims to be all-embracing, but in practice—which is what matters—each discipline has its own techniques. In making certain suggestions about anthrolopogical field-work I wish it to be understood that I have no sort of animus against anthropology, even where those suggestions may be critical. As an archaeologist I know how greatly one can profit by taking a course in anthropology, the more so because when I took one the founder of anthropology himself was still lecturing in the University of Oxford. Indeed I am sure that archaeologists would be better at their own job if they were able to pass through the purlieus of anthropology first.

Now, although in theory an anthropologist who writes about a primitive community should describe every aspect of its culture, in practice certain aspects are often more fully described than others. Such non-material matters as customs, social organization, and religion often occupy far more space than the description, if any, of the way in which that community solves the basic problems of existence. It is of the utmost importance, of course, that these non-material matters *should* be described, as fully and as quickly as possible, not only because they are vanishing, but also because they are themselves of the greatest intrinsic importance. Moreover they lie in a field that is of necessity almost inaccessible to archaeology, except occasionally by a hazardous inference from material finds. But is not the anthropologist who sets out to study and describe a primitive community —let us say, a village in the Nuba hills or in the Aures mountains of Algeria—simply doing for it what his archaeological colleague is trying to do, with far less evidence, for the one that he is excavating? The latter is merely an anthropologist in the past tense employing another technique; and one might also call the other an archaeologist in the present tense. The work of each should amplify and supplement that of the other. In order that he may help the archaeologist, the anthropologist should, for instance, make a plan of his village and of some of the huts or houses, marking on the plan the purpose served by the houses (habitation, storage, ritual, etc.) and rooms.[1] He needs no technique for this; he just has

[1] As is done, for instance, Dr S. F. Nadel's excellent book on the Nuba people, though the plans are diagrammatic and rather small (*The Nuba*, by S. F. Nadel, Oxford, 1947).

to ask questions and observe habits. Archaeologists would welcome the fullest possible descriptions of granaries—are they communal, with one building for a small village, or individual? In the Aures mountains there is one big building—often the biggest and most conspicuous in the village—but it is divided up into locked rooms, each of which is individual or family property. In the Roseires region of the Blue Nile there are many separate granaries of mud or straw (like the houses), each individually owned (Plate 20). What procedure is adopted for threshing and grinding corn? How far from the village is the furthest regularly cultivated field, and how are the fields owned? What are the ploughs or hoes like? How and whence do they get water? Are there specialized potters or does every household make its own? Where is the clay got, and are the pots fired there or the clay taken home? Are pots traded and if so how far? How are houses built? How long do things last in use? (Heirlooms are always a possible snag in archaeological chronology, and virtually nothing certain is known about them).

These are merely a few examples, chosen almost at random, from amongst the hundreds of details that anthropologists could supply so easily and so rarely do. Perhaps that is because it is always difficult to bring one's self to record the obvious and commonplace things. A student living in a primitive community tends, if he is any good, to become for the time being a member of that community; and so to accept as obvious and well-known what is so to all its members. But it is just these things that we most want to know; they are not at all obvious or well-known to the rest of the world, yet they are basic, for without them existence would not be possible. There is a good historical reason for ignoring basic things. Both archaeologists and anthropologists belong usually to a class that is not brought into direct contact with them at home. They do not have to grow or store corn, or to grind it, or to make pots or other implements of daily use, or build their own houses. They buy these things ready made, and often do not know where they come from. They may be more alive to the importance of trade, especially if they belong to the 'nation of shopkeepers'. But their scale of relative values is still, or was until quite recently, that of a leisured class, sheltered from the struggle for necessities by family accumulations or by special endowments. (So too the classical writers, similarly sheltered, rarely mentioned the processes which maintained their lives; and the history of such things as mills is thereby rendered obscure.) Standards of value are largely determined by education, which reflects those of the ruling class. The anthropologist has already acquired a set of values at school and college, perhaps half consciously, long before he goes abroad; and when he sets out to observe and record the culture of a primitive community his selection of culture-traits is determined by his education. He selects those which seem to him most interesting, the things that will interest others at home; and if, as often, his background is a university, his choice will fall on abstract rather than on concrete things—belief and custom rather than pots and ploughs. He is himself as much the product of his culture as are the people he is observing. *His* behaviour as an anthropologist is just as much a culturological phenomenon as is the behaviour of the subjects of his inquiry; and it is to be equally explained in terms of culture. His interests differ from those of his subjects because their culture and his are different. This comes out very plainly in the questions asked; he will be continually enquiring about matters which do not greatly interest them and vice versa. One often finds one's self talking thus at cross purposes. I may be interested in some abstract belief or legend; while my native friend keeps asking me how many wives I have, whether I have any cattle, how much my boots cost or what my income is. Such things as these interest him far more than the others. He lives closer than I do to the basic facts of existence. Ask him about *his* wives and cattle, or about corn and fields, granaries, querns, pots and the like and you will find that he is full of information, and probably pleased and surprised to meet such an intelligent European. His opinion is sound; man can live without philosophy but not without food, and the more highly industrialized his culture, the more important does food become—and food cannot be grown in towns.

The foregoing generalizations, like all such, need some qualification; one can think of many exceptions. Whatever his education, the countryman's view of life is always closer to basic realities than the townsman's; and some of the best field-work in archaeology and anthropology has been done by countrymen—by country doctors like Williams-Freeman and by the sons of country parsons. General Pitt-Rivers, who emphasized the importance of common things, was a countryman, and so were many of the best of the earlier archaeologists, such as Colt Hoare. But these exceptions themselves prove the truth of the generalization that the field-worker's outlook has been largely determined by the culture of his social environment, and his selection of facts to record influenced by its values.

In the record of anthropological facts that will help archaeologists, air-photography has already begun to play a part. One of the first demonstrations of its value in this sphere was given by those taken by Richard and Mary Upjohn Light just before the Second War during a cruise from Capetown to Cairo.[2] Some of the air-photographs taken show hut-settlements and corrals in Northern Rhodesia which, consisting as they do of many elements (such as thorn-hedges, ill-defined straw buildings and tracks) that are difficult to represent satisfactorily by conventional signs on plans, are particularly well-adapted to air-photography. Such views enable one to visualize these settlements far more clearly and completely than one could from a general ground view or plan. Supplemented of course by a more leisurely investigation on the spot, they provide comparative material that assists the excavator in his imaginative reconstruction of prehistoric sites. They also have an intrinsic value of their own for the anthropologist who is concerned with primitive economy. The result of this one cruise was a series of vivid pictures of primitive life in Africa such as had not before been seen. These native villages represent a stage in the development of human society that, as the other photographs taken show, is rapidly giving place to another. The time to record these is *now*, before they have passed away. In my note in *Antiquity*, I urged the importance of such work for British anthropologists, whose concern with them is particularly close and widely spread; and also of a central depot for air-photographs in general. The second proposal has been adopted, but it will need an enlargement of their outlook before anthropologists generally appreciate the value to their work of such photographs. How useful it would be to an excavator to have a series of them, together with details of construction and usage, both in words and in diagrams amplifying the photograph!

Other examples of the sort of air-photographs that should interest field archaeologists are to be found scattered through the publications of learned societies and in books such

---

[2] *Geographical Review* (of the American Geographical Society), October 1938: mentioned in *Antiquity*, XIII, 1939, 1–3, where two of the air-photographs are reproduced. I have repeated here some sentences from my Editorial Notes there.

as *Découverte aérienne du monde*.[3] Here are views of primitive villages in Asia and Africa, complete with all the tracks leading to them and the village fields. Sometimes, as at the Kotoko village of Divel in Northern Cameroon (Plate 19), the huts stand in a group surrounded by a wall with entrances where, for better defence, it makes a V-shaped re-entrant angle, to which tracks converge. On the hillside below and just outside the wall are reservoirs of water for drinking and irrigation. As M. Chombart de Lauwe says: 'No map would so well show this distrustful architecture [i.e. the wall and its gaps] . . . nor the oblong shape of the roofs, nor the number of huts, nor the distribution of trees within the wall nor of the palms in the immediate outskirts. Within the enclosure one can trace [on the open, unoccupied portions] the square lines of the winter fields which are almost invisible during the dry season.' This excellent summary, quite adequate for its purpose in the book mentioned, could profitably be expanded by ground-work. An air-photograph cannot tell us all we should like to know—what the wall and houses are built of, for instance, less still the social organization of the community. That is the task of anthropologists, and the book is intended, we imagine, to call attention to the potentiality of air-photography in this (and other) subjects. It does so well, particularly in showing as no map can, the nature of the surrounding vegetation—wild and cultivated. What greater contrast could there be than that between the scattered patches of cultivation in the Sudanese landscape of Bamako (Afrique Orientale Française), the neat terraces of Java and the long narrow strips of Sundgau on the Upper Rhine?[4] These things, for which we have to thank geographers, belong properly to the discipline of a modernized anthropology which should concern itself with the whole structure of a community, not merely with the superstructure.

Elsewhere in this book I have alluded to the opportunities which North Africa—the Mediterranean coast and Morocco—offers for the study of 'the past in the present'. Hilltop communities where the boom of the rotary quern may be heard daily are not yet extinct there. Egypt must be full of 'survivals' and the Balkans certainly are. In Bulgaria even the goats belong to a prehistoric breed.[5] And, speaking of goats, I would remark that the study of different breeds of domesticated animals—sheep, cattle and dogs[6] as well as goats—is of considerable culturological importance. The research must be done by a zoologist who can handle archaeological and historical evidence; but field-workers can help by taking photographs of animals they meet with during their travels. Such photographs of animals are not easy to take; animals are as suspicious of the stranger with a camera as is an Arab woman. The most useful view is the side view; but they dislike exposing their flanks. These animal-photographs are, apparently, not at all common. When the late Dr Hilzheimer was writing his articles[7] for *Antiquity* on domestic animals, I managed to take for him one of a Soay sheep on the island of Harris, outer Hebrides; and that photograph has since been in great demand.

The anthropology—in the limited and specialized sense here used and explained above —of the countries round the shores of the Mediterranean is an almost unworked field. Who has ever troubled to describe and publish illustrations of the various ceramic types

---

[3] By Paul Chombart de Lauwe of the Musée de l'Homme; Horizons de France, 30 rue du Général Foy, Paris, 1948 The author in his text emphasises the ethnographical importance of the air-photographs.

[4] Pages 203, 214, 221.

[5] *Antiquity*, XII, 1938, 81–2 (Kish goat).

[6] See, for instance, *Antiquity*, X, 1936, 358–9 (Inca bull-dog).

[7] Cut short by the War and then by his death.

in use there? Yet they are both anthropologically interesting and as often as not aesthetically satisfying. The late Stanley Casson was beginning to collect materials for a study of the pot-fabrics of Greek lands and islands; and he published some notes in *Antiquity*.[8] But he died before he could write the article or book that he was contemplating. There is a very great variety of types; I have seen and obtained specimens from south-east Spain (bought in the island of Majorca), Algeria, Jerba (where the potteries of Guellala produced glazed ware of an Arab type), Athens and Bulgaria. At the fair of Tschumen I saw set out on the ground a display of bowls, plates and pots for domestic use such as would fill a monograph. The shapes were practical and the designs and colours more satisfying than most of the productions of modern artists. Colonel Gordon has made a beginning in India, where he has studied modern painted pottery directly descended from wares of the Harappa culture of 3,000 years ago.[9] Sporadic notes on modern pottery may be found here and there in anthropological publications; but they should be regarded as a necessary part of every anthropological study of a primitive culture.[10] But too often we see page after unreadable page on the systems of relationship, and little or nothing about the pots. Not long ago I wanted, for archaeological reasons, to find an illustrated description of modern Shilluk pot-types. Books have been written about the Shilluks, but the pottery is nowhere described or illustrated. And pottery everywhere is tending to be ousted by containers fashioned from petrol-tins. Soon it will disappear altogether, and an age-old craft will be lost to anthropology and pass into the sphere of archaeology. The same happens with basket-work. Once the most beautiful baskets were made on the Blue Nile and in Dongola Province. They were mentioned by a seventeenth-century traveller and were still being made when I was at Sennar in 1914. I have, and use, one. They are no longer made there and, though still made elsewhere, aniline dyes have ousted the old colours. Basketry is as important in culturology as is pottery—in fact it is almost more important because, being perishable, it rarely survives in an archaeological context; and we therefore need all the help we can get by analogy from modern fabrics. All that I have said above applies equally to many other things of daily use such as clothes, for example. I could go on multiplying instances. My point is that sudents of modern cultures should realize the importance of these common basic things and record them with as much care and respect as they show for the other elements of those cultures. The foundations are just as important as the superstructure.

There is a small region where history, anthropology and archaeology meet; that is where primitive culture still survives or has only recently become extinct. In south-east Australia, for instance, there are many summer camp sites of aborigines round Port Philip Bay near Melbourne. They consist of middens and are covered with a scatter of stone implements. In early colonial days they were still frequented and they are mentioned in published descriptions; they were then within the sphere of anthropology (though the science was as yet unborn). Now they are deserted and there are no aborigines anywhere near, so that they have passed into the sphere of archaeology. But being mentioned in written documents they belong also (albeit rather loosely) to history. A detailed description of one such camp site, written at a time when it was still frequented, would be (if it exists) classified as anthropological. A modern investigator of the same site would have

---

[8] XII, 1938, 464–73: 'Modern Pottery Trade in the Aegean'.   [9] *Journ. Indian Anthrop. Inst NS.* 2, II, 1948, 9–18.
[10] There is an excellent account of Kikuyu pottery in Mrs Routledge's book on these people.

to employ only the techniques of archaeology, amplified by the historical document of his anthropological predecessor. This is not an imaginary case. These camp sites *have* been subjected to one of the techniques of archaeology, namely air-photography. Major Williams-Hunt has described them and shown by illustrations how they may be discerned and recognized in air-photographs.[11] It is not, however, the middens that reveal them, but the topographical conditions which caused the sites to be selected, such as reefs or a wide extent of beach uncovered at low tide where sea food was abundant and easily collected. Other examples in Malaya are cited. Major Williams-Hunt rightly classes all these sites as archaeological, with a tenuous historical link; and emphasizes the necessity of following up air-photography by field-work.

In these Australian sites, then, there is an excellent opportunity of testing the value of what I said earlier in this chapter. I claimed that anthropologists would help archaeologists by recording certain facts about the material culture of a community, because many such facts necessarily elude their technique. Our colonial investigator, visiting such a site, would find out by enquiry, for instance, how often it was visited and at what times of year, how long the aborigines remained there, how many of them were there at one time, whether they ate other than sea food and whether they ate it raw or cooked, whether they had boats and fished with a line, whether they erected any sort of shelters and so on. Many of these facts must necessarily elude the archaeologist whom we assume to come along later and dig there in the middens; yet all of them are facts that he would like to be able to discover if he could. If they had been recorded while the camp was still in use, there would be little left for him to do. Thus we see how very closely the objectives of the two disciplines coincide when they meet on a single site. It is therefore quite legitimate to claim that they coincide over a much larger field of enquiry.

Actually it is still not too late to study the habits of the living Australian aborigines. Though greatly reduced in numbers they still survive in their fantastic land in the centre of the continent, where Mr Charles Mountford recently visited and lived with them. His account of his experiences[12] forms, in my opinion, a landmark in anthropological literature, not only because of his superb and dramatic photographs but because of the essential *humanity* which it reveals. We had already been taught to regard these people as interesting specimens, but we never suspected, from the manuals, that they were also 'one of the most lovable races of men'. We find them kind and courteous, simple-minded and interested in small things, also sometimes less charming—in fact, just such people as our own friends. Nor are they just 'people'; compare for instance the faces of Tjallrina and Jabiaba (pp. 112, 128). Here is something to give pause to the archaeological fanatic, 'so careful of the type . . . so careless of the single life'. True, he can never come to love the prehistoric men who died many centuries ago, and the limitations of his technique exclude any recognition of the 'single life' in the way in which Mr Mountford, with his Australians, reveals it to us. But he can, and should, remember that that is the ultimate fact behind all his generalizations; and he can also get *en rapport* by long and sympathetic immersion in his study, by getting to know the country and the remains that are left of their handiwork. There is also the ancestral link; these men too lived in our land and may have loved it, as do the Australians.

[11] *Antiquity*, XXII, 1948, 103–5.
[12] *Brown Men and Red Sand*, Phoenix House Ltd., 1950. Reviewed in *Antiquity*, XXV (June 1951), 108–9.

The coincidence between archaeology and anthropology is nowhere seen so clearly as in the study of primitive houses. Excavators rarely find much left of the superstructure of these houses; when they do, as at Skara Brae in Orkney and Lepcis Magna in Tripoli (where even the roofs of the Roman baths were intact) it is because they have been preserved by sand-drifts. More often they have to reconstruct their houses in imagination from a group of post-holes. This disciplined use of the imagination is the highest function of the archaeologist; it is creative work of the highest order, in the exercise of which he finds his greatest pleasure and the fullest intellectual satisfaction. The process by means of which an archaeologist reconstructs and brings back to life again a prehistoric house or village is a work of art exactly comparable to that performed by, for instance, a writer of plays or novels. The observed facts (whether behaviour or post-holes) are assimilated, mated in the mind with the memory of others, and a book or article is born. The process has much in common with that by which living things are created. The nature of the product varies in accordance with that of the producer. If he has a mind well-stocked with pertinent knowledge and is endowed with a creative imagination that can use it, what he produces will be good and alive; if he has not, no matter how good his work may be in other more mechanical ways, it will be stillborn. There are many people who, when digging, obey all the rules and record details with painful care and precision, but who, lacking the power of creative imagination, cannot interpret their discoveries. Their work is technically well done, but the final results are defective. No serious attempt is made to interpret what has been revealed. Each post-hole, each layer is well observed, but one sees at once from the printed report that neither during the excavation nor afterwards was an earnest attempt made to understand what these features meant and what purpose they served while the structure was still standing. The lack of this imaginative thinking may lead, and has often led, to erroneous interpretation, when such is attempted; and it affects also the direction of the excavations themselves, because possibilities are not tested. People either have or have not this gift of creative imagination; if they have it not, they cannot learn it, and will never know what excavation can achieve. They are apt to regard excavation as merely a mechanical process whereas it is a creative one. It goes without saying that the objective study and record of observed facts must be kept apart, in the record itself, from the imaginative interpretation of these facts, which must be checked over and over again.

It is in this imaginative process that anthropology can so greatly help. An archaeologist whose mind is well stocked with observations of primitive houses, for instance, will be able to reconstruct the house he has excavated far more easily than one whose mind is not so stocked. If he has lived in such houses and shared the life of their occupants, he will be better equipped than if he has merely read about them in books. But even to have read about them only is helpful, especially in minor matters. One does not need to have actually used a modern three-pronged fish-spear, for example, to spot the resemblance to the so-called harpoons of the Mesolithic Period; it is enough to see them or even only drawings of them.[13] Dr Stone, I am sure, has never dried a skin with the aid of a perforated pot; but his note based on a drawing is a perfectly adequate and legitimate explanation of our Bronze Age 'incense-cups'[14]. What is essential is that the archaeologist should be on the

---

[13] See Dr Grahame Clark's note in *Ant. Journ.*, XXVIII, 1948, 58–60.
[14] *Antiquity*, XXII, 1949, 215–16.

23a. (*above*) Hut-circle formed by burning a round straw hut, Abu Geili, 1950; see page 148
23b. (*below*) Squatter's shack amid the departed glories of Suakin; see page 231

24. Wansdyke, looking east from Morgan's Hill (*see* fig. 41 *and* page 254)

look-out for these resemblances, that he should realize that it is part of his job to interpret as well as to record, and that in the living primitive cultures of to-day, and in the records of those now extinct, he has a rich store of material lying ready for his use. He will not realize this if he regards excavation as a mechanical process of observation and record merely, however technically excellent his work may be in these respects. He will do so only if he realizes that all his work is ultimately the means to an end—the reconstruction of past life, that, though his means are post-holes, houses, etc., the end is the people who made them, and that the problem of adaptation to environment (a house is such) has had to be solved by people living the same sort of life to-day, and has often been solved in similar or identical ways, and that he can learn from them. But even though he may realize all this intellectually it will not avail him if he have not the gift of a creative imagination which alone can enable him to use this knowledge. He will never be an archaeologist but will remain an antiquary; and that is the end of the matter.

FIG. 37a. Section of Wansdyke, after Sir Richard Colt Hoare.   See plate opposite.

CHAPTER 22

Living 'Prehistory' in Central Africa[1]

THIS BUSINESS OF using the present to interpret the past is so important that I am going to devote another chapter to it, illustrating the generalities of the last chapter by particular instances. That has been made possible by a tour which I made in the Anglo-Egyptian Sudan in the first part of 1950, immediately after I had written that chapter. During this visit I was able, thanks to the generosity of the Sudan Government and the hospitality and generous help of its political officers, to visit Darfur and other regions where primitive conditions of life still prevail. I was supposed to have gone out there in an archaeological capacity and for the purpose of contributing something of value to Sudanese archaeology. How far I succeeded I do not know, but I do know that, like good King Wenceslas, I myself 'found blessing', and returned home enriched by my experience. And in retrospect I am certain that the enrichment consisted not so much of archaeological observations as of anthropological ones. The people in many regions are still living a life which is 'prehistoric' in the European sense, so much so that it is often difficult to distinguish the remains of huts which have been only recently abandoned from ancient ones. When Mr Shinnie, Abdelrahman Effendi and I were exploring the region round Kutum, north-west of El Fasher, we found hundreds of hut-circles and fields which looked ancient and were unoccupied, but which we were told had only been deserted a year or two ago. The cause is climatic; northern Darfur has an annual rainfall, but it is small in amount, sporadic and apt in some years to fail altogether. It is a marginal region between one desert in the north and the permanently sown further south, and is inhabited by nomads, who move over it with their flocks and herds. They live chiefly in groups of straw huts, but they do not live there permanently. When the water or pasture round the huts is exhausted they move on elsewhere. It is therefore quite usual to find one of these villages uninhabited, or with only one or two of the huts occupied. But they also cultivate; and when rain has fallen over a cultivatable region, they move and settle there, remaining as long as is necessary to reap the corn. We saw many remains of these temporarily abandoned fields (Plate 22). The method employed is to scrape away the loose stones from the surface and leave them in parallel rows, sowing the seed in between. The width of the rows is very small, never more than three or four feet; and they are also often divided by shorter rows of stone into patches of about a yard square—surely the smallest 'fields' on record! The primary object is no doubt to clear the soil for sowing, but when (as nearly always) the ground is sloping, subsequent rainfall washes the soil downwards and it forms a slight accumulation or lynchet on the lower side. If the process continues long enough perceptible terraces are formed, but those we saw never had a height of more than a foot and were usually less. Some excellent examples were seen and photographed beside the road from Ain Farah to Kutum, about ten miles south of Ain Farah (Plate 22a and c). We were told they had been in cultivation a few years ago. Others cover the slopes of the hillside at Ain Farah just below the spring, on the east side of the gorge opposite Jebel Danga, on which are situated the remains of a hill-fort and ruins of a mosque.[2] Here the surface stones scraped into rows are of basalt, and there is the same incipient lynchetting, but it must be some years since the last cultivation, for the *kittir* has again grown and now covers the whole area with an almost impenetrable forest of thorn-bushes. Actually, the cultivation must surely belong to the hill-fort opposite, whose age is unknown, but it is to be measured in centuries.

Near the cultivations are always to be found small circles of stones. Some are obviously the collapsed walls of huts; others, which I was assured on the spot by natives of the district were the same, consist of quite small boulders only a few pounds in weight set in the ground in a perfect circle. Several occurred quite close together. They are abundant all along the first stretch of the road from Kutum to Ourei (which is a ridgeway), and there are some about four miles from Kutum on the Melit road. The diameters of those I measured ranged from five to seven yards, but some are smaller than this.

Circles of both kinds are extremely numerous all over the Kutum district; we saw hundreds beside the roads we went along, and there must be as many more elsewhere. Those which were certainly remains of huts were seen in every stage of decay. At Jaatek, a few miles from Ourei on the Kutum road, is a group of huts abandoned only the year before. One is more or less intact; the roof has begun to fall in, but the wall on which it rests still stands, and in the foreground are stones defining the forecourt (Plate 9). Another has lost its roof, and inside the hut one sees the quern and rubber which were too heavy or not worth carrying away, and hearthstones. The last stage is a shapeless ring of stones, remains of the dry wall on which the roof rested. This wall might be of stones only, or of mud with some stones, or of mud only, or of straw. When a mud hut is abandoned or burnt, the walls dissolve and melt away into a small low bank.

These remains closely resembled the hut circles so common in the west and north of Britain (except of course for the absence of grass). There was no essential difference to be seen between one of these Darfur examples and one on Dartmoor or on a Scottish mountainside. One of the lessons to be learnt in Darfur is that great numbers of *contemporary* hut-circles do not prove the existence of a large population. This part of Darfur is inhabited almost exclusively by nomads and there are very few of them. We travelled about quite a lot, and it was quite an event to see a human being. The prehistoric hutmakers of Britain may also have been nomadic or semi-nomadic, even when they also cultivated, for exhaustion of pasture may have caused migration here as much as in Darfur. In both countries we find these little hut-and-cornplot complexes, and it is a reasonable inference that the life led by their makers was not dissimilar. Though the shape of the plots differs, I was constantly reminded in Darfur of the Dartmoor plots described by Dr Cecil Curwen.[3]

[2] The mosque is of basalt bricks, some very large indeed ($20'' \times 10\frac{1}{2}'' \times 5\frac{1}{2}''$), some no bigger than modern ones. Some have alphabetic signs marked on them. It is surrounded and protected by a dry stone wall with core of rubble and an external parapet on the outer side. The fort above has an encircling dry stone wall (now collapsed) and inside are remains of huts of stone and also of brick. Remains of window-glass can be picked up on the site of the huts. The name Jebel Danga means Brick Mountain. For further details see *Sudan Notes and Records*, XIX, 1936, 301.

[3] *Antiquity*, I, 1927, 282.

In this context it is not only the things seen but the way they are looked at that matters. Constantly I kept saying to myself: What would an archaeologist make of this, if he were to dig and plan the site years hence? Would he realize that some groups of huts had only been occupied once and that for a few months only? He would of course have no difficulty with the huts themselves, and their contents of querns and hearthstones and pots. But what would he make of a hut-circle consisting of mud or earth with *a few* big stones? Would he draw the correct conclusion that here the walls were of mud with a few big stones set in it?—a transitional type. He might or might not; he would certainly be less likely to go wrong if he had travelled in a region like the Sudan and studied existing conditions there—in other words if he were something of an anthropologist.

In Darfur it is not possible to date sites by the potsherds lying about on them. Nothing whatever is known about the ancient wares of this huge region. When therefore, we found postherds on a site they told us nothing, for we did not even know what the modern pots were like. This utter ignorance could soon have been overcome, but it will be a long time before we learn, from excavation, what the ancient wares looked like.[4] It is not yet possible, therefore, to use in Darfur the technique that can still be applied, in a rudimentary way, to sites in the Nile valley, where one can distinguish periods and date ruins and sites approximately by means of potsherds.

To get an idea of the local wares it is a good thing to study them at the cemetery, where there are always some on the graves. This is easier than doing so in the village itself and attracts less attention.

Darfur provided the answer to another question that crops up regularly at archaeological field-meetings in hill-forts—Where did they get their water from? There are many villages which still have no water and where occupants have to go several miles for it. Wara, when we were there in March, had to fetch it from El Fasher, twelve miles to the west. The transport is by camels or donkeys, in skins. The people who lived in the hill-fort at Ain Farah must have got their water from the permanent pools several hundred feet below, and no doubt it was stored in large pots. The nomads who keep cattle drive them to the pools daily, often from pasturage several miles away. The reservoir at Melit is visited at regular intervals by nomads with camels, sheep, goats and cattle; water-skins are then filled and have to last till the next visit. The chalk downs of Wessex are not now so dry as the African steppes, though they may have been drier in the Neolithic period. But there are many sites known to have been occupied that are a mile or more from water, and I have no doubt that a similar procedure was followed—at Windmill Hill, for example.

At Melit an important weekly market has come into existence, chiefly as a result of the making of the reservoir (by a small dam). The nomads coming in to water their flocks and herds, bring their goods (chiefly mats) for sale and buy what they cannot themselves produce. The goods I saw there included food of all kinds, vegetables and fruit grown on the rich alluvial soil above the reservoir, coffee, dukhn, rice, natron, shoes, pots. The market did not begin till about 2 p.m. when the visitors had time to come in (often from a considerable distance) and get their watering done. Most Sudanese villages have a market (suk); the bigger ones—such district centres as Roseires or Kutum—usually now have a

---

[4] See Arkell's article on 'Darfur pottery' in *Sudan Notes and Records*, XXII, 1939, 79–88. Arkell thinks there is very little difference between ancient and modern, except that some of the ancient sherds (from Merbo, near Sayah) were thinner and less fragile, and others (from Ourei) thicker. At Jebel Danga we found fragments of pots very like the Darfur birmas of to-day; they seemed to be ancient, one being more or less embedded in the soil of a stone hut.

shop or two. There is not enough regular business for more. Nowadays in the Sudan the station platform is an intermittent market, functioning only during the halt of trains at whatever hour of the day or night; and it was interesting to observe the variety of goods offered at the different stations, indicating a special section of industry. Shendi specialized in gaily-painted straw baskets and incense pots, but also sold strips of damur, mats, walking-sticks, coffee-pots, coloured handkerchiefs, as well as such travellers' refreshments as tea, eggs, oranges and illustrated magazines in Arabic. The station market thrives because local products are not saddled with the costs of transport, which, in a land of great distances and no roads, are heavy; so that they can be sold cheaper. A pair of Geneina slippers (the best) which at El Fasher cost 45 piastres (about 9s. 6d.) cost twice that amount in Omdurman, 500 miles away. Melit mats (also famous) fetch double the price at Omdurman.

The market must have been an important feature of prehistoric life. We know that it was so in medieval England. Probably those greater medieval markets called fairs have their origins in prehistoric or Romano-British times, though there is no evidence that they did, and one relies merely upon the known tenacity of ancient custom. However this may be, one cannot travel in this part of Africa without learning much about primitive—and so also prehistoric—commerce. One observes, for instance, that there is a special quarter for the market, usually (but not always) outside the village. It is generally rectangular, and the best stalls are those along the sides. Was there anything like this in prehistoric Europe? Shelter would be necessary, not (as in the Sudan) from the sun, but from rain, and shelter implies post-holes at the least. One must remember, of course, that there is a difference between semi-nomadic and agricultural societies; but both need markets, and one finds them just as much in the Nile valley as on the dry steppes.

Archaeologists are closely concerned with house-types and the Sudan can teach us much about them. The materials used vary in accordance with those most readily available. Mud and mud-bricks are used in the Nile Valley, especially in the rainless region; wood and straw in the bush and forest regions of the south, not only because it is plentiful but also because it stands up better to heavy rain.[5] For the same climatic reason the flat roofs of the north are replaced by conical ones in the rainlands—a change observed by the early travellers to begin south of the Bayuda. Now, however, improved building methods have pushed the limit much further south, and it is unusual to see many round conical-roofed huts north of Sennar, except in the poorer villages. The conical hut is merely a room, and the unit of occupation is not a single hut but a group, usually partly or wholly enclosed by a zareeba (hedge) of thorn-bushes or a fence. This zareeba type of homestead, the African kraal, is found everywhere in Africa south of the Sahara (Plate 15). But the flat-roofed rectangular mud buildings of the north are also no more than rooms, too small for the needs of a family; and although the addition of an upper floor is in their case possible, it is technically difficult and expensive and rarely found. It is easier to build another room on the ground. These rooms are enclosed within a mud wall instead of a thorn zareeba, so that the resulting plan is the same as before, with one difference. In order to economize, the houses themselves often form part of the enclosing wall whose length is

[5] Stone was also used with or in place of mud when it was readily available. The contrast between these two types of building material was observed as long ago as the fourth century A.D. by Aizanas, King of Axum, who distinguishes between the towns of stone (Alwa and Daro) and those of straw (Kammerer, *Essai sur l'histoire antique de l'Abyssinie*, 1926, 96).

shortened by that much. This economy is not possible when the walls of the conical huts are of straw, which forms an inadequate protection against robbers and animals —the goats eat the straw walls.[6]

The homestead which consists of rectangular flat-roofed buildings of mud or mud-brick connected by a rectangular wall of the same materials may be called the Courtyard type. There is a single entrance consisting of a door in the wall, over which the wall is carried in the form of steps. This type is normal in the towns and villages between Shendi and Berber, and seems (to judge from Cailliaud's description) to have extended to Halfaya, whose houses (he says) were of stone. It may have had, and still have, a much greater extent; my knowledge of the country is not extensive enough for me to say whether it does. One thing, however, is quite evident. The 'mud castles' of the Shaigia,[7] whose centre is the Merowe reach, are simply enlarged versions of the courtyard house, strengthened for defence. The rooms on the perimeter have another storey added and become towers. The enclosing wall is built thicker and has loopholes and a kind of triangular crenellation added. Where stone is available it is largely used.

The age and origin of the Courtyard type of homestead are unknown. It is tempting to regard it as genetically related to the Zareeba type, of which it is a mud or stone version, but that would be difficult to prove. We know practically nothing of house-plans in earlier times in this part of Africa; the only ones recovered by excavation (at Abu Geili) certainly do not belong to the courtyard type.

Equal in importance to house-types is the study of pottery. This has already been discussed elsewhere in this book, and here I will mention only two instances where modern Sudanese pots proved to have a direct bearing upon archaeological problems.

The first example is a modern Nuban pot, now in the Khartoum Museum, collected in the Nuba mountains by Mr A. J. Arkell. It is of burnished black ware, covered with a graphite slip, and in every respect except one[8] it is identical with the Fung bowls found in the Abu Geili cemetery. That there is a connection between them is quite certain, and I think it probable that the modern Nuba pot represents a lingering survival, in a backwater, of a Blue Nile tradition, rather than that the Nuba hills were the original home of the Fung pots. Unfortunately I could not visit the Nuba mountains to enquire into the antecedents of the makers; but if this were done, we might find out the correct answer. It is the most striking example I have ever come across of the light which a study of modern pottery might throw upon a purely archaeological problem.

Also in the Khartoum Museum, and also collected by Mr Arkell, is a Nilotic basket which has been smeared with mud to render it less leaky. It may be conjectured that the basket was made to hold some fine grain rather than a liquid, for which its bulk is unsuitable. But the point of interest here (as of course Arkell observed) is that just such a mud smearing has often been postulated as a possible cause of the invention of pottery itself; for if the basket were burnt, the mud would be baked and a sort of rude pot would remain. That would easily lead to the deliberate burning of receptacles made more substantially

---

[6] When the hut wall is of mud or stone it is possible, but then only when the wall is high enough to raise the straw roof beyond reach. When the hut stands outside a zareeba it has thorns laid against it to keep away the goats; and when (as at Kutum and elsewhere) the enclosure is a fence of straw, thorn bushes are laid along its base for the same reason.

[7] For a full account see my *Fung Kingdom of Sennar*, Chapter 3.

[8] It is round bottomed, whereas the Fung bowls are all flat bottomed. Their date is probably late sixteenth century. See *Abu Geili*, by O. G. S. Crawford and F. Addison, Oxford, 1950, Chapter 4.

of mud—perhaps always at first on a basket framework. The value of the Nilotic basket lies in the fact that here we have an actual concrete instance of what would otherwise remain merely an *a priori* guess.

The last example of 'the past in the present' comes from Suakin and belongs rather to social anthropology. Suakin was once a flourishing port, serving the Nile Valley and the Fung kingdom of Sennar. Ships came to it from as far away as India, but it was in the nineteenth century that it achieved the culmination of prosperity. Merchants thrived and grew rich, and invested their profits in building fine houses for themselves. But the boom was short-lived; and when Port Sudan was built in 1905 trade deserted Suakin. It is now a dead city, and the palaces of its merchant-princes are empty and falling into ruin. But amongst the debris of fallen stone squatters have built ramshackle straw and wooden shacks, made out of the wooden balconies and of other nondescript material (Plate 23b). They are detribalized nomads who have come there with their goats which are penned up on the ground floors of abandoned palaces, whence come their incongruous bleatings. One is forcibly reminded of the sort of conditions that must have obtained in the Roman towns of Britain after the Roman power was withdrawn. We know that the Saxons avoided these towns, but we may suppose that their shelter was taken advantage of by the human riff-raff of these days in much the same way as now at Suakin.

At the beginning of the chapter I said that I proposed to illustrate the generalities of the previous one by particular instances. Perhaps that promise has been inadequately fulfilled. But at any rate it will have been evident that there is much to be learnt from the observation of modern life by an archaeologist whose mind has been already prepared by some sort of anthropological training. That is, I think, what is essential—that he should have learnt to see the past in the present and vice versa. In other words, he must look at both with the same eyes. Such a person will recall a Roman town at Suakin and Darfur on Dartmoor. It is not only knowledge but an attitude of mind that is needed. (The late Sir Douglas Newbold had it and used it in all his work). Given that attitude, the field-worker will ask the right questions, (such as those given on p. 219 above) and many others. That is far easier for a resident administrator than for a traveller on a hurried visit, for it needs ample time, knowledge of the language and a recognized position.

CHAPTER 23

The Significance of Field-work

ENOUGH HAS BEEN said in the earlier parts of this book to show that field-work is a fundamental and necessary part of archaeological technique; and field-work of course includes excavation which for practical reasons has been deliberately excluded from this book. Archaeology, in fact, *is* field-work, and the student who ignores it may be a good scholar or linguist, but he is not an archaeologist. What happens when archaeology is divorced from field-work has been shown several times over in its history. The best examples are in the field of typology. The basic assumption of typology is that if a sequence of evolving types can be established, those types can then be used for dating purposes. Properly handled by a field archaeologist the method is useful, as Petrie showed in Egypt. Sir John Evans and Montelius attempted with a considerable degree of success to divide the Bronze Age into periods by means of typology, chiefly of copper and bronze implements. But when Evans wrote, it was not possible to correlate the implements of the Late Bronze Age with the pottery and habitation sites of the period, for the necessary excavations had not been carried out; nor was the study of geographical distribution then invented. Consequently he failed fully to appreciate that fundamental division between the Late Bronze Age and the preceding period which was caused by invasion. Without his great work, however, it would have been much more difficult to make that discovery.

A classic instance of the dangers of pure typology is provided by Reginald Smith's attempt to prove that the flint mines of Grime's Graves in Norfolk and of Cissbury in Sussex were of Palaeolithic (Mousterian) date. He produced implements of almost identical type from the flint-mines and from Le Moustier itself; but excavation has produced Neolithic pottery from Grime's Graves and thus annihilated the hypothesis. It should be added that this unfortunate lapse must not be allowed to obscure the immense amount of valuable work he did at a time when British archaeology was (apart from Pitt-Rivers and Haverfield) in its dilettante stage.[1]

Another classic instance of the same danger is to be found in the study of the plans of megalithic burial-places. A single element—the burial-chamber—was isolated from the barrow or cairn of which it formed an integral part, and was called a 'free-standing dolmen'. A wholly hypothetical sequence of plans was then promulgated and arranged in an equally hypothetical chronological order. This fantastic structure was built by arm-chair students upon defective field-observation.

---

[1] See, for instance, his contributions to the *Victoria County Histories* and to the *Proceedings* of the Society of Antiquaries and *Archaeologia* from 1900 onwards.

The construction of castles in the air is not peculiar to archaeology. The same kind of thing took place in cartography. An accurate map can only be constructed by making measurements in the field, starting with a carefully-measured base-line. The process of making a map of the world began well and cúlminated in Ptolemy's work; but during the Dark Ages his principles were forgotten, and though Ptolemy's work was used, every kind of distortion was introduced by a failure to work scientifically. Idrisi's twelfth-century maps are little better than caricatures of cartography. Not only did they differ from those of others, but they differ in each version of his own work. They are strictly comparable with the different philosophic systems which have emanated from comfortable professorial chairs ever since Plato. The nature of the universe cannot be discovered by introspection, nor is it possible by introspection to construct a map of the world, or a chronological chart, or a typological sequence that corresponds with reality. These tasks can only be performed by measurements and observations made in their respective fields by astronomers and physicists, surveyors, archaeologists and historians; in other words, by field-work.

It thus becomes plain why field archaeology is of such fundamental importance. It is merely the archaeological equivalent of a procedure common to all other branches of science. To attempt archaeological work without doing field-work is exactly the same as to try to make a map of a country without going there, or even questioning those who have done so. Compare, for instance, the Hereford map of the world with that of Fra Mauro. Neither is satisfactory by modern standards, but Fra Mauro's, based upon the best in formation available in 1459—i.e. upon the field-work of travellers—is far nearer the truth than the other, based upon mere speculation.

All this argument may perhaps be met with the retort that it is unnecessary nowadays, that the case has already been decided and that I am merely flogging a dead horse. I wish that it were so; but I am not sure that it is. The horse may be practically dead in this country, but it is still alive and kicking in others. A constant stream of articles and books still comes from the archaeologically backward lands, full of pictures of potsherds and flints and devoid of plans and sections, or, if they are present, mere caricatures drawn from memory in an office. This may be due merely to bad field-work or excavation, not to its absence. But the impression still exists, and finds expression in print, that it is enough to live in a museum to be an archaeologist. Museums are, of course of vital importance, and I should be the last person to decry them. But they are not enough. They must be supplemented by field-work if they are not to degenerate into charnel-houses containing the desiccated corpses of potential archaeologists. The best museum curators, of course, realize this to the full, and would welcome opportunities for field-work. They are often still hampered by an obsolete and pernicious tradition which regards museums as bank-vaults rather than dynamos of research; and all of them are overworked. My criticisms are directed not against them but against the system of ideas of which they are the victims. So long as that system prevails, and so long as museums are understaffed, archaeology must suffer from deficiency. When all this has been said it still remains true that there are some countries where museums abound and field archaeology is non-existent. If the statements—and perhaps overstatements—in this book succeed in remedying such a state of affairs, it will have achieved one of its main purposes.

APPENDIX 1

Dene-holes

(see Chapter 8)

THE FOLLOWING LIST is not of course complete; there must be hundreds of dene-holes in existence —and thousands if those which have collapsed are included. It may, however, be useful to give a few examples, all in Hampshire, except the last.

CLANVILLE PARK (15 SE.): this was formerly open and used as a rubbish-pit.

OLD ALRESFORD (34 SE.): west of Bighton Wood, an OS. air-photo (No. 628) shows a trefoil mark: this may be the hole, or one of the holes, that gave the name *Pyt leage* to the Down (see Grundy in *Arch. Journ.*, LXXVIII, 75, 107).

CHAWTON PARK (35 SE.): two, collapsed in Holm Wood on the southern boundary of the park.

HEADMORE FARM (43 NW.): a dene-hole only 3 to 5 feet wide, with dome-shaped chamber 45 feet below surface and no side galleries; pick-marks and lines scratched on sides. *Proc. Hants Field Club*, XVI, 1945, 192-3.

FARLEY CHAMBERLAYNE (49 NW.): one close to the church, between it and the old semaphore house: the sides are lined with flints; perhaps an old well, not a dene-hole.

BASING PARK (52 NW.): several on the line of the old and probably Celtic lynchets and linear earthworks. Another west of the park close beside the round barrows called the Devil's Jumps, marked on the map and called 'shaft'; several others near it now filled in.

WOOTTON ST LAWRENCE (18 SW.): a quatrefoil revealed by an air-photo (No. 02622) ½ mile north-west of Worting Junction. (Plate 2b).

CHUTE FOREST, Wilts (49 NW.): in a wood called Biddesden Corner Ride, immediately east of Home Farm, are the remains of at least one dene-hole which has become filled up with soil and the sides partly removed by subsequent quarrying.

The use of chalk for marling fields continues even today, but the chalk is of course obtained now from open quarries. Dene-holes continued to be made down to within living memory, so that those enumerated above may be of any age. They were made by itinerant specialists who travelled round the country with a donkey and a windlass. I owe this information to the late Mr Nicholson of Woodcote and earlier of Basing Park.

APPENDIX 2

Meres

(see Chapter 11)

ALBEMERE: probably Folly Pond, Rogate, Sussex, near the border of Hants (44 SE.).

ANMORE (King's Pond): in the parish of Denmead, Hants (68 SW.).

ASHMANSWORTH, Hants (8 NE. SE.): Ekwall derives this name from a hypothetical personal name Æscmær, but the earliest recorded form *Æscmeres wierth* seems to me to be more likely to mean 'the worth of the ash-pond', thus bringing the name into association with other names similarly compounded (Ashmore).

ASHMORE POND: in north-west corner of Conholt Park, Wilts (43 SW.); Asshemere 1300 (Crawford, *Andover District*, 82): 'ash pond'.

ASHMORE (Dorset 9 SW.): there is a large round pond in the middle of the village, which is about 700 feet above O.D.

BALMER LAWN (Hants 72 SW.): an open space in the New Forest on which there is a large pond.

BEGMÆRE: on the bounds of Hurstbourne Tarrant combined with Vernham's Dean, Birch, *Cart. Sax.* 1080, A.D. 961; the exact location of this and the next two items (*cogan mere* and *tan mere*) is uncertain, but all three must have been situated on the Tangley ridge between the villages of Vernham's Dean and Upton on the north, and Tangley on the south. The area is covered by Hants 15 NE. Possibly *begmaere* may be the large depression marked by hachures immediately south of the point where the Vernham's Dean boundary meets the county boundary ½ mile east of Hampshire Gate: see *Huddesmere.*

BLACKMOOR (Hants 44 NW.): Blackemere (stagnum), Birch, *Cart. Sax.* 640, A.D. 931-40, 'Black Pond'.

BLACKMOOR POND: Whitsbury Common, Hants (54 SE.).

BLACKWATER POND: on Baddesley Common, on the boundary between North Baddesley and Romsey, Hants (57 NW.): *brod mere* BCS. 1187, A.D. 975

BRIDMORE: a district name in Cranborne Chase, Wilts (74 NE.).

BRIDMORE HOLE: a depression, probably a spring-pond, in the bottom of a valley (between 300 and 400 feet above O.D.) in Maddington, Wilts (53 NE.): the edition of 1901 shows water in it.

BROADMORE COPSE: contains a large old pond and is ¼ mile west of Blackmoor Pond on Whitsbury Common (Hants 54 SE.).

BUTTERMERE (Wilts 37 SE.): the pond is in the village which is 837 feet above O.D.

COGAN MERE: next bound-mark north of *begmære*, q.v., see also *Knightes mere.*

COLLMOORE POND: now Melchet Pond, a bound-mark of Melchet Forest in A.D. 1620, at the junction of the parishes of Plaitford, Sherfield English, Melchet Park and Whiteparish; Hants 48 SW., Wilts 73 SW.

COLMORE (Hants 43 SW): no pond is marked on the map here, but the Domesday spelling Colmere shows that it was a pond name.

CRANEMOOR LAKE: a large but artificial expanse of water in Englefield Park, Berks (36 NE.). 'Cranes pond.'

CRANMER BOTTOM: in Woolmer Forest, Hants (44 NW.). The same.

DUMMER (Hants 26 NW.): 530 feet above O.D., pond in the middle of the village: *dunmere*, 1196. Dummer stands on the highest ground in the district and is a conspicuous landmark all over N. Hants. 'Hill pond'.

DUNMORE POND: Brightwalton, Berks (26 NE.) ¼ mile west of church, on the Chaddleworth boundary: *dunian mere*, BCS. 743, A.D. 939; 600 feet above O.D. 'Hill pond'.

ENGLEMERE POND: Winkfield, Berks (39 SE.). elliptical in shape but probably artificial.

GATMOORE POND: a bound-mark of Melchet Forest, A.D. 1620, on the Hants (48 SW.) and Wilts (73 SW.) border, between East Dean, Hants and Whiteparish, Wilts.

GORMOOR POND: a dammed fishpond, Easthampstead, Berks (47 NW.).

HUDDESMERE: a bound-mark of Vernham's Dean in 1460 (*Proc. Hants Field Club*, IX, 268), between *Oldhurne* (perhaps the cross-roads east of Whistler's Farm) on the east, and *Les Walles* (the hill-fort of Bevisbury at Hampshire Gate) on the west; Hants (15 NE.). It is probably the pond earlier called *begmære*, q.v.

IMBER (Wilts 45 SE.): the name undoubtedly refers to a pond and not to a boundary; the village lies at the meeting-place of two valleys, the longest of which (running ESW.) is the *ymman dene* of BCS. 1215.

JANESMOOR POND: south-east of Fritham in the New Forest (Hants 63 NE.).

KING'S MERE and QUEEN'S MERE: dammed ponds in the parish of Wokingham Without, Berks (46 NE.).

KNIGHTES MERE: a bound-mark of the parish of Vernham's Dean in A.D. 1410 (*Proc. Hants Field Club*. IX, 267); the pond is where Conholt Lane enters Wilts and is marked but not named on the map (Hants 7 SE.); it may well be the same as the earlier *cogan mere*, q.v. It is 700 feet above O.D.

LARMER GROUNDS, Tollard Royal, Wilts (74 SE.): *lafres mere*, BCS. 917, A.D. 955. 'The pond of the yellow iris.'

LIMMER POND: beside Chute Causeway, 1¼ miles west of Ashmore Pond, above Hippenscombe Bottom, Wilts (43 SW.): 800 feet above O.D.

MERE POND: 1¼ miles north-east of Washmore Hill (q.v.), 600 yards east of Fawley Church, Berks (20 SW.) and in Fawley parish: 676 feet above O.D.

MERE POND: at the south-east corner of Basing Park, Hants (52 NW.).

OXNA MERE: a large round pond on the bounds of Stanton St Bernard and Alton Barnes, Wilts (35 NW.), mentioned in BCS. 998, A.D. 957; called Pennings Pond in A.D. 1784. It is about 960 feet above O.D. and is on Milk Hill, ¼ mile south of Wansdyke.

PEASEMORE (Berks 26 NE.): the name means 'pond where peas (or some wild plant like them) grew'.

PIMMER: a field-name one furlong east of Pill Heath Farm, Hurstbourne Tarrant, Hants (15 NE.): *penemere*, a bound-mark of the bailiwick of Finkley in Chute Forest, A.D. 1298 (*Proc. Hants Field Club*, IX, 263): about 650 feet above O.D.

RINGMERE POND: now Ringmoor, on Bell Hill near the boundary between Okeford Fitzpaine and Turnworth, Dorset (23 NE.): on the hill east of it is a prehistoric settlement with its fields: 830 feet above O.D.

ROCKMOOR POND: at the present meeting-point of the counties of Hants, Berks and Wilts, and of the parishes of Linkenholt, Vernham's Dean, Coombe and Buttermere: *throcmere*, BCS. 508, A.D. 863; *thorocmere*, BCS. 1080, A.D. 961; *trokkemere*, bounds of Vernham's Dean, A.D. 1410 (*Proc. Hants Field Club*, IX, 267). 'Trestle pond.'

RODLEAGE MÆRE: now Bitham Pond, Savernake Forest, Wilts (36 NE.); a bound-mark in Bedwyn, A.D. 968, BCS. III, 1213. See my field-notes in *Wilts Arch. Mag.*, XLI, 1921, 289.

RUSHMOOR POND: at the meeting-point of five roads and three parishes, Wield, Bradley and Bentworth, Hants (34 NE.): *risc mære*, BCS. 625, A.D. 909: see my remarks in the *Hampshire Observer*, 19 August, 1950. 'Rush pond.'

RUSHMOOR FLASH: Aldershot, Hants (21 NW.).

RUSHMERE POND: in a hamlet suburb of Hambledon, Hants (67 NE.), possibly the original site of the village, which now lies in a dry valley 160-180 feet lower down; the pond is on the top of a hill to the south, 340 feet above O.D.

RUSHMORE POND: on the top of the escarpment, 780 feet above O.D., 1 mile east of Ogbourne St George, Wilts (23 SW.): the name is taken from A. C. Smith's map of 25 miles round Avebury.

RUSHMORE POND: in a Celtic field 1 mile north-east of Ogbourne St George, on Whitefield Hill, Wilts (23 SW.).

RUSHMOOR POND: Lower Common, Verwood, Dorset (26 NE.).

STURTMOOR POND: on Plaitford Common, Hants (55 SE.).

SUTH MERE: now Seymour Pond, Burbage, Wilts (36 SE.): so called in medieval perambulations of Savernake Forest.

TAN MERE: was east of *begmære* (q.v.) and may have been near Tangley Clumps. The parish boundary runs along the top of the ridge, which is about 750 feet above O.D., and the Clumps are a land-mark, visible from afar. There are Celtic fields on the northern slopes (Ordnance Survey air-photos 5108, 5094), and two large oval enclosures a little further east (5090, 5111).

THYRRAN MERE: was the bound-mark next on the west following after Rockmoor Pond (q.v.), and must have been on the ridge about 1 mile south of Buttermere. An identification with Rymer's Pond, 1582 (*Proc. Hants Field Club*, IX, 275) is topographically impossible. 'Dry pond.'

TUTAN MERE: on the bounds of St Mary Bourne and Hurstbourne Priors, BCS. 594, A.D. 901, at some point south of the village of Woodcott, Hants (16 NE.).

WADSMERE DOWN: there is a pond at about 850 feet above O.D. in the parish of Coombe, Berks (41A NE.).

WÆLLES MÆRE, Savernake Forest, Wilts (36 NW.); now called Thornhill Pond: a bound-mark in Bedwyn, A.D. 968. BCS., III, 1213. See my field-notes in *Wilts Arch. Mag.*, XLI, 1921, 289.

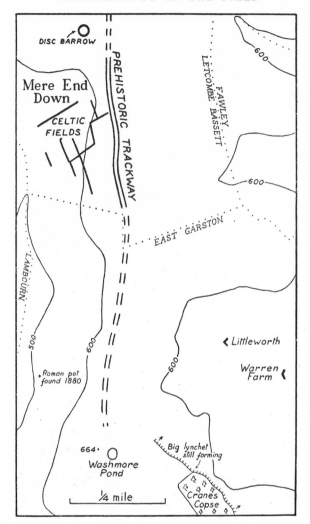

FIG. 38. Washmore Pond on the Berkshire Downs, East Garston.

WASHMORE HILL, East Garston, Berks (20 SW.): what is called an 'old clay pit' on the O.S. map is nothing of the kind, but is in fact a fine old embanked pond which, when seen on 4 March 1931, had some water in it. It stands at the meeting-place of many tracks, on the top of a ridge 670 feet above O.D. A prehistoric ditch, which seems also to be a lynchet way, runs north from the pond over Mere End Down, which is covered with the lynchets of pre-historic fields (Fig. 38).

WERMERE Pond, Alvediston, Wilts (74 NE.): this is a fine, deep, old pond, surrounded by a big bank 177 yards in circumference; it is situated on the top of the chalk escarpment, at a height of 753 feet above O.D.; between it and the Ridgeway are some old diggings. It was a bound-mark of Cranborne Chase; the name comes from an old map of the Chase repro-duced in Dr Wake Smart's history of the Chase. It was surveyed and described by H. S. Toms, *Wilts Arch. Mag.*, XLVI (Fig. 39).

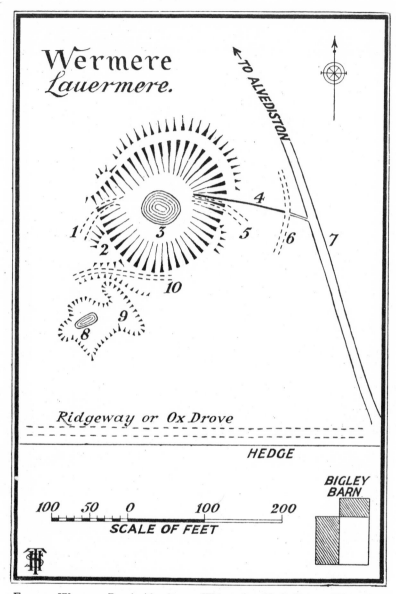

FIG. 39. Wermere Pond, Alvediston, Wilts, after H. S. Toms (*Wilts Arch. Mag.*, XLVI) by permission.

WIDEMERE: a bound-mark in Damerham, formerly in Wilts, now in Hants (62A NE.), BCS. 817, A.D. 940-6 (medieval copy): *Wydemoore Copse*, A.D. 1563 (*Survey of Pembroke Lands*, ed. C. R. Straton, Roxburghe Club, Vol. I, 1909, 312, where Bollesborough = Boulsbury Wood). The name may survive in Little Wigmore Copse in Boulsbury Wood.

WOOLMER POND: gave its name to the royal forest of that name; Hants (44 SW.): *Uulfamere*, BCS. 1266, A.D. 970. 'The wolves' pond.'

APPENDIX 3

Defensive Linear Earthworks

(see Chapter 17)

BERKSHIRE

AELFTHRYTHE DIC   Berks, 9 NE.

Mentioned in the bounds of Fyfield, A.D. 956 and 968. The identification of the bound-marks is easy and enables one to locate the 'dic' on the map at a point where the Witney road is crossed (at B.M. 261.1) by the boundary between Fyfield and Kingston Bagpuize. The bank is plainly visible for a distance of more than a quarter of a mile S. of the road, where it forms the E. boundary of Kingston Bagpuze park. N. of the road are two fairly well-preserved fragments, one having the ditch plainly on the E. The total length (with gaps) now visible is exactly ¾ of a mile. The road is called Teles weg and Wattes Weg in the bounds, and is a branch of the Faringdon ridgeway (see text, p. 86) leading to Abingdon. Leman records that 'in leaving the town [of Kingston Bagpuze] a bank resembling much a Roman road crossed the turnpike [from Faringdon to Oxford] at right angles.'

T. Leman, manuscript notebook in library of Wilts Arch. Soc. at Devizes, fol. 154 (A.D. 1802). Birch, *Cart. Sax.*, Nos. 977, 1221.
Berks, Bucks and Oxon Arch. Journ., xxix, 1925, 108–12 (Grundy on the bounds of Fyfield. My field-work and identification was made independently.)

BLACK DITCH, SNELSMORE   Berks, 34 NE. 35 NW.

A short bank with ditch on N. running for 500 yards across the plateau of Snelsmore Common, W. of Arlington Manor. Its ends rest on the valley slopes on either side of the plateau.

BURY'S BANK   Berks, 43 NW.

Runs for 1,600 feet from N. to S. across Greenham Common, from the head of a valley running through the grounds of Greenham Lodge on the N. to the same at 'The Ark' on the S. Ditch on W.

Arch. Journ. C, 177–87.   *Berks Arch. Journ.* L, 1947, 107.

CROOKHAM COMMON   Berks, 43 NE.

There are four banks running from N. to S. across the road at the extreme E. end of the common where it narrows in width from a quarter of a mile to a point. The westernmost is marked as a bank on the edition of 1932; the next two on the E. are described as ditches between two banks, and the easternmost as a slight ditch. I discovered all of them many years ago and marked them on the 6-in. map, but selected only the westernmost for insertion in the published edition, as the others seemed to be rather enclosure banks of later date.

Peake, *Arch. of Berks*, 184.

GRIM'S DITCH, ALDWORTH   Berks, 27 NE. 28 NW.

Runs from S. of Woodrows Farm, Aldworth, to S. of Westridge Green; a subsidiary bank forks off at the S. end. Ditch on N. CD vertical, 4–6 feet.

Another short length is in Broom Wood, 1¼ m. to the SE.; ditch on N.

Antiquity, V, 1931, 162–4.

CAMBRIDGESHIRE

BRAN DITCH   Cambs., 58 NE. SE., 59 SW.

Also called Heydon Ditch and Green Ditch.

Runs for 3¼ miles SE. from watercress-beds at source of stream in Fowlmere, along boundary between Fowlmere and Melbourne parishes to Heydon, being called Green Ditch for the last mile.

Fox, *Camb. region*, 127.
Fox and Palmer, *Proc. Camb. Ant. Soc.*, XXVII, 1926, 16–35.
Lethbridge, Palmer and Duckworth, *ib. id.* xxx, 1929, 78–96.
A. Gray, *ib. id.* xxxi, 1931, 77 ff.
Palmer, Leaf and Lethbridge, *ib. id.* xxxii, 1932, 54–6.
V.C.H. Cambs., i, 1938, 310 (plan, Plate III).
Lethbridge, *Merlin's Island*, 1948, 21–2.

BRENT DITCH   Cambs., 54 SE. 55 SW.

Also called Pampisford Ditch; length 1½ miles. First visible in the grounds of Pampisford Hall, ¼ m. SE. of the edge of the fen at Home Farm. Thence it can be followed continuously for 1½ m. south eastwards. The ditch is not visible in the portion I visited in January 1934, but seems to be marked on the NE. side of the bank at its SE. end (55 SW.).

Fox, *Camb. Region*, 126.

DEVIL'S DITCH   Cambs., 35 SE. 41 NE. SE.
                                                    42 SW. 49 NW.

Runs for 7 miles from the fen at Reach southeastwards in a direct line to a point near Camois Hall. Ditch on SW. Proved by excavation in 1949 to be later than the fourth century A.D.

Fox, *Camb. Region*, 124–5.   *Proc. Camb. Ant. Soc.*, XXVI, 1925, pp. 90–129.
cf. Lethbridge, *The Car Dyke, the Camb. Ditches and the Anglo-Saxons*, Proc. C.A.S., XXXV, 1935, pp. 90–96: *Jour. Roman Studies*, XL, 1950, 105.

FLEAM DITCH   Cambs., 48 SW. 55 NW. NE.

Runs for 3¼ m. from the fen at Shardelowes Well and forms the boundary between Great Wilbraham and Fulbourne. Passes Mutlow Hill and ends 1¼ m. NW. of Balsham. Ditch on SW. Probably once a little longer.

Fox, *Camb. Region*, 125–6.
Fox and Palmer, (1) *Proc. Camb. Ant. Soc.*, XXIV, 1923, pp. 21–52.
                 (2) *Proc. Camb. Ant. Soc.*, XXV, 1924, pp. 21–36.

CORNWALL

BOLSTER BANK   Cornwall, 47 SE. 50 NE.

Runs southwestwards from SW. of St. Agnes on the NE. to the head of a coombe called (lower down) Chapel Coombe. Observed length ½ m., but there are slight probable traces of it in St. Agnes itself (47 SE.). Ditch on S. The name Bolster Bank was given to me as a local one for the earthwork by the occupier of the small farm called (doubtless after the bank) Bolster. (For the giant Bolster at St. Agnes, see Hunt.) Where the bank is exposed by digging the top is 8 feet above the old surface. Visited 12 February 1935.

> Robert Hunt, *Popular Romances of the West of England*, 1881, 73–5, and frontispiece.
> *Antiquity*, X, 1936, 174.

GIANT'S GRAVE   Cornwall, 68 SE.

A bank with ditch on SE. running for ¼ m. from boggy ground ¾ m. S. of Ludgvan NE. to the road-fork 400 yards SW. of Ludgvan Leaze, where it falls into line with the Hayle road. Here I saw a section of it exposed, 8 March 1936. The banks is of earth, is well preserved in places and is about 5 feet high.

> Robert Hunt, *Popular Romances of the West of England*, 1881, 56 (legend of Tom and the
>   Giant's Hedge at Ludgvan Lees).
> *Antiquity*, X, 1934, 173, fig. 4 (plan).

GIANT'S HEDGE   Cornwall, 43 SW. SE. 53 NW.

A linear earthwork with ditch on N. running E. from near the head of the estuary at Lerryn, on a sinuous course to Muchlarnick in Pelynt. There is a gap of more than 1½ m. until it reappears in Kilminorth Wood, and runs along the S. side of the West Looe estuary to the town of West Looe itself. In places its course is doubtful because it has been obscured or obliterated by a lynchet and by lanes and hedges; but the general course is certain. The distance in a straight line from Lerryn to West Looe is 7¼ m.

CUMBERLAND

SCOTS' DIKE   Cumb., 6 NW. SW. SE.

> Marks the boundary between England and Scotland, as agreed in 1552; first mentioned in 1590.
> *The Place Names of Cumberland*, Part I, 1950, 39.

DERBYSHIRE

GREY DITCH   Derbyshire, 10 SW.

Runs from NW. to SE. across the Roman road called Batham Gate, and the Bradwell Brook. Total length, including gaps, five-sixths of a mile (as recorded in the field by me). Ditch on N.

> *Antiquity*, XIX, 1945, 11–19 (plans).

DORSET

BATTERY BANKS   Dorset, 49 NW. NE.

Near Wareham. Ditch on N.

BINDON   Dorset, 55 NW.

A linear earthwork runs from W. Lulworth due E. to Cockpit Head at the E. end of Bindon Hill, a distance of 1⅓ miles. Excavation has proved it to be prehistoric, about 400 B.C.

> O'Keeffe's *Recollections*, ii, 1826, 191–2.

BOKERLEY DYKE   Dorset, 9 NE. 10 NW. SW.

Fully described below, the account of Hawkes being the latest and best general analysis. Belongs to the fourth century A.D., but was twice altered during that century.

> Pitt-Rivers, *Excavations in Cranborne Chase*, Vol. iii, 1892.
> Heywood Sumner, *Earthworks of Cranborne Chase*, 1913, 54–7: *Local Papers*, 1931, 89–105.
> C. F. C. Hawkes, *Arch. Journ.*, CIV, 1948, 62–78.

COMB'S DITCH   Dorset, 33 NW. NE.

Runs from Whatcombe Down on the NW., thence W. of Charisworth and over Charlton Down to Great Coll Wood, where it ends. Ditch on N. and NE. Known length 2½ miles. See text, p. 185. It was called *cunucces* or *cunnuces dic* in the tenth century.

Edwin Guest, *Origines Celticae*, ii, 1883 (1850), 207.
Heywood Sumner, *Local Papers* (Chiswick Press, 1931), 89 ff.
Birch, *Cartularium Saxonicum*, Nos. 775, 781.
Rune Forsberg, *A Contribution to a Dictionary of Old English place-names* (Uppsala, 1950), 204–5.

GLOUCESTERSHIRE

BAGENDON   Glos., 43 SW.

Several distinct sections: (1) 'Scrubditch camp', between North Cerney and Bagendon running E. and W., and a little less than half a mile long; ditch on S. (2) a bank with ditch on E. and S., running close beside Cletham Lane on its W. side and across Perrott's Brook: E. of it are two discontinuous short sections of ditch. Inspected 3rd August 1930.

HAMPSHIRE

BEAULIEU HEATH (EAST)   Hants, 73 SW. SE.

Marked by a line on the 6-in. map (editions of 1909 and 1910). Runs from boggy ground, the source of the Dark Water, on the N. to the Valley of the Dark Water at Pits Copse in Holbury Purlieu. Ditch on NE., CD. vertical about 4 feet, overall width about 20 feet.

Antiquity, XXVI, 1952, 196 (there numbered 4).

BEAULIEU ROAD   Hants, 72 SE.

A bank with ditch on NW. running from SW. to NE. across the Beaulieu–Lyndhurst road ½ m. SE. of Beaulieu Road station; begins at SW. end at head of small valley called Stephill Bottom (which is enclosed by the Bishop's Dike), and ends at NE. end near another valley going down to Culverley Farm. Just E. of where it crosses the Beaulieu road, the earthwork cuts through another older one. Length 1,200 feet.

Antiquity, XXVI, 1952, 196 (there numbered 2).

DEVIL'S DITCH   Hants, 16 SW. 24 NW.

Runs southward from the Roman road (Silchester–Sarum) on the N. to Tinkers' Hill, a little S. of the Harroway, on the S. Known length 1⅙ m. Ditch on W.

Williams-Freeman, *Field Archaeology*, 1915, 33, 239–40.
Crawford, *Andover District*, 1922, 64.

DIBDEN   Hants, 73 SW.

Runs westwards from the 'ancient road' at a house called 'Forest View' in 1909 to the head of a small valley; length 1,600 feet. Discovered O. G. S. C. about 1940. Ditch on N.

Antiquity, XXVI, 1952, 194–5 (there numbered 1).

'FAESTEN DIC', EVERSLEY   Hants, 12 NW.

This undoubtedly defensive linear earthwork was discovered by Mr A. H. A. Hogg, who deliberately set out to find it, on the evidence of the bounds of Crondal. It is 1,900 feet long, with ditch on W., and runs from near the head of a valley (*efers cumbe* of the bounds) on the N., across the Basingstoke-London road 1,000 feet W. of the milestone (Bas. 11½) to a gravel-pit where it is lost. The road crossed is an ancient highway of great age, and this earthwork was certainly constructed to bar traffic along it.

A. H. A. Hogg, *Proc. Hants Field Club*, xiii, 70–4

FROXFIELD DYKES   Hants, 52 NW. NE. SW.

These are fully described by Dr Williams-Freeman, and have also been examined in the field by me pretty thoroughly. Unfortunately the most important field-sheets (52 NE. SW.) containing my field-notes are missing and must be written off as lost (though not by me).

Williams-Freeman, *Field Archaeology*, 1915, 286–92.

GRIM'S DITCH, SILCHESTER   Hants, 4 NE. SE.

Two, one with a total length of 2½ miles, called Grim's Ditch; the other a short one of 1,000 feet on Mortimer Common. Fully described below.

Antiquity, XVIII, 1944, 113–22.

HATCHET   Hants, 80 NE.

Runs from N. to S. near the head of Hatchet Pond, 1¾ m. SW. of Beaulieu; ends on the N. at a spring, the source of a rivulet. Length 2,200 feet.

Proc. Preh. Soc., 1943, 2, fig. 1.
Antiquity, XXVI, 1952, 197–8, fig. 3 (there numbered 3).

OCKNELL   Hants, 63 NE.

Marked as a bank merely on O.S. 2-in. MS. drawing of 1807–8. Length 850 feet. Runs from N. to S. between springs, the sources of rivulets.

Proc. Preh. Soc., 1943, 3, fig. 2.

PYOTT'S HILL   Hants, 11 SW. 19 NW.

This earthwork, hitherto regarded as the rampart of a huge promontory fort, is certainly nothing of the kind but simply a medieval park bank. Within its area is a farm called Basing *Lodge*.

Williams-Freeman, *Field Archaeology*, 1915, 312–13, 396.

HEREFORDSHIRE

ROWE DITCH   Hereford, 11 SW. 18 NW.

A cross-valley dyke over the R. Arrow near Pembridge: length 2 miles, 300 yards; ends on the sides of the valley: controls access to Mercian farmlands.

Arch. Camb., 1930, 67: 1931, 49.
R.C.A.M., *Herefordshire*, III, p. xxxi.

HERTFORDSHIRE

GRIM'S DITCH, CHILTERN   Herts and Bucks, 32 NE. 34 SE. 33 NW.
                                                                        38 SW. NW. 37 SE. 41 NE.

In three sections, fully described below.
Antiquity, V, 1931, 167–9.

MILE DITCHES Herts, 4 NE., Cambs., 58 SW.

A complex affair, fully described below.

Fox, *Camb. Region*, 127.   *Antiquity*, VIII, 1934, 216–18 (air-photos).

KENT

CHARTHAM DOWNS Kent, 46 SW.

A short length with ditch on west, due north of Swarling, on Chartham Downs. Discovered 20th December 1933. Present length 150 yards. It is called Deadman's Bank.

Hasted, *Hist. of Kent*, vii, 1798, 301.   *Arch. Cant.*, xlvi, 1934, 60–1.

'FAESTEN DIC', JOYDEN'S WOOD Kent, 8 SE. 9 SW.

In the north part of Joyden's Wood is a bank, part of whose N. end is buried beneath a lynchet. There is another bank with ditch on W. $\frac{1}{2}$ m. further S., which may be a continuation of it, but there is a break (ancient) between them. Neither is to be confused with the so-called 'British Road'.

Antiquity, VIII, 1934, 218–22.

LANCASHIRE

DANES' PAD Lancs., 51 NW. SW. SE. 59 NE.

This seems to have been some kind of a causeway and not a linear earthwork. I have not seen it nor has it ever been properly examined in the field, or described. At the time when the large-scale revision of Lancashire was being carried out during the early 1920's I was informed by a local correspondent that it did not exist, and its course, recorded on the 1st edition of the 6 in. maps, was therefore omitted. This was a mistake; it should not have been omitted without conclusive evidence from field-work and excavation that nothing existed there. It seems, however, that much confusion was caused by the writings of a parson called Thornber about 1850. For this information and the reference I am indebted to Mr T. G. E. Powell, through the Archaeological Branch of the Ordnance Survey.

Amounderness, by T. H. Mawson and others. Batsford, 1937, 16 ff.

NICO DITCH Lancs, 104 SE. 105 SW. 111 NE.

Runs through the S. and SE. suburbs of Manchester, from Fallowfield to Audenshaw. Only in one place is the bank at all well preserved, and even there it has been much lowered. Visited 27th February 1935 (notes on 6-in. maps at the O.S.).

C. H. Melland, *Journ. Manchester Geogr. Soc.*, 1936.

LEICESTERSHIRE

KING LUD'S BANK Leic., 14 NW.

Runs in two detached sections (probably once continuous) from a swallow-hole at the source of the Eye to the county boundary at Wyville Lodge. Length (including gap) 3,360 yards.

Bateman, *Ten Years' Diggings*, 1861, 109.   Nichols, *Leicestershire*, i, 305, Plate 53.

MIDDLESEX

GRIM'S DITCH, PINNER Middx., 5 SW. SE. 10 NW.

Runs NE. from the junction of Albion Road and Broadway (10 NW.) roughly parallel with the county boundary, to Harrow Weald Common. Length $1\frac{2}{3}$ m.

NORFOLK

BICHAM DITCH   Norfolk, 46 SE. 58 NE. SE.

Runs for $3\frac{1}{3}$ m. from near the Nar at Narborough Hall (where is a circular earthwork) on the N. due S. along Chalk Lane and then across Narborough Field. It is last marked on the map at the road 1,100 yards NW. of Beechamwell Hall. The ditch is on the E. On the O.S. map it is called Devil's Ditch.

DEVIL'S DITCH   Norfolk, 82 NE. SE. 92 NE. SE.

Runs for $5\frac{3}{4}$ m. southwards from the alluvium of the River Wissey on the N. to the Ouse on the S., but not seen further S. than a point $\frac{1}{4}$ m. N. of the river. Ditch on E. Also called Foss Ditch. Excavation near the S. end in 1949 by Mr Rainbird Clarke proved its age to be fourth century A.D. or later.

Fox, *Camb. Region,* 132.
Norfolk Archaeology, xxx, 1952 (full report of excavations to be published).
ib. id. xxvii, 1940, 233–4 (Norfolk linear earthworks in general).

DEVIL'S DITCH   Norfolk, 104 NW. SW.

Runs S. from the East Harling road at East Harling Heath, between Gasthorpe Heath and Garboldisham Heath to the alluvium of the Little Ouse. The ditch is on the W. and in places there is another bank on the W. of the ditch. Total known length 1 m. 1,600 ft. R. Rainbird Clarke points out (in a note on margin of 104 SW. at the O.S.) that this earthwork is incorrectly marked on the O.S. Dark Ages map.

LAUNDITCH   Norfolk, 48 NW.

Called Devil's Dyke on the O.S. map (edition of 1907). The existing portion is only about $\frac{3}{4}$ m. long with breaks included. Southwards the course is continued by the boundary between the parishes of Wendling and Longham. In one place near Bell Hall the CD. vertical is from 6 to 8 feet, and the ditch is on the W.

T. Leman, MS. notebook in library of the Wilts Arch. Soc. at Devizes, f. 51.

OXFORDSHIRE

GRIM'S DITCH, MONGEWELL   Oxon, 49 SE. 50 SW. 53 NW.

Grimisdic, *c.* 1219: Sandford Cartulary. Length 3 to 4 miles, ditch on S., fully described below.
Antiquity, V, 1931, 165–7.   *Sandford Cartulary,* Oxford Record Society, 1938, 29.

GRIM'S DITCH, WYCHWOOD   Oxon, 21 NW. SW. SE. 25 NE. SE. 26 NE. SW.
                                                                                      32 NW.

A complex affair of many pieces, with subsidiary works. Fully described below.
Antiquity, IV, 1930, 303–15 (maps).
Oxoniensia, ii, 1937, 74–92 (result of Excavation); xv, 1950 (1952), 108 (ditto.)

SHROPSHIRE

LONG MYND   Salop, 55 NE. SE.

Two short dykes, one on each sheet.

E. C. Cobbold, *Church Stretton,* III, 1904, 51–5.   Cyril Fox, *Arch. Camb.,* 1930, 64.

WAT'S DYKE — Salop, 19 SE. to Flint, 6 NW.

The standard account is of course that of Sir Cyril Fox in *Arch. Camb.*, 1934, 205–78. See also *Trans. Yorks. Soc. for Celtic Studies*, I, 1937–8, 1–8, *Proc. Brit. Acad.*, XXVI, 1940, 3–28.

SOMERSET

PONTER'S BALL — Somerset, 52 NE. SE.

Runs for 1 m. across the ridge at Havyatt, which connects Glastonbury with the mainland. Thus, running from fen to fen across this 'bridge' it completely isolates Glastonbury. Ditch on E.

Allcroft, *Earthwork of England*, 1908, 69 (plan). *Proc. Som. Arch. Soc.*, lxxii, 1926, Pt. I, pp. lvii, lviii.

SUFFOLK

BLACK DITCHES — Suffolk, 32 NE. SE.

Two separate stretches: (1) from near the River Lark, ½ m. SW. of Icklingham: length ⅔ m., ditch on W. (2) on the boundary between the parishes of Cavenham and Lackford, length a little over 1 m., ditch not recorded on the map.

Fox, *Camb. Region*, 123–4.

WILTSHIRE

WANSDYKE — Wilts, 37 SE., to Som., 12 NE.

Fully described on pp. 252–8. Stuart Piggott (*Stukeley*, 1950, 70) considers that it was 'built in the fifth century A.D. as a northern frontier-work defending the still romanized province lying to the south against the Saxons of the Upper Thames.'

Pitt-Rivers, *Excavations in Cranborne Chase*, Vol. 3, 1892.
Wilts Arch. Mag., XLI, 396–406 (its course in E. Wilts).
Wilts Arch. Mag., XLII, 497–500 (excavations).
Wansdyke is mentioned in pre-Conquest charters printed in Kemble's *Codex Diplomaticus*, Nos. 335, 378, 467, 482, 486, 502, 516, 566, 1109, 1120: ranging in date from A.D. 903 to 970.

YORKSHIRE

BECCA BANKS — Yorks (WR.), 204 SW. SE.

A bank with ditch on S. first seen ¾ m. NE. of the church of Barwick-in-Elmet (204 SW.) and running eastwards parallel to the Cock Beck Valley on its N. side to Hayton Wood, 1 m. NE. of Aberford, where it ends. On the S. border of Becca Park and elsewhere remains of walling can be seen in the bank, and in one place, where the CD. vertical height (from present bottom of ditch to top of bank) is at least 25 feet, five courses of stone are visible. This linear 'earthwork' must therefore have been a stone wall. Total length a little more than 2½ m.

On the S. side of the Cock Beck are two banks, with ditches on S. and SW. which cross; one parallel to the beck is ⅔ m. long; the other, running SE., is just over 1 m. long, ending at Lotherton Cottages, NE. of Lotherton Hall.

An 'intrenchment', so called on the O.S. map, at Lead Hall seems to be an old road and not a linear earthwork. Field-work done March 1935.

Hayton Wood is on Middle Permian Marl, which is described as 'red clay'. The two earthworks S. of the beck both run over Lower Magnesian limestone, both ending (apparently) on the red clayey Permian Marl.

FLAMBOROUGH HEAD — Yorks, 128 NE. SE. 129 NW. SW.

See Pitt-Rivers in *Journ. Anthr. Inst.*, xi, 1882, 455–70 (map of dykes opp. p. 455). The excavations were carried out in October 1879, and the paper read on 15th January 1882.

ROMAN RIDGE   Yorks, 283, 289, 294

Begins in Mexborough and runs for about 11 m. W. and S. by Wentworth Park to Sheffield. Roughly parallel to it on the S. is another between ½ m. and 1 m. distant and 7,288 yds. long. Both have a CD. vertical in places of 9 ft., and the ditch on the SE. Walked, Christmas 1932.

Antiquity, IX, 1935, 283, note 12 (mention only).
See p. 274 below, under Preston.

ROMAN RIG   Yorks, 204 SW. 219 NW. SW.

Runs from Swillington Bridge on the River Aire near Woodlesford to Scholes near Barwick-in-Elmet. Ditch on E., length about 7,900 yards. Walked, March 1935.

Thoresby's Diary, i, 368 (sub anno 1702).
Thoresby's Diary, i, 417 (sub anno 1703).

SCARBOROUGH   Yorks

For these, see Dr Mortimer Wheeler's appendix to his article on Prehistoric Scarborough in the *History of Scarborough*, edited by Arthur Rowntree, 1931, pp. 38–9.

SCOTS DYKE   Yorks, 25 NW. SW. 39 NW. SW.

Runs northwards from just S. of Richmond to Aldborough near Stanwick. Ditch on E. Total length 7¾ m. Inspected 16th March 1935.

Antiquity, IX, 1935, 283, Plate I, opp. p. 277.

WALES

CARMARTHENSHIRE

CLAWDD MAWR   Carm., 23 NW.

Runs north and south for one mile at an elevation of about 1,000 ft. between Nant Bargoed and Afon Cloddi, parishes of Penboyr and Conwil Elvet. Overall width 50 to 62 ft.; depth of ditch (where tested) 5 and 3 ft.; height of bank above natural ground level 6½, 3½, 5 ft. It isolates and provides a boundary for the kingdom of Dyfed: A.D. 720 (?)

Bull. Board of Celtic Studies, viii, 1937, 383–5 (E. G. Bowen).

GLAMORGANSHIRE

BEDD EIDDIL DYKE   Glam., 18 NW.

Faces NW. and bars access along a ridgeway to the coastal plain. Length 103 yds.; overall width 16 ft. Height above sea 1,300 ft. Not on O.S. maps.

Bull. Board of Celtic Studies, viii, 1936, 282.

BWLCH Y CLAWDD DYKE   Glam., 27 NW.

Two dykes (*a*) lower, 180 yd. long, 48 ft. wide overall: (*b*) upper, 174 yd. long, 63 ft. wide overall: controlling traffic along the ridge to the coastal plain.

Bull. Board of Celtic Studies, vii, 1935, 221.
Ant. Journ., xix, 1939, Pl. LXXVI (general map).

BWLCH YR AFAN DYKE   Glam., 17 SE. 26 NE.

A double-banked ditch; length, 150 yd., overall width 30 ft.; elevation 1,700 ft. It is 350 yd. S. of Crug yr Avan.

Bull. Board of Celtic Studies, vii, 1935, 221 (Aileen Fox).
Bull. Board of Celtic Studies, viii, 1936, (Aileen Fox).
Ant. Journ., xix, Pl. LXXVI (general map).

CEFN GELLIGAER   Glam., 12 SE. 19 NE.

1. Bank and ditch, 80 yd. long, overall width about 18 ft.
2. Bank and ditch, slightly larger, 200 yd. long, overall width 24 ft.; bank 10 ft. on scarp and 2 ft. high.
Both face N. and control traffic proceeding southwards along the ridge.

Bull. Board of Celtic Studies, vii, 1935, 418–19.
Bull. Board of Celtic Studies, viii, 1936, 283.

CEFN MORFYDD DYKE   Glam., 16 SW.

Faces N. and bars access along ridgeway to the coastal plain. Length $\frac{1}{4}$ m. Overall width 30–40 ft. Elevation 850–80 ft.

Bull. Board of Celtic Studies, viii, 1936, 280–2.

CLAWDD MAWR (Mynydd Caerau)   Glam., 26 NE.

Length, 170 yd.; overall width, 24 ft.; elevation, 1,550 ft.

Bull. Board of Celtic Studies, vii, 1935, 221 (Aileen Fox).
Bull. Board of Celtic Studies, viii, 1936, 283 (Aileen Fox).
Ant. Journ., xix, 1939, Pl. LXXVI (general map).

FFOS TON CENGLAU   Glam., 10 SE.

Facing E. and barring access along a ridge to the coastal plain. Length, $\frac{3}{4}$ of a mile; overall width, 27 ft. The bank partly stone revetted and partly dry stone walling, has been dug from above. Height, *c.* 1,650 ft.

Bull. Board of Celtic Studies, viii, 1936, 280 (Aileen Fox).

MYNYDD MAENDY DYKE   Glam., 27 NW.

Probably part of the upper dyke at Bwlch y Clawdd: length, 33 yd.; height above sea, 1,500 ft.

Bull. Board of Celtic Studies, 1935, 221; 1936, 283.
Ant. Journ., xix, 1939, Pl. LXXXVI (general map).

TOR CLAWDD   Glam., 8 NW.

In parish of Llangyfelach, on Mynydd-y-Gwair. Length about 925 yd.; elevation, 1,000 ft.
Ditch on N. Overall width, 30 ft.; scarp, 17 to 18 ft., measured on slope. Ditch rock-cut, bottom 4 ft. below present surface at one place where it is exposed. A formidable work controlling the approach to the Gower peninsula from the uplands.

Bull. Board of Celtic Studies, ix, 1939, 368–72, with map (C. and A. Fox).

MONMOUTHSHIRE, Etc.

OFFA'S DYKE   Mon., 31 NW., to Flint, 5 NW.

The standard account is of course that of Sir Cyril Fox, published seriatim in:

Arch. Camb., 1926, 133–79; 1927, 232–68; 1928, 33–110; 1929, 1–60; 1930, 1–73; 1931, 1–74.

See also *Trans. Yorks. Soc. for Celtic Studies*, I, 1937–8, 1–8; R.C.A.M., *Herefordshire*, III, pp. xxx, xxxi; *Antiquity*, III, 1929, 135–54; *Proc. Brit. Acad.*, xxvi, 3–28 (Boundary line of Cymru, the Rhys Lecture for 1940).

MONTGOMERYSHIRE

DOUBLE DEYCHE   Mont., 43 SE.

Runs across Cryggun Bank, Kerry; length, ½ m.; elevation about 1,400 ft. Controls access to the Midland Plain.

Arch. Camb., 1930, 67 (Fox).
R.C.A.M., *Mont.*, 293.

DOUBLE DEYCHE   Mont., 43 SE.

Runs across the Kerry Ridgeway and controls access to the Midland Plain. Length, 630 yd.; elevation above sea level, 1,650 ft.

Arch. Camb., 1930, 66 (Fox).
R.C.A.M., *Mont.*, 293; *Rad.*, 86.

LOWER SHORT DITCH   Mont., 44 NE. SE.

Runs across the Kerry Ridgeway and controls access to the Midland Plain; length, 800 yd.; elevation, 1,523 ft.

Arch. Camb., 1901, 289 (Lloyd); 1930, 66 (Fox).
R.C.A.M., *Mont.*, No. 291.

SHORT DYKES   Mont., 43 SE.; Rad. 4 NE.

See R.C.A.M., *Mont.* and *Rad.* under 'Dykes' in Index.

Arch. Camb., 1901, 279 ff. (Lloyd); 1929, 43–5, fig. 14 (Fox); 1930, 59–70, figs. 25, 26 (Fox); 1931, 49 (Fox); 1935, 279–87 (Jerman).

UPPER SHORT DITCH   Mont., 44 SW.

Runs across the Kerry Ridgeway and controls access to the Midland Plain; length, 930 yd.; elevation, 1,500 ft.

Arch. Camb., 1901, 291–3 (Lloyd); 1930, 66 (Fox).
R.C.A.M., *Mont.*, 292.

WANTEN DYKE   Mont., 37 SW. 44 NW. NE.

A cross-valley dyke over the Caebitra; length, 2 m.

Arch. Camb., 1901, 279 ff. (Lloyd); 1930, 67 (Fox).
R.C.A.M., *Mont.*, 58 ff.

RADNORSHIRE

CEFN-Y-CRUG DYKE   Rad., 24 NW.

Runs across col between Cwm Ffrwd and Cwm Merwys; length, 729 ft., elevation about 1,500 ft. Ditch on S. to obstruct traffic from England into Wales. This is unusual and shows that it is not part of any Mercian scheme.

Arch. Camb., 1935, 286–7 (H. Noel Jerman).

DITCH BANK   Rad., 24 SE.

A dyke running across the Summergil Brook, SW. of New Radnor, and ending on the steep flanks of the valley. Controls access to the Mercian farm-lands? Length, 400 yd.

Arch. Camb., 1930, 67 (Fox).
R.C.A.M., *Rad.*, 358.

PEN-Y-CLAWDD DYKE   Rad., 17 NW.

Runs across col between Fan Brook and Cwm Frank, 1½ m. WSW. of Llangunllo Church; length, 1,192 ft.; elevation, 1,050 ft.

SHEPHERD'S WELL DYKE   Rad., 24 NW.

Runs across very narrow col between Harley's Dingle and Cwm y Gerwyn, across a west-east route over Radnor Forest; length, 347 ft.; elevation, 1,980 ft.

Arch. Camb., 1935, 282–5 (H. Noel Jerman).

SHORT DITCH   Rad., 10 NW. SW.

Runs across Llan Lluest and Bugeildy; length, 700 yd.; elevation, 1,523 ft. Controls access to the Midland Plain.

Arc. Camb., 1930, 67 (Fox).
R.C.A.M., *Rad.*, 85.

SCOTLAND

PERTHSHIRE

DUNNING   Perthshire, 109 SW.

A short length (430 ft.) of bank and ditch ½ m. NNE. of Dunning Church, in Kincladie Wood, on the W. side of the road from Dunning to Forteviot. Ditch on N. CD. vertical between 3 and 4 ft. Possibly not a true linear earthwork. Found by chance observation (independently of Macfarlane), 17th April 1940.

Crawford, *Topography of Roman Scotland*, 1949, 59.
Macfarlane, *Geographical Collections*, I, 121.

SELKIRKSHIRE

WALLACE'S TRENCH   Selkirk, 7 SW.

Barrier across the old Selkirk-Peebles highway over Minchmoor. Not seen. Described as 'a fine breast-work 4 to 6 ft. high right across the road' (Inglis). The north end rests on a marsh. Ditch apparently on west.

P.S.A.S., lviii, 1924, 207 (Inglis).
Crawford, *Topography of Roman Scotland*, 1949, 7.

APPENDIX 4

Wansdyke

(see Chapter 17)

WANSDYKE IS THE most famous linear earthwork of southern England, and the next longest in England after Offa's Dyke. The length in a straight line between its terminal points, as at present known, is 48 miles.[1] Throughout the ditch is on the north side. The western terminus is at the hill-fort of Maes Knoll in Norton Malreward parish, 4 miles south by east of Bristol, and the eastern the North escarpment of the north Hampshire Downs at Inkpen, where that escarpment is climbed by the boundary between Berkshire and Wiltshire, 6 miles WSW. of Newbury. Wansdyke was well known to the Saxons who called it Woden's ditch (*Wodnes dic*), a name that must go back to the sixth century; it bore that name throughout its whole course, and there are several mentions of it in Saxon boundaries. Though it is not mentioned by name in the Saxon Chronicle, the battles in 592 and 715 at Woden's Barrow (*Wodnes beorg*), where it is crossed by the Ridgeway 6 miles south-west of Marlborough, were surely connected with it, and the name suggests that the earthwork also had already acquired its name. Most of the early antiquaries mention it; Colt Hoare published a sectional drawing of it (see above, p. 225), almost the first of its kind ever made.[2] Pitt-Rivers dug two sections across it, one in 1889 near Shepherd's Shore, and proved it to be late Roman or post-Roman.[3] The only book devoted to it, Albany Major's *Mystery of Wansdyke* (1929), though based on extensive field-work, is entirely untrustworthy; the author, who did good service to field archaeology as Hon. Secretary of the Earthworks' Committee, unfortunately had no eye for earthworks, and mistook modern field-banks for the remains of Wansdyke. Besides his book there are many articles dealing with Wansdyke, especially in the *Wiltshire Archaeological Magazine*, published by the county society at Devizes. But a bad book has more publicity than many good articles, and in order to counteract its influence I propose to give a short description of its course, based throughout on my own observations in the field.

Wansdyke falls naturally into four sections: (1) from Maes Knoll to a point south of Bath (10½ miles); (2) from the hill above Bathford on the east to Morgan's Hill above Calstone, Wilts, the escarpment of the chalk downs, throughout which section it follows the Roman road (14 miles); (3) thence to New Buildings 2 miles south of Marlborough where it breaks off (11 miles); (4) from Chisbury hill-fort above Little Bedwyn to Inkpen (6 miles).[4]

1. *Maes Knoll to near Bath* (Fig. 40). Throughout this section Wansdyke can be traced continuously (apart from negligible gaps) except for a break of 1¾ miles between a northern tributary of the River Chew at Cottle's Farm and the Chew at Compton Dando. The fact that it is plainly

[1] In my Ordnance Survey pamphlet on *Field Archaeology* (1932, 30), the length is wrongly given as 10 miles.
[2] The first seems to be Stukeley's, of a barrow; Bodleian Gough Maps 229, fol. 45.
[3] *Excavations* III, 1892, 252; see also *Antiquity* VI, 1932, 349–50.
[4] This total of 41½ miles is less than the length given above because of gaps between (1) and (2) and between (3) and (4).

visible right up to the west bank of the stream at Cottle's Farm, but that no trace can be seen on the east bank opposite suggests that the stream and, below, the Chew itself were used as a substitute line of defence. But that is not certain, for the Ordnance Survey Map of 1811 marks Wansdyke running parallel with the Chew for a short distance north-east of Woollard. I could, however, find no trace of it anywhere, in spite of a careful search. Albany Major's course south of

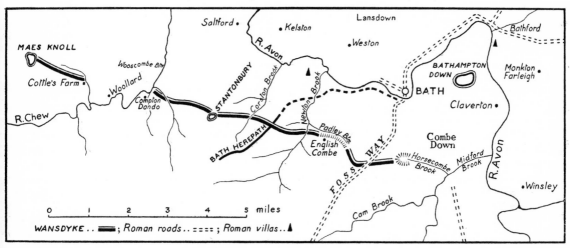

FIG. 40. Wansdyke, section 1.

Wooscombe Bottom was composed of modern field-banks and is wrong.[5] It is well preserved in a field 600 yards due east of Compton Dando church, and thence goes as marked to the cross-roads at Wansdyke House, where it is called *Wodnes dic* in a charter of A.D. 963.[6] Thence it goes south-east to Stantonbury Camp. The half-mile between Park Farm and the Newton Brook was not marked on the 6-inch map of 1903 (Som. 13 SE.), but is quite clearly traceable. At Park Farm it is crossed by a road which in A.D. 963 was called *Bath herepath*. East of English Combe, a significant name, it seems to have used the steep scarp above Padley Bottom for about $\frac{1}{4}$ mile, for it is not to be seen until we come to the east part of Breach Wood. Thence it goes south-east to Vernham Wood, and east through it and round the head of a coombe to the Foss-way cross-roads at Burnt House Inn. Thence it goes due east and dead straight to the Cross Keys at the head of Horsecombe Brook (*Horsecumbes broc*, A.D. 970) and is there mentioned in a charter of A.D. 961 (*Wodnes dic*). There it stops and I have little doubt that the gap is original, and that the line of the stream and beyond that of Midford Brook and Avon was used instead. It used to be identified with some remains on Combe Down above (east and south of) Prior Park, and it is possible that they may represent its course. South of Bathford the Ordnance Survey Map of 1904 marked two banks which it called Wansdyke, the eastern on the western slopes of Bathford Hill and the western on the ground below. Between them is a gap with no trace of an earthwork. The eastern alleged portion consists of a scoop on the hillside more likely to be an old quarry. The western portion coincides with a field-bank and is probably that and no more. It does not align at all with the eastern portion.

It will be observed that in this section Wansdyke used two and perhaps three hill-forts, Maes Knoll, Stantonbury and perhaps Bathampton Down. That other such hill-forts were *used* in the Dark Ages is amply attested by documentary evidence.

[5] By an unfortunate mistake this portion was incorporated in the revised 6-inch Ordnance Map, subsequently corrected.
[6] Kemble, *Codex Diplomaticus*, III, 460 (bounds of Stanton).

2. *Near Bathford to Morgan's Hill.* Throughout this section the makers used the Roman road which, except for a southward bend at Sandy Lane, runs dead straight and almost due east. There are parts of this section that I have never seen (the only ones), and as its course is clearly marked throughout on the map, no detailed description is necessary. The coincidence of Roman road and Wansdyke was observed by Colt Hoare, but needs clarifying by excavation; about the fact of it there is no doubt—the bank of Wansdyke is plainly visible at several points, for instance, midway between the hill on which Daniel's Wood stands on the east and the road from Melksham to Gastard. On the low ground (Oxford Clay) further east, between the railway and the Avon, the causeway of the Roman road was made of imported stone which I noted as Oolitic in character. The deep ditch is visible south of Bowden Hill House (Wilts 26 SE.), at the south end of Griffin's Wood. From the point where the accompanying parish boundary leaves it one furlong due south of Bowden House, the course can still be clearly followed without any change of direction to below the fish pond south-east of Spye Park House. No doubt it crossed this valley in a loop as it does the next one. It is interesting to note that the two ends of the Roman causeway are plainly visible ending abruptly on each side of this valley, separated by a distance of about 40 feet which was probably covered by a wooden bridge.[7] Wansdyke is very clearly visible by the old quarry in the east part of Spye Park, but only for a short distance. At Wans House it turns and runs south-eastwards for ¼ mile, and then resumes its former alignment and runs over low ground to Morgan's Hill, where dyke and road diverge. It was from above this region that George Allen took one of his best air-photos of it (Plate 24).

3. *Morgan's Hill to south of Marlborough* (Fig. 41). This is by far the finest section of the whole earthwork. It runs along the back of the downs behind the Vale of Pewsey escarpment in almost undiminished magnificence, and there are no more than a few small breaks in its course. A description from the map alone is unnecessary and would be flat without the spice of recent memories. The downs are covered with relics of the past and there could be no better beginning for a field archaeologist than to walk along Wansdyke from Morgan's Hill to near Marlborough. (This can easily be managed by staying at Avebury and Marlborough and using the bus service.) There is, moreover, no finer downland in the whole of England, though no doubt it is doomed, like the rest, to be turned into arable.

One or two things should be observed by the way. At *Old* Shepherd's Shore is a wide gap where the old Bath road went through; here branched off the Devizes road whose track can be seen in the corn, curving up the north-east spur of Stone Pit Hill—Bagdon Hill in 1773—a little over ½ mile to the south-west. Between Tan Hill where once a famous fair was held, and Red Shore, a cross-dyke and several older linear earthworks of the ranch-boundary type can be seen curving up to Wansdyke from the south and passing beneath it. On Milk Hill is a round pond that is certainly a thousand years old. It was called Oxnamere in 960 and Penning Pond in 1784 (Fig. 42). We then come to the road from Marlborough and Lockeridge to Alton Barnes which runs along the bottom of a valley called Woden's Dene (*Wodnes dene*) in A.D. 939.[8] A quarter of a mile east of Shaw Farm (35 NE.), a break and some old enclosure banks mark the site of the old Shaw House, shown here on the plan of 1734 (now at Devizes). Wansdyke then plunges into the West Woods, formerly part of Savernake Forest. Here again it is mentioned in pre-Conquest charters, one of the gaps in it being described as '*titferthes gate*'.[9] It eventually emerges into a rather dull expanse of modern enclosures, marked as such by the severely regular lines of the field-boundaries, and dies away towards New Buildings. In order to test whether it ever continued further Mr H. C. Brentnall dug a trench across the ground to the east, and found traces of the ditch, showing that it continued here.[10]

---

[7] Compare the like case on Akeman Street near Asthally in Oxfordshire: *Antiquaries Journal*, VI, 1926, 42–53.
[8] BCS., 734.   [9] Ib. id. The point is at the south-east corner of Heath Plantation.
[10] Marlborough College Nat. Hist. Soc. Report for 1924.

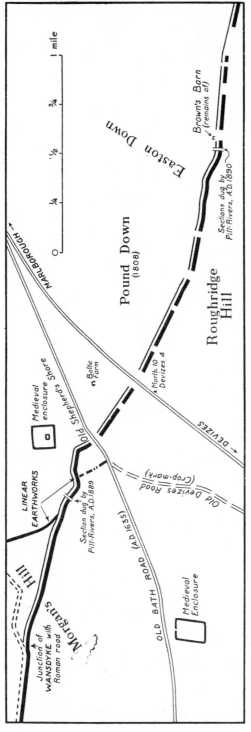

FIG. 41. Wansdyke, section 3 (west part). This is continued on the east on Fig. 42.

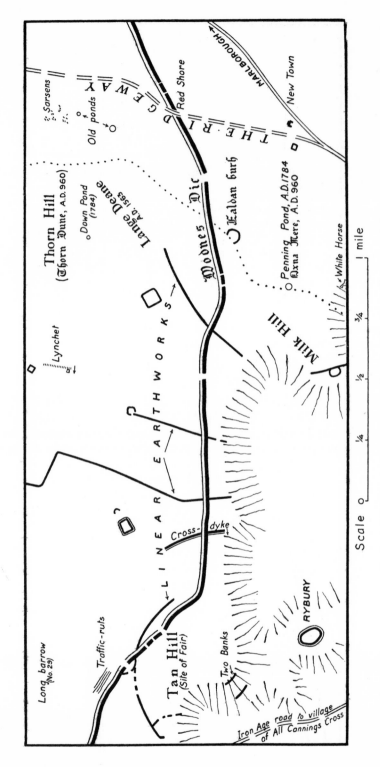

FIG. 42. Wansdyke, section 3 (central part). This joins Fig. 41 on the west.

4. *Chisbury to Inkpen* (Fig. 43). Many attempts have been made to find traces of Wansdyke in Savernake Forest. If it ever existed there it should still be visible, for this is a virgin forest. I have known and wandered about every part of it ever since I was a boy, but have never seen any certain remains of Wansdyke. A bank ½ mile south-west of Savernake Lodge (36 NE.) is merely part of that enclosing the medieval lodge of Bailiwick of Bagden. Another, faintly visible as a curved bank in arable between Belmore Copse and Birch Copse, may represent that marked by Colt Hoare, but is too far gone for any certainty and needs excavation. I once thought I had found remains of Wansdyke in the northern part of Chisbury Wood, but should not like to say anything about the bank there without re-inspecting it. Both are called 'Wansdyke' on the revised large-scale Ordnance Maps, for which I was responsible; but the revision was done thirty years ago when I had less experience.

The lane which leads out of the hill-fort of Chisbury follows the line of Wansdyke, whose banks can still be seen in places beside it. It crosses the Bedwyn stream just below Burntmill Lock (formerly Little Bedwyn Mill), and can be followed up the hill into the woods and is lost. The last part marked on the map (Wilts 37 SW.) is at Round Copse, where the Saxon bounds of Bedwyn—a good document of A.D. 968[11]—refer to 'the ditch-gate at the old (or white) valley'. But there Wansdyke, if such it is, has turned to go southwards. The bank seems to be continuous with that coming out of Chisbury, except for the break across the stream.

The next certain remains are in the east part of Shalbourne parish, between the Shalbourne on the west and Prosperous Farm[12] on the east. I traced it here on the ground before the first war, but my field-maps were lost. The course was revealed again by an oblique air-photograph of George Allen's, and an R.A.F. one (Ramsbury 85) which latter shows it continuing the line of Daniel's Lane to the river.

The last portion is along Old Dyke Lane, 600 yards west of Inkpen church. This portion was found by Harold Peake from a mention of the name in the Award Map of Inkpen which he was examining in connection with his work for the Victoria County History.[13] It was inserted at his suggestion at the revision of 1913 and duly appears on Berks sheets 41 NE. and SE. This portion is continued as a crop-mark southwards for 1,100 feet beyond the right-angle bend in the Ham-Inkpen road in an air-photograph taken by Major Allen. The mark extends across and a little beyond the rivulet here marked—a very insignificant affair. The field was called *Stan ceastla* (stone castle) in the bounds of Ham, A.D. 931.[14] On the top of the escarpment, beside Bull's Copse, is a round barrow which I dug into in 1907; in the charter it is called *Oswaldes berghe*. Immediately east of the barrow the steep hillside is scored by a broad shallow depression running vertically up and down it. This is not an ancient traffic-rut; I strongly suspect it to be a continuation of Wansdyke, which at this eastern end seems not to have been continuous but to have consisted of disjointed fragments.

[11] BCS. 1213. See my article on these bounds in *Wilts Arch. Mag.* XLI, 1921, 281–301, and the accompanying map, which has been used in compiling Fig. 43.

[12] The home of Jethro Tull, a famous early agriculturist. It is now called Prosperous House.

[13] See *Berks*, IV, 1924, 200: the name Wans Dyke appears on the Common Award Map of 1733, near Old Dyke Lane. Query, should it be Wan's *Ditch*, not Dyke?

[14] BCS., 677. For *Stan ceastla* see Grundy in *Arch. Journ.*, LXXVI ,1919, 224, note 2.

R

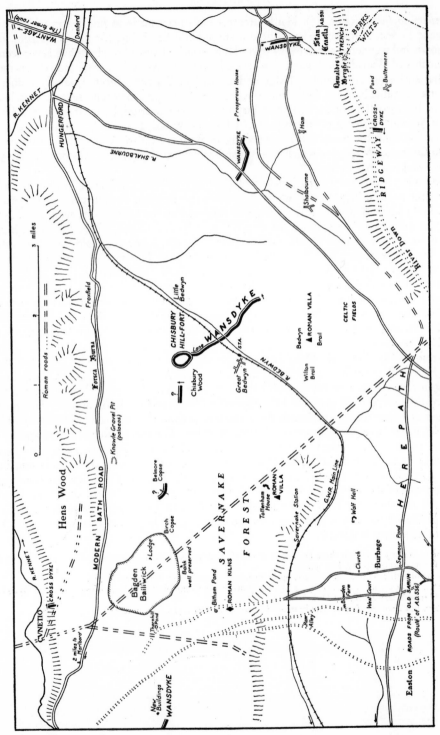

FIG. 43. Wansdyke, section 4.

APPENDIX 5

Field-work in Africa

(see Chapters 20 and 22)

THERE IS MUCH field archaeology in Africa, where the path was blazed by Cailliaud in 1819–22,[1] and Lepsius in 1842–5.[2] They were followed by Budge (who also excavated), Crowfoot, Sir Douglas Newbold, Kennedy Shaw, Addison, Jackson, Dunbar, Whitehead, Arkell, Edmonds, who published their observations in *Sudan Notes and Records* (Khartoum, 1918 onwards) and elsewhere, and by many other officials of the Sudan Government travelling on their lawful occasions. All these have from time to time made valuable contributions to knowledge by reporting antiquities inaccessible to most people, and that in spite of the fact that most of them were not trained archaeologists. The collection of a few potsherds from an ancient site that may not be visited again for perhaps a century is a valuable piece of work; stored in the local or national museum they are available for future students. Need it be said that the exact site of their discovery is the most important fact to record?

The sort of thing that needs to be done can best be gathered from articles published by the authors mentioned above. Edmonds, for instance, has described[3] some stone-walled enclosures in Dar Hawawir, an area of north-eastern Kordofan on the fringe of the desert south of the Nile bend at Debba, extending southwards to Lat. 16° north. It is a pastoral region and has now no permanent habitations. The enclosures 'seeming to be the handiwork of a people living much the same sort of pastoral life as the present-day inhabitants', who know nothing about these remains except that they exist, are associated with *hafirs* for water-storage. Those found by Mr Edmonds were found quite by accident, and he rightly suggests that there must be many more still undiscovered. A few air-photographs would reveal them; they are exactly the things that show up well if photographed from the air at sunrise or sunset, when the shadows show them up. The collection of surface potsherds would provide a clue to their age.

I have suggested elsewhere[4] the possibilities of excavation that are offered by the Shilluk and Dinka mounds on the White Nile. Even without excavation the collection of specimen potsherds from their surface would be both easy and valuable. Arkell has already collected many potsherds and made them available for study in the Khartoum museum where I profited much from an examination of them in 1950.

Ethiopia is still not an easy country to travel in, but it is probable that people will continue to travel about it as in the past. It is no more difficult to-day than it has been for the last century or two, during which travellers have described its antiquities. Their accounts might

[1] *Voyage à Meroé* (etc.), by Frédéric Caillaiud, 4 vols., Paris, 1826; Atlas of maps and illustrations, 2 vols. folio, 1823.
[2] *Denkmäler aus Aegypten und Ethiopen*, Berlin, 1849; *Discoveries in Egypt, Ethiopia* (etc.), translated from the German edition of 1852 by Kenneth R. H. Mackenzie, London, 1853. Contains a wealth of topographical information.
[3] 'Some Stone-walled Enclosures in Dar Hawawir', by J. M. Edmonds: *Sudan Notes and Records*, XXIII, 1940 (Part 2), 295–303, with sketch-map and photographs.
[4] *Antiquity*, XXII, 1948, 8–12 ('People without a History').

have been far more useful if they had known what to look for and describe. How often in reading them have I read on, hoping each time to find a mention of some place or ancient site that the writer must have seen or passed near, only to be disappointed each time! Why did he not mention them? Why does a Newbold tell us what we want to know and a Baker (to mention only one of many Victorian travellers) rarely do so? Because he has or has not the historical mind and eye. The pleasures of travel are heightened, and its discomforts borne more easily, if the traveller feels that he can learn and perhaps discover something of permanent value. The things that need doing in Ethiopia (apart of course from such obvious and important ones as recovering or copying manuscripts, etc.), and which can be done by any historically-minded visitor, are not quite the same as in some other lands. There is the same need for the field archaeologist's eye to discover hill-forts and the like; but there are also certain historical matters that need investigation. Ethiopia has been visited by Europeans since at least the middle of the fifteenth century. They have left records and maps, and many of the places named—even some of the most important ones—still have not been identified. Ethiopia has no government maps, and many of the villages are not marked on any maps. Even the site of the former chief temporary residence—or 'capital' —of the Emperor, a place called Barara, has not been identified. It was close to Addis Ababa, and a few local enquiries made at my suggestion narrowed down the choice of sites considerably. A little more work on these lines would probably settle the matter. Apart from local names and traditions the site itself, though it may have been no more than a temporary camping-ground, may nevertheless have some remains of habitation. Field-work would at any rate eliminate unsuitable sites.

Then there are the 'gates of Badabeja' on the frontiers of Amara and Shoa, mentioned by Alvarez (1520-6). Where exactly were they? The site is on a famous road and is fairly closely identifiable. So far as I know no traveller has followed that route since Alvarez, or, if he has, he left no description. It would still be a difficult journey, but not an impossible one. There are also very many other places mentioned not only in European sources but also in the Ethiopian annals; a simple question by a well-informed traveller would often be enough to locate them.[5]

The more ancient Ethiopian sites—Axum, Yeha, Kohaito, Gondar—have mostly been described, and Axum was excavated, and well for the period in which the work was done, by a German expedition. Has anyone looked for Palaeolithic remains in Ethiopia? It is possible that there may have been inhabited caves; if so, flint implements would be found, at any rate in the debris below the caves.

In the south of Abyssinia are great numbers of standing stones, some phallic, others with crude representations of the human figure. These were discovered by Fathers Azais and Chambard, but their published descriptions[6] need supplementing and there is ample scope for photography and field archaeology of all sorts. There must surely be ancient habitation-sites to be found of the people who made them. Then there are those most important inscribed Arabic tombstones, testifying to early Arab penetration there from the north during the thirteenth century.[7] There must be many more awaiting discovery.

In the next country, Somaliland, are many ruined villages of the medieval Arab period. The only published description of them is one by Alexander Curle.[8] There is ample scope here for the field archaeologist.

---

[5] The sort of problems awaiting solution can be inferred from my article on the Nile Sources, *Geographical Journal*, Sept. 1949, 6–29.

[6] *Cinq années de récherches arch. en Ethiopie*, Geuthner, Paris, 1931, 2 vols. (text and illustrations).

[7] Published in *Cinq années*, I, 283–309. See Enno Littmann, *Zeitschrift für Semitistik und verwandte Gebiete*, ed. by E.L., Band 3 (Leipzig, 1924), 236–46, severely criticizing an article by Paul Ravaisse in *La France Illustrée*, 27th Oct. 1923. Two of the inscriptions have dates (A.H. 662 = A.D. 1263–4, and A.H. 666 = A.D. 1267–8); one of these was from Munessa near Lake Zuwai, south of Addis Ababa.

[8] *Antiquity*, XI, 1937, 315–27.

Almost equally unknown are the ruined Arab cities of the East African coast—Kilwa and the like. They are mostly rather difficult of access, but well worth a visit. They have been ignored by almost everyone; no plans and nothing but a few bad photos of them are available.

The reader may be getting weary of this long list of *addenda et corrigenda*. 'Has nothing been done properly anywhere by anybody?' he may ask. 'Is everyone out of step except you and a few of your friends?' The most telling reply is to point to work already done on the lines suggested. Perhaps the best examples in this part of the world are the two articles published in 1911 by Mr J. W. Crowfoot on 'The Island of Meroe' and on 'Some Red Sea Ports'.[9] Both describe work done in the field—if one may so describe the Red Sea and the Butana. No excavation was attempted, but there was a rich harvest of new knowledge. Lepsius did the same sort of thing half a century earlier.

As we go westwards across the Sudan we pass out of the old world—*orbis veteribus notus* in Kiepert's Atlas—into one which, though not without historical documents, still has no history. There was an Empire of Bornu in the European medieval period, and Barth[10] collected and published some of its records and Sir Richmond Palmer[11] others. Timbuctoo is marked on Fra Mauro's world-map of 1459. Idrisi in the twelfth century described some of the oases and caravan-routes across the Sahara.[12] In some of these oases are castles still waiting to be surveyed and planned—a pleasant winter task for an enterprising student. An oasis, like an island, is convenient for study because it has clearly defined limits, and the ever-present temptation to stray beyond one's allotted region is made impossible. South of the Sahara is a vast region ranging from the parklands on the edge of the desert to tropical forest on the coast. The archaeology of the whole of this region is still a virgin field. Nowhere has the technique of modern excavation been used to build up a sequence of types, to date earthworks, and to do for it what has been done for some European countries. Yet the Ife heads[13] show that the culture at some unknown date had reached a high technological and artistic standard. Excavation will one day set this culture in its proper perspective. But before it is undertaken, adequate conservation and publication of the results should be guaranteed. Meanwhile there are many things to be done—if it be not already too late to do them. The walls of Kano and Katsina are crumbling fast and it may now be too late to survey them. In 1947 it was proposed, and the proposal recorded without comment in an official report,[14] to destroy what remained of the walls of Katsina to fill up some stagnant pools which were a breeding-ground of the malaria mosquito. A photographic survey of the best remaining fragments of the walls should be made, and plans of at least the gates. They are certainly some centuries old, and the tactical arrangements which only planning and air-photography can record, might well throw light on the origin of the culture and its connections (if any) with regions east or north. In this region the old culture is not yet extinct, and archaeology merges imperceptibly into cultural anthropology. That is of no practical consequence, for so should merge archaeologists and anthropologists. If, for instance, I were to be doing any of the things suggested above, I should certainly include photographs of such decorated porches as that of a Wasuri trader's house at Katsina illustrated by Sir Richard Palmer;[15] it may be quite modern, but such decoration is not likely to be made for much longer. I should also take close-up photographs of such details as the guns on the wall on the left.

[9] 19th Memoir of the Arch, Survey of the Egypt Exploration Fund (Meroe): *Geographical Journal*, May, 1911, 523–50 (Red Sea Ports).

[10] See Henry Barth, *Travels and Discoveries in North and Central Africa*, 1849–55: 5 vols., 1857.

[11] *The Bornu Sahara and Sudan*; John Murray, London, 1936: see also the same author's *Sudanese Memoirs* (vol. III 1928) printed at Lagos.

[12] *Géographie d'Idrisi*, traduite par A. Jaubert, 2 vols., Paris, 1836–40.

[13] See *Antiquity*, XV, 1941, 72–80; *Man*, XLIX (June 1949), 61.

[14] *Annual Report of the Nigerian Medical Department for 1947*, 12 (published by the Government Printer, Lagos, 1949).

[15] *The Bornu Sahara and Sudan*, 1936, Plate xxvii.

There are plenty of things for a field archaeologist to do in Nigeria,[16] and no one has even begun to do them. In the neighbouring country of the Gold Coast earthworks exist and have been mapped and excavated by geologists heroically striving to save and record valuable archaeological data.[17] Near Abodum and Manso are huge enclosures surrounded by ditches more than a mile in circumference and twenty feet deep. The pottery found is unlike that now in use, and the habitation-sites were probably deserted before the sixteenth century or earlier. 'It is clear', says Mr Braunholtz, 'that there is here a large, interesting and almost untouched field awaiting the spade of the trained archaeologist. Aerial photography might prove a valuable help, not only in bringing out details of known sites invisible on the ground, but also in revealing new and unsuspected sites.'

Further southwards in Africa we lose even such dim light as history throws, or may one day throw, on the past and are wholly dependent upon an archaeology that is only just beginning. In Kenya Mr Huntingford has described[18] hut-sites, linear earthworks, hollow ways, irrigation channels and other fieldworks that recall similar things in Britain where he learnt to recognize them. Clearly there is here a vast scope for field-work and for air-photography as a prelude to the excavation of some key sites. Such excavation has already been begun by the Leakeys,[19] who have done so much for the earlier history of man in that country. It is to be hoped that their initiative will be followed up; with modern techniques a skeleton outline of the prehistoric cultures could be built up in much less time than it has taken in Europe, where we have had first to invent and make our tools for the job. It is also to be hoped that a few first-class sites will be scheduled for protection.

The problems that such excavation may one day solve can as yet only be faintly seen. It is thought that the Shilluk tribes of the White Nile migrated thither from somewhere in or near Uganda.[20] The evidence is linguistic and traditional, but seems valid. When the Shilluk mounds and some ancient sites in their presumed southern home have been excavated it should be possible to provide an archaeological test of the evidence from the other two sources; and if, as may well happen, stratified finds in the mounds include dateable imported objects, it may become possible to date the Uganda sites, where such objects, though possible, seem less likely to occur.

Beyond the equator southwards there is a blank area of some 1,500 miles before we reach archaeological sites again at Zimbabwe. That does not mean that there are none; merely that what must exist is still unknown or unrecorded. South Africa is the land of the men of the Old Stone Age *par excellence*, and I fear that those ancient hunters have been rather overlooked in this survey. That is partly because the archaeology of the Old Stone Age is a special subject in itself, in which I have had no experience, partly because many Old Stone Age sites require excavation, and highly skilled excavation, to produce results. They do not therefore lend themselves as readily as later sites to the technique of field-work, though this cannot be wholly excluded, as will be seen later on. Between the Old Stone Age and the next period represented is a vast gap of thousands of years. There are in Rhodesia and the Transvaal remains of dwellings and fields which have been shown by excavation to belong to the European medieval period. The most famous

---

[16] In a letter Mr H. J. Braunholz, Keeper of the Department of Ethnography in the British Museum, confirms this statement, adding that the N.E. region (Chad and Bornu), which was one of the gates of entry into Nigeria from the east, contains many remains of ancient settlements.

[17] In the Annual Reports of the Geological Survey of the Gold Coast, in the *Gold Coast Review* and elsewhere. See 'Archaeology in the Gold Coast', by H. J. Braunholz, *Antiquity*, X, 1936, 469–74, plan of earthworks (p. 470), drawings of pot-herds (pp. 471, 473).

[18] *Antiquity*, VII, 1933, 153–65: 'The Azanian Civilization of Kenya'.

[19] Report on the Excavations at Hyrax Hill, Nakuru, Kenya Colony, 1937–8, by Mary Leakey, *Trans. Royal Society of S. Africa*, XXX, Part 4, 271–409. Cape Town (reviewed in *Antiquity*, XXII, 1948, 54–5).

[20] Rossini, *Rivista degli Studi Orientali*, XI, 1927, 70–1. He divides the Nilotic languages into two groups, Ciol (Chol or Shilluk) and Dinka-Nuer, extending from Lake Victoria to the middle White Nile. Westermann (*The Shilluk People*, 1912) gives the Shilluk traditions.

is Zimbabwe, a village of stone-built houses. Twice excavated,[21] its age has been conclusively proved by the discovery of fragments of imported Chinese celadon ware sealed up beneath an unbroken (later) hut-floor. This dating is supported also by beads—the universal trade-goods of all periods—which must have been brought to ports on the coast by Chinese or Arab traders, both of whom are known to have reached the east coast of South Africa at a very early date.[22] Sofala, a port in Portuguese East Africa on Lat. 20° South (the same latitude as Bulawayo) was known by name in Venice nearly half a century before the Portuguese sailed round Africa and discovered it.

At 150 miles south-west of Zimbabwe is the ancient village site of Mapungubwe[23], perched on the top of a precipitous plateau. Here have been found 'hoards of gold beads and ornaments, masses of coloured glass beads from the Near and Middle East, Chinese porcelain, ivory, copper, bronze, iron, and a great mass of pottery, and human, faunal and vegetable remains.' Another site belonging to the same culture at Bambandianalo has yielded somewhat similar remains. There was a 'great midden containing about 40,000 tons of material that reached a maximum depth of 20 feet. . . . Masses of burnt matter and hundreds of grinders of the pestle and mortar type were found.' The conclusions drawn were that 'the Northern Transvaal contains remains of extensive medieval settlements. . . . The oldest material culture encountered (at Bambandianalo) is apparently that of a Bantu-speaking people who worked in copper. They were potters and pastoralists and apparently of Sotho stock.' The Mapungubwe culture arrived at the site fully fledged and is homogeneous throughout. Its pottery has resemblances to that of the second occupation period of Zimbabwe, but it is much more varied.

With these sites must surely belong the terraces of the Inyanga region, some 300 miles north-east of Bulawayo. They were first described by Dr Randal MacIver,[24] who went there in 1905 and a fund has recently been established to excavate there. The remains consist of thousands of narrow cultivation-terraces built (not naturally formed, as are lynchets) on the steep slopes of the hills. Scattered about amongst them, often perched on eminences, are simple dwellings consisting of a round stone hut or two with a small round-walled compound. Between the terraces are narrow lanes between stone walls on each side, leading to the dwelling-sites. The whole of the remains are most impressive and are very well displayed by air-photographs taken by Mr R. A. Bourlay, from an examination of which the above description has been made possible. The remains are being gradually levelled by erosion, which makes their early investigation a matter of urgency. It also suggests that they cannot be very ancient or they would have been entirely eroded away.

If these terraces and huts were in a more accessible place they would be an ideal subject for field study. The hut-groups need planning and their features describing. But they are most inaccessible. It may be a little presumptuous for one with so very slight a knowledge of Inyanga even to make a suggestion about its future conservation. Would it not be possible to make the whole region into a National Park? The time is surely coming when the people of southern Africa will have both the desire and the leisure to study the history of their homeland. One can imagine a vacation-course held here amid what would appear to be pleasant scenery and climatic conditions. Surveying, geography, archaeology would all seem capable of being taught here; it would certainly be a good region to teach contouring! But I make the suggestion with much diffidence, for the reasons stated above.

[21] First by Dr Randall MacIver in 1905 (see his *Medieval Rhodesia*) and then by Miss Caton Thompson in 1929 (see her article in *Antiquity*, III, 1929, 424–33 and her book *The Zimbabwe Culture*, Oxford, 1931). For other references see my note in *Antiquity*, XXIV, 1950, 96–8 (Rhodesian cultivation-terraces).

[22] *Antiquity*, X, 1936, 290–1.

[23] See Dr C. van Riet Lowe's article in *Antiquity*, X, 1936, 282–91, and *Mapungubwe; reports on the excavations 1933–5*, edited by Leo Fouché, Cambridge Univ. Press, 1937 (reviewed at length by Miss Caton Thompson in *Antiquity*, XIII, 1939, 324–35, with a note on the skeletal remains by Dr G. M. Morant, pp. 335–41). The second volume has not yet been published.

[24] *Medieval Rhodesia*, Macmillan, 1906. See my note in *Antiquity*, XXIV, 1950, 96–9, giving short bibliography.

One of the chief needs in a new country would appear to be to record the exact position, on some fairly large-scale official map, of as many as possible of the ancient sites known. That is a matter for the Survey Department in co-operation with archaeologists. It is not too much to say that British archaeology owes much of its excellence to the fact that, right from the start exactly 150 years ago, the Ordnance Maps have marked the sites of antiquities. If that had not then been done not only would it never have been possible to know where many vanished sites (and sites of finds) were, but many archaeologists (including the present writer) whose interest was first aroused by those intriguing names in Old English letters ('Camp', 'Tumulus', etc.) might never have been aware that such things existed at all. That official notice singled them out as objects worthy of attention and sent one to look at them; the rest followed naturally from this early field-work. But it was the maps that began it. That must often have happened.

Conscious of my utter inadequacy for the task of writing about field archaeology in a region I have never seen, I consulted Professor van Riet Lowe, Director of the Archaeological Survey of the Union of South Africa, and through him was put in touch with Mr Roger Summers, Keeper of Antiquities in the National Museum of Southern Rhodesia. By kind permission of the former I am able to give here an extract from his reply. That of Mr Summers which is longer, is printed as Appendix 6. I would express my gratitude to both for their courtesy and for the trouble they have taken in this matter.

Professor van Riet Lowe refers first to the terracing—I wrote chiefly to inquire about that at Inyanga—saying that similar terracing occurs also in the northern and eastern Transvaal, but not on nearly so large or spectacular a scale as in Rhodesia. He then proceeds to describe how air-observation (and even ground observation of the flora in some cases) can help to locate even sites of the Old Stone Age.

'On one occasion I met with a most unexpected success which will, I am sure, interest you. While flying over the northern Transvaal in 1937 I noticed a dirty creamy coloured area undergoing surface erosion. As the implements which characterise our Middle Stone Age (which is characterised by Mousterian- and Solutrean-like tools integrally associated with a developed prepared core or Levallois technique) invariably occur in a ferruginised or calcified subsoil of dirty creamy colour, I made a sketch plan of the locality, and visited it some months later—and reaped a rich reward. The sheet erosion had exposed the calcified Middle Stone Age factory and living-site, the exposed portion of which showed up most strongly in its green setting. Whether the subsoil has been calcified and is in consequence a dirty creamy colour, or ferruginised (when it is a russety ochreous or brick colour), the colours show up sharply during the rainy seasons when the grass is green, but not nearly so well in the dry seasons when the vegetable growth is dead and straw-coloured.

'Another factor which is helpful in Africa is to be found in the fact that different rock formations often support different vegetations. It is, for example, quite easy to spot a dolerite dyke in quartzite from the air, even where the contours are smooth, simply because the plant growth on the two rocks differs. The same applies to our dolomites (with their breccia-filled caverns, many of which were occupied in prehistoric times), where these occur in granitic or generally quartzitic areas—again simply because the plant growth over the dolomite differs from that over the granitic or quartzitic rocks.

'In Rhodesia and the Transvaal I have frequently seen a quite distinctive flora on sites which the ancients used as dumps for rubbish— a fact to be noted by your field archaeologist. I actually had an interesting experience in this connection when I revisited Zimbabwe with Summers last year. While we were standing on the Acropolis and looking down upon the Valley of Ruins and the so-called Temple, I noticed (through my binoculars) an area covered by grass and a particularly unpleasant thorny ground-creeper with masses of small yellow flowers and, indicating the area to Summers, said: "There is a large midden." With us was an experienced Rhodesian who expressed surprise—which, but for our code of politeness, would have been doubt. However, when we had descended into the valley, we went on to my entirely uninviting patch and judiciously cleared and dug into a few small areas from every one of which we extracted handfuls of potsherds encased in ash. The whole proved to be an extensive midden which will, I hope, some day be systematically excavated.

'Another very important fact to be noted by the field archaeologist in Africa is the geology of the area he wishes to explore. For example, the rock outcrops in the Orange Free State (which is almost as large as England) are almost exclusively soft or friable sandstones and shales which were quite useless to Stone Age Man. It is, therefore, extremely improbable that Stone Age Man will have spent much (if any) time in an area where there are no other types of rocks. Consequently field archaeologists looking for stone implements cannot expect much in such areas. But if a dolerite or any other igneous dyke happens to have extended through the shales or sandstones one knows at once that one's chances are good; for where an igneous mass cut through the softer sedimentary rocks it baked or indurated the sandstones or shales, thus producing the finest rock (after flint) that Stone Age Man could hope to find. That is why we have such a wealth of Stone Age remains in the shale areas north of the southern limit of the Karroo dolerites —a wealth which depended entirely on the extensive outcrops of indurated shale or lydianite.

'Another interesting geological factor in Africa is that in the eastern rift valley in Tanganyika and Kenya the lava is acid, and there is much obsidian, a most popular rock during the Stone Age, whereas in the western or Albertine fork of the rift (Lakes Edward, George, Albert, etc.) the lava is basic, and there is no obsidian, and Stone Age Man had to look for other rocks.'

S

APPENDIX 6

Field Archaeology in Southern Rhodesia

by ROGER SUMMERS

OPEN SITES. A country with markedly seasonal rainfall offers peculiar advantages to the field archaeologist. Rains are concentrated and consequently heavy, cutting new sections in the banks of rivers and streams all over the country. The passing of the rainy season (November-March) makes it possible to examine these sections for the full height of the banks.

In the dry season the weather in the higher and more settled areas is usually cool enough to make walking pleasurable and it is then that most field-work is undertaken.

As the debris from these natural excavations are carried downstream and deposited in the bed of the river the obvious technique is to examine the dry bed for artifacts and then to examine exposed banks upstream for occurrences *in situ*. If the artifacts found in the stream bed are fresh, one knows that the search will not be a long one, but the occurrence of rolled implements often, although not inevitably, leads to a fruitless search. (In passing, the degree of abrasion of artifacts found in the beds of intermittent streams and in torrent gravels seems to be related to the distance travelled in the stream rather than to the age of the artifact: I have found tools typologically similar but with different degrees of abrasion side by side in gravel deposits here.)

This particular technique is useful both when making a local survey and when undertaking a large-scale exploration of a new area. In the latter case one follows a road and stops at each bridge or drift (= Ford) and in each stream carries out the drill of searching bed and, if necessary, banks upstream; this sounds superficial, but in a country which is so rich in stone implements it yields quite useful results. Naturally the lateral tributaries and downwash introduce material from higher levels and in an intensive survey, particularly when looking for stratigraphy, the search may be prolonged.

Torrential rain when it falls on gently sloping areas impoverished by over-cultivation, over-stocking or undue cutting of veld trees causes rapid soil erosion, at first gullies and, if unchecked, sheet erosion or 'washouts' are formed. These are disastrous for the farmer but a delight to the archaeologist, for they provide an area of an acre and upwards from which humus has been stripped off, leaving the subsoil bare. Sometimes more than the humus goes and one may be faced with a mixture of cultures. This can however sometimes be resolved by a careful study of the banks of the 'washout'. I know such a place where there is a large Late Chelles-Acheul (originally Stellenbosch V) working floor exposed on which lay hundreds of handaxes, cleavers and stone balls mixed with Middle Stone Age flakes with an advanced facetted platform (Levallois) technique; the Middle Stone Age material was found *in situ* in the banks of more recent alluvial deposits which originally overlay the Chelles-Acheul floor and so a cultural separation was possible.

Very few of our roads are tarred; local roads are gravelled, and main roads have two tarmac strips about two feet wide and three feet apart like a single track railway line—a method of road-making which provides many of the advantages of a tarred road without its expense, and which is quite adequate for the comparatively small amount of traffic here. Beside and between the strips local gravel is spread; all road metal is local, and this often provides a few artifacts which can easily be tracked down to one of the very numerous road metal pits near the road.

Our railway cuttings here are fairly new and as vegetation dies down in the dry season they too provide useful sections. As trains are few and far between, there is no reason why these sections should be neglected by the field archaeologist.

There is a much-searched section in the cutting near the Victoria Falls Station, but the enclosed reprint refers to one near Umtali which was brought to Mr Jones's notice by a railway permanent-way engineer.

CAVES. Caves have fatal fascination for the amateur who too often spoils a deposit by unskilled digging and, despite the existence of a Monuments Act forbidding such practices, they are most difficult to prevent.

Without digging the field archaeologist can find much useful material by searching along the drip-line where falling water has disturbed the ashy layers which form the topmost horizon of our cave deposits. The talus outside caves in this country is usually too overgrown with trees and scrub for any outwash of stone implements to take place, but a search here will sometimes produce useful results.

A useful piece of field-work undertaken by a number of people here is the copying of rock paintings ('Bushman Paintings' is the incorrect local term). Of these there are many thousands of examples scattered amongst the granite kopjes of the Colony. It is surprising to find that these paintings have never been scientifically studied as a whole; there have been local studies and studies of special subjects, but probably the subject is so vast that nobody has yet dared to tackle it. Literature is still scanty.

RUINS. The term 'ruins' in Southern Rhodesia covers all stone built structures no longer occupied and is applied equally to complicated ruin-fields like Zimbabwe and to a mere stone wall which once surrounded a single hut. All represent Bantu occupation.

These monuments attracted the attention of early travellers and consequently many were ransacked for gold believed to be buried within. The treasure seekers met with sufficient success to lead them to do irreparable damage to many ruins.

Despite the damage to stratified deposits there is much that the field archaeologist can do in the way of recording and planning, for, although many ruins have been known since the 1890's the only comprehensive list (Hall and Neal, *Ancient Ruins of Rhodesia*, 1902) has a highly inaccurate map and a few plans of equally doubtful accuracy.

A feature of many of our ruin sites is the accumulation of rubbish in the form of middens. Where these are on the sides of kopjes the loose ash of which they are mostly composed, washes away and leaves sherds, beads, fragments of metal, etc., on the surface. As these middens are really surface deposits it is almost as useful to collect the washed-out finds as it is to dig and sieve in them. Even without digging it is possible to get some idea of the contents of the midden by turning over the upcast from ant-bear holes (the local equivalent of rabbit burrows but more like badger earths in their size).

OTHER BANTU SITES. Not all Bantu sites are marked with stonework. Some of the early Bantu, practicing a culture somewhat akin to that of the Early Iron Age in Europe, lived in huts hidden amongst the rocks of granite kopjes, whilst others lived in open country. The sites of their kraals can sometimes be detected by an unusually spongy feeling underfoot when the ground is wet. In certain circumstances a rank, weedy growth covers these patches, but such differences in vegetation are difficult to see in the thick bush which covers so much of this area.

Another indication of Bantu occupation sites is the presence of U-shaped holes sunk vertically into the surface of rocks. These holes are anything from 4 to 9 inches in diameter at the top and usually anything up to a foot deep (the deepest I have seen was 16 inches, but that was exceptional). These holes are in the hardest rocks and were originally used for quartz crushing in gold extraction.

These sites yield a characteristic pottery.

Sites of kraals of Ndebele origin (post A.D. 1838) can sometimes be detected at a distance by a clump of well-grown trees with straight trunks. These have grown from some of the posts of the stockade round the cattle kraal. Such kraal sites yield a good series of nineteenth-century beads including some very interesting ones from Arab sources used by the slavers.

Recent kraal sites of Kalanga and Shona origin can sometimes be detected by searching in the neighbourhood of iron-smelting sites. Native iron-smelting leaves much slag, and in recent sites this can be readily recognized on the surface of the veld. In a few sites parts of the furnace remain, but broken tuyères are of more common occurrence. Such sites yield ironworkers' tools: stone anvils, stone hammers and (very rarely) lost metal tools. Beads can sometimes be recovered.

As elsewhere, field archaeology in Southern Rhodesia is a necessary preliminary to more detailed work. Excavation can be undertaken at a few sites only, but straightforward field-work enables us to work out distributions and, in the case of Bantu cultures, to trace migration routes.

TOOLS. The Africans of Southern Rhodesia are very skilful with the hoe (*badʐa*) and this tool has proved very useful in excavation: in the hands of the uninstructed it is capable of damaging buried structures but used carefully it can be as sensitive as a trowel and very much quicker. For skimming off humus it is invaluable and for digging in anything stony it is extraordinarily useful.

The modern tool is of similar design to the ordinary English garden hoe but about six times the size. This tool is made in Britain and is here known to the hardware trade as a '2½ lb hoe'. (I imagine it would be very useful instead of a pick in ditches.)

ANTS. In Southern Rhodesia (and probably everywhere else in the tropics) ants and termites play havoc with archaeological deposits. (*a*) Their workings make the ground very hard indeed, too hard for the hoe usually; if active, the deposit is gluey, if abandoned, it becomes like a moderately ferruginised gravel; in either case work is very slow indeed. (*b*) Although stone artifacts can be got out of such a deposit bone tools and glass beads are almost impossible to recover—fortunately the bone hardens but the glass is so glued up to sand grains that beads cannot be sieved out. (*c*) Ant workings cause deposits to swell and so falsify stratigraphy in places. (*d*) Finally, they destroy differences in local texture and so make it impossible to identify the commencement of disturbances (e.g. graves).

APPENDIX 7

Crankeries

THE SERIOUS STUDENT, whether whole or part-time, is not always serious, and he has a sense of humour. It is fed by a perennial stream of absurdities rising on the lower slopes of Parnassus. He soon comes to classify them into certain groups, one of the largest of which is concerned with the alleged mysteries of numbers and direction. Others derive civilization from a 'lost' continent in the Atlantic or Pacific; others again attribute the remains of prehistoric Britain to the Romans, Jews, Phoenicians or Egyptians. Modern British place-names are (it is asserted) derived from oriental languages. The divining-rod is claimed to be able to locate burials as well as water. Mummy wheat is made to germinate.

The onus of proof that these things are able to do what is claimed lies on those who make that claim; there is no obligation to disprove them. Archaeologists are concerned with facts and only with such theories as are put forward to explain observed facts by persons qualified to do so by training and hard work. If it be claimed that human beings lived on a 'lost' continent, evidence must be produced by the claimant that such a continent existed during the human period, i.e. during the last million years or so, and that it was inhabited. Neither of these things has been done and, failing the production of evidence, the theory can be ignored. If it be claimed that there is some mystical or other significance in the measurements or proportions of the Great Pyramid, these should be correctly given; they are not. The errors of fact made by the Pyramidiots have been repeatedly demonstrated, most recently by Noel Wheeler,[1] and the prophecies 'when disproved by events are then shifted to new dates'.[2] Flinders Petrie used to tell an amusing story of an incident that happened in 1881 when he was measuring the side of the Great Pyramid. When he came to the corner he met another person apparently doing the same thing, but armed with a chisel as well as a tape-measure. Petrie asked why he needed a chisel and the man, slightly embarrassed, explained that it was to 'adjust' the length of the side which did not quite conform to the length required by his theory.

One of the craziest books ever written about British archaeology was Watkins's *Old Straight Track*. The author found that, if he drew a straight line on a small-scale map with a broad-pointed nib it passed through a number of objects on the ground, such as haystacks, cathedrals, ponds and large stones. (How could it not do so?). These were supposed to mark the courses of aligned tracks laid out by prehistoric man! As we have already seen, the feature which distinguishes prehistoric from Roman and some modern roads is precisely the sinuosity of their course. Such an inversion of the facts reveals a complete failure to understand the nature of a primitive culture.

Closely allied to such fantasies are the theories about orientation. They are more difficult to deal with, because they are sometimes based upon facts. Some prehistoric monuments do have

[1] *Antiquity*, IX, 1935, 292–304.
[2] Flinders Petrie, quoted in the preceding, p. 302.

an orientation of a kind; long barrows, for instance, usually have their 'business' end at the north-east, east or south-east end. But so do Christian churches. What does this prove? Nothing.

The theory that the early inhabitants of Britain were migrants from the east is a hang-over from the days when the Bible and other literary sources were used to explain prehistoric monuments. That was before archaeology had elaborated its own technique, before it had achieved independence. Similar reasoning attributed sarsen stones to the Saracens, hill-forts to Oliver Cromwell or the heroes of legend. By a similar process hill-forts and medieval castles are attributed to the Romans. Basically this is an attempt to explain the unknown by the known. Oliver Cromwell and the Romans, and also the Jews, Phoenicians and Egyptians were known; but the successive prehistoric peoples whose culture has been revealed in recent years by purely archaeological methods were then unthought of, and are still unknown even by name to many educated people. A curious instance of this attitude of mind is seen in the Sudan. In the north are many Egyptian temples; elsewhere there are none. The conclusion is drawn that the north is therefore an 'archaeological' region, and that there is no 'archaeology' in the south. There is, of course just as much 'archaeology' there as in any other part of the world that has been continuously inhabited for a long time; but the remains are less obvious. They have been found and classified by purely archaeological techniques (dating by pottery, etc.), and have non-historical, non-ethnical names given to them. In the Sudan we have the Early Khartoum and Shaheinab cultures, in Britain the Beaker-folk and Iron Age A, B, C and so on. Such 'people without a history' are quite a modern discovery; they are to be found in all countries, and they are the makers of the monuments and remains attributed in pre-archaeological times to the only peoples then known—the Romans, etc. When, therefore, one is asked, as one often is, whose ancient remains one was excavating in the southern Sudan—were they ancient Egyptians?—the reply is—no, they were just ancient Sudanese.

The theories which derive cultures from hypothetical ones on 'lost' continents are usually based upon geological speculations, imperfectly understood. Some geologists have thought that in former ages large land areas may have existed where now the Atlantic and Pacific oceans are to-day. Such ideas were admittedly speculative and never formed part of the accepted body of geological knowledge, and current geological opinion regards them as unlikely to be correct. But whether correct or not, they cannot be used to support any 'lost continent' theories, for no reputable geologist has ever suggested that these continents existed as late as the human period. Recent examination of deposits of foraminifera deposits at the bottom of the Atlantic prove that that ocean existed at least at the beginning of the Ice Age, more than half a million years ago. The existence or non-existence of these 'lost' continents is a geological problem; the origin of cultures is an archaeological one. Neither problem can profitably be discussed with persons who have not taken the trouble to study geology or archaeology, and are ignorant of their methods, and too often of logic also.

The inventors of these crazy theories make free use of place-names to support them. One of the best specimens in my collection is an article called 'The Secret of Salisbury Plain',[3] by a person who called himself 'Appian Way', purporting to be a review of my monograph on 'Air Survey and Archaeology'. After summarizing its contents, the writer himself leaves the ground and sets out on a flight of fancy. His opening sentences are at least arresting. 'Palestine contains no traces whatsoever of its alleged past, or any antiquities which can be traced back beyond the Roman age. There are certain places, of course, as there are in Asia Minor, but nothing to identify it with the original land of Palestine.' One wonders how he would have accounted for the recently-discovered Hebrew scrolls in Palestine, or why that land and Asia Minor are the only ones that contain 'places'. He thought that the day was approaching when we should 'identify the Holy Land as being Britain, and as having always been Britain'. The early Celts were the Canaanites;

[3] *The Watchman*, 15th August 1924.

Salisbury Plain, which he calls the Plain of Sarum, was the Plain of Saron (he means Sharon),
'where Shitrai pastured the royal flocks'. Old Sarum was two places at once—Gibeah and Byblus;
'Devizes or Lydd' was Lydda; 'Gibeon itself, the great high place where Solomon went to offer
sacrifice when he became king, is Stonehenge'; Oxford 'stands on the site of the ancient city of
Hebron', and is a double city, for it is also 'the real original, many-gated Thebes', and Avebury
is Mizpah. Saul was buried under Silbury Hill. The Vale of Pewsey is a double vale, being both
the Arthurian Avalon and the 'Avaris or Abaris . . . where the Pharaohs shut up the Hebrews in
the time of Moses'. After this uncontrolled flight in the stratosphere, where philological rules do
not function, we are assured that 'these statements are not guess-work, nor are they coincidences
arrived at by certain similarities of name', as one might well have been led to think. What, then,
is their basis? We read on hopefully, but if we expect to be given evidence we shall be disappointed.
'They are the result of 15 years' close study of the subject.' Well, well! *Parturiunt montes, nascetur
ridiculus mus.*

One always runs the risk, by mentioning these lunacies in a sane book, that their authors may
claim to have been treated seriously by competent students. It is unlikely that 'Appian Way' is
still pursuing his studies, which would now (1951) be in their forty-fourth year; but if he should
be, let me assure him that I have quoted him for entertainment purposes only.

APPENDIX 8

Bibliography

THE PREPARATION OF a bibliography that will be of use to those who wish to do field-work is not an easy task. Of the many principles of selection one might adopt I have not adopted any one to the exclusion of the rest. Thus I have included some books which, thought not directly concerned with field archaeology, are written by archaeologists with wide experience in the field and which, therefore, provide general information of an essential kind; and a few merely because they are referred to in the text. Many of the best examples of archaeological field-work are in the form of articles in the Proceedings of learned societies, references to which will be found in the footnotes, and in Appendix 3. It is not possible for a student to depend solely upon books; he *must* consult articles in those Proceedings. The chief ones are the *Antiquaries Journal* (Soc. of Antiquaires of London), *The Archaeological Journal, Antiquity*, the *Proceedings* of the Society of Antiquaries of Scotland, of the Prehistoric Society, of the Society of Antiquaries of Newcastle and their publication, *Archaeologia Aeliana* (both of which are much concerned with Hadrian's Wall); and *Archaeologia Cambrensis*. Then there are the Proceedings of county societies, of varying merit, amongst which those of Wiltshire and Sussex deservedly rank highly. It should not be thought that these articles are more difficult to read then books; the reverse is true. Dealing as they do with particular matters, and illustrated by large-scale plans, they are easier to understand because they provide the concrete examples that illustrate the more general statements in books.

ALLCROFT, A. Hadrian	*Earthwork of England.* Macmillan, 1908.
ASHMOLEAN MUSEUM	*Notes on Archaeological Technique*, Ashmolean Museum, 3rd edn. 1950.
ATKINSON, R. J. C.	*Field Archaeology*, 2nd edn., revised. Methuen, 1953.
BAILLIE-GROHMAN, W. A.	*The Master of the Game by Edward, Second Duke of York: the oldest English book on hunting,* 1904.
CHILDE, V. Gordon	†*Prehistoric Communities of the British Isles.* W. & R. Chambers, 3rd edn. 1949, 274 pages. (The standard text-book.)
CHRISTISON, David	*Early Fortifications in Scotland.* Blackwood, 1898.
CLARK, Grahame	'Earthen Long Barrows.' *Proc. Preh. Soc.* NS. III, 1937, 173–5. *Archaeology and Society.* Methuen, 1939. *Prehistoric England.* Batsford, 1940.
COLLINGWOOD, R. G.	*Roman Britain.* Oxford, 1934.
COPLEY, GORDON J.	*The Conquest of Wessex.* Phoenix House, 1954.
CRAWFORD, O. G. S.	*Man and His Past.* Oxford, 1921. 'The Anglo-Saxon Bounds of Bedwyn and Barbage.' *Wilts Arch. Mag.* XLI, 1921, 281–301. *The Long Barrows of the Cotswolds.* Bellows, Gloucester, 1925. *Air Survey and Archaeology.* Ordnance Survey, 2nd edn. 1928.

CRAWFORD, O. G. S.   *Air-Photography for Archaeologists.* Ordnance Survey, 1929.
† *Field Archaeology: Some Notes for Beginners,* issued by the Ordnance Survey. (Out of print; last edition 1932.)
Topography of Roman Scotland North of the Antonine Wall. Cambridge, 1949.

CRAWFORD, O. G. S. and
   KEILLER, A.   *Wessex from the Air.* Oxford, 1928.

CUNNINGTON, M. E.   *An Introduction to the Archaeology of Wiltshire.* Woodward, Devizes, 3rd edn. 1934.

CURWEN, E. Cecil   *The Archaeology of Sussex.* Methuen's County Archaeologies, 1937.

DANIEL, Glyn E.   *A Hundred Years of Archaeology.* Duckworth, 1950.

DOBSON, Dina P.   *The Archaeology of Somerset.* Methuen's County Archaeologies, 1931.

ELGEE, F. and H. W.   *The Archaeology of Yorkshire.* Methuen's County Archaeologies, 1932.

FOX, Sir Cyril   *The Archaeology of the Cambridge Region.* 1st edn. 1923; 2nd edn. 1948.

FOX, Sir Cyril   *The Personality of Britain.* Nat. Mus. of Wales.
GODWIN, H.   'Prehistoric Trackways in the Somerset Levels.' *Phil. Trans.,* Series B, No. 599 (Vol. 233, 1948, 249–73).

GRINSELL, L. V.   *The Ancient Burial-mounds of England.* Methuen, 1936. New edition 1953.
† *White Horse Hill and the Surrounding Country.* 1939. (A little book of a kind that might well be much commoner if the people able to write them were more numerous.)

HALDANE, A. R. B.   *The Drove Roads of Scotland.* Nelson, 1952.

HAWKES, C. F. C.   'Britons, Romans and Saxons round Salisbury and in Cranborne Chase.' *Arch. Journ.* CIV, 27–81. (A re-examination of some of the sites excavated by Gen. Pitt-Rivers, and a revaluation thereof in the light of the knowledge since acquired.)

HAWKES, Jacquetta   *Discovering the Past.* Nat. Council of Social Service, Local History Series No. 8.

HAWKES, Jacquetta   *Early Britain.* Collins, 1945.
Prehistoric and Roman Monuments in England and Wales. Chatto & Windus, 1951.

HAWKES, Jacquetta and
   Christopher   *Prehistoric Britain.* Pelican Books, 1943.
ib. id. Chatto & Windus, 1947. (An enlarged and more elaborate edition of the same book.)

HENCKEN, H. O'Neill   *The Archaeology of Cornwall and Scilly.* Methuen's County Archaeologies, 1932.

HOARE, Sir Richard Colt   *Ancient History of Wiltshire,* 2 vols. 1812, 1819. (One of the best and earliest of the open-air books.)

HOPE-TAYLOR, Brian   'Celtic Agriculture in Surrey'. *Surrey Arch. Colls.,* L, 1949, 47–72

HOUGHTON, F. T. S.   'Salt-ways'. *Trans. Birmingham Arch. Soc.,* LIV, 1932, 1–17 (maps).

HATT, Gudmund   *Oldtidsagre*. Copenhagen, 1949. (The standard book on prehistoric fields in Denmark, illustrated by many plates. In Danish with 15 pages of summary in English.)

JESSUP, R. F.   *The Archaeology of Kent*. Methuen's County Archaeologies, 1930.

JOHNSON, Walter   *Byways in British Archaeology*. Cambridge, 1912.
Folk Memory. Oxford, 1908. (A useful compendium of facts; deals with such subjects as dene-holes and flint mines.)

JOHNSON, Walter and WRIGHT, William   *Neolithic Man in North-east Surrey*. 1903. (An early essay in field archaeology, now completely out of date, but good for its time.)

KENDRICK, T. D. and HAWKES, C. F. C.   *Archaeology in England and Wales*, 1914–32. London, 1932.

KENDRICK, T. D.   *British Antiquity*. Methuen, 1950.

KENYON, Kathleen   †*Beginning in Archaeology*. Phoenix House, 1952. Revised edn. 1953.

LETHBRIDGE, T. C.   *Merlin's Island*. Methuen, 1948.

MacDONALD, (Sir) George   'General Roy and his Military Antiquities of the Romans in North Britain.' *Archaeologia*, LXVIII, 1917, 161–228.

MARGARY, Ivan D.   †*Roman Ways in the Weald*. Phoenix House, 1948. (A thorough field-survey, supplemented by excavation and fully illustrated by plans.)

MARPLES, Morris   *White Horses and Other Hill Figures*. Country Life, 1949.

MILLER, S. N. (Editor)   *The Roman Occupation of South-western Scotland* (Maclehose Glasgow), 1953.

OAKLEY, K. P.   *Man the Tool-maker*. British Museum, 1949.

PEAKE, H. J. E.   *The Archaeology of Berkshire*. Methuen's County Archaeologies, 1930.

PETRIE, W. M. Flinders   *Methods and Aims in Archaeology*. Methuen.

PETRIE, Sir Flinders   'The Hill Figures of England.' *R. Anthr. Inst. Occasional Papers No. 7*, 1926. (Useful if used with caution; see my review of it in *Antiquity* III, 1929, 277–82.)

PHILLIPS, C. W.   'The Long Barrows of Lincolnshire.' *Arch. Journ*. LXXXIX, 1933, 174–202. (An excellent example of the value of field-work alone.)

PIGGOTT, Stuart   †*British Prehistory*. Home University Library, Oxford, 1949.
†*William Stukeley, an Eighteenth-century Antiquary*. Oxford, 1950.

PRESTON, F. L.   'A Field Survey of the "Roman Rig" Dyke in South-West Yorkshire.' *Trans. Hunter Arch. Soc*. VI, 1950. 197–220, 285–309.

SUMNER, Heywood   'Archaeological Benefactors of Hampshire, Dorset and Wiltshire.' *Proc. Bournemouth Natural Science Society*, XIX, 1928.
Earthworks of Cranborne Chase. (This and the companion book on the New Forest are perhaps the best of their kind.)
Earthworks of the New Forest.

THOMAS, Edward   *The Icknield Way*, 1913. (The book has considerable charm and recalls a pleasant epoch that has vanished within a lifetime; but it is not a serious study of the Icknield Way.)

† Books containing bibliographies

TOMS, H. S.   *Ancient Ponds near Cissbury. Sussex County Magazine*, I, 1926–7, 404–7.

Ancient Ponds near Falmer. SCM, VIII, Sept. 1934.

Ancient Ponds near Patcham. SCM, VIII, Aug. 1934

'Chettle Down Earthwork: An Ancient Pond.' *Proc. Dorset NH and Arch. Soc.* LI, 1930, 192–203. (See Chapter 11.)

'The Destruction of Eastwick Pond.' *SCM*, X, May 1936.

'Notes on the Larmer, Wermere, Ashmore and Tollard Royal Ponds.' *Wilts Arch. Mag.*, XLVI, 1934, 8–15.

'Some Sussex Meres.' *SCM*, VIII, Nov. 1934.

'The Welesmere Quest.' *SCM*, IX, June 1935.

'The Younsmere near Rottingdean.' *SCM*, IX, Jan. 1935.

VARLEY, W. J. and JACKSON, J. Wilfred   *Prehistoric Cheshire*. Cheshire Rural Community Council, Chester, 1940.

VULLIAMY, C. E.   *The Archaeology of Middlesex and London*. Methuen's County Archaeologies, 1930.

WHEELER, R. E. M.   'The Linear Earthworks of the Scarborough District.' Appendix to his article in the *History of Scarborough* edited by Arthur Rowntree, 1931, pp. 34–9.

Prehistoric and Roman Wales, Oxford, 1925.

WILLIAMS-FREEMAN, J. P.   *An Introduction to Field Archaeology as illustrated by Hampshire*. Macmillan, 1915. (The best of the earthwork books and a pioneer effort in scientific field archaeology; also extremely well written.)

'Linear Earthworks: Method of Field Survey.' Notes prepared at the request of the Research Committee of the Society of Antiquaries of London. *Antiquaries Journal*, 1946, 175–9; also sold as a separate pamphlet.

I have to thank Professor van Giffen of Groningen for most kindly sending me the following bibliography of his work on prehistoric Dutch fields:—

Grafheuvels te Zwaagdijk, gem. Wervershoof, N.-H.

'West-Friesland's Oud en Nieuw', XVII, 1944, pp. 121–221, afb. 1–38.

Oudheidkundige aantkeningen over Drentsee vondsten VII. Nederzettingen, grafheuvels, leemkuilen en rijengrafveld tusschen Rhee en Zeijen, gem. Vries. Nieuwe Drentse Volksalmanak 1940, pp. 192–200, spec. p. 198, afb. 17–19.

Oudheidkundige aantkeningen over Drentsee vondsten VIII. Tweeperioden-heuvel N. van Gasteren, gem. Anl. Nieuwe Drentse Volksalmanak 1941, pp. 129–131, afb. 29–32.

Oudheidkundige aantekeningen over Drentse vondsten XVI. Het 'Noordse Veld' bij Zeijen, gem. Vries. Nieuwe Drentse Volksalmanak 1949, pp. 93–148, Afb. 1–27.

Opgravingen in Drente. In: Drente, een handboek voor het kennen van het Drentssche leven in voorbije eeuwen, onder redactie van J. Poortman. Eerste deel, Meppel, 1943, pp. 391–564, afb. 1–65. Tweede druk, 1944, pp. 393–568.

See also *Antiquity* II, 1928, 85.

INDEX